Managing IT as a
Strategic Resource

Managing IT as a Strategic Resource

Leslie P. Willcocks MA (Cantab), MA, MIPD
Fellow in Information Management
Templeton College, Oxford

David F. Feeny MA, MBA
Vice-president, Templeton College, Oxford
Director, Oxford Institute of Information Management

Gerd Islei MA, Dipl.,Phys, PhD
Fellow in Information Management
Templeton College, Oxford

The McGraw-Hill Companies

London · New York · St Louis · San Francisco · Auckland
Bogotá · Caracas · Lisbon · Madrid · Mexico · Milan
Montreal · New Delhi · Panama · Paris · San Juan · São Paulo
Singapore · Sydney · Tokyo · Toronto

Published by
McGraw-Hill Publishing Company
Shoppenhangers Road, Maidenhead, Berkshire, SL6 2QL, England
Telephone 01628 502500
Fax: 01628 770224

British Library Cataloguing in Publication Data
The CIP data of this title is available from the British Library

0-0 7-7 09-36 4X

Library of Congress Cataloging-in-Publication Data
The CIP data of this title is available from the Library of Congress,
Washington DC, USA

McGraw-Hill

A Division of The McGraw-Hill Companies

Copyright © 1997 McGraw-Hill International (UK) Limited

6 7 8 BB 4 3 2 1

Printed and bound in Great Britain by
Marston Lindsay Ross International Ltd,
Oxfordshire

To Jenny, Pam and Sue at OXIIM—for their immense contribution to the work represented in this book, and for continually making things possible.

Contents

About the Contributors

EDITORS

- Leslie P. Willcocks is Fellow at the Oxford Institute of Information Management (OXIIM), University Lecturer in Management Studies at Templeton College, University of Oxford, and Visiting Professor in Information Systems at Universiteit van Amsterdam, and at Erasmus University, Rotterdam.
- David F. Feeny is Director of OXIIM and Vice-President of Templeton College, University of Oxford.
- Gerd Islei is Fellow of Information Management and University Lecturer in Management Studies at Templeton College, University of Oxford.

OTHER CONTRIBUTORS

- Barry Cox is Section Manager of ICI Pharmaceuticals, Macclesfield, UK.
- Wendy Currie is Reader in Management at the Sheffield Business School, University of Sheffield. She has been a Visiting Fellow at Templeton College and continues as a Research Affiliate of OXIIM.
- Michael J. Earl is Director of the Centre for Research in Information Management and Professor at London Business School. A former Director of OXIIM, he remains a Research Affiliate of the Institute.
- Brian Edwards is an independent consultant and a Research Affiliate of OXIIM.
- Guy Fitzgerald is Cable and Wireless Professor of Business Information Systems at Birkbeck College, University of London. He continues to be a Research Affiliate of OXIIM.
- Steve Gisbourne is Consultant with ICI Corporate Management Services, Wilmslow, UK.
- Catherine Griffiths is Research Fellow at IC Parc, Imperial College, University of London.

- Blake Ives is Professor of Information Systems and Decision Sciences, Ourso School of Business, Louisiana State University, USA. He has been the John M. Olin Distinguished Fellow at Templeton College, and continues as a Research Affiliate of OXIIM.
- Mary C. Lacity is Associate Professor in Management Information Systems at the University of Missouri, St. Louis. Previously a Visiting Fellow at Templeton College, she continues as a Research Affiliate of OXIIM.
- Stephanie Lester is Technology Change Manager at Lloyds Register, London.
- Geoff Lockett is Professor of Management Science at the University of Leeds.
- K. Pelly Periasamy is Senior Lecturer in The Institute of Systems Science, National University of Singapore. He completed his D.Phil at Templeton College, University of Oxford, and is a Research Affiliate of OXIIM.
- Jonathan Reynolds is Fellow in Retail Marketing, Dean and University Lecturer in Management Studies at Templeton College, University of Oxford.
- Kep Simpson is an independent consultant and a Research Affiliate of OXIIM.
- Mick Statford is Consultant with ICI Corporate Management Services, Wilmslow, UK.
- Ashok Subramanian is Associate Professor in Management Information Systems, at University of Missouri, St. Louis, USA.
- Andrea Taylor-Cummings is Managing Director of recruitment consultants LKRC. She completed her D.Phil at Templeton College, University of Oxford, and is a Research Affiliate of OXIIM.

Acknowledgements

Earlier versions of the chapters in this book appeared first in the Oxford Institute of Information Management Working Papers series. The exception is Chapter 15, a more detailed version of which appeared as a joint Oxford Institute of Retail Management/KPMG report: *The Internet: its potential and use by European Retailers*.

Versions of several of the chapters have also been published in journals. Thus Chapter 1 is a reprint of 'Is Your CIO Adding Value?' *Sloan Management Review*, **35,** (3), pp. 11–20. An earlier version of the research in Chapter 2 won the Best Paper award at the Thirteenth International Conference in Information Systems and was subsequently published in MIS Quarterly, **16,** pp. 435–448. An abridged version of Chapter 5 appeared in *Interfaces*, **21,** pp. 4–22, while an earlier version of Chapter 9 appeared as 'Predicting Risk Of Failure in Large-scale Information Technology Projects' in Technological Forecasting And Social Change, **47,** pp. 205–28. Chapter 11 has appeared as 'The Value of Selective IT Sourcing' in *Sloan Management Review*, **37,** (3), pp. 13–25. An earlier version of Chapter 12 won the Best Paper award at the Third European Conference in Information Systems, and was subsequently reprinted in the *International Journal of Information Management*, **15,** (5), pp. 333–351. Material in Chapters 6, 7, and 16 has also appeared in Earl, M. (ed.) *Information Management: The Organizational Dimensions*, Oxford University Press, Oxford. Full details of all the above are given in the relevant chapter references.

Sources of figures and tables are indicated in the text. We gratefully acknowledge the permissions granted to reproduce materials listed above. Every effort has been made to trace copyright and gain permissions, but please contact the authors if there are any omissions or oversights.

We would like to thank all at McGraw-Hill, but especially Alfred Waller, Elizabeth Robinson and Rosalind Comer, for their unfailing speed, enthusiasm and professionalism. We would like to thank all our administrative and academic colleagues at Templeton College for their humour and support, and who make the college the stimulating and unique place it is. Our greatest debt of gratitude goes to Jenny Peachey, Pam Reeder and Sue Kitt to whom this book is dedicated.

Introduction—Information Management: Lasting Ideas within Turbulent Technology

DAVID F. FEENY

In 1984 the Oxford Institute of Information Management (OXIIM) was established at Templeton College, Oxford. At that time the relevant parts of the British Government seemed pre-occupied by supply-side questions, by the nation's potential to be major providers of the new technologies. And the IT professional community was most visibly concerned with another aspect of supply—the availability of analysts and programmers to meet the burgeoning demand for new systems development. By using the phrase 'information management' our intention was to highlight another dimension of IT exploitation, the management dimension. The mission statement of OXIIM was:

> To improve the body of knowledge on how to manage information resources, so that information technology can be fully exploited in business, government and other large organizations to the advantages of the host organization, its members, and society at large.

The underlying thesis was that successful exploitation of IT is critically dependent on the actions of business managers and senior levels of IT management.

Currently, both mission and thesis remains in place. We continue to believe that IT exploitation, not IT adoption, is the appropriate goal. We perceive that an emphasis on technology and technology-related skills guarantees adoption but not exploitation. Our research has consistently confirmed that it is management that makes the difference.

CRITICAL QUESTIONS

But how well positioned are managers to take up the challenge? It is common wisdom that most executives are particularly uncomfortable when addressing IT issues. Their typical concerns are:

- How do I assess the 'value for money' of my existing investments in IT? It is difficult enough to keep track of IT costs, as expenditure is increasingly incurred by end users of IT beyond the formal IT budget. And when it comes to benefits I must somehow choose between the sophisticated but dubious arithmetic of investment documentation; and the general rhetoric which assures me of better decisions, faster outcomes, lower costs and higher quality. Overall we seem to have invested a great deal without significantly changing the business.
- Given that we have a limited IT budget and an abundance of bids for it, how do I choose between application opportunities? Should I prioritize bids based on rate of return or payback period? Or ration the budget between functional areas of the business? Is a new personnel information system more or less important than a further refinement of production scheduling? Or should we just increase the IT budget to allow for all 'viable' investment cases?
- How can we ensure that the investments we commission are achieved within budget and timescale? Our track record is notoriously patchy even though we build in contingencies to figures which are already too large for comfort. Will using the new 'breakthrough' set of IT tools mean that things really are different this time?
- When we finally achieve the rollout of new systems why are the users of these systems so ungrateful? Given that the whole purpose of the system was to improve the business, why do I often end up dealing with a series of complaints about lack of 'user-friendliness', or coping with business problems which are reportedly due to systems' deficiencies?

The wider question is surely: Why do so many organizations and executives still exhibit these concerns after more than three decades of rapid development in IT hardware, software, and service components? In organizations which embrace the best CASE tools or object-oriented programming techniques, do new systems get delivered on time and do they delight users? Does the engagement of highly qualified consultants result in identification of an IT strategy which resolves the dilemma of investment priorities? Are all these concerns going to be addressed more successfully if the next head of IT is a proven business manager, plucked from another part of the organization? And/or should we invest in intensive IT education for business people, and business education for IT people, to achieve a 'hybrid' culture in which everyone is comfortable with the issues? Is the ultimate solution to outsource the IT function to expert external service providers ('strategic partners') who will resolve these issues for us on a permanent basis? OXIIM's research challenges the likely effectiveness of any such initiatives in isolation. It suggests that the fundamentals of successful information management lie in attitudes, relationships, organizational arrangements and processes. If (and only if) these fundamentals are properly addressed, we find the organization can capitalize on new technologies, tools, consultancy and services to further improve its performance. In other words there are fundamentals which have lasting relevance despite the turbulence of the IT industry. To understand why, we need to identify some prevailing characteristics of IT – factors which help to explain why the executive concerns described earlier remain so familiar across the years of IT 'progress'.

For many years now I have been using Figure I.1 to explore with executives why information technology provides them with such a challenge. Figure I.1 suggests there are four IT domains. While the content of each may vary over time, the separate existence of each remains an important phenomenon.

The first domain is labelled 'IT hype'. Throughout the history of IT

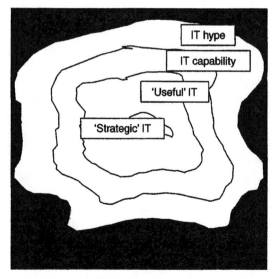

Figure I.1   Four IT domains

there has been a rhetoric which goes beyond the actuality, a focus on potential capabilities and outcomes. The most obvious area of example recently has been the information highway which we are encouraged to believe will shortly transform the existence of every individual, organization, and nation in the universe. IT hype is not just the creature of optimistic IT providers. Heavyweight newspapers, journals and politicians have found it *de rigueur* to issue visionary statements on the subject.

Within the IT hype lies an ever-increasing domain of 'IT capability', comprising the products and services which are available today for organizations to exploit. Here, the counterpart of the information highway is the Internet. It truly exists, and has substantial functionality. But its limitations in performance and security dimensions alone make it a questionable operational tool of real significance for most corporations currently. Clearly there are many other more mature strands of IT where the current capability is truly quite remarkable, so that the domain as a whole represents a huge toolkit available to organizations.

How much of this toolkit is of use? We have probably all experienced some IT products wc would characterize as solutions in search of problems. If we define the 'Useful IT' domain to consist of all the investments which potentially provide at least a minimum acceptable rate of return for the organization, we can reasonably depict this domain as large. While not as large as the IT capability domain, most will feel it is quite large enough to overwhelm any conceivable level of IT budget!

The fourth and smallest domain is labelled 'Strategic IT'. It is probably an unfortunate label to choose as some will assume it refers exclusively to grandiose examples such as the use of airline reservation systems as competitive weapons. However, when I define it as that subset of potential investments which can make a substantial rather than a marginal contribution to organizational achievement, I find most managers intuitively recognize its existence – even if they have not directly experienced it.

Figure I.1, albeit simplistic, now enables us to further examine organizational goals for IT, to provide some explanation for historic disappointment, and to suggest in outline a more convincing and robust way forward.

First, we can define organizational exploitation of IT to be successful navigation through the domains, so that organizational resources become consistently focused on the achievement of 'strategic' rather than 'useful' IT investments. By definition this will provide significantly better value for money. Using the next section as illustration, we may size the possible significance.

'STRATEGIC' VERSUS 'USEFUL' IT

In the early 1990s company A was experiencing a series of poor financial results. Others were also suffering within the industry of global giants, but executives of company A particularly noted the generally excellent performance of company B – a competitor with comparable scale and product lines. Company A therefore initiated a series of benchmarking studies which yielded performance data against industry success factors, including the following:

- Company A took 50 per cent longer than company B to develop a new product.
- Company A's time to deliver against a specific customer order was 2–3 times that of company B.
- Labour productivity in company B was up to twice that of company A.

The contribution of IT to this situation? Further studies provided conflicting evidence:

- Company A's IT activity was assessed by third party consultants to be world class in its efficiency.
- Company A was spending more than twice as much on IT as company B as a percentage of revenue or spend per product shipped.
- In the specific area of computer-aided engineering, which might contribute to shorter product development times, company B invested more than company A.

In the language of the diagram we can suggest that while company A had a cadre of excellent IT professionals, they were supporting a portfolio of 'useful IT' investments which contributed far less benefit (at twice the cost) than the more 'strategic' portfolio of company B.

How had company A ended up in this position? And why have so many of the executives I have worked with positioned their own company's experience to be like that of company A rather than company B? Figure I.1 provides potential insights into this all too common experience.

Consider three ways of navigating through the domains of Figure I.1. The first we can refer to as IT-led. Faced with the complexities of IT hype and IT capabilities, senior management look to their IT function to professionally assess these domains and propose an agenda for IT investment – subject of course to executive approval. Most organizations have operated in this way for some part of their history. Company A did so until the mid-1980s. Why have they (and most others) moved away from an IT-led process? IT professionals are the obvious people to develop and maintain an authoritative view of IT capability. The difficulty lies in moving from capability to application.

Here we encounter a unique characteristic of IT, its inherent lack of application purpose. If I explain to someone any of a range of traditional technologies – balance scales, bulldozers, or blast furnaces – the application is obvious. The technology's purpose was defined at the point of manufacture, and its relevance, or lack of it, to any particular business is easy to discern. However, if I explain what is meant by a multi-media workstation, who knows what relevance it may have within a bank, a supermarket chain, or a government department. Its application is defined at the point of use, not the point of manufacture. Its relevance is a function of the imagination of the user, not the product designer, and may take any of a number of forms. For example, in the UK the Direct Line insurance company moved rapidly from entrant to a mature market to market leader. It used the same core IT products as its entrenched competitors, but it applied them to support a new and superior business model. The technology was embedded in strategic rather than useful initiatives.

This lack of application specificity is the stumbling block within an IT-led process of navigation. Having identified a new area of IT capability, IT professionals are understandably keen to put it to use. They exhibit energy and creativity in identifying how the technology could be used, and in constructing a supporting cost/benefit analysis. Senior management find themselves in the uncomfortable position of adjudicating on a series of strongly argued investment cases. Any negative decision feels like the rejection of an opportunity for improvement. 'Useful IT' is the common result.

In the mid-1980s, company A abandoned the IT-led approach, and adopted what we can call a user-led process. All investment cases for IT would now be developed and argued by the potential beneficiaries – the users of technology. The role of the IT function was now to efficiently implement the applications for which users had won approval. Many organizations still largely operate such a user-led process. It seems eminently rational, particularly as end-users become more sophisticated in their understanding of IT.

Unfortunately, as company A discovered, the user-led approach tends to parallel the IT-led approach in producing a large portfolio of 'Useful IT' investments. There seem to be two reasons for this. First, only a subset of users take up the challenge, and the members of the subset of those users are those who have become enthusiasts for IT. They are at least as energetic and creative as the IT community in pursuing opportunities to embrace the exciting technology they have discovered. Secondly, each is operating within a bounded domain of responsibility, and their proposals therefore represent potential improvements to what may be non-critical aspects of the business. More 'Useful IT' results as senior management now find it even more difficult to deny business-side people the opportunity to improve their performance.

BUSINESS-LED APPROACH

So how do the company Bs of this world achieve their focus on 'Strategic IT' investments which leverage key dimensions of organizational performance? What is the 'Business-led' approach to navigating the four domains which results in an organization understanding what should be done, rather than what could be done, with IT? A business-led approach (Figure I.2) requires one of the three paradigm-shifts which characterize successful information management.

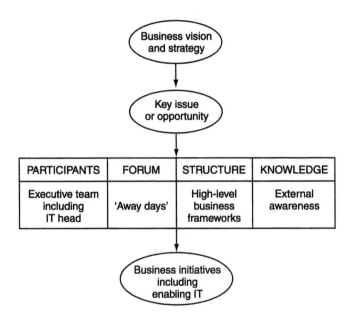

Figure I.2   The business-led approach

The accumulated evidence of our research and experience identifies six characteristics of a business-led approach to IT investment:

● The trigger point is articulation of a business issue or opportunity which, if successfully addressed, would radically advance the organization's achievement of its vision and strategy. Examples might include a breakthrough in unit costs, reduced time to market, or differentiation through new value-added customer services. The start point is not IT capability or an existing business process.

- The business issue is owned and addressed by the organization's executive team, including its head of IT. Each brings a functional perspective, but all are focused as a team on how best to address the key issue.

- The team accepts that 'breakthrough' thinking is unlikely to be achieved amid the hurly burly of day-to-day business or routine board meetings. They adopt an 'away day' culture, taking significant time out from operational activity.

- The team adopts some high-level methodologies – positioning frameworks, value chain concepts, etc—which serve as a common language and structure for debating the issue at hand.

- Through its own membership or through guest members the team has access to knowledge of how other organizations have addressed this type of issue, including organizations in other sectors and including examples of potential IT contributions.

- The target output is not an IT investment case, but an integrated design for a new business initiative, which spells out requirements for IT as well as for other functional areas.

We can describe this as a paradigm shift because the traditional process of navigation through the domains of Figure I.1 is reversed—from outside in to inside out. The business-led process works on the assumption that anything is possible, envisions the ideal business initiative, then checks to see if the necessary IT is available to support it.

If the first paradigm shift has been made, the second is relatively straightforward. It involves evaluating IT investment in a way that flows naturally from a business-led navigation process. Most organizations still operate investment appraisal processes that demand cost/benefit analyses of proposed IT expenditure. The second paradigm shift involves recognizing that IT expenditure does not lead to business benefits. Only the adoption of new business ideas can lead to business benefits. If there is no new business idea associated with IT investment, the most that can be expected is that some existing business idea will operate a little more efficiently as old existing technology is replaced by new. On the other hand, as I.3 depicts, if there is a new business idea associated with IT investment it will not be delivered by IT activity alone. There must be implied a wider set of changes to business processes, skills, structures, measurements. All of these must be identified, costed, planned for, and championed by relevant line management if the investment is to succeed. Analysis of IT investment in isolation does not make sense. A holistic picture delineates all the elements required to deliver a new business idea and articulates how we shall measure if the new idea has been put in place. It then invites

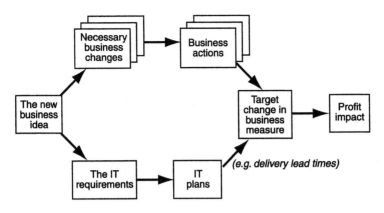

Figure I.3   Evaluation of IT investment

management to judge the value of that idea in profit impact terms, and decide whether the likely value justifies all (or none) of the necessary investment.

SYSTEMS DEVELOPMENT AND DELIVERY

There is a third paradigm shift to be made if we are to transform the track record of systems development. The traditional approach to systems development is based on a rational/engineering perspective which leads to a well-structured sequential process, driven by IT professionals but with regular involvement from the business side to confirm satisfaction at checkpoints along the way. The process begins with a statement of requirements and proceeds through external design, internal design, coding and testing. If the application in question is essentially a new technology platform for an existing business idea this is all well and good. If the application is a 'strategic' component of a new business initiative this traditional process is a route to disaster.

The basic problem comes in the initial phase, the specification of requirements. In a radically new business initiative the fact is that the business has only a general understanding of its need at the outset. But, confronted by a process which presses for a full specification ('Tell me what you need and promise not to change your mind'), users resort to specifying everything they *might* need, in order to be 'safe'. As the specification grows, timescales extend and risks escalate. We are confronted with the all too familiar phenomenon of the two-year development in which few have confidence. And a succession of poor experiences generates an environment in which the business feels unable to base its strategy on untimely and uncertain IT developments.

The paradigm shift establishes a new culture, based on the following elements:

- A single project team is set up, comprising all the required resources from both the business and the IT function. Ideally all team members are committed to the project full time, and are co-located in order to build good relationships and successful communication.
- The team is made responsible not for creating a system but for delivering clearly specified benefits to the business. There are no other success criteria. Hence, if it becomes clear during the project that specifications and plan should change, all team members are motivated to show the necessary flexibility.
- Executive management *mandate* at the outset the timescale within which the project must deliver the target benefits. They deliberately specify (and stick to) a challenging timescale even though expert opinion may say it is impossible. Nine months is the maximum timescale and it may well be significantly shorter.
- This 'time-boxing' forces the team to make decisions about what is really required, to target the adequate rather than the gold-plated system. It drives adherence to the Pareto Principle, that 20 per cent of the effort achieves 80 per cent of the available result.
- Time-boxing also encourages the use of prototyping. Instead of creating a full requirements specification, the team iterates through a series of prototypes and achieves the target learning of what is really required.
- The project may be planned as a series of phases within an overall architecture if the team remains convinced that it cannot be achieved within a single nine-month time-box. This is still a major step forward. A series of six month steps which each deliver business benefits is a far better route than a two-year monolith.

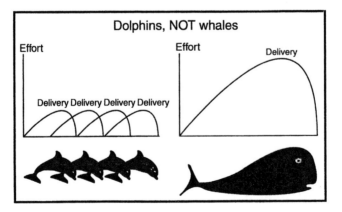

Figure I.4   Dolphins, NOT whales

Figure I.4, entitled Dolphins not Whales, is not a product of my imagination. It was produced by one major corporation which was seeking to implement the findings of our research, and proved particularly effective in winning hearts and minds. This is surely what paradigm shifts are all about, leading people to a different but better approach which depends on changes in attitudes, understanding and relationships.

ABOUT THIS BOOK

Through its research-based chapters this book sets out to provide the relevant understandings to develop more detailed insights into successful information management.

- Part 1 has five perspectives on the strategic exploitation of IT, ranging from the top level teamwork implied by a strategic orientation, through questions of opportunity and evaluation, to IT support for strategic decision making.
- Part 2 focuses on the organizational arrangements which underpin information management. It addresses both structural and relationship issues.
- Part 3 homes in on the management of major IT-based projects, drawing lessons from a wide range of project successes and failures.
- Part 4 looks at the sourcing of IT services and resources, considering how organizations can best utilize the rapidly growing market for external services.
- Part 5 addresses a number of other contemporary issues and assesses how previously established information management principles can be interpreted into emerging fields.
- Part 6 reflects on evolution and learning in information management and seeks to draw an overall picture of the emerging IT function.

At least one of the authors of each chapter is a current member of the Templeton College faculty, (David Feeny, Gerd Islei, Jonathan Reynolds, Leslie Willcocks). Others are mainly former or visiting faculty (Michael Earl—OXIIM's Founding Director, Guy Fitzgerald, Wendy Currie, Blake Ives, Mary Lacity), recent OXIIM doctoral students (Pelly Periasamy, Andrea Taylor Cummings), or OXIIM Research Affiliates (Brian Edwards, Kep Simpson). This is not of course to suggest that OXIIM has a monopoly of information management wisdom. Each chapter references the external work that has most influenced our thinking. But after more than twelve years of research and education activity, it seemed appropriate to draw together the knowledge we have acquired, the OXIIM approach to information management. We hope our readers will experience a body of work that is at once scholarly, relevant, and accessible. These are the values to which OXIIM continues to aspire.

Part One

Information Technology: Leveraging the Business

CHAPTER ONE

Is your CIO Adding Value?

MICHAEL J. EARL AND DAVID F. FEENY

INTRODUCTION

Despite most businesses being dependent on information technology (IT) today, the information systems (IS) function is often seen by chief executives (CEOs) as a problem area – or more accurately as a dilemma. Many general managers are tired of being told that IT can create competitive advantage and enable business transformation. What they observe and experience are IS project failures, unrelenting hype about IT, and rising information processing costs. CEOs often do not know how to evaluate the IS function's performance and the IT Director's, or Chief Information Officer's (CIO), contribution (see also Chapter 4). Not only are radical IS management prescriptions, such as outsourcing and downsizing being applied, (Lacity and Hirschheim 1995; Willcocks and Fitzgerald, 1994; see also Part 4) but CIOs are being fired (Earl, 1996; Rothfedder and Driscoll, 1990; see also Chapter 18). These include some heroes of the IT profession whose photographs not long ago graced the covers of business magazines.

For several years now we have been researching the leadership of IS, interviewing extensively among CEOs and CIOs. This work has included three formal studies of the CIO. The first study (Feeny *et al.*, 1992) examined the factors which determine the relationship between the CEOs and the CIOs in 14 organizations. A second project focused on the survival of the CIOs. Ten matched pairs of surviving and non-surviving CIOs in different industries were studied (Earl, 1996). In the third investigation, 10 individuals who had been interviewed in a CIO study in the 1986 (Hirschheim *et al.*, 1988) were revisited in order to understand their experience and learning over a five-year period (see Chapter 18). All of these studies involved CIOs in leading corporations across the spectrum of industries. Face to face interviews with CIOs and CEOs explored not only their actions and experiences, but also their personal backgrounds, attitudes and values and the organizational contexts in which they operated. CIO interviews were supplemented by administration and psychometric tests. Through these studies and others on IS management which have involved CIOs and CEOs, we have research data on the leadership of IS in more than 60 organizations.

Across the whole experience, two patterns stand out. First, there is an apparent polarization of CEOs in attitude and behaviour, between those who see IT as a strategic resource and those who see IT as a cost. Second, the role and actions of the CIO turn out to be crucial in ensuring that IT is deployed for strategic advantage and that the IS function delivers value for money. The CIO can and must add value in order to make the difference between an organization where IS is seen to be a problem and one where it is a recognized strength. Here are some examples of what we have seen, which illustrate contrasting pictures of IS added value. In the following three companies, taken from our research, IS was seen as a problem:

1. In a telecommunications company, the CEO revealed that only one thing kept him awake at night. He was never sure whether his CIO was doing a good job or not. He knew that IT mattered in that industry and he found the IT strategy seductive, but delivery and benefits were elusive. The strategy centred on building a new state of the art IT infrastructure which, it was claimed, would provide an efficient and flexible platform to meet both current and future business needs. The CIO concerned had spent his career in the IT industry and was an avid scanner of emerging technologies. While the CEO was attracted by the promise of future excellent IS capability, he wanted adequate applications now to support a rapidly growing business. After wrestling with this dilemma for some time, he fired the CIO. Soon afterwards a successor CEO strongly reinforced the emphasis on rapid support for immediate needs and formally reversed most of the IS policies of the past.

2. In a chemicals company, the CIO believed fervently that IT could yield competitive advantage across the business. Given his previous background as a business general manager, the CIO's beliefs were based more on a sense of business opportunities than a long familiarity with IT. He was an ardent evangelist who would regularly create occasions to promulgate his message to the Company's management teams. He was appointed and initially backed by a CEO who was himself a well-known visionary on the transformational capabilities of IT. The CIO led investment in a corporate-wide infrastructure ahead of many of the business units adopting and owning such visions. The environment changed

sharply when a successor CEO took office and in his eyes, IT was a source of cost and rarely delivered its promise. He was a persuasive and public orator on these points and the recent infrastructure investment provided some ammunition for such views. The CIO retired early and his own successor found that even charting a middle way was extremely difficult in this management context.

3. In a high-growth financial services company, IT had underpinned much of the aggressive marketing of recent years. The CIO enjoyed being a high-profile member of the executive team and found it difficult to adjust when the company entered a period of consolidation with a new emphasis on cost and efficiency. In this new environment, the CEO felt that teamwork at the top was particularly important; he was critical of the CIO's behaviour. According to the CEO, the CIO stonewalled whenever the question of the IS budget was questioned and resented being asked about his department's contribution. Further, the CEO felt patronized when the CIO suggested that the CEO could not appreciate the complexity of the issues involved. The relationship became unsustainable.

By contrast, the CIO and the IS function were perceived as adding value in these companies:

4. Following privatization, a utility had to make the transition from monopoly supplier to one of an increasing number of rival providers competing on price and reliability. Faced with the need to make radical changes in the company's culture, business processes and cost structure, the CEO recognized IT's enabling potential. He recruited a CIO who accepted the responsibility to rapidly deliver a new set of systems to underpin the new way of doing business. Now the CEO sees the CIO as his principal ally in driving the fundamental business changes. A critical factor in the relationship is the CIO's personal ability to contribute to business thinking, the vision of change, and management of the change process. Interestingly, the CIO's background is in IT and in quite different industry settings, yet his business acumen is clearly appreciated.

5. In an insurance company, the CIO was recently appointed CEO of the largest division in order to turn it round from loss to profit. He was judged to know and understand the working and economics of that division's business better than anyone, because of the perspectives gained from years of systems work done there. He had also gained credibility through his management of IS as a line of business.

6. In a retail group, which has now become an industry leader, the CEO recognized some years ago that he could not match entrenched

rivals on the most obvious bases of competition. Instead, he identified the innovative use of IT as his best route to competitive advantage and recruited a CIO with that in mind. With the CEO's backing, the CIO has helped take the company to a position of leadership in areas such as logistics and promotion management. The philosophy has been to deliver lean systems that can be implemented in a few months and expanded over time. The CEO now states publicly that the IS function has given most value to the building of the business.

In the first three cases, we see some familiar experiences. One CEO finds it difficult to evaluate the performance of IS and the contribution of the CIO. Another CEO is a born sceptic; stories of IT-based competitive advantage are to be distrusted and do not apply to his industry where the clear goal should be to minimize the costs of the IS function. At another company, the CIO believes that IT budgets should not be subject to the same disciplines as the rest of the business, the IS function is beyond challenge and business executives must trust in the superior and specialist knowledge of IS professionals.

In the contrasting cases the companies, and in particular the CEOs, are very clear that IT is adding value and that the CIO's contribution has been significant. These CEOs believe that IT can enable new and smarter ways of doing business and that the CIO, and the IS function in general, should therefore be actively brought into the business team. Indeed, the CIOs are valued for their business thinking and change management capabilities as much as their IT knowledge.

Collectively these cases illustrate the more general divide in perceptions of IT, which we have characterized in Table 1.1. We have found that the CIO's ability to add value is the biggest single factor in determining whether the organization views IT as an asset or a liability.

ADDING VALUE

What is striking in the organizations we have studied is that nearly all have found it difficult, when challenged, to formally assess value for money from their IT. This is a well-documented problem (Strassmann, 1990; Willcocks, 1996; see also Chapter 4). This is often because the returns are not due to IT investments alone, there are many unanticipated costs and benefits, and measurement tools and methods are immature. In many organizations, this difficulty is compounded by an inability to point to any conspicuous IT successes, so that an atmosphere of unhappiness and uncertainty prevails. In other organizations, however, top management still recognizes the difficulty of measuring IS performance but is not so obsessed by the question of

Table 1.1 Perceptions of IT

Issue	'IT is a liability'	'IT is an asset'
Are we getting value for money	ROI difficult to measure and the organization is notably unhappy with IS as a whole	ROI difficult to measure but the organization believes IS is making an important contribution
How important is IT?	Stories of strategic use of IT dismissed as relevant to 'this' business	Stories of strategic use of IT seen as interesting and instructive
How do we plan for IT?	IT plans are made by specialists or by missionary zealots	IT thinking subsumed within business thinking
Is the IS function doing a good job?	General cynicism about the track record of IS	Performance of IS is no longer an agenda item
What is the IT strategy?	Many IT applications under development	IS efforts focused on a few key initiatives
What is the CEO's vision for the role of IT?	Sees limited role for IT within the business	Sees IT as having a role of the transformation of the business
What do we expect of the CIO?	CIO positioned as specialist functional manager	CIO valued as contributor to business thinking and business operations

IT value for money. They are collectively aware that at least some IT applications have been central to important business achievements. For example, when recent legislative change created the opportunity for a new financial services product, one company took a leadership position because the systems support necessary to launch its product was available well in advance of rivals. The CIO's added value here was that he had focused, obsessively and continuously, on identifying and supporting the emerging business imperatives. He was able to judge when an IT application should be rolled out quickly.

Stories of how businesses have gained competitive advantage from IT have been important in stimulating management interest in IT (Benjamin *et al.*, 1984; McFarlan, 1984; see also Chapter 3). In the chemical company mentioned, the CIO delighted in relating such stories but executives routinely dismissed them as being irrelevant to the industry. Meanwhile a competitor was implementing a business strategy of differentiation by successfully adapting an IT application which had been established in a different industry. A second attribute of CIOs who add value is their ability to conceptualize how success stories from elsewhere may or may not have relevance for their business.

A recurring theme of recent years has been how to connect IT investment to business strategy. All too frequently the connections are attempted through special exercises led by IS, or they are not made at all because some missionary zealot drives through an investment unrelated to business direction. By contrast the most successful approach we have experienced is where there are no IT strategies, only business strategies (Earl, 1993). The added value required for the CIO is that he or she builds excellent and informed relationships with key executives, so that IT requirements become an integral component of business strategy. We can compare two automotive companies. In one the CIO is the trusted confidant of the CEO, automatically included in strategic deliberations so that the need for IT applications emerges as business directives evolve. In the other the CIO has found it difficult to establish relationships with a succession of top executives, and the IT plans are no more than a synthesis of new requests from other functions and systems work-in-progress.

The CIO also adds value by building a demonstrable track record of delivery. As one CIO remarked, 'You can't sell the sizzle of IT if you don't deliver'. If promises of IS lead times and service availability are consistently missed, there arises a general cynicism which results in business plans and operations that avoid reliance on IT. An important added value of the CIO therefore is to build such a demonstrable track record of delivery to promise that IS performance drops off the management agenda.

The tasks of IS strategic planning include identifying IT applications which can support business strategies or create new strategic options, and allocating scarce IS resources (Earl, 1989; Henderson and Venkatraman, 1993). Organizations which view IT as a liability typically possess 'application portfolios' which appear to cover most of the business. By contrast, and as argued in the Introduction to this book, the perception that IT is an asset is associated with strongly focused IT efforts, each tackling an area of business weakness or leveraging a unique organizational capability. The CIO's added value here is to lead the resistance to myriad proposals of how IT *could* be used, in order to concentrate effort on areas where IT *should* be used.

The CEO's attitude toward and vision for IT may influence the organization's strategic orientation (see Chapter 2). A CIO's targeted approach to IT investment has often been helped by the CEO's publicly expressed belief that IT is an enabler of business transformation. More diverse application portfolios, and more limited achievements, are found where the CEO and top management see IT as having an administrative or support role – or where executives have mixed views of the scope of IT's contribution. CIOs add value by working to achieve a shared and challenging vision of the role of IT among the executive team, a common conception of the nature (not the specifics) of IT's potential contribution to the business.

Finally, it is our experience that CEOs and their organizations are sharply divided in their expectations of the CIO. In some organizations the CIO is positioned as a specialist functional manager, and therefore is only involved by the business in what are identified as IT-related issues. In other organizations, the CIO is valued as a regular contributor to business thinking and business operations (see Stephens *et al.*, 1992). Part of the added value of the CIO is to spot and create opportunities to make such contributions, in contexts that may have little or nothing to do with IT.

Table 1.2 summarizes what we have consistently identified as the added value of CIOs in organizations which perceive IT as an asset. It is the added value which makes the difference between failure and success.

Table 1.2   The added value of the CIO

1. Obsessive and continuous focus on business imperatives
2. Interpretation of external IT success stories
3. Establishment and maintenance of IS executive relationships
4. Establishment and communication of IS performance record
5. Concentration of the IS development effort
6. Achievement of a shared and challenging vision of the role of IT
7. Personal contributions beyond the IT function

HOW CIOs ACHIEVE THE ADDED VALUE
(AND HOW CEOs HELP)

What exactly does the CIO do to create the added value we have identified? And how can the CEO ensure that the CIO has every chance of delivering it? We can describe what we have found to be important for each of the components of added value.

To achieve the *focus on business imperatives*, successful CIOs consistently invest their personal time in discussions which develop and test their vision of the business. They never relent. They look for the one or two business themes which capture strategic intent and which can drive IS development. Formal statements of business goals and strategy may be taken as starting points, but are not seen as definitive inputs to IS activity. Such statements can never be rich enough to capture the full essence of critical business needs as they emerge. It is only through dialogue with the CEO and other executives that the CIO can tease out the motivations, meanings, and priorities, know the mind of the business, sense the impending changes, and maintain the relevance and timeliness of the IS effort. Without such insight from the CIO, the IS function becomes like a supertanker with a broken radio – lurching ponderously in response to ambiguous semaphore messages, more likely to prove an expensive liability than a company asset. We recall the huge investment made by one IS function in a global communications network because, 'the Bank has said it wants to be a global competitor'. The Bank's CIO soon found that business colleagues did not share his interpretation of the strategic rhetoric, and hence did not value the facilities the network provided. 'They did not believe in it; they did not understand,' he complained. After a high-level audit by consultants, he lost his job.

Two actions by the CEO are important in creating this component of added value. The first and most obvious is to make the CIO a true member of the top management team. The CIO who attends as of right all key executive meetings directly gains a new level of understanding of the business, and indirectly gains enhanced access to fellow executives who can provide the next level. Note that we are not prescribing any particular reporting structure for the CIO; in our research we have consistently found that team membership rather than reporting structure is critical. The second and related action for the CEO is to ensure that at least once or twice a year this top management team takes time out to debate the business directions. Executive team retreats and 'away days' can be instrumental in educating the CIO – as well as serving their primary purpose of challenging the continuing validity of business thinking.

CIOs who add value through their *interpretation of external IT success stories* tend to be skilled analysts and natural tutors. They avoid the perils of making naïve suggestions about transferring a technology or application from outside, or advocating what may be well-founded ideas in a proprietorial and offensive style. They are good business theorists and systems thinkers who can capture the kernel of an exemplar and conceptualize its potential relevance to the business, where it may relate to a business need or create new strategic option. They communicate with fellow executives by translating new ideas into pictures and understandable benefits. And they draw satisfaction from facilitating the learning of others, unconcerned about who ends up claiming to have originated the idea.

A CIO's propensity for tutoring is one of the keys to *establishing and maintaining executive relationships*. It is very easy for CIOs who have built their career in IS to spend their time with, and identify with those within the IS function, managing within and perpetuating the specialist values of the IS function. More surprisingly, perhaps, we find that CIOs who are ex-general managers are equally fallible in this area. Some succumb to the temptation to avoid the hard work of building substantive relationships with their peers; they look for some very visible but shallow initiatives to make a careerist splash – internal publicity through newsletters, presentations and IT exhibitions are examples we have encountered. Others become ardent converts who know exactly how IT should be deployed in all parts of the business, even if their peers do not share the same enthusiasm. In all these cases the IS function ends up isolated from the rest of business, and unable to implement initiatives which require whole-hearted collaboration from senior business executives.

Whatever their backgrounds, CIOs who succeed in adding value recognize and act upon the importance of executive relationships. They look upon alliance-building as an important component of their job. Most often they work at it through informal one-to-one meetings – the soft, opportunist, rather than the formal approach. But opportunities are sought out and firmly grasped as they arise. In the words of one CIO: 'It is never too much trouble to explain when a business colleague asks for help. It is my job to make the technology accessible in the eyes of the management team'. Another, who had been fired from his previous company but had now re-emerged as a CIO, explained how his approach has changed: 'In my previous company I now realize that I constructed win/lose situations with business peers. I was determined to fight the IS corner, to prove that problems were not of our making, and I generated enemies not allies. Today I work hard at constructing win/win situations which secure the relationships I need'.

CEOs help to enable these relationships by making the CIO a member of the management team, as we have already urged. This one action greatly increases both the number and the quality of relationship-building opportunities available to the CIO. We have also found that CEOs can set powerful examples through their own two-way relationships with CIOs.

Establishing and communicating a strong IS performance record is a component on which some CIOs spend most of their time. Unfortunately it often avails them little, and serves only to ensure that they have no time to deliver the other components. Overseeing what may be independently rated as highly efficient data centres has not saved CIOs from being fired or their empires out-sourced. In our experience, the successful CIOs do care about and achieve this component of added value, but spend little of their personal time in the process. Rather they set up and monitor a regime which delivers. Characteristic elements of this regime include:

- selection of subordinates who are outstandingly good at operations management, often better than the CIOs themselves;
- procedures which require feedback to the business on all actions taken in response to any request of/complaint to IS;
- procedures which require feedback from the business on their satisfaction with most actions taken by IS;
- communication of service and business satisfaction data, with the CIO closely and visibly monitoring results, getting personally involved early if things start to go wrong.

The CEO can help stimulate such a regime by making clear to the CIO that the perceptions of users in the business are the only relevant performance criteria. Awards from peers in the IT community, even the CEO's personal sympathy, will count for nothing if users are unhappy. It is also very helpful if the CEO ensures that the IS function is fully integrated into any company performance initiative, such as a TQM programme, and IS is therefore perceived as neither forgotten nor special.

We have seen many CIOs who generate or agree to IS application portfolios which proliferate across the business. Their (forlorn) hope is that this will be a means of satisfying everyone. In practice, in our experience, they end up satisfying no-one. CIOs who add value work hard to ensure that the business *concentrates the IS development effort*, invests solely and successfully in projects which are integral to business strategy. This is the component which most directly adds value; it represents the ultimate pay-off enabled by several other components of the CIO's work. Again we can talk of a regime which characterizes the success stories of our experience, the elements in this case including:

- **Sponsorship by the Business**   While the CIO takes responsibility for IS related cost elements, he or she insists that all investment cases are presented for approval by business executives, who relate them to stated business strategy or agreed business imperatives, and agree to be held accountable for the target benefits. Proposals which achieve 'useful' rather than 'strategic' benefits are strongly challenged as potential diversions of management effort and attention (see Introduction).
- **Maximum Elapsed Time**   A development environment in which the CIO mandates that there is a maximum elapsed time (6 or 9 months) within which any project must deliver new functions and benefits to the business. Huge monolithic projects consistently re-emerge as disaster stories.
- **The 80/20 Rule**   An agreement between IS and the business that, faced with an 'impossible timescale', they will identify and implement the 20 per cent of the requirement that delivers 80 per cent of the benefit. Again, it is the inclusion of the 'nice-to-have' features that turn potentially sound projects into looming catastrophes.

The rewards in this area can be very high. One large multinational recently benchmarked its leading competitor and found its own IT spend was more than twice that of the competitor. But by targeting and limiting its spend to critical projects, the competitor still manages to outperform them on the vital dimensions of time-to-market and manufacturing productivity.

CEOs can stimulate the introduction of the appropriate regime by demanding that projects are appraised against strategic criteria rather than simplistic cost/benefit analysis, and ensuring that they are managed as business projects rather than IS developments. All too often, in our experience, CEOs still do exactly the opposite!

Working to achieve a *shared and challenging vision of the role of IT* within the executive team is another added value component which requires much of the CIO's personal time. In the most successful organizations we have encountered, this shared vision positions IT as an agent of business transformation – a technology which is only applied to achieve radical rather than incremental improvement in the business. Such a vision is the precursor and enabler of the concentrated IS development effort described above. In the short term a CIO can operate successfully with the 'sponsorship' of only a few executives who share this vision – perhaps the CEO alone. But longer term success requires the vision to be shared across the whole executive team. Successful CIOs recognize this and can provide detailed profiles of the understandings and attitudes of every key executive of the business. They have clear plans for obtaining the desired buy-in to the vision, tailored to each individual. The plans may include formal events such as application demonstrations, or visits from appropriate gurus; but again they are likely to be centred on quality one-to-one contact between CIO and executive over many months or more. These CIOs realize that attitudes, visions, and values seldom change quickly; and they are prepared to find whatever time and resources are necessary. The CIO of a large manufacturing company went so far as to bring in a psychologist to help him think through how to work with one key executive. In the words of another CIO, 'the day you stop working on developing a shared vision for IT, you are gone'.

Finally, CIOs who add value make important general *contributions to business thinking and business operations*. We have cited the CEO who sees the CIO as his principal ally in driving fundamental business change. Why should CEOs expect such a contribution? It is clearly not sensible to expect the CIO to have better marketing insights than the marketing director, or sharper ideas for improving the manufacturing process than the production director. But the nature of the IT is such that the CIO is one of those executives who gets a view *across* the business, with a requirement and a curiosity to 'know how things work'. They are well placed to understand the connections and interrelationships between functions and organizational units; and it is by improving these linkages that the greatest opportunities for business advantage often occur (see also the discussion on the role of the CIO in Chapter 17). Thus we have seen CIOs who become highly valued members of task forces – charged with improving logistics, reducing the time taken between customer order and delivery, taking significant cost out of the business without damaging its competitive capability. It is in the CEO's interest to ensure that the CIO is made a member of such task forces and working groups, to contribute a business-wide perspective without allegiance to one of the historic power bases within the company.

From our description of how the added value is delivered, it will be obvious that there are many connections and overlaps between the components. Figure 1.1 demonstrates this graphically. For example, CIOs who have built excellent executive relationships are better able to focus on business imperatives, achieve a shared vision of the role of IT, link that focus and vision into a concentrated IS development effort – and through those actions sustain the excellent relationships. Because of the inter-dependencies, CIOs are likely to deliver on *all* or *none* of the added-value components. This is the primary explanation for the polarity between the views of the CEOs on the contribution of IS to their business.

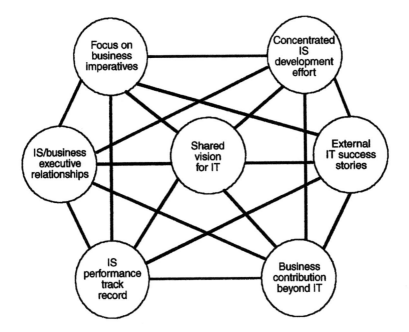

Figure 1.1   The Added-value framework

As pointed out in later chapters in this book, some CEOs see outsourcing as the answer to their dissatisfaction with IS. This outsourcing may include the CIO role and its incumbent (Hamilton, 1989; Willcocks and Fitzgerald, 1994). Our added-value framework highlights the implications of this step. It is very difficult to see how an outsider could deliver any of the components of added value, operating in the way we have described. Even the achievement of a good performance record through outsourcing involves substantial management of the supply activity from within the organization and continuous attention to the organization's perception of IS performance. More obviously, building executive relationships which are so fundamental cannot be sub-contracted. To outsource the CIO role will ensure that IS remains a liability, albeit perhaps a smaller one. This argument is pursued and substantiated in more detail in Chapter 17.

QUALITIES OF THE CIO WHO ADDS VALUE

Through our research we have accumulated extensive data on CIOs who succeed in adding value: the CIOs' own descriptions of what they do, and what abilities they draw upon; their CEOs' perceptions of the qualities they look for and experience; and behavioural data from a number of psychometric tests we have administered to the CIOs (the Myers Briggs Psychological Preference Test (MBTI, 1986) and Belbin's (1981) team-role self-perception inventory). Collectively this data provides a consistent profile of the CIOs who add value, which we have brought together in Figure 1.2 under the headings of behaviour, motivation, competencies and experience.

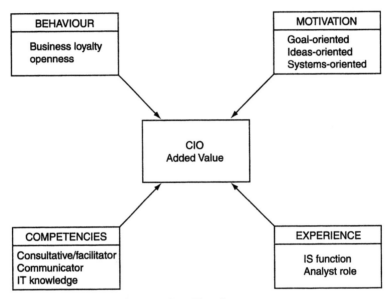

Figure 1.2   Profile of the CIO who adds value

For many CEOs the first requirement of a CIO is 'integrity'. This might be considered an essential quality of any executive, but where CIOs are concerned it relates to some specific anxieties. CEOs can feel particularly vulnerable in the area of IT, aware of how difficult it is to assess project status, technology risk, functional performance. They know that CIOs can use their specialist knowledge and language to camouflage problems, advance or defend their own empires and budgets, pursue their own interests. The integrity sought of the CIO therefore extends to the two elements of behaviour in Figure 1.2 – business loyalty and openness. The CEO needs to have confidence that the CIO's first loyalty is to the business as a whole, and that every IT initiative will be driven by business imperatives, not technology aggrandisement. Second, the opaqueness of IT activity leads the CEO to value the CIO who will 'report impending problems as quickly and openly as they report triumphs'.

The next element of Figure 1.2 looks at the motivation of CIOs who add value. Psychometric data shows that these CIOs are strongly goal-oriented. They derive great satisfaction from knowing that they have influenced the course of the business. They demonstrate stamina and steely determination in pursuit of goals related to business change. They are also fascinated by new ideas and usually devote considerable time to scanning and networking beyond their own company and industry. They think instinctively of business as systems, whose current working must be understood so that superior new systems can be devised, analysed and successfully applied. The combination of these motivation elements is captured in the words of one CIO who told us 'I am not interested in running an IS department, I want to transform this business'. This was not a bid for the CEO's job, but a perception of his mission as CIO!

Nevertheless, such ambitions may seem threatening and inappropriate in a CIO, and we have found that some of those who are hard drivers for business change do indeed accumulate powerful enemies. This situation becomes counter-productive in terms of achieving the sought after change, and has often resulted in the demise of the CIO. What saves CIOs like the one quoted above, is that they seek to be the facilitators not the formal leaders of change. They want the satisfaction of achievement, but do not demand the public credit. In short, they have the compensating competencies of Figure 1.2. Such CIOs are adept at working through others, at consulting and involving their peers, at constructing those 'win/win situations'. Linked to the consultative style is a second competency, the CIO as communicator. We are not here referring to oratory, though some of them are indeed excellent speech-makers. They key requirement is communication in the literal sense, these CIOs are able to absorb and utilize the language of a colleague in production or marketing, show understanding of and sensitivity to their issues. And allied to a profound knowledge of IT, their communications capability allows them to de-mystify any aspect of IT that needs to be discussed. It is the combination of motivation and competencies that allows the goal-hungry CIO to operate effectively, the iron fist in the velvet glove.

Perhaps the most surprising element of the profile comes under the heading of experience. The successful/value-adding CIOs in our research have invariably come from the IS function. Most have never had a job outside the IS function. It is those who are transplanted from other areas of the business who have struggled, uncomfortable with the technology, unclear of their careers, typically equipped to operate as forceful managers rather than bridge-builders and facilitors. It seems that a lengthy apprenticeship in the IS function, particularly in systems analysis and development, is the appropriate background for a CIO.

Before assuming the leadership, the CIO will then be well accustomed to operating by consent, from a function that is not a traditional power base, with a mission to explain and a focus on systemic business change.

SOME ADVICE FOR THE CEO

'With my previous CEO', one ex-CIO said ruefully to us, 'anything was possible', with his successor, nothing was possible'. The statement may be extreme, but the sentiment is widespread. CIOs who are intrinsically capable of adding value in the ways we have described know very well that the CEO's position on a number of issues is critical to their own ability to achieve. They believe that IT has evolved to the point where leadership must come from executive line management (Rockart, 1988). Table 1.3 summarizes the requests that value-adding CIOs would make to CEOs. It is also the advice we now give to CEOs on their behalf.

Table 1.3   Key message for CEOs

- Position IT and the CIO as agents of change
- Focus on achieving effectiveness not efficiency from IT
- Institutionalize business values for IT
- Build an executive team which includes the CIO
- Manage IT as an integral not an adjunct to the business

First, as CEO you are of course in the business of change, particularly in the turbulent 1990s. Position IT and the CIO as agents of change. See IT and the CIO as part of the solution, not part of the problem. Involve the CIO early in the debate about the nature of change required and the options available, not after the new way forward has already been defined.

Second, make sure that you and your organization focus on how and where the application of IT can be effective. The key idea is to exploit IT within initiatives which deliver some element of business transformation, and substantial benefits. Do not think of IT as a cost displacement technology, which may contribute, after much effort, some incremental gains in 'efficiency'. The major gains come from applying IT to 'doing the right things' not to 'doing things right'. So when appraising IT-related investments, apply the same market-oriented criteria that you would use for investments in new production capacity, distribution channels and so forth. As one CEO remarked: 'Ask the question – does this IT proposal make business sense?'

Third, use the personal time you give to IT to help institutionalize business values across the organization. The CEO of a chemicals group transformed attitudes to IT within his corporation through his consistent questions to business executives about how IT featured in their business strategies. Lead by example. Focus on establishing a business context and language which is conducive to IT exploitation. Get in place the regimes required for achieving excellent IS performance, identifying strategic IS developments, and delivering them fast. Value for money will follow without your having to continually review IS projects and budgets, or preside over painful post-mortems.

Fourth, build an executive team that includes an appropriately qualified CIO. Whatever the organization structure and reporting lines, the CIO needs to be, *de facto*, part of the top management group. And the group needs to operate as a real team. It is very difficult to surface and do justice to new business thinking unless there is a top-level culture in which executives regularly meet – formally and informally – to discuss potentially challenging and far-reaching ideas in an atmosphere of mutual trust.

Finally, manage IT as integral to the business not an adjunct. If you have special steering committees for putting the business into IT, disband them. If the CIO is a full member of the business team, that team can take the issues as and when required, to much better effect. Equally, whenever projects, task forces, special initiatives arise, involve the CIO and ensure that a systems and IS perspective is brought to bear on devising solutions to business problems.

CONCLUSION

We have described how CEOs tend to be polarized in their views of the value for money being delivered by IT. In recent years there has been a tendency among organizations who view IT as a liability to resort to outsourcing the IS function. This action may reduce IT costs, at least in the short term, but it does nothing to change the dominant variable, the value being delivered by IT. Organizations where IT is viewed as an asset, where IT plays a role in transforming the business, have quite a different IT environment, as we have detailed. This environment is not achieved by outsourcing. It is achieved primarily by the actions and qualities of a value-adding CIO, irrespective of whether the bulk of IT activity is outsourced or remains in-house. But the critical dependency for the CIO is the attitude and influence of the CEO. The CEO can help by inspiring a receptive and constructive climate for IT across the organization. Alternatively, the CEO can, through a personal example of hostility or detachment, inhibit any worthwhile IT achievements. Ultimately you get what you deserve from IT.

REFERENCES

Belbin, R. (1981) *Management Teams: Why they Succeed or Fail*, Heinemann, London.

Benjamin, R., Rockart, J., Scott Morton, M. and Wyman, J. (1984) 'Information Technology: a Strategic Opportunity', *Sloan Management Review*, Spring, pp. 3–10.

Earl, M. (1989) *Management Strategies for Information Technology*, Prentice-Hall, London.

Earl, M. (1993) 'Experiences in Strategic Information Systems Planning', *MIS Quarterly*, **17,** pp. 1–20.

Earl, M. (1996) 'The Chief Information Officer: Past, Present and Future', In Earl, M. (ed.), *Information Management: The Organizational Dimension*, Oxford University Press, Oxford.

Feeny, D., Edwards, B. and Simpson, K. (1992) 'Understanding the CEO/CIO Relationship', *MIS Quarterly*, **16,** (4), pp. 435–448.

Hamilton, R. (1989) 'Kendall Outsources IS Chief', *Computerworld*, 8th April, pp. 1–4.

Henderson, J. and Venkatraman, N. (1993) 'Strategic Alignment: Leveraging Information Technology for Transforming Organizations', *IBM Systems Journal*, **32,** (1), pp. 4–16.

Hirschheim, R., Earl, M., Feeny, D. and Lockett, M. (1988) 'An Exploration into the Management of the Information Systems Function: Key Issues and an Evolutionary Model', Information Technology Management for Productivity and Competitive Advantage, IFIP TC-8 Open Conference, Singapore, March.

Lacity, M. and Hirschheim, R. (1995) *Beyond the Information Systems Bandwagon*, Wiley, Chichester.

MBTI (1986) Myers-Briggs Type Indicators (MBTI), Consulting Psychological Press, Palo Alto, California.

McFarlan, W. (1984) 'Information Technology Changes the Way you Compete', *Harvard Business Review*, May–June, pp. 98–103.

Rockart, J. (1988) 'The Line Takes the Leadership—IS Management in a Wired Society', *Sloan Management Review*, Summer, pp. 57–64.

Rothfeder, J. and Driscoll, L. (1990) 'CIO is Starting to Stand for Career Is Over', *Business Week*, February 26th.

Stephens, C., Ledbetter, W., Mitra, A. and Ford, F. (1992) 'Executive or Functional Manager? The Nature of the CIO's Job', *MIS Quarterly*, **16,** pp. 449–468.

Strassman, P. (1990) *The Business Value of Computers*, Information Economics Press, New Canaan, Connecticut.

Willcocks, L. (ed.) (1996) *Investing in Information Systems: Evaluation and Management*, Chapman and Hall, London.

Willcocks, L. and Fitzgerald, G. (1994) *A Business Guide to Outsourcing IT*, Business Intelligence, London.

CHAPTER TWO

Understanding the CEO–CIO Relationship

DAVID F. FEENY, BRIAN EDWARDS AND KEP SIMPSON

INTRODUCTION

'We have a tough relationship, but spend a lot of time together. I have a lot of confidence in him, whereas his predecessors used to talk arcane impenetrable stuff'.

'We have no difficulty talking to each other. We talk good shorthand. He is a strong ally of mine in the drive to change this company'.

These comments are from the CEOs of two multi-billion pound businesses; they were describing their firm's CIO. The CEOs quoted were interviewed in a study reported in this chapter exploring the relationship between CEOs and CIOs. The assumption underlying the study was that good relationships are enablers of successful exploitation of IT. The connection has been asserted directly by one well-known industry observer, who claims that 'IT successes generally reflect an effective relationship between business managers and IS managers', and 'the dialogue is needed most right at the top', (Keen, 1991, pages 214 and 219). More broadly it can be argued that good CEO/CIO relationships will contribute to success in at least three respects: strategic information systems planning, business/IS partnerships, and CEO involvement in IT management.

Contribution to Strategic Information Systems Planning

SISP was consistently identified to be the most critical issue facing IS executives through the 1980s, and its importance continues into the mid-1990s (Brancheau and Wetherbe, 1987; Dickson *et al.*, 1984; Galliers and Baker, 1994; Grindley, 1995; Hartog and Herbert, 1986).

SISP involves the alignment of IS plans with strategic business plans. Much attention has been devoted to the development and evaluation of methodologies to assist this alignment, but research by Earl (1990; 1996) emphasizes teamwork between business and IS representatives (see also Chapters 7 and 8). Other studies point to the importance for SISP of a direct two-way relationship between the CEO and IS Executive (Lederer and Mendelow, 1987; Watson, 1990).

Contribution to Business/IS Partnership

When discussing how 'information technology changes the way you compete', Cash *et al.*, (1988) assert that a partnership is necessary between IS and business (see also Chapter 1). Henderson (1990) proposes a model of such partnership; while his focus is on organizational partnership, he also recognizes the importance in effective partnerships of personal relationships and attitudes.

Contribution to CEO Involvement

Line management leadership of IS has been urged as essential to the multi-organizational, multifunctional systems era resulting from evolving communications capabilities (see Chapter 8). In support of this notion, Rockart (1988) describes case studies of CEO leadership in the planning and implementation of strategic systems. Along these same lines, Jarvenpaa and Ives (1991) reviewed the historic arguments for executive involvement in the management of information technology and determined that 'few nostrums have been prescribed so religiously and ignored as regularly as executive support in the development and implementation of MIS' (for some examples see Chapter 9).

It is our experience that the nostrum is in fact seldom ignored but often unattained (see Introduction; also Chapter 18). The involvement of executive management as partners in the exploitation of information technology is surely dependent on effective relationships between top levels of IS and business line management. But articles in business and professional magazines record how turbulent such relationships can be (for examples see Carlyle, Rothfeder and Driscoll, 1990). This chapter describes an exploratory research study into the factors that may drive the quality of the central relationship, that between the CEO and the CIO.

METHODOLOGY

'Relationship' is a nebulous concept, not easily amenable to traditional forms of empirical research. Relationships can be expected to be a complex product of multiple factors, including business context variables, individual backgrounds/values/cognitive styles, and professional skills and contributions. It is also difficult to get meaningful data, especially from busy CEOs. As one example, Jarvenpaa and Ives (1991) had to discard much of the data from their questionnaire survey of CEOs because of a low response rate and the lack of differentiation in responses to structured questions. We therefore decided to conduct an exploratory study using personal interviews with CEO/CIO pairs. This would allow in-depth investigation of a wide range of variables. Fourteen UK-based organizations were selected for study, with the characteristics summarized in Figure 2.1. Organizations were selected across industry sectors to allow for different 'information intensities' (Porter and Millar, 1985); these included examples of state and private ownership to capture potential differences in management regimes. Ten of the CEO/CIO pairs were focused on a single business – either because their corporation was itself a single business (for example the utility company) or because we were interviewing executives of a business unit within a multi-business corporation (for example the CEO and CIO of the insurance subsidiary of a conglomerate). The remaining four CEO/CIO pairs operated at business group level in the sense that they were corporate officers of a multi-business corporation. The organizational units represented were mostly large or very large: four of the CEOs were responsible for annual revenues in excess of $5 billion; only one managed an annual revenue of less than $200 million. Interviews with CEOs lasted for an average of one hour, while those with IS executives averaged more than 90 minutes.

Industry Sector	Central government	1	Process	2
	Distribution	2	Retail	2
	Financial services	3	Transportation	1
	Manufacturing	2	Utilities	1
Ownership	Private sector	10	Public sector	4
Interview level	Business group	4	Business unit	10

Figure 2.1   Study organizations

The interview design was guided by the overall model depicted in Figure 2.2, which was constructed to capture the propositions of various prior authors as well as the previous experience of the researchers. As Figure 2.2 suggests, the interviews sought data on a variety of factors which might affect CEO and CIO pre-dispositions, together with an in-depth picture of the relationship achieved.

In order to gain insights on pre-dispositions, CEOs were asked about their career backgrounds, the business environment with particular reference to the level of change desired or experienced, their view of the potential contribution of IT to achievement of business critical success factors, their personal experience of IT, and their general view of the role of IT in organizations. In interviews with CIOs we gathered data on their backgrounds, achievements and aspirations, and organizational position; we also probed their understanding of the business – its environment, culture and needs – as well as their views of the generic and specific contributions of IT.

Our exploration of the CEO/CIO relationship required the participation of both in order to grade the quality of their relationship using a five-point scale; to underpin that assessment through relevant anecdotes commenting on causal factors, and potential for change, contrast the relationship with others they held or had held at executive level. Both parties' views were sought on the organization's level of achievement in the IT field – their perception of the business's position versus key competitors in each major area of IT application, and of their own level of IT spend versus the IT budgets of those same

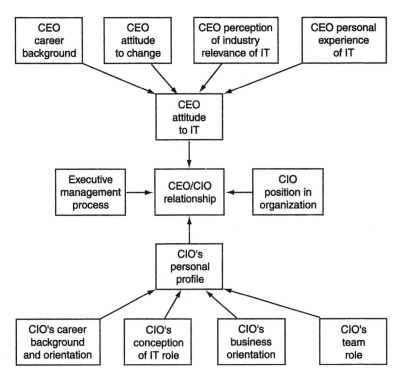

Figure 2.2   Interview design model

competitors. Each CIO was further asked to predict his or her CEO's response to IT-related questions.

The interview process was semi-structured, with a typical interview section consisting of a series of open-ended questions plus a summary categorization or Likert-type scale. The Likert scale requests a response score within a range of (say) 1–5. See the appendix to this chapter for an example. For example, to assess the CEO's personal experience with IT, we started with open questions pertaining to hands-on use, historic project responsibilities, relevant education events, influence of friends/family. We then requested the CEO's response to a five-point positioning scale, whose extremes were labelled from 'Badly burned by IT' to 'Significant beneficiary of IT'. As other examples, the sections assessing attitudes towards IT included categorizations based on the prior work of Schein (1989) and Parsons (1983).

Finally, after their interviews each CIO was asked to complete and return for analysis the 'self-perception inventory' developed by Belbin (1981) from his research into management teams. The subjects' responses to a standard series of statements about teamwork are used to assess what behavioural contributions they are likely to make to the management teams in which they work.

ANALYSIS OF RESULTS

Given the small size of the sample, it is inappropriate to formally test the research propositions implied by the model of Figure 2.2 through conventional data analysis. The study was instead intended to build insights using the depth rather than breadth of the data. This, we felt, would lead to stronger propositions which could be tested by subsequent work.

The first step in our analysis was therefore to place each relationship into one of three categories – loosely labelled as 'excellent', 'fair' and 'poor'. The positioning was based principally on the direct (five-point scale) evaluations of the relationship by the interviewees. However, in two cases responses to the questions about 'contrasting relationships' and 'scope for improvement' led us to downgrade the reported relationship quality (see this chapter's appendix for a more detailed explanation of the categorization process). As a result, five organizations were seen to enjoy an 'excellent relationship, five more were in the 'fair' category, and in four cases the strong dissatisfaction of at least one of the interviewees led to a categorization of 'poor'. Interestingly, each of the five in the top category represented a different industry sector – distribution, financial services, retail, transportation, and utilities. In all five of these companies, IT was a centralized function headed by the CIO concerned. The central IT function served multiple businesses in the distribution and financial services companies, but in each case there was a small number of business units (four) which were perceived to be strongly inter-related.

It is important to note that an excellent CEO/IT director relationship does not necessarily equate in the short term with *leadership* in the exploitation of IT – though one might expect it to correlate with *progress* in exploitation. Three of the organizations represented by our top five have been recognized elsewhere as leading IT users in their respective sectors – for example, all featured in business and trade articles, and their CIOs were regular speakers at public events. Meanwhile, two would be seen as moving into leadership from a weak initial position. On the other hand, one of the 'poor' relationships was in an organization which has been regularly cited as outperforming its competitors in the use of IT. This did not protect the CIO concerned from fierce criticism, nor from the eventual decision by his CEO to sever the relationship.

In the second step in the analysis we contrasted the data from the five 'excellent' situations with the four 'poor' ones, looking for attributes which were consistently and distinctively present in the 'excellent' relationships. Common attributes were indeed identified in those five organizations, and they are summarized in Figure 2.3. These attributes are not totally absent from the 'fair' or even the 'poor' relationships.

CEO attributes

- General management and/or marketing background
- Change-oriented leadership
- Attended 'IT awareness' seminars
- Experienced IT project success
- Perceives IT as critical to the business
- Positions IT as agent of business transformation

Organizational attributes

- Personal/informal executive style
- Executive workshops on strategic issues
- CIO accepted into executive team

CIO attributes

- Analyst background and orientation
- Promotes IT as agent of business transformation
- Contributes beyond IT function
- Accurate perception of CEO views on business and IT
- Integrates IT with business planning

Figure 2.3   Attributes of excellent CEO/CIO relationships

But case by case analysis demonstrates that at least some of these attributes are missing from each of the 'fair' relationships, and many of them are missing from each 'poor' relationship. The attribute set is at least a reasonably consistent basis for explaining the different qualities of relationship found within the three categories.

DISCUSSION

The attribute set becomes more powerful if it can be seen to be supported by other evidence, to have a legitimacy beyond the 14 organizations in our study. In this section we examine and interpret each attribute in turn, and consider its possible relationship with previous theory and research.

The CEO attributes

All five CEOs with excellent relationships had career backgrounds in marketing or general management. Of the nine CEOs with less successful relationships, another four came from marketing or general management; the remaining five had spent their previous careers in production or process engineering. Although we are not suggesting that only CEOs from marketing or general management can enjoy successful relationships, it can be argued that such backgrounds are helpful on a number of counts. They encourage a focus on business strategy and an organization-wide perspective which will be important when a wide variety of IT-based projects are considered. Such people may also be expected to place more value on relationships generally, and to be more prepared to work at them. They would be classified by Hambrick and Mason (1984) as 'output'-oriented, interested in innovation and opportunity, versus the 'throughput' orientation of those from production and process engineering, who may be more focused on efficiency and automation. Jarvenpaa and Ives (1991) report an association between the CEO's functional background and the 'progressive use of IT'.

The five CEOs within the excellent relationships group also demonstrated a track record of leading organizations through periods of change. This was not a major discriminator in our sample, since almost all of the organizations interviewed were confronted with a turbulent external environment and pressures for change. However, it was clear that in at least one case the conservatism of the CEO was seriously damaging his relationship with the CIO because initiatives for IT-use consistently represented more change than the CEO would countenance. One experienced CIO (Seddon, 1988) has described how his whole approach to strategic IS planning came to be dominated by considerations of the change orientation of business management.

Attendance at IT executive seminars, plus personal association with successful IT projects, were also common attributes of the CEOs with excellent relationships. By contrast, only three of the nine of the other categories shared these attributes. Lederer and Mendelow (1987) found that IS executives regularly suggested education as a means to improve communication with top management, and to facilitate strategic IS planning. At OXIIM, where we have run many IT seminars for executive teams, we have direct experience of how significant these events can be in changing attitudes towards IT. Looking at the personal experience of successful IT projects within the top group, our study provides support for the Jarvenpaa and Ives (1991) finding, that 'executive participation' influences 'executive involvement'. Favourable personal experiences (the 'participation' element) predispose CEOs to an 'involvement' which was defined by Barki and Hartwick (1989) as a 'subjective psychological state' in which IT issues are perceived as 'important and personally relevant'.

On the other hand, *personal use* of IT by CEOs was not a discriminating factor in our study. With an overall six out of 14 CEOs as 'hands-on users', our small sample shows much higher use than the 21 per cent reported by *Personal Computing* magazine's surveys of CEOs in 1989 and 1986 (Nelson, 1989) – probably because some of the CEOs we interviewed were heading businesses within a multi-business corporation. However, our study provides no support for the contention in that publication that CEOs should 'find a reason, any reason' for personal use. Only one of the CEOs with an 'excellent' relationship was a hands-on user, compared to all four of those with 'poor' relationships. In highlighting the significance of IT project experience rather than personal use, our study is supportive of Keen's view that 'familiarity with small-scale technology and its applications affords surprisingly little real insight into the complexities of IT design, development and use' (Keen, 1991, page 126).

CEOs were each asked about the critical success factors for their business, and about the existing and potential contribution of IT to those success factors. In their response to a subsequent five-point scale question on the importance of IT to their business, the CEOs with excellent relationships averaged 4.8 – well above the average of 3.6 for the other nine CEOs. It can be argued that the CEOs in the top group were influenced by the information intensity of their businesses (Porter and Millar, 1985). However, on that basis the CEOs of a high technology manufacturing business and of the second financial services business would have been expected to give high rather than low ratings to IT importance. In practice, the assessment of IT importance seems at least as much a function of the CEO as of the business or industry. For example, the CEO of the transportation company (an airline) had arrived from a different industry and immediately uprated the perception of IT importance, elevating the CIO to be his direct report. The retail CEO claimed he had identified IT as a strategic resource at least two years before his main competitors reached the same view.

The single most powerful discriminator in our study was labelled 'CEO attitude to IT'. This we tested by inviting each CEO to position his view of the role of IT against the four 'IT visions' developed from CEO interviews by Schein (1989). Our description of these visions, as presented during interviews, is reproduced in Figure 2.4. All five CEOs in the 'excellent' group aligned themselves with the 'vision to transform' while only one of the other nine CEOs made the same choice. Since 12 of the 14 CIOs also identified with the 'vision to transform' (including all five in the 'excellent' group), it becomes clear that excellent relationships only occurred when CEO and CIO shared the same conception of the role of IT.

The CEOs with excellent relationships seemed to have reached the 'vision to transform' by various routes. One pointed to a transformational experience in his previous role as COO (chief operating officer) of a car rental company; there he had inherited a project to make that company the first in the industry to introduce an IT-based reservation

---

Vision to automate   the role of IT to replace expensive, unreliable human labour, or at least transform its productivity, with sophisticated robots, systems etc . . . promise of IT to save money, improve quality, make organization more effective.

Vision to informate up   the data and the transactions required to automate also allow more clear and organized management views of the state and dynamics of the business. This can add further increments of performance through management's possession of new levers, micro as well as macro control of the business.

Vision to informate down   the data and transactions can provide a far fuller picture at 'operator' level with members of the workforce gaining greater insights into their own activities. With looser job specifications and more emphasis on self-management against objectives, this can lead to employee-driven performance improvement. The need for traditional control hierarchies is reduced.

Vision to transform   the organization and/or industry can be fundamentally changed through the use of IT, including the terms of 'our' relationship with suppliers and customers and the boundaries among us. There will be opportunity for more local problem-solving and lateral information sharing, more centralized and informed strategy and goal setting, more decentralized implementation and control.

Figure 2.4   Visions of the role of IT

system. Three other CEOs described how they had been aggressively seeking growth in their sectors, and had fastened on the innovative use of IT as the way to achieve the sought-for competitive advantage. The fifth CEO explained how his CIO persuaded him to attend a series of educational programmes; these had the intended result of persuading him that IT was a strategic resource for a company in financial services. These contrasting examples support the implied propositions of Figure 2.2, that CEO personal experience of IT, CEO attitude to change, CEO perception of industry relevance of IT, are influencers (along with CEO career background) of the CEO attitude to IT.

This part of our model is consistent with that developed by Jarvenpaa and Ives (1991). They suggest that executive involvement in IT (roughly analogous to our model element 'CEO attitudes to IT') is a function of organizational conditions (CEO perception of industry relevance of IT), and of executive background (CEO career background). On the other hand we identify CEO attitude to change as a fourth predictor variable; Jarvenpaa and Ives see attitude to change as a function of executive background, related to CEO age and CEO tenure in the organization and position. In our study the CEOs who had excellent CIO relationships were both older than CEOs with poor relationships (average age 52 versus age 46) and longer in post (7.6 years versus 2.5 years).

There seems to be widespread popular belief that problems with IT exploitation will disappear once a younger generation of managers reaches the boardroom. Clearly our study provides no support for this view if a link between CEO/CIO relationships and exploitation is accepted. There is support for the idea that younger CEOs are more likely to be hands-on users of IT (the average age of hands-on users was 47, for non-users it was 52); but we have already noted that hands-on use is not a distinctive attribute of the CEOs with excellent relationships.

Organizational attributes
A potential obstacle for innovative applications of information technology is the opposition of territorial senior executives who perceive their empires being threatened. This sort of difficulty may particularly be encountered in what Burns and Stalker (1961) would refer to as mechanistic organizations, where the top team is comprised of the heads of functional fiefdoms who come together at regular meetings to progress a formal agenda. It is less likely to occur when there is an integrated management team with close personal relationships and a shared focus on the goals of the overall business (the organic organization).

We asked both CEOs and CIOs how new ideas were advanced and

approved in their organizations. The consistent responses in the organizations enjoying excellent relationships was that individuals would make informal contact with relevant peers to discuss ideas and build support before a formal proposal was made. This reflects the 'personal informal' style which has previously been suggested as particularly effective in identifying new IS applications (Pyburn, 1983). A further characteristic of these organizations was that all had a culture of off-site workshops for the top management team to discuss strategic issues. These were the occasions when radical new business and IT thinking could be surfaced, debated and progressed.

The CIO in each of these organizations was positioned as a member of the top management team. He attended the strategy workshops and was well positioned to make the informal contacts with colleagues. Only two of these five CIOs were actually direct reports to the CEO. In the other three cases the CEO had very few direct reports, but the recognized top management team extended to the next level which included the CIO. Each of the these CIOs therefore had ready access to other members of the team, including the CEO. The emphasis on team membership rather than direct reporting is in conflict with Raghunathan and Raghunathan (1989) who found that only direct reporting made a significant difference to the IS planning effort. But it is consistent with Watson's (1990) study which identified two-way communication between CEO and CIO as the key factor. All of the CIOs with excellent relationships achieved that two-way communication. The three CIOs who were not direct reports had immediate superiors who were concerned with shorter term issues in IT management; their CEOs focused on broader and longer term issues of IT use.

In the remainder of the sample, four of the nine CIOs with less successful relationships were neither direct reports nor members of the top management team. These individuals commonly expressed frustration at their exclusion from the top level of briefing and debate. And their perceptions of the critical issues facing the business rarely matched the responses given by their CEOs.

The CIO attributes
With the exception of one who had moved out of IT for a period, the CIOs enjoying excellent relationships had spent their entire careers within the IT domain – moving through systems analysis to the management of systems development and then to overall responsibility for the IT function. Another pattern in their career histories was a learning orientation. When asked to describe which parts of their careers they had enjoyed most and least, they consistently seemed surprised at the question and insisted they had enjoyed virtually everything; several went on to volunteer what they had learned from

each stage of their careers. These responses bring to mind the high 'growth need strength' first detected in IT professionals by Cougar and Zawacki (1980); and also perhaps the 'variety' career anchor added by DeLong (1982) to Schein's (1975) original list of 'motivational/ attitudinal/value syndromes' which 'guide and constrain' the careers of individuals. The background of these successful CIOs challenges popular wisdom during the second half of the 1980s, sometimes reiterated in the 1990s, which suggested that business line managers should be transferred into the top IT management posts. Five such transferees were among the nine CIOs experiencing 'fair' or 'poor' relationships.

Despite (or maybe because of) their IT-centred careers, the CIOs in the top group all subscribed to Schein's 'vision to transform'. What distinguished them more from their colleagues was the vigour of their views and the extent to which they promoted those views. One of the top group stated 'I do not want to run an IS department, I want to transform this business'. His expressed career ambition was 'to take over the human resources function so that I bring together both the key levers for change'. Without expressing it quite so strongly, his peers in the top group shared this fascination with the achievement of business change. Each of them had incorporated transformation concepts into a formal IT mission statement which was widely publicized inside the IT function and elsewhere in the organization. The emphasis of these CIOs' on communication and promotion was in sharp contrast to their four colleagues with 'poor' relationships who either had mission statements stressing cost and service, or no mission statement at all. Lederer and Mendelow (1988) highlight the importance of a selling orientation in IS executives if top management are to be convinced of the strategic potential of IS.

The business orientation of CIOs was further tested when CEOs were asked which of the statements in Figure 2.5 applied to their CIO. Statements 4 to 9 were designed to test various aspects of business orientation, such as sensitivity to business priorities. On these the CIOs enjoying excellent CEO relationships were all given perfect scores, with the CEO commonly emphasizing statement 8 – 'contributes beyond the IT functional role'. Each of the other nine CIOs were seen to be lacking at least some of the business orientation qualities. On the other hand, several of these nine were rated more highly than two of the top group against statements 1–3 which relate to aspects of managing IT resources. The appropriate balance of strengths for successful CIOs apparently matches the popular conception (for example Bock *et al.*, 1986); the softer skills and business orientation are vital, while weaknesses in operational management can be tolerated provided competent subordinates are in place.

1. Manages consistently within budget

2. Can be relied on to deliver on commitments

3. Good manager of his or her own people

4. Good relationships with other members of the executive team

5. We talk the same language

6. Sensitive to business priorities

7. Identifies with the business

8. Contributes beyond the IT functional role

9. Good ambassador for the business

Figure 2.5   CIO qualities

Another common attribute of those CIOs with excellent relationships was their remarkable perception of and congruence with their CEO's views. Looking across each pair of interviews, there were numerous points at which we could directly contrast CEO and CIO responses including:

- their separate statements of the business critical success factor;
- their separate descriptions of the executive management style;
- the CIO's predictions of how his CEO would rate:
    - the importance of IT (five-point scale);
    - the role of IT (Schein's vision statements which none of the interviewees had seen before);
- their separate ratings of:
    - IT achievement vs competition (in each major application area)
    - IT spend vs competition (five-point scale)
    - the quality of their relationship (five-point scale)

In the CEO/CIO pairs where relationships were excellent, 76 per cent of all responses indicated full agreement; there was at least partial agreement in a further 19 per cent of responses. In the organizations where there were poor relationships, CEOs and CIOs showed full agreement in only 28 per cent of responses, with partial agreement in a further 10 per cent. The congruence achieved in the excellent relationships, and the sometimes startling lack of it within the less successful ones, might be considered as either cause or effect. The partnership model proposed by Henderson (1990) suggests that shared knowledge is a critical factor which results from access plus a conscious investment in learning. At the very least, shared understanding must serve to reinforce a successful relationship.

In a similar fashion, the integration of business and IT planning described by CIOs in the group with excellent relationships can be seen as both enabled by and supportive of their relationships. These CIOs used a combination of what Earl (1990; 1996) called the 'business-led' and the 'organizational' approaches to strategic IS planning. Earl sees both approaches to be potentially successful in linking IT investment to critical business issues, but their viability would be in question without the business understanding and relationships which these successful CIOs have achieved.

The final piece of data collected from CIOs concerned their team role profile. Behavioural researchers (Belbin, 1981; Hambrick, 1987) have directed attention to the importance of balance in top management teams, to enable successful team process. Belbin's work identified nine different types of team contribution which in various combinations could bring to a team an appropriate mix of leadership, creativity, evaluation and implementation. A typical individual provides two or three such contributions to a team, and with conscious effort may be able to provide two or three more. While Belbin makes no association between team roles and functional roles, we looked for and found some evidence in our study of a pattern of team roles for CIOs. The results must be treated with caution, because of the small sample size and because we were limited to collection of self-perceived data without corroboration of the CIO's team behaviour from colleagues. Nevertheless, the data suggests some interesting potential insights, with the profiles of the CIOs who enjoyed successful relationships differing quite sharply from their less successful peers. Each of the five in the top group had a profile in which three strands were prominent:

- consultative leadership, stressing communication and relationships, and achievement of good group process;
- entrepreneurial leadership, providing drive and commitment and goal orientation;
- creativity, based either on lateral thinking ability, or on strong external networking and scanning.

Only one of these strands – consultative leadership – was common in the other nine CIOs; their profiles were otherwise dominated by some combination of Belbin's four evaluation/implementation roles, (formally labelled implementer, completer/finisher, teamworker, monitor/evaluator), which were conspicuously absent from the profiles of all but one of the top group of CIOs.

This team role data is consistent with many of the themes emerging from the interview data. The top group of CIOs are interested in ideas, with a strong drive to achieve change, but with the communications and relationship capabilities needed to bring others down the path to change. The CIOs are more clearly differentiated from their less successful peers (on both team role and interview data) than are their CEOs. Belbin's methodology may well prove to be a helpful tool in developing a further understanding of the CIO's task in achieving successful integration into the management team.

QUALITIES OF THE 'IDEAL' CIO

An additional advantage of an interview methodology is the collection of qualitative data which can richly illustrate the interviewee's response to a structured question. Synthesizing and paraphrasing this softer data provides a potential profile of the 'ideal' CIO. The profile may be 'idealized', in that such an individual may never exist, but it is an opportunity to review the combined opinions of some experienced CEOs and CIOs. In this respect it should be noted that the average time in post for those with excellent relationships was 7.6 years for CEOs, and 6.4 years for CIOs. Components of the profile, some of them by now familiar, are:

- *Honesty, integrity, sincerity, openness* 'As CEO I can stop worrying about looming IT catastrophes because this CIO will be as open about problems as he or she is about triumphs'.
- *Business perspective, motivation, language* 'This CIO discusses (in English!) how we might achieve what I want, not (in technobabble) why we can't achieve what I want; he or she doesn't patronize me by saying "It's all very complicated and would take a long time to explain (to someone like you)"'.
- *Communicator, educator, motivator, leader, politician, relationship builder* 'I'm fed up with all of my executives complaining about IT, I can't tell whether their complaints are valid; I need a CIO who can conciliate and defuse and explain instead of confront, someone who eventually can even enthuse the executive team'.
- *Continuously informed on developments in IT, able to interpret their significance to the business* 'I can stop worrying that a competitor might pre-empt us, or that I shall suddenly discover we are spending twice as much on IT as we need; this CIO can be relied on to choose the right technology, and won't suggest that each new IT product heralds a new world order'.
- *Change-oriented team player, catalyst to business thinking* 'As CEO I need someone who is a sharp creative thinker across the business, not committed to any of the company's traditional power bases; I need an ally and a sounding board when I'm thinking of the future of the organization'.

Both the 'ideal CIO' profile and the CIO attribute list of Figure 2.3 can be seen as strikingly consistent with the set of information executive attributes identified a decade ago by Rockart *et al.*, (1982). Of the six attributes described by those authors, three are particularly emphasized in our study – political/organizational/communication skills, strategic orientation, and technological understanding. Only one of the six – the CIO as manager of managers – is missing from our profiles; this is more than a matter of selected emphasis, since two of our CIOs with excellent relationships were perceived to have real but tolerated weaknesses here.

The requirement for integrity/openness etc., highlighted earlier in this section might be considered an essential virtue in any executive role. The prominence it received from our interviewees suggests it is particularly important in a CIO, since the average CEO feels more personally exposed in this area than in any other.

CONCLUSIONS

This study set out to explore a wide range of ideas associated with CEO/CIO relationships, and to gain some tentative insights into how those ideas might fit together. The study sampled a small number of organizations but was unusual in achieving substantive direct inputs from CEOs of large corporations.

Where the study overlapped with previous work its findings were mostly consistent with that work. However, the study highlights a number of ideas and issues:

- It identifies Schein's vision statements as a potentially powerful way of categorizing the CEO's attitude to IT.
- It suggests that attitude can be altered through some (planned or unplanned) action which affects the CEO's personal experience of IT, his or her perception of the industry relevance of IT, or attitude to the needed level of business change.
- It challenges the findings of some earlier research by suggesting that CIO membership of the top management team may be more important than direct reporting.
- It introduces to this arena a potential method of classifying and researching the contribution of the CIO to the top management team.

It is important to restate that the study was exploratory in nature, and hence there are numerous limitations to be kept in mind. The most obvious concern is that the sample is small and in most respects diverse. On the other hand it was restricted to large corporations in the UK, while company and national contexts may be important influences on the culture within which relationships exist. At another level, we lack independent verification of some key data – for example, third party perceptions of whether CIOs possess the qualities attributed by CEOs with whom they have excellent relationships.

Looking forward, the model depicted in Figure 2.2 may serve as a helpful framework for identifying issues for practitioners and researchers. We are already finding that it stimulates CEOs and CIOs to formally review their relationship, and that it provides at least a structure for review and some guidance on actions likely to achieve desired improvements.

Further research may include a large-scale survey of CIO team role profile and an assessment of any dependence on organizational context. Additional case study research may be particularly valuable to an understanding of how CEOs acquire the vision to transform, a critical element according to this study (see also Chapters 1 and 18).

Finally, it would be interesting to formally test the association between CEO/CIO relationships and successful exploitation of IT, to verify or otherwise the underlying assumption of this study.

REFERENCES

Barki, H., and Hartwick, J. (1989) 'Rethinking the Concept of User Involvement', *MIS Quarterly* **13**, (1), March, pp. 53–64.

Belbin, R. (1981) *Management Teams: Why they Succeed or Fail*, Heinemann, London.

Bock, G., Carpenter, K., and Ellen, J. (1986) 'Management's Newest Star: Meet the Chief Information Officer', *Business Week*, October 13, pp. 84–92.

Brancheau, J. and Wetherbe, J. (1987) 'Key Issues in Information Systems Management', *MIS Quarterly*, **11**, (1), March, pp. 23–45.

Burns, T., and Stalker, G. (1961) *The Management of Innovation*, Tavistock Publications, London.

Carlyle, R. (1989) 'Careers in Crisis', *Datamation*, August 15, pp. 12–16.

Cash, J., McFarlan, F., McKenney, J. and Vitale, M. (1988) *Corporate Information Systems Management: Text and Cases*, (2nd edition) Irwin, Homewood, IL.

Couger, J., and Zawacki, R. (1980) *Motivating and Managing Computer Personnel*, Wiley-Interscience, Chichester.

DeLong, T. (1982) 'Re-examining the Career Anchor Model', *Personnel*, **59**, (3) May-June, pp. 50–61.

Dickson, G., Leitheiser, R., Wetherbe, J. and Nechis, M. (1984) 'Key

Information Systems Issues for the 1980s', *MIS Quarterly*, **8**, (3), September, pp. 135–159.

Earl, M. (1990) 'Approaches to Strategic Information Systems Planning: Experience in 21 UK Companies', *Proceedings of the Eleventh International Conference on Information Systems*, pp. 271–277.

Earl, M. (1996) 'The Chief Information Officer: Past, Present and Future', In Earl, M. (ed.) *Information Management: the Organizational Dimension*, Oxford University Press, Oxford.

Galliers, R. and Baker, B. (eds.) (1994) *Strategic Information Management*, Butterworth Heinemann, London.

Grindley, K. (1995) *Managing IT At Board Level*, Pitman, London.

Hambrick, D., and Mason, P. (1984) 'Upper Echelons: the Organization as a Reflection of its Top Managers', *Academy of Management Review*, **9**, (2), pp. 193–206.

Hambrick, D. (1987) 'The Top Management Team: Key to Strategic Success', *California Management Review*, **30**, (1), Fall, pp. 88–108.

Hartog, C. and Herbert, M. (1986) '1985 Opinion Survey of MIS Managers: Key Issues', *MIS Quarterly*, **10**, (4), December, pp. 351–361.

Henderson, J. (1990) 'Plugging into Strategic Partnerships: The Critical IS Connection', *Sloan Management Review*, **31**, (3), Spring, pp. 7–18.

Jarvenpaa, S., and Ives, B. (1991) 'Executive Involvement and Participation in the Management of Information Technology', *MIS Quarterly*, **15**, (2), June, pp. 205–227.

Keen, P. (1991) *Shaping the Future: Business Design through Information Technology*, Harvard Business School Press, Cambridge, Mass.

Lederer, A., and Mendelow, A. (1987) 'Information Resource Planning: Overcoming Difficulties in Identifying Top Management's Objectives', *MIS Quarterly*, **11**, (3), September, pp. 389–399.

Lederer, A., and Mendelow, A. (1988) 'Convincing Top Management of the Strategic Potential of Information Systems', *MIS Quarterly*, **12**, (4), December, pp. 525–534.

Nelson, R. (1989) 'CEOs: Computing in High Places', *Personal Computing*, **13**, (4), April, pp. 70–84.

Parsons, G. (1983) *Fitting Information Systems Technology to the Corporate Needs: the Linking Strategy. Case Study 183176*, Harvard Business School, Cambridge, Mass.

Porter, M. and Millar, V. (1985) 'How Information gives you Competitive Advantage', *Harvard Business Review*, **63**, (4), July-August, pp. 149–160.

Pyburn, P. (1983) 'Linking the MIS Plan with Corporate Strategy: an Exploratory Study', *MIS Quarterly*, **7**, (2), June, pp. 1–14.

Raghunathan, B., and Raghunathan, T. (1989) 'Relationship of the Rank of Information Systems Executive to the Organizational Role and Planning Dimensions of Information Systems', *Journal of Management Information Systems*, **6**, (1), Summer, pp. 111–126.

Rockart, J. (1988) 'The Line Takes the Leadership – IS Management in a Wired Society', *Sloan Management Review*, **29**, (4), Summer, pp. 57–64.

Rockart, J., Ball, L., and Bullen, C. (1982) 'Future Role of the Information Systems Executive', *MIS Quarterly*, (Special Issue), pp. 1–14.

Rothfeder, J., and Driscoll, L. (1990) 'CIO is starting to Stand for Career is Over', *Business Week*, February 26, pp. 47–48.

Schein, E. H. (1975) 'How Career Anchors Hold Executives to their Career Paths', *Personnel*, **52**, (3), May-June, pp. 11–24.

Schein, E. H. (1989) *The Role of the CEO in the Management of Change: The Case of Information Technology. Management in the Nineties Working Paper (89-075)*, Sloan School of Management, August.

Seddon, D. (1988) 'Experiences in IT Strategy Formulation at ICI', In Earl, M. (Ed.), *Information Management: The Strategic Dimension*, Clarendon Press, Oxford.

Watson, R. (1990) 'Influences on the IS Manager's Perceptions of Key Issues: Information Scanning and the Relationship with the CEO', *MIS Quarterly*, **14**, (2), pp. 217–231.

APPENDIX TO CHAPTER 2: CATEGORIZATION OF CEO–CIO RELATIONSHIPS

Categorization of relationship quality was based on each interviewee's responses to five questions. The wording of these questions to CEOs is reproduced below; the equivalent five questions were put to the CIO.

Q1 How would you rate the effectiveness of your relationship with your CIO?

Ö ----------Ú-------------Ú ------------Ú ----------Ú ------------Ì
  °   1   °   2   °   3   °   4   °   5   °
Û ----------Ù-------------Ù ------------Ù ----------Ù ------------ì
   Bad   Poorish   Average   Good   Excellent

e.g. – avoid seeing   e.g. – trusting
     – critical   – fertile
     – his/her job on the line   – synergistic
     – I use other contacts/routes   – comfortable
     – he/she uses other contacts/routes

Q2 Please give any recent anecdotes that illustrate your view.

Q3 If improvement in the relationship is needed, what action might be effective? By you? By the CIO?

Q4 Is there any other CIO you have known/met who you particularly admire? Why?

Q5 Is there another member of the executive team with whom you have a particularly good relationship? What is the basis of the success?

In allocating CEO/CIO pairs between 'excellent', 'fair' and 'poor' categories, we were cautious about directly accepting interviewee responses to Q1. If at least one party to the relationship claimed its quality was bad/poorish, we put the pair in the poor category – good relationships cannot be one-sided.

However, where both parties claimed a high quality relationship in response to Q1, it was still possible that this implied social compatibility rather than effectiveness. In these cases we reviewed the (often lengthy) responses to Q2–Q5. Where these responses disclosed significant reservations or unfavourable contrasts we excluded the pair from the excellent category. While this may have allowed an element of subjectivity to enter the process, we felt there should be no doubts about relationships in the top category, given the study's objectives and the small sample size.

The five relationships classified as excellent each had combined scores from Q1 of greater than eight; and no negative responses from Q2–Q5. The four relationships classified as poor each received one score of 2 or less to Q1.

CHAPTER THREE

IT as a Basis for Sustainable Competitive Advantage

DAVID F. FEENY AND BLAKE IVES

INTRODUCTION: IT AND COMPETITIVE ADVANTAGE

In the second half of the 1980s, a series of articles, books and seminars proclaimed the emergence of a new competitive weapon – information technology. Despite some scepticism it does appear that companies have increasingly accepted the central idea, that IT should be viewed as a potentially strategic resource. More problematic has been the question of how companies can move from general awareness of the idea to the actual achievement of business advantage.

The IT for competitive advantage message has been conveyed to researcher and practitioner in many ways. The message has included descriptions of how a small number of companies successfully deployed their IT weapons for strategic advantage (Clemons and Row, 1988; Ives, 1990; Linder, 1987; Stoddard, 1988; Vitale, 1986a). Perhaps most compelling to the practising manager are tales of the firms such as Frontier Airline (Vitale, 1984) and People Express (Burr, 1989), that have been beaten down by information technology. The message has included frameworks, such as those proposed by Ives and Learmonth (1984), Parsons (1983), Porter and Millar (1985), and Wiseman (1985), intended to help managers identify applications that can bring competitive advantage to their own business. Rackoff et al., (1985) describe the use of such a framework within an organization, while Vitale, Ives, and Beath (1986) describe alternative approaches to identify strategic applications. Some investigators have looked at

43

specific types of strategic applications, including customer service (Learmonth and Ives, 1987), after-sale service (Ives and Vitale, 1988), and strategic pricing opportunities (Beath and Ives, 1986). Others have looked at differences across industry. McFarlan *et al.*, (1983) for instance, have suggested via their strategic grid model that IT will have varying applicability across industries, a notion that has been verified empirically by others (Jarvenpaa and Ives, 1989). Copeland and McKenney (1988) have traced the history of competitive advantage applications of IT within the airline industry.

Others have considered the role of telecommunications (Clemons and McFarlan, 1986) or database (Madnick and Wang, 1988) infrastructure in contributing to strategic applications. Cash and Konsynski (1985), following on the work of Barrett (1982), have drawn attention to the strategic possibilities of inter-organizational systems, and both Clemons and Kimbrough (1986) and Malone *et al.*, (1986) have proposed using Williamson's (1979) theory of transaction costs to further investigate the economic underpinnings of such systems. The realities of inter-organizational systems are empirically explored by Runge (1988). Runge also demonstrated the crucial role often played by a project champion in identifying and implementing strategic applications, a finding that has been reconfirmed by others (Lockett, 1987; Vitale, 1988). Methods for fostering the involvement and cooperation of such champions have been explored in Beath and Ives (1988).

We note that all of this material promotes and elaborates upon the potential for creating competitive advantage through IT. The further question is whether companies which pioneer such ideas in their own marketplace can achieve rewards substantial enough to justify the costs and risks associated with being the prime mover. After all, the technology is increasingly within the grasp of even the smallest follower company, either directly or through well-developed IT service supply segments. Management requires clearer insights into the relative merits of pioneering versus following with particular IT initiatives. Prime movers face the traditional risks associated with innovation, and the changing economics of IT also guarantee the later entrant a lower-cost equipment platform. Vitale (1986b), for example, warns that some supposed strategic applications of IT may provide limited advantages to the innovator before being readily copied by competitors. The result, he worries, may often be 'an extension of the current competitive situation at an increased level of cost'.

There has been little attention in the literature to the sustainability of strategic IT applications. A notable exception is the work of Clemons and his associates at Wharton. Clemons (1986) notes the importance of imposing switching costs on customers to ensure sustainability. Clemons and Row (1987) propose that applications taking advantage of 'unique structural characteristics of the innovating firm' will be more likely to contribute to sustainability. Customer adoption rate has also been proposed (Clemons and Row, 1987) as critical to sustainability for systems that establish customer switching costs. Recognizing that a particular application may be necessary but not sustainable, Clemons and Knez (1988) have described several approaches for evaluating whether a given application should be developed independently or as part of a consortium of competitors.

A FRAMEWORK FOR DETERMINING SUSTAINABILITY

Much of the previous work has focused on frameworks to support 'idea generation', but 'idea filtration' may be a considerably richer target of investigation. There is an extensive cost-benefit literature and a smaller risk analysis literature, but there is no comprehensive analytical tool for assessing the strategic implications of IT-based competitive edge projects. Drawing on our own experience, some theoretical underpinnings, and the work of Clemons and others, we have sought to provide a useful conceptual model. We propose the pillared framework depicted in Figure 3.1 as a means to assess the sustainability of IT-based competitive advantage.

The first and most obvious support pillar involves analysis of the project development cycle to understand what we term the 'generic lead time' faced by a follower company. The second pillar identifies the extent to which the project is protected through 'competitive

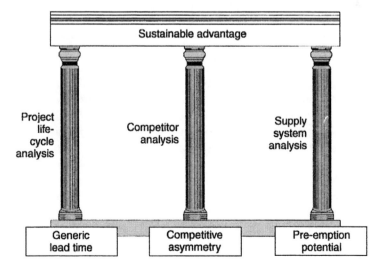

Figure 3.1   The three pillars supporting sustainable advantage

asymmetry'. This analysis is based on the theory of competition popularized by Chamberlin (1933), and is used to assess what handicaps, if any, each competitor will be under in attempting to respond to the pioneer. Finally, we turn to supply chain analysis and the ideas of McMillan (1983) to consider the 'pre-emption potential' of the proposed application. The three pillars suggest the questions:

1. How long before a competitor can respond to our idea?
2. Which competitors can respond?
3. Will a response be effective?

In the following three sections we examine each of these questions. We then consider a number of developments in the field since our model was first published (in Feeny and Ives, 1990), before drawing conclusions for organizations seeking to pursue these ideas.

Project life-cycle analysis: how long before a response?

A 'sustainability analysis' for an IT application can produce a much different profile than a risk analysis. An expensive system that takes two years to build may be high risk indeed, particularly if the payoff is dubious. But a high-risk system is unlikely to be copied by a competitor unless the motivation is compelling. And, if the application is a large one, there may be considerable delay for the build itself. As Merrill Lynch demonstrated with their cash management account, a large high-risk application that bears fruit can provide a nicely biased playing field for pleasant years of increased profitability or market share growth (Wiseman, 1985).

The time line in Figure 3.2 depicts the components of generic lead time – the time it would take the competitor to approximately duplicate the application, given similar starting points. The prime mover must go through some preliminary stages before the application can be built. A planning process or emerging vision leads into a project approval and resource allocation process. Interestingly, we now understand that applications with strategic or competitive implications often manage to side-step traditional project approval processes (Lockett, 1987; Runge, 1988; Vitale, 1988). But whatever the process, the resources are allocated and the application build initiated. Depending on the nature of the application, 'the build' may be a lengthy and complex process – particularly if new technologies are required or if implementation requires installing systems in unfamiliar environments. Eventually, the application will be launched and market advantages begin to accrue. By the time the competitors respond, system enhancements may provide an opportunity to keep the originator's application out in front.

Lead time is the amount of time from project launch until a competitor or competitors have a substantive response in place. If the

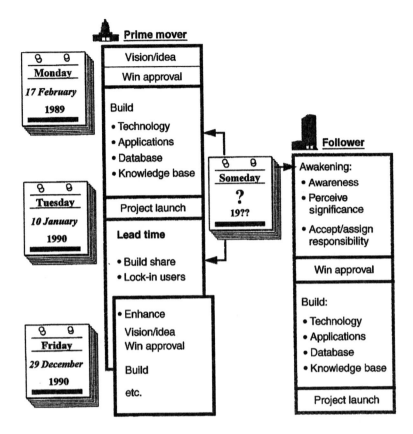

Figure 3.2   The components of generic lead time: how long to respond

change required is merely a few parameters within an existing application then the response is immediate and lead time non-existent. But lead time is usually far longer. The actual length of time will be dependent on the variables discussed below.

The awakening

How does a follower respond to the competitive initiative of a prime mover? Followers require no vision or planning process. Instead, they become aware of the change in the playing field and aroused as they begin to recognize the costs associated with the unfavourable tilt of the field. But they still must come to understand what is causing the haemorrhage in revenues, profits, goodwill, etc., and someone in the organization must be found to repair the damage. Each stage can be problematic. Each can contribute to the innovator's lead time.

The first hint of a competitive initiative can come quickly. A new employee may report on a systems initiative at her old firm, newspaper advertisements may suggest that company X is looking for people with experience in a leading edge technology, or the field salesforce may bring back interesting insights or rumours from the field. Even if the initiative is not picked up prior to project launch, it will probably be spotted when the application goes live, particularly if it is a basis of differentiation that will need to be sold to the customer. But, if the application is focused on an internal process, such as a data base for deriving market intelligence or an expert system for authorizing bank loans, it may take considerably longer to realize that something unusual has happened. However, even when the competitive initiative has been recognized, the follower may not respond until sales have fallen off, profits declined, or customers have clamoured for comparable capabilities. This is particularly likely if the prime mover is a small player or a new entrant rather than a feared major competitor.

There may be still further delay as the follower organization decides who is responsible for responding. One solution, turning the problem over to the information systems group, may result in a poorly crafted or inappropriate approach that inadequately addresses the range of potential business responses. Feeny (1988) describes how competitive response to a pioneer in the UK travel industry was misdirected for three full years.

Once the problem is recognized and someone assigned to lead the defence, there can be problems deciding how to respond. There may be issues of proprietary technology, unavailable data, or an unknown solution. For example, Fidelity Investments was the first mutual fund to introduce hourly pricing to the marketplace. Prior to Fidelity's innovation mutual funds had been priced once a day. Once Fidelity announced this new capability it became obvious to the followers what the customer implications were. It took somewhat longer to determine the extent of the damage attributable to the uneven playing field. But even as competitors began to see market damage, it was not a simple matter to understand the rather complex mechanisms required to implement hourly mutual fund pricing.

Winning approval
Now funds will need to be allocated to mount a defence. If the follower believes they are being hurt the monies will be quickly allocated, even for a project that had previously been sidelined. For instance the IT manager of a UK firm some years ago proposed to senior management that the firm introduce point-of-sale (POS) terminals in their retail outlets. The suggestion died an inglorious death during an early round of that year's application portfolio deliberations, and met the same fate the following year and again the year after that. But when *The Times*

published an account of a major competitor's intention to roll out POS terminals during the next 12 months the attitude of the follower's senior management team changed dramatically. The original proposal was quickly revitalized, enthusiastically endorsed, and generously funded.

In another industry a prime mover's management team, understanding their competitor's conservative attitude about IT, went ahead with an application that they realized could be easily imitated. From past experience they felt confident that their competitors would not respond until the new application was demonstrated to be a *commercial success in the marketplace*. The resulting lead time, which proved to be over two years, guaranteed them significant gains in marketshare, before the competitive response was put in place.

Building the system

The system build may present an opportunity for the follower to make up lost time. This is particularly true if the application depends to a large extent on off-the-shelf packaged software or expertise readily brought in from outside (perhaps from previous employees, vendors, or former consultants of the prime mover). The follower has opportunities that were not available to the prime mover. The follower begins from a well understood starting point – the original application developed by the prime mover. The follower can also consider whether joining a syndicate of other competitors might be an appropriate way to meet the prime mover's initiative (thus decreasing the costs but probably increasing the lead time).

The prime mover will be in a stronger position at this stage if no short-cuts exist for the follower. This is more likely to be the case if the application is built around an existing data or knowledge base.

Project launch

Project launch may again offer time advantages to the follower because the system's intended users will now understand the value of the application. If the users are customers, distributors, or suppliers, they are likely to be aware of the application's potential due to the successful efforts of the prime mover. If the users are internal, competitive pressures will have likely paved the way for the new system. For instance, if the expert system for approving loans has increased the quality of the prime mover's loan portfolio, then the follower will soon see that they are beginning to lose the best risks.

Competitor analysis: who can respond?

Projects that rely on generic lead time for advantage are at risk. Word may leak out sooner than expected or a competitor may find a short-cut solution. Delays in the initial build or problems during implementation may give the competition an opportunity to field a timely response. Worse, the competitive response may leapfrog the original initiative, particularly if they have greater resources (Vitale, 1986b). Sustainability is much more likely either where the prime mover earns a decided advantage by going first or where competitive asymmetry makes it difficult or impossible for a competitor to respond. In this section we discuss competitive asymmetry, and in the following section focus on ways that the prime movers can pre-empt subsequent challenges.

Chamberlin (1933) used the term 'monopolistic competition' to describe industry rivalry between businesses which possess significant unique features within their resource and asset bases. He demonstrated that monopolistic competition was associated with the achievement by some industry participants of superior financial returns for sustained periods. The implication is that heterogeneity is a potential source of competitive advantage, and companies should seek to base their strategies around such distinctive capabilities. Thus, a new application which leverages dissimilarities between the prime mover and likely followers makes it difficult or impossible for followers to mount an effective response. In such a situation the follower is required not only to build the new application, but to also address the fundamental dissimilarity that the system relies on for success.

We have found three categories of such differences that can be usefully exploited with information technology. The first focuses on the firm's scope of operations, the second on issues revolving around the firm's chosen organizational structure and culture, and the last on the firm's existing information base. Each is described below and depicted in Figure 3.3.

Competitive scope:
- geographic
- segment
- vertical
- industry

Organizational base:
- structure
- culture
- physical assets

Information resources:
- technology
- applications
- databases
- knowledge bases

Figure 3.3   Sources of asymmetry

Competitive scope

Michael Porter claims that competitive scope can have 'a powerful effect on competitive advantage' (Porter, 1985, p. 55). In essence, scope is the range of markets, locations, channels, and products within which the firm chooses to compete. Porter describes four types of scope:

- *Geographical scope* refers to the geographical area that a firm chooses to compete in or the places that it chooses to locate particular types of work.
- *Segment scope* refers to the breadth of products sold and the buyers served.
- *Vertical scope* is the extent to which the firm has elected to pursue backwards or forward integration strategies.
- *Industry scope* is 'the range of related industries in which the firm competes with a coordinated strategy'.

Differences in scope can provide powerful starting points for leveraging IT. Merrill Corporation, a financial printer, has located its production operations in their headquarter's facility in St. Paul, Minnesota. Their primary competitors historically have located both production and sales facilities in local offices across the US. A communications network ties Merrill's sales offices to St. Paul, where inexpensive and well educated labour is easily obtainable. Merrill's competitors, though saddled with much higher costs for labour, equipment, and rent, have invested heavily in facilities in their present offices and would face huge cost penalties if they elect to redo their current infrastructure. In the industry downturn which followed the stock market crash of October 1987, Merrill fared well due to its low fixed costs (James, 1989).

Merrill has taken what was once a geographical advantage for its competitors – downtown locations near their prestigious clients – and used IT to leverage it to advantage. Similarly, firms with a worldwide presence and corporate network often have opportunities to move work loads and expertise across time zones, giving them an advantage over firms located in a single country. Expert negotiators in Boston, for instance, can be preparing tomorrow's negotiating ploys while the sales staff wine and dine the hapless customer in London.

Large multinationals can use worldwide electronic networks to take advantage of their geographical scope, but special familiarity with a local market also can provide unique opportunities as RHP Ltd has demonstrated. Initially RHP, a UK manufacturer of ballbearings, found themselves at a disadvantage when a multinational competitor established electronic links to the offices of major customers. RHP responded with a system specially tailored for their own UK-based customers. The system took advantage of technology readily available in the UK that was not available worldwide. RHP's offering quickly won them back lost marketshare. Moreover, the multinational competitor, facing the constraints of developing a common system for a geographically dispersed marketplace, had little incentive and less latitude to properly respond.

Segment scope and product breadth can also provide exploitable opportunities. Thomson Holidays, the largest participant in the UK holiday industry, was not the industry leader in providing direct links to the offices of travel agents. But, unlike the smaller competitor who initiated the concept, Thomson offered a wide enough assortment of tours and constituted a big enough share of the travel agent's business that the agents quickly accepted their new system. Thomson's market position was so great that they could downgrade service on manned phone lines, thus forcing the travel agents to use the system and further improving Thomson's cost position. Similarly, in the well-worn story, American Hospital Supply's (AHS) links to customers brought them preference even after competitors had responded because AHS had much the widest product line in the industry and represented the best chance of 'one-stop shopping'.

The now defunct airline, People Express, was victimized by information technology that took advantage of the airline's narrow product scope. People Express offered one price for every seat, while higher-cost competitors such as American Airlines used information technology to fine tune the prices for a much broader set of products. The sophisticated yield management software of the major carriers turned People's low-cost advantage into a fatal flaw. Donald Burr, founder of People Express, described the role of IT in the demise of his airline: 'The reason People Express didn't roll on ... had everything to do with information technology ... the goal (of the competition) was to sell every seat at every price point' (Burr, 1989).

Firms that compete within several elements of the overall supply system may also have unique opportunities. For example, Otis Elevator both manufactures and services elevators. In the former business they have few competitors but in the latter they have hundreds – including many set up by former Otis employees. Otis began embedding a remote diagnostic computer within the elevator which was connected via the in-car phone to an Otis repair facility. The closed loop system establishes an entry barrier for the independent service operators. Going in the other direction, the Otisline service database provides information on elevator reliability which will help Otis to design and build better elevators in the future (Stoddard, 1988).

When a firm competes in numerous related industries, advantages in industry scope may provide opportunities to exploit information technology. For example, if a unit of a larger industrial company equips its sales force with portable computers containing marketing information on products from across other units of the business, the sales person calling on a customer to sell one product can now intelligently talk about others. The sales force becomes considerably more useful to the customer, perhaps differentiating what had previously been a product bought strictly on the basis of price and availability.

Organizational base

Competitive scope takes an outward look at the firm, focusing on its products, target markets, and degree of integration. Looking within the organization, however, can point to other unique attributes that can be leveraged. Differences in organizational structure, culture, or asset base all provide exploitable opportunities.

One of the most powerful competitors damaged by American Hospital Supply's ASAP order entry system was Johnson & Johnson (J&J), a manufacturer and distributor of hospital supply products (Vitale, 1986a). Unlike AHS, J&J had for many years maintained a very decentralized organizational structure. This meant, among other things, that each J&J business unit had its own outgoing logistics operations. Responding to the AHS order entry system was therefore a difficult challenge. After considerable heart-searching, J&J set up a hospital services company in 1982 to centralize its order taking and distribution functions across the product companies. A decade after the AHS initiative the J&J response is still perceived as a tentative one by many industry observers.

The firm's existing asset base can similarly constrain the range of responses available to the follower. Mercury Communications in the 1980s enjoyed such an advantage over its far bigger rival – British Telecom. Mercury is a relative newcomer in the recently deregulated UK telecommunications industry. They differentiated themselves from British Telecom by providing call detail reporting on customer bills. British Telecom, whose switching equipment was installed many years ago, was unable to collect the required information and still charged by metered time, with customers receiving a lump sum bill every quarter.

Information resources

Competitive scope and organizational base provide likely sources of exploitable competitive asymmetry. The firm's existing information resources provide another. The existing technological infrastructure, applications inventory, data resources, and knowledge base all provide potential opportunities.

Recurring investments in distinct technological infrastructures can produce significant and exploitable differences among firms. In their history of the airline industry, for instance, Copeland and McKenney (1988) found that 'the multiprocessor systems that today belong to American and United, as well as TWA, Delta and Eastern/Texas Air, make them different in kind, not just degree, from the uniprocessor systems common to the rest of the airline industry'. Such differences permitted these large carriers to implement sophisticated yield management software, frequent flyer programs, and the sale of reservations services to those very same competitors. Copeland and McKenney conclude that, 'technical competence is a necessary requirement for gaining competitive advantage from information technology'.

But adherence to a technological architecture can also present a potential Achilles' heel to competitors. For instance, for years prominent information technology consultants strongly suggested that firms settle on an IBM-based architecture and thereby simplify life. A company that ignored that seemingly sound advice, perhaps by choosing instead to go with Digital minicomputers or Apple microcomputers, now finds themselves with a computer architecture that is far different from their competitors. If the uniqueness of these architectures can be translated into a business advantage it may be difficult and extremely expensive for a competitor to mount an effective challenge.

Uniqueness in the applications inventory can be another source of potential advantage as Commercial Union, a UK insurance company, demonstrated. When new regulations required UK life insurance brokers to choose between complete independence or alliance with a single underwriter, those insurance companies with advanced IT applications bases prospered at the expense of their rivals. Many companies were still running on batch-based centralized systems. But Commercial Union was able to offer a range of customer service applications such as on-line policy enquiry and the downloading of customer information to the broker's office – because these facilities were extensions of the facilities already developed for their own branch offices. Such capabilities helped Commercial Union to sign up a big UK bank and 500 smaller firms as dedicated agents, giving them thousands of new sales staff for their products.

Existing databases can present another rich source of leveragable uniqueness. The International Trucks division of Navistar, for instance, had for some years been collecting information from existing customers so as to give their engineers some understanding of how the trucks were holding up in use. Eventually, it was discovered that this database could be used to provide analytic tools of use to the fleet owners that Navistar often sold to. Personal computer-based models were developed that assisted fleet owners in determining appropriate staffing levels for maintenance facilities or investments in spare parts inventories.

Competitive response was slowed by the lack of a comparable historical database upon which to base the models (Ives and Vitale, 1988).

A similar approach has been taken by Hartford Steam Boiler Insurance Company, who have taken a database of information on boiler operations, originally developed to assist their underwriters, and made it available to their customers' boiler room managers (Heskett, 1987). And, in the future, as expert systems become more commonplace and as more expertise is captured within their knowledge bases, we expect to see them presenting innovative firms with similarly exploitable opportunities.

Supply chain analysis: will copying help?

Lead time and competitive asymmetry have been discussed as two contributing factors to sustainable advantage. 'Generic lead time', tells us how long we have until competitors can put together the same application and 'competitive asymmetry' tells us if they will be able to copy the application. The final question is whether, once the competition has the application in place, it will do any good. Here we are concerned with the potential of the prime mover to seriously pre-empt retaliation by the follower.

Some of the best known examples of using IT for competitive advantage involve pre-emption – perhaps that accounts for their fame. The Merrill Lynch Cash Management Account was targeted at the wealthy individuals of North America; competitors struggled to respond, and eventually brought out equivalent offerings. However, Merrill Lynch retained its customer base even after competitive response. Five years after the introduction of the Cash Management Account, the nearest rival was reported to have only one tenth as many accounts as Merrill Lynch (Wiseman, 1985). In 1986 Merrill's market share was still reported to be more than 50 per cent due to 'account stickiness' (Clemons, 1986). Similarly, American Airlines and United Airlines between them signed up nearly 60 per cent of US travel agents for their systems, putting airlines like Frontier at a decided disadvantage. These and other examples illustrate the three components of successful pre-emption which we term:

- Finding the exploitable link.
- Capturing the pole position.
- Keeping the gate closed.

Finding the exploitable link
Whereas Chamberlin (1933) and the concept of competitive asymmetry focus our attention on the asset base of the business contrasted with that of competitors, McMillan (1983) suggests that the research for pre-emption potential should take us into the upstream and downstream

elements of the supply chain. There we should look for a concentration point within the supply chain where resources are finite and where a limited number of participants control the link in the chain. Examples of such exploitable links could be restricted supply sources for a key input, concentrated distribution channels, or a limited number of customers within the target segment. In Merrill Lynch's case, customers represented the exploitable resource; in the airline industry it was first the travel agents (via computer reservation systems) and then the customers (via frequent flyer programmes). For the John Hancock Insurance Company (described below) it might be the employee benefits managers within their corporate customer set. For paint manufacturer Benjamin Moore it is the major outlets retailing paint to customers.

Capturing the pole position

Having identified such target groups within the supply chain, we must then seek out IT applications which can propel the business into a unique and superior relationship with that group. IT will provide a superior relationship if, in return for the benefits provided by the application, the user will be prepared to put the prime mover into the position of preferred business partner. The relationship must be unique in the sense that the user will not want more than one such partner – there is only one pole position, denoting clear and unchallenged leadership. The leader may be displaced in time, but he will not be joined. Thus no customers want or need two cash management accounts – that would damage the whole service concept; they either have a Merrill Lynch account or transfer to a competitor. In providing the retailer with a service which mixes paint to the precise colour of a customer's sample, Benjamin Moore achieved the same position, increasing sales by 5–10 per cent. Having gained benefit from the provision of a new service to the customer, will the retailer want to incur the expense, space loss, and set-up time required to take a second and equivalent machine from a rival paint supplier?

In true pre-emption the prime mover's continued leadership position is secure against any competitive response which is *equivalent* to his own offering. For example, guarding against leaving scope for a follower to come in with an application that is clearly *superior* in the sense that it offers significant extra benefits to the user. Only then will the user be prepared to incur the switching costs which are the subject of the next section.

Keeping the gate closed

From the earliest days of computing, it has been clear that users perceive there to be significant tangible and intangible costs incurred in moving from one system to another. As a result, COBOL programmers generally have resisted using the apparently more elegant C or ADA programming languages; professionals and secretaries alike resist transferring from one word processing package to another. This phenomenon represents the prime mover's initial base for sustaining advantage, the gate which bars the way of the follower.

The switching costs associated with today's IT applications can be considered under three headings, relating to the application interface, the database, and the community of users. In the first case, even the simplest IT application requires its user to learn and remember an interface comprising sign-on procedure, password, command language, etc. As Feeny (1988) notes from his research in the UK package holiday industry, travel agents who had grown accustomed to the prime mover's system were not prepared to learn new interfaces in order to use a follower's system in parallel. Only when Horizon Holidays introduced a system which looked to the travel agent to be identical to that of the prime mover, Thomson Holidays, did Thomson's advantage begin to erode. In an elementary parallel, most of us now carry several plastic cards which can be used to obtain cash from ATMs; how many of us actually use more than one such card in this way, the one whose PIN we remember?

In some applications, transfer of allegiance also involves the user in loss or re-creation of data – for instance a US travel agent transferring from American Airlines SABRE to United's APOLLO loses his sales history file; a customer moving from Merrill Lynch's Cash Management Account has to transfer all the information which describes his probably complex financial status. These switching costs are additional to the investment in learning the rival's system and increase the likelihood that switching will not occur unless the follower can offer substantial advantages over the prime mover, or unless the relationship between user and prime mover has seriously deteriorated.

The third potential source of switching costs is represented by the users themselves if they form a community of interest. For example, in the John Hancock system the users are the employee benefits managers of different corporations. In addition to accessing John Hancock for insurance services, they use the system to communicate with each other via electronic mail on matters of common interest. If one user were to switch from John Hancock to a rival it would mean separation from the circle of fellow professionals. Similarly Foreign Exchange Dealers would find it difficult to move from the Reuters' Monitor system and still have enough people to trade with. In cases like these, the prime movers' systems have become part of the infrastructure of the supply chain. Individual defection to a follower system become most unlikely;

only wholesale defection makes sense, and that will only be organized if the user community as a whole loses faith in the prime mover's system.

SUSTAINABILITY: THE LITERATURE REVISITED

Since our model was first published in 1990, there have been a number of further articles in the field of which the most prominent are Clemons and Row (1991), Kettinger et al., (1994), and Mata et al. (1995). Each of these has particularly emphasized the idea of firm specific resources as a foundation for achieving IT-based sustainable competitive advantage. This emphasis reflects the dominant contemporary focus of authors on strategy, the link between strategy and the firm's resources, skills, and competences (see for example, Grant 1991). It is analogous to the assessment of competitive asymmetry, the central pillar of our model.

Clemons and Row (1991), while acknowledging the legitimacy of other strands of analysis, including their own prior work, consider the role of 'strategic resources' in explaining the allocation of benefits from an IT innovation. They assume that any successful innovation will be imitated in due course by industry competitors, and suggest that sustainable advantage will flow to the owners of those resources which best 'complement' the technology in achieving the innovation. If there is competitive asymmetry in this respect, and barriers to duplication, sustainable advantage will accrue to the firm dominating those resources whether or not that firm is the prime mover. Thompson Holidays among our examples, illustrates the point. Interestingly Clemons and Row argue that, in the absence of lasting differences in ownership of complementary resources, the benefits of an IT innovation will ultimately flow to customers rather than industry competitors. They cite the provision of ATMs by banks, which rapidly became a strategic necessity for all competitors rather than a source of advantage for a few.

In the language of our model Clemons and Row (1991) focus particularly on 'competitive scope' as a source of asymmetry. They suggest that companies with little 'vertical scope' may actually be better placed than more vertically integrated competitors to achieve IT-based competitive advantage. By contrast, broad 'industry scope' is seen to provide significant and largely untapped opportunity.

Kettinger et al., (1994) make a brave attempt to establish empirical evidence of sustainable competitive advantage being achieved through IT-based innovation. They track from public sources the achievements of 30 businesses which have been regularly cited as innovators (though their list includes only three of the examples we have used). Only 15 of these businesses are seen to have both established gains (in profitability and/or market share) in the five years following innovation, *and* to have sustained those gains over a further five years. All 13 of the firms which gained marketshare in the first five years sustained those gains in the next five – the phenomenon familiar to marketeers, that market shares re-stabilize at new levels after innovations have been successfully imitated. However, the analysis also highlights the difficulties of isolating the performance effects of specific innovations within the wider complexity of competitive dynamics. For example, Merrill Lynch, which undoubtedly achieved lasting domination of the market for cash management accounts, is shown to have lost profitability and market share overall as their more familiar lines of business failed to prosper.

Before Mata *et al.*, (1995) address their main theme of resource-based competition, they strongly attack the 'create-capture-keep' paradigm represented by the pre-emption leg of our model. They argue that customers will not allow themselves to be 'captured' through switching costs and 'exploited'. We find the first part of this assertion surprising, since the trend in so many industries has been for firms to move towards single sources and intensive relationships with suppliers – away from the commodity style purchasing which electronic markets might support. These firms are consciously accepting that the accumulation of significant switching costs is a disadvantage outweighed by the efficiencies which can flow from close interworking with suppliers. The Walmart/Proctor and Gamble relationship provides one well-known example. Of course customers will not tolerate being 'exploited' by suppliers who seek excessive margins. But suppliers who achieve 'pole position' can enjoy sustainable marketshare gains and increases in absolute profit levels without having to resort to margin exploitation.

When Mata *et al.*, address resource differences between firms, their interest is specifically IT resources. They conclude that three categories of IT resource – access to capital for investment, proprietary technology, technical skills – represent 'mobile' resources which are easily duplicated. These cannot be the basis for sustainable competitive advantage. However, they find that 'managerial skills' – which include the ability of IT managers to understand business needs, work successfully with business colleagues, manage market and technical risk of innovations – are difficult to achieve and 'immobile'. Managerial IT skills can be the foundation for sustainable advantage. The importance of these skills is acknowledged and addressed elsewhere in this book, particularly in Chapters 1 and 2.

CONCLUSION

In our experience, most large organizations are now alert to the concept of using IT to achieve competitive edge, particularly in the form of building new services to customers and distributors. But ideas in this area need careful analysis before investments can be made with any confidence. We have seen a major car rental company put touch-sensitive screens on its airport desks to allow drivers to request directions from airport to local destinations. The technology is very user-friendly; the application is genuinely helpful to many. But will that free service application really sway the customer to choose that company's rental in preference to those of its rivals on the adjacent desks? And if it does, how long will it be before every rival desk also carries such a device? The application fails all the tests of generic lead time, competitive asymmetry, and pre-emption potential.

The frameworks we have proposed allow management to consider the probability that an application, if successful, will provide advantage for long enough to properly repay the investment required. Further, the framework can give insights into the actions which will lead to an increased chance of sustainable advantage. For example, if an application is seen to be dependent on generic lead time, it will be important to ensure that it is developed in a secure environment so that competitive reaction is triggered as late as possible; a series of upgrades should be planned from the start so that leadership can be consistently renewed and follower companies disoriented. Or taking the concept of competitive asymmetry, we can be confident that the business as a whole invests in monitoring competition, but how many IS departments have invested in building a picture of the competitor's IS capability which can be the basis of understanding which initiatives the competitor can respond to? Finally, if the application represents an attempt at pre-emption, two questions are particularly important: can the application scope be expanded to more completely meet the user's need, thereby denying followers the superior response which might displace the prime mover? And can switching costs be built up by adding database facilities and/or establishing the type of community of users we have described?

Greater attention to the analysis of sustainability can, we believe, help to restore the credibility of IT as a competitive weapon at a time when many are wondering whether the concept is another example of IT industry hype. And if the analysis shows that an application, despite offering attractive benefits, cannot be defended against the competition, management should forego the excitement (and cost!) of pioneering the idea and settle for a fast, cheap, and effective follower role.

REFERENCES

Barrett, S. and Konsynski, B. (1982) 'Inter-organizational information sharing systems', *MIS Quarterly*, **6,** (5) December, pp. 93–105.

Beath, C. M. and Ives, B. (1986) Competitive information systems in support of pricing', *MIS Quarterly*, **26,** (1) March, pp. 85–96.

Beath, C. M. and Ives, B. (1988) 'The information technology champion: aiding and abetting, care and feeding', *Proceedings of the Twenty-first Annual Hawaii International Conference on Systems Sciences*, pp. 115–123.

Burr, D. (1989) 'Coming of age', *Inc.*, **11,** (4), April, pp. 38–77.

Cash, J. L. and Konsynski, B. (1985) 'IS redraws competitive boundaries', *Harvard Business Review*, **63,** (2), March/April, pp. 134–142.

Chamberlin, E. H. (1933) *The Theory of Monopolistic Competition*, Harvard University Press, Cambridge, Mass.

Clemons, E. K. (1986) 'Information systems for sustainable competitive advantage', *Information & Management*, November, pp. 131–136.

Clemons, E. K. and McFarlan, W. F. (1986) Telecom: hook up or lose out', *Harvard Business Review*, **64,** (4) July/August, pp. 91–97.

Clemons, E. K., and Kimbrough, S. O. (1986) 'Information systems, telecommunications, and their effects on industrial organization', *Proceedings of the Seventh International Conference on Information Systems*, San Diego, December, pp. 99–108.

Clemons, E. K. and Knez, M. (1988) 'Competition and cooperation in information systems innovation', *Information & Management*, **15,** pp. 25–35.

Clemons, E. K. and Row, M. (1987) 'Structural differences among firms: a potential source of competitive advantage in the application of information technology', *Proceedings of the Eighth International Conference on Information Systems*, Pittsburgh, December, pp. 1–9.

Clemons, E. K. and Row, M. (1988) 'McKesson Drug Company: a case study of Economost – a strategic information system', *JMIS*, **5,** (1) Summer, pp. 36–50.

Clemons, E. K. and Row, M. C. (1991) 'Sustaining IT Advantage: the role of structural differences', *MIS Quarterly*, **15,** (3), September.

Copeland, D. G. and McKenney, J. L. (1988) 'Airline reservations systems: lessons for history', *MIS Quarterly*, **12,** (3) September, pp. 353–370.

Feeny, D. F. (1988) 'Creating and sustaining competitive advantage', In Michael Earl, (ed.), *Information Management: the Strategic Dimension*, Oxford University Press, Oxford.

Feeny, D. F. and Ives, B. (1990) 'In Search of Sustainability: Reaping long-term advantage from investments in Information Technology', *Journal of Management Information Systems*, **7,** (1), Summer.

Grant, R. M. (1991) 'The resource-based theory of competitive advantage: implications for strategy formulation', *California Management Review*, **33,** (3), Spring.

Heskett, James L. (1987) 'Lessons in the service sector', *Harvard Business Review*, **65,** (2), March/April.

Ives, B. (1990) 'Wingtip Couriers', *Southern Methodist University Case Study*, #SMU/MIS/90–01, January, Edwin L. Cox School of Business, Dallas, Texas.

Ives, B. and Learmonth, G. P. (1984) 'The information systems as a competitive weapon', *Communications of the ACM*, **27,** (12) December, pp. 1193–1201.

Ives, B. and Vitale, M. R. (1988) 'After the sale: leveraging maintenance with information technology', *MIS Quarterly*, **12,** (1), March, pp. 7–21.

James, E. L. (1989) 'Casualties and hard times follow', *Wall Street Journal*, September 10.

Jarvenpaa, S. L. and Ives, B. (1989) *Information technology and corporate strategy; a view from the top*, (Working paper), University of Texas, Austin, August.

Kettinger, W. J., Grover, V., Guha, S. and Segars, A. H. (1994) 'Strategic Information Systems Revisited: a Study in Sustainability and Performance', *MIS Quarterly*, **18,** (1), March.

Learmonth, G. P. and Ives, B. (1987) 'Information system technology can improve customer service', *Database*, Winter, pp. 1–25.

Linder, J. (1987) *Frito-Lay Inc: a Strategic Transition (A)*, Harvard Business School Case Study, #9–187–065, March, pp. 1–25.

Lockett, Martin. (1987) *The factors behind successful IT innovation*, (Working paper) Oxford Institute of Information Management, Templeton College, Oxford University.

Madnick, S. E. and Wang, Y. R. (1988) 'Evolution toward strategic applications of databases through composite information systems', *JMIS*, **5,** (2), Fall, pp. 5–22.

Malone, Thomas W., Yates, J. and Benjamin, R. I. (1986) 'Electronic markets and electronic hierarchies: effects of information technology on market structures, and corporate strategies', *Proceedings of the Seventh International Conference on Information Systems*, San Diego, December, pp. 109–112.

Mata, F. J., Fuerst, W. L. and Barney, J. B. (1995) 'Information Technology and Sustained Competitive Advantage: a Resource-based analysis', *MIS Quarterly*, **19,** (4), December.

McFarlan, W. F., McKenney, J. L. and Pyburn, P. (1983) 'The

information archipelago – plotting a course', *Harvard Business Review*, **61**, (1) January/February, pp. 145–156.

McMillan, I. C. (1983) 'Pre-emptive strategies', *Journal of Business Strategy*, **3**, (2) Fall, pp. 16–26.

Parsons, G. L. (1983) 'Information technology: a new competitive weapon', *Sloan Management Review*, **25**, (1), Fall, pp. 3–14.

Porter, M. (1985) *Competitive Advantage*, Free Press, New York.

Porter, M. and Millar, V. E. (1985) 'How information gives you competitive advantage', *Harvard Business Review*, **63**, (4) July/August, pp. 149–160.

Rackoff, N., Wiseman, C. and Ullrich, W. A. (1985) 'Information systems for competitive advantage; implementation of a planning process', *MIS Quarterly*, **9**, (4), December.

Runge, D. (1988) *Winning with Telecommunications*, Washington: ICIT Press, December.

Stoddard, D. (1988) *Otisline*, Harvard Business School Case Study, #9–186–304, pp. 1–14.

Vitale, M. R. (1984) 'Frontier Airlines Inc.', *Harvard Business School Case Study*, #9–184–041, pp. 1–24.

Vitale, M. R. (1986) *American Hospital Supply Corp. (A) the ASAP System*, Harvard Business School Case Study, #9–196–005, March, pp. 1–17.

Vitale, M. R. (1986) 'The growing risks of information systems success', *MIS Quarterly*, **10**, (4), December, pp. 327–334.

Vitale, M. R. (1988) *Finding and fostering innovative applications of information technology part 2: the lessons*, (Working paper). The International Center for Information Technology, Washington DC.

Vitale, M. R., Ives, B. and Beath, C. M. (1986) 'Identifying strategic information systems: finding a process or building an organization', *Proceedings of the Seventh Annual International Conference on Information Systems*, San Diego, December.

Williamson, O. E. (1979) 'Transaction cost economics: the governance of contractual relations', *Journal of Law and Economics*, **22**, pp. 233–261.

Wiseman, C. (1985) *Strategy and Computers: Information Systems as Competitive Weapons*, Dow Jones Irwin, Homewood, IL.

CHAPTER FOUR

Assessing IT Productivity: Any Way Out of the Labyrinth?

LESLIE P. WILLCOCKS AND STEPHANIE LESTER

INTRODUCTION

Labyrinth – An intricate structure of intercommunicating passages, through which it is difficult to find one's way without a clue.

(OED definition)

There's no way a mathematical cost/benefit analysis is worth the paper it is written on.

(IT Executive quoted in Grindley, 1995)

There are mosquito bites, and there are snake bites. Good managers can tell the difference.

(J. Titsworth, vice-president, Xerox)

Industrial-age control ratios persist as a way of thinking about IT costs . . . (but) the effects of computers are systemic.

(Strassmann, 1990)

The history of numerous failed and disappointing information technology (IT) investments in work organizations has been richly documented. The 1993 abandonment of a five-year project like Taurus in the UK London financial markets, in this case at a cost of £80 million to the Stock Exchange, and possibly £400 million to City institutions, provides only high profile endorsement of underlying disquiet on the issue. Earlier survey and case research by the present authors established IT investment as a high risk, hidden cost business, with a variety of factors, including size and complexity of the project, the 'newness' of the technology, the degree of 'structuredness' in the project, and major human, political and cultural factors compounding the risks (Willcocks and Griffiths, 1994; Willcocks and Lester, 1996; see also Chapter 9). Alongside, (indeed we would argue contributing to) the performance issues surrounding IT, is accumulated evidence of problems in IT evaluation together with a history of general indifferent organizational practice in the area.

But at the same time it is now widely acknowledged that the evaluation and management of IT investments is shot through with difficulties. Increasingly, as IT expenditure has risen and as the use of IT has penetrated to the core of organizations, the search has been directed towards not just improving evaluation techniques and processes, and searching for new ones, but also towards the management and 'flushing out' of benefits. But these evaluation and management efforts regularly run into difficulties of three generic types. First, many organizations find themselves in a Catch-22 situation (Willcocks, 1992). For competitive reasons they cannot afford not to invest in IT, but economically they cannot find sufficient justification, and evaluation practice cannot provide enough underpinning, for making the investment. Secondly, for many of the more advanced and intensive users of IT, as the IT infrastructure becomes an inextricable part of the organization's processes and structures, it becomes increasingly difficult to separate out the impact of IT from that of other assets and activities. Thirdly, and despite the high levels of expenditure, there is widespread lack of understanding of IT and information systems (IS – organizational applications, increasingly IT-based, that deliver on the information needs of the organization's stakeholders) as major capital assets. While senior managers regularly give detailed attention to the annual expenditure on IT/IS, there is little awareness of the size of the capital asset that has been bought over the years (Keen, 1991; Willcocks, 1994). Failure to appreciate the size of this investment leads to IT/IS being under-managed, a lack of serious attention being given to IS evaluation and control, and also a lack of concern for discovering ways of utilizing this IS asset base to its full potential.

Solutions to these difficulties have most often been sought through variants on the mantra 'what gets measured gets managed'. As a dominant guiding principle, more (and more accurate) measurement has been advanced as the panacea to evaluation difficulties. In a large body of literature, while some consideration is given to the difficulties inherent in quantifying IT impacts, a range of other difficulties are downplayed, or even ignored. These include, for example:

- the fact that measurement systems are prone to decay;

- the goal displacement effects of measurement;
- the downside whereby only that which is measured gets managed;
- the behavioural implications of measurement and related reward systems, and;
- the politics inherent in any organizational evaluation activity.

In practice, counter evidence against a narrow focus on quantification for IT/IS evaluation has been gathering. Thus some recent studies point to how measurement can be improved, but also to the limitations of measurement, and areas where sets of measures may be needed because of the lack of a single reliable measure (Banker, Kauffman and Mahmood, 1993; Farbey, Targett and Land, 1995; Willcocks, 1996a). They also point to the key role of stakeholder judgement throughout any IT/IS evaluation process. Furthermore, some published research studies point to the political-rational as opposed to the straightforwardly rational aspects of IT measurement in organizations. For example, Lacity and Hirschheim (1996) provide an important insight into how measurement, in this case benchmarking IT performance against external comparators, can be used in political ways to influence senior management judgement. Currie (1989) detailed the political uses of measurement in a paper entitled 'the art of justifying new technology to top management' (see also Walsham, 1993; Willcocks, Currie and Mason, 1997). Additionally, there are signs that the problems with over-focusing on measurement are being recognized, albeit slowly, with moves toward emphasizing the demonstration of the value of IS/IT, not merely its measurement (see Banker, Kauffman and Mahmood, 1993; Gillin, 1994; LaPlante, 1994; and LaPlante and Alter, 1994 for examples). Elsewhere we have argued for the need to move measurement itself from a focus on the price of IT to a concern for its value; and for a concomitant shift in emphasis in the measurement regime from control to quality improvement (Willcocks and Lester, 1991, 1996).

These difficulties and limitations in evaluation practice have become bound up in a widespread debate about what has been called the IT productivity paradox. This is the notion that despite large investments in IT over many years, it has been difficult to discover where the IT payoffs have occurred, if indeed there have been many. In the words of Solow (1987), 'Computers (are) everywhere except in the productivity statistics'. In this chapter we will address critically this overall sense, held by many, that despite huge investments in IS/IT so far these have produced disappointing returns. We will find that while much of the sense of disappointment may be justified, at the same time it is fed by limitations in evaluation techniques and processes, and by misunderstandings of the contribution IT can and does make to organizations, as much as by actual experience of poorly performing information systems. The focus then moves to how organizations may seek to improve their IT/IS evaluation procedures and processes. Taking into account the many limitations in evaluation practice identified by a range of the more recent research studies, a high-level framework is advanced for how evaluation can and needs to be applied across the systems life-cycle. The chapter also suggests that processes of evaluation, and the involvement of stakeholders, may be as, if not more, important than refining techniques and producing measurement of a greater, but possibly no less spurious, accuracy.

IS THERE AN IT 'PRODUCTIVITY PARADOX'?

Alongside the seemingly inexorable rise of IS/IT investment in the last 15 years, there has been considerable uncertainty and concern about the productivity impact of IT being experienced in work organizations. This has been reinforced by several high profile studies at the levels of both the national economy and industrial sector, suggesting in fact that if there has been an IS/IT payoff it has been minimal, and hardly justifies the vast financial outlays incurred. Two early influential studies embodying this theme were by Roach (1986) and Loveman (1988). At time of writing the most recent advocate of this argument was Landauer (1995). A key, overarching point needs to be made immediately. It is clear from reviews of the many research studies conducted at national, sectoral and organization specific levels that the failure to identify IS/IT benefits and productivity says as much about the deficiencies in assessment methods and measurement, and the rigour with which they are applied, as about mismanagement of the development and use of information-based technologies (Brynjolfsson, 1993; Glazer, 1993; Willcocks, 1994). It is useful to chase this hare of 'the IT productivity paradox' further, because the issue goes to the heart of the subject of this chapter.

Interestingly, the IT productivity paradox is rarely related in the literature to manufacturing sectors for which, in fact, there are a number of studies from the early 1980s onwards showing rising IT expenditure correlating with sectoral and firm-specific productivity rises (see for example Brynjolfsson and Hitt, 1993; Loveman, 1988; Weill, 1990). The high-profile studies raising concern also tend to base their work mainly on statistics gathered in the US context. Their major focus in fact tends to be limited to the service sector in the USA (see Hackett, 1990; Roach, 1988; 1991). Recently a number of studies question the data on which such studies were based, suggesting that the data is sufficiently flawed to make simple conclusions misleading

(Brynjolfsson, 1993; Quinn and Baily, 1994). It has been pointed out, for example that in the cases of Loveman (1988) and Roach (1986) neither personally collected the data that they analysed, thus their observations describe numbers rather than actual business experiences (van Nievelt, 1992).

Still others argue that the productivity payoff may have been delayed but, by the mid-1990s, recession and global competition have forced companies to finally use the technologies they put in place over the last decade, with corresponding productivity leaps (Gillin, 1994; Roach, 1994; Sager and Gleckman, 1994). This explanation fits quite well with the fact that the research periods of many of the studies uncovering lack of IT productivity were restricted to the early 1980s or before. By way of example, Barua, Kriebel and Mukhopadhyay (1991) studied 20 firms in the 1978–82 period, Loveman's (1988) study covers 1978–82 while Morrison and Berndt (1990) covered 1968–86. Gillin (1994) makes the additional point that productivity figures always failed to measure the cost avoidance and savings on opportunity costs that IS/IT can help to achieve.

Others also argue that the real payoffs occur when IS/IT development and use is linked with the business process reengineering (BPR) efforts coming onstream in the 1990s (for example, Brynjolfsson and Hitt, 1996; Davenport, 1993; Hammer and Champy, 1993). However, recent UK evidence develops this debate by finding that few organizations were actually getting 'breakthrough' results through IT-enabled BPR. Organizations were 'aiming low and hitting low' and generally not going for the radical, high-risk reengineering approaches advocated by many commentators. Moreover, there was no strong correlation between size of IT expenditure in reengineering projects, and resulting productivity impacts (see also chapter 10). In business process reengineering, as elsewhere (see below) it is the management of IT and what it is used for, rather than the size of IT spend that counts (Willcocks, 1996b).

On a related issue, Bakos and Jager (1995) provide interesting further insight. The latter argue that computers are not boosting productivity, but the fault lies not with the technology but with its management and how computer use is overseen. Along with Quinn and Baily (1994), Bakos questions the reliability of the productivity studies, and, supporting the positive IT productivity findings in the study by Brynjolfsson and Hitt (1993), posits a new productivity paradox: 'How can computers be so productive?'

In the face of such disputation Brynjolfsson (1993) makes salutary reading. He suggests four explanations for the seeming IT productivity paradox. The first is measurement errors. In practice the measurement problems appear particularly acute in the service sector and with white-collar worker productivity – the main areas investigated by those pointing to a minimal productivity impact from IT use in the 1980s and early 1990s. Brynjolfsson concludes, from a close examination of the data behind the studies of IT performance at national and sectoral levels, that mismeasurement is at the core of the IT productivity paradox. A second explanation is timing lags due to learning and adjustment. Benefits from IT can take several years to show through in significant financial terms, a point also made by Keen (1991) and Strassmann (1990) in arguing for newer ways of evaluating IS/IT performance at the organizational level. While Brynjolfsson largely discounts this explanation in his 1993 paper, there is evidence to suggest he is somewhat over optimistic about the ability of managers to account rationally for such lags and include them in their IS/IT evaluation system (Willcocks, 1994). Moreover, in a later paper Brynjolfsson and Hitt (1996) do offer an 'investment in learning' explanation for lack of productivity in the early 1980s, feeding through into a 'substantial and significant' IS contribution to firm output in the 1987–91 period they studied.

A third possible explanation is that of redistribution. IT may be beneficial to individual firms but unproductive from the standpoint of the industry, or the economy, as a whole. IT rearranges the share of the pie, with the bigger share going to those heavily investing in IT, without making the pie bigger. Brynjolfsson (1993) suggests, however, that the redistribution hypothesis would not explain any shortfall in IT productivity at the firm level. To add to his analysis one can note that in several sectors, for example banking and financial services, firms seemingly compete by larger spending on IT-based systems that are, in practice, increasingly becoming minimum entry requirements for the sector, and commodities rather than differentiators of competitive performance. As a result in some sectors, for example the oil industry, organizations are increasingly seeking to reduce such IS/IT costs by accepting that some systems are industry standard and can be developed together.

A fourth explanation is that IS/IT is not really productive at the firm level. Brynjolfsson (1993) posits that despite the neoclassical view of the firm as a profit maximizer, it may well be that decision-makers are, for whatever reason, often not acting in the interests of the firm: 'instead they are increasing their slack, building inefficient systems, or simply using outdated criteria for decision-making' (p. 75). The implication of Brynjolfsson's argument is that political interests and/or poor evaluation practice may contribute to failure to make real, observable gains from IS/IT investments. However, Brynjolfsson appears to discount these possibilities citing a lack of evidence either way, though here he seems to be restricting himself to the economics literature. Against his argument however, there are frequent study findings showing patchy strategizing and implementation practice where IS is concerned, (for overviews see Currie, 1995; Robson, 1994). Furthermore, recent studies in the IT evaluation literature suggest more evidence showing poor evaluation practice than Brynjolfsson has been willing to credit (see below).

It is on this point that the real debate on the apparent 'IT productivity paradox' needs to hinge. Studies at the aggregate levels of the economy or industrial sector undoubtedly conceal important questions and data about variations in business experiences at the organizational and intra-organizational levels. In practice, as we will discuss further, organizations seem to vary greatly in their ability to harness IS/IT for organizational purpose. Furthermore, as we address the evidence it will become clear that significant aspects of the IT productivity paradox, as perceived and experienced at organizational level, can be addressed through improvements in evaluation and management practice. In particular the distorting effects of poor evaluation methods and processes need close examination and profiling; alternative methods, and an assessment of their appropriateness for specific purposes and conditions need to be advanced; and how these methods can be integrated together and into management practice needs to be addressed. These are large issues but, using recent research, a preliminary attempt to address them at the organizational level will now be made.

ASSESSING THE BUSINESS VALUE OF IT: RECENT RESEARCH

The rest of this chapter concentrates not on assessing IT/IS performance at national or industry levels, but on the conduct of IT/IS evaluation within work organizations. As already suggested, IT/IS expenditure in such organizations is high and rising. The US leads the way, with government statistics suggesting that, by 1994, computers and other information technology made up nearly half of all business spending on equipment – not including the billions spent on software and programmers each year (Sager and Gleckman, 1994). Globally, computer and telecommunications investments now amount to a half or more of most large firms' annual capital expenditures. In an advanced industrialized economy like the UK, IS/IT expenditure by business and public sector organizations was estimated at £33.6 billion for 1995, and expected to rise at 8.2 per cent, 7 per cent and 6.5 per cent in subsequent years, representing an average of over 2 per cent of turnover, or in local and central government, an average IT spend of

£3546 per employee (Keen, 1991; Kew Associates, 1995; Willcocks, 1994). If organizational IS/IT expenditure in developing economies is noticeably lower, nevertheless those economies may well leapfrog several stages of technology, with China, Russia, India and Brazil, for example, set to invest into telecommunications an estimated 53.3, 23.3, 13.7, and US$10.2 billion respectively in the 1993–2000 period (Engardio, 1994). Within this wider context recent research points to three major issues that need to be addressed. The next three sections will do just that.

IT expenditure: containing a rising trend

There were many indications by 1996 of managerial concern to slow the growth in organizational IS/IT expenditure. Estimates of future expenditure based on respondent surveys in several countries tended to indicate this pattern (see for example, Kew Associates, 1995; Moad, 1994; Price Waterhouse, 1994). In the UK anticipated trends varied according to sector. In one recent study 63 per cent of financial service companies expected immediate IT expenditure rises to exceed 10 per cent per annum. Over half of manufacturing and distributive trade companies expected IT cost rises in 1996, but several companies in retailing, wholesaling and distributive trades expected to cut IT budgets by up to 50 per cent in 1996 (Kew Associates/CBI, 1996). However, the broad emphasis in recent studies seemed to fall on running the organization leaner, ringing more productivity out of IS/IT use, attempting to reap the benefits from changes in price/performance ratios, while at the same time recognizing the seemingly inexorable rise in information and IT intensity implied by the need to remain operational and competitive. In particular, there is wide recognition of the additional challenge of bringing new technologies into productive use. The main areas being targeted for new corporate investment seemed to be client/server computing, document image processing and groupware, together with 'here-and-now' technologies such as advanced telecom services available from 'intelligent networks', mobile voice and digital cellular systems (Price Waterhouse, 1994; Taylor, 1995). It is in the context of these many concerns and technical developments that evaluation techniques and processes need to be positioned.

Organizational variation in IT performance

In 1996 Brynjolfsson and Hitt published a study of 367 large US firms generating $1.8 trillion in 1991 output. For 1987–91 they found 'IS spending making a substantial and statistically significant contribution to firm output'. They concluded that the productivity paradox, if it had existed, had disappeared by 1991 for their sample firms, which together represented a large share of total US output. Though they used similar models to previous researchers, Brynjolfsson and Hitt (1996) attributed their different findings mainly to the larger and more recent data set they used. At the same time they pointed to further analysis being needed of the factors which differentiate firms with high returns to IT from low performers. In an early study, Cron and Sobol (1983) pointed to what has since been called the 'amplifier' effect of IT. Its use reinforces existing management approaches dividing firms into very high or very low performers. This analysis has been supported by later work by the Kobler Unit (1987) and Strassmann (1990), who also found no correlation between size of IT spend and firms' return on investment. Subsequently, a 1994 analysis of the information productivity of 782 US companies found that the top 10 spent a smaller percentage (1.3 per cent compared to 3 per cent for the bottom 100) of their revenue on IS, increased their IS budget more slowly (4.3 per cent in 1993–4 – the comparator was the bottom 110 averaging 10.2 per cent), thus leaving a greater amount of finance available for non-IS spending (Gillin, 1994).

The calculation of information productivity in this study does make a rather large assumption – that management productivity is synonymous with information productivity because management is so highly dependent on information. This is probably not sustainable (Willcocks, 1994). Notwithstanding this, not only did the top performers seem to spend less proportionately on their IT; they also tended to keep certain new investments as high as business conditions permitted while holding back on infrastructure growth. Thus, on average, hardware investments were only 15 per cent of the IS budget while new development took more than 50 per cent, with 41 per cent of systems development spending incurred on client/server investment (Sullivan-Trainor, 1994). Clearly the implication of this analysis is that top performers spend relatively less money on IS/IT, but focus their spending on areas where the spend will make more difference in terms of business value. An important aspect of their ability to do this must lie with their evaluation techniques and processes.

van Nievelt (1992) adds to this picture. Analysing database information on over 300 organizations he found shortcomings in the commonly used indices of economic performance, especially where these were included in how IT's contribution was then measured. Empirically he found that customer satisfaction relative to all leading competitor's performance (relative customer satisfaction – RCS) was the key variable helping to then diagnose IT contribution, and how it should be made. His work found that IT as a coordinating, communicating and leveraging technology was capable of enhancing customer satisfaction, flattening organizational pyramids and supporting knowledge workers in the management arena. At the same time many organizations did not direct their IT expenditure into appropriate areas at the right time, partly because of an inability to carry out evaluation of where they were with their IT expenditure and IT performance relative to business needs in a particular competitive and market context.

van Nievelt's work and conclusions are worth pursuing, based as they are on strong empirical and statistical analysis because they show ways out of the IT productivity paradox. van Nievelt (1997) rejects the paradox as faulty. His statistical analysis of business unit level data provides strong evidence for a significant, positive, but multi-faceted IT effect on productivity.

However, timing and placement of IT expenditure emerge as all important. As one example, he found that when customer perceptions of the firm are unfavourable relative to those of competitors, executing such a broadly recommended move as making large investments in 'strategic IS' has a strong probability of causing significant economic damage to the firm. Some explanation is needed. Unhappy with traditional measures of economic performance, van Nievelt developed the organizational performance index (OPI – briefly, this is 1 plus economic profit before taxes divided by full overhead costs). He found that economics performance as represented by OPI was strongly correlated with two factor rather than one factor interactions. A particularly strong correlation is found between relative customer satisfaction and percentage of overhead budget spent on IT. However, increased expenditure on IT does not raise RCS and OPI in a linear way. Thus, an organization with low relative customer satisfaction and low IT spend would do best *not* to increase its percentage of overhead budget spent on IT. Here enhanced customer satisfaction derives either from non-IT based improvements or from directing the spend into commoditized IT operations. It is only at later stages, once customer satisfaction has been raised significantly, that higher IT expenditure becomes correlated to improved economic performance of the firm. The optimal path to higher performance is then building IT infrastructure, followed by channelling additional investments into strategic, systems to secure competitive advantage(s).

The work reported in this section shows how complex it is to identify IT impacts and effects, and points to the need to examine a range of correlated factors before rushing to judgement. At the same time it does serve to highlight how macroeconomic studies of IT productivity can mislead, and that microeconomic studies of how individual organizations and markets behave are altogether more helpful. At the same time it becomes clear that IT events must become continually correlated to business performance measures in ways frequently not represented in existing assessment practice, a fact we now turn to examine.

Standards of IT evaluation: continuity and change

Many mid-1990s' UK studies show both difficulties in establishing the business value of IT, and also indifferent evaluation practice (see for example, Ballantine, Galliers and Stray, 1996; Grindley, 1995; Ward, Taylor and Bond, 1995; Willcocks and Lester, 1996). One 1995–96 study points to sectoral differences, with a majority of financial companies getting 'good' or 'very good' value from IT, while manufacturing and distributive trades are less certain about the IT payoff now, and less optimistic about IT payoffs in the next five years (Kew Associates/CBI, 1996). One noticeable – and worrying – feature of such studies is how often their findings on weaknesses in evaluation practice replicate those of much earlier studies (see for example, Butler Cox Foundation, 1990; Farbey, Land and Targett, 1992; Hochstrasser and Griffiths, 1990; Strassmann, 1990).

Our own research reinforces and extends these points (see Harvey, Islei and Willcocks, 1996). A survey of 150 senior IT managers carried out in February 1996 attracted a 37 per cent response rate. The sample was opportunistic rather than random, but nevertheless provided interesting insight into evaluation practice in 44 organizations. Respondents were drawn from large organizations in financial services, energy, pharmaceuticals, publishing, transport, manufacturing, public and private service sectors. Two thirds of IT respondents admitted that they encountered scepticism when trying to demonstrate the effectiveness of IT services. The majority of the survey sample expressed their assessment of performance predominantly in terms of technical efficiency or project evaluation, sometimes a mix of the two. By contrast IT's overall contribution to the business was the predominant focus in only 16 per cent of organizations. The strong bias towards technical project assessment is reflected in the detailed breakdown of measures applied by organizations. Most widely used of all was system and network reliability (93 per cent). This was followed by project completion to time and budget (90 per cent), and user satisfaction with technical service (88 per cent). Project and efficiency-related measures were almost twice as widely used as financial measures. Return on investment and financial cost benefit analysis for example, were each used by only half the sample. This reduced emphasis on some aspects of financial measurement represents a change from earlier surveys, but is somewhat more consistent with more recent studies. Thus Ballantine, Galliers and Stray (1996) for example found 72 per cent of UK respondents using finance-based cost benefit analysis, 60 per cent payback methods, and only 43 per cent ROI (return on investment) measures.

Of the business-related performance measures covered by the survey, the most frequently used was customer/user satisfaction with the business impact of IT services. But this was applied in only 40 per cent of organizations. The next most commonly used – by a quarter of respondents respectively – were measures that reflect the effectiveness in meeting specific business goals, broad-based quality rating of IT services and improvements in business process operations. The most frequently mentioned (50 per cent) 'most useful' measures fall into the business improvement category. Additionally, 36 per cent claimed that customer satisfaction ratings were valuable, but only two respondents extended this beyond the boundaries of the organization to include external customers.

Much of this points to continuing patterns of indifferent evaluation practice. The reasons cited for this were diverse, but a number had to do with corporate circumstances of a long-standing and intractable nature. Fifty-five per cent of respondents pointed out that the absence of a clearly articulated business strategy, or poorly defined business goals, were fundamental to their problems in closing the loop between IT and its contribution to business performance. Thirty per cent complained of the absence of good working relationships with the rest of the organization. This absence of close liason was reflected by the relative scarcity of forums for IT and business managers to discuss IT performance measurement issues. Closely related to specific weaknesses in communication links is the standing of IT within organizations. Forty-three per cent complained that unfavourable business attitudes towards IT was a fundamental obstacle to developing an improved measurement system.

At the same time the survey indicated changes in the use of measurement systems. While business-related measures were still the least commonly used, they were the most fast-evolving. Almost three quarters of these types of measures had been introduced within the last 12 months. However, by far the most widely cited set of problems were associated with developing such new sets of measures – 80 per cent cited difficulties in this area. Some IT managers were clearly low down on the learning curve and handicapped by ignorance of the options: 'lack of understanding of possible methods', 'identifying what to measure', or, more plaintively, 'how to measure performance' exemplified their difficulties. In other cases the problems were information-based and related to concerns about 'the accuracy of source data' or 'the availability of data on business performance enhanced by IT'. Elsewhere it was the indirect contribution of IT investment entailed in 'assessing the benefits of infrastructure projects' and 'trying to quantify soft measures' that blocked faster progress.

Much of this section points to the need for a family of measures that cover technical and business performance of IT in an integrated manner. Measures are needed that point to cost effectiveness and containment, but that embrace additional key IT/business performance criteria. In this respect there is potential value in drawing on emerging practice in applying models developed to extend the range of corporate performance measurement (for example, Kaplan and Norton, 1992; van Nievelt, 1992). On this theme, our recent survey found that 35 per cent had adapted, or planned to adapt a balanced scorecard approach in order to produce a new 'dash board' of IT performance indicators. The second issue is to integrate these measures over time, right into decisions about whether existing IT needs to be replaced, enhanced or dropped. Past studies have shown this to be a particularly weak area in evaluation practice (for summaries see Willcocks, 1994; 1996a). A third intractable area is building evaluation as a process which includes a large range of stakeholders and improves IT/business relationships over time by sharpening understanding of IT's business value, while not just monitoring but also improving IT's business use. An attempt to address these concerns is made in the remainder of this chapter.

EVALUATION: A SYSTEM'S LIFE-CYCLE APPROACH

At the heart of one way forward for organizations is the notion of an IT/IS evaluation and management cycle. A simplified diagrammatic representation of this is provided in Figure 4.1. Earlier research found that few organizations actually operated evaluation and management practice in an integrated manner across systems' life-cycles (Willcocks and Lester, 1991; 1996). The evaluation cycle attempts to bring together a rich and diverse set of ideas, methods, and practices that are to be found in the evaluation literature to date, and point them in the direction of an integration approach across systems' lifetime. Such an approach would consist of several interrelated activities:

1. Identifying net benefits through strategic alignment and prioritization.
2. Identifying types of generic benefit, and matching these to assessment techniques.
3. Developing a family of measures based on financial, service, delivery, learning and technical criteria.
4. Linking these measures to particular measures needed for development, implementation and post-implementation phases.
5. Ensuring each set of measures run from the strategic to the operational level.
6. Establishing responsibility for tracking these measures, and regularly reviewing results.
7. Regularly reviewing the existing portfolio, and relating this to business direction and performance objectives.

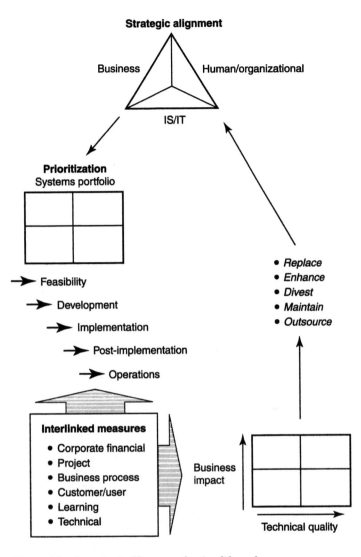

Figure 4.1   Investing in IS – an evaluation life-cycle

A key element in making the evaluation cycle dynamic and effective is the involvement of motivated, salient stakeholders in processes that operationalize – breathe life into, adapt over time, and act upon – the evaluation criteria and techniques. Let us look in more detail at the rationale for, and shape of such an approach. In an earlier review of front-end evaluation, Willcocks (1992) pointed out how lack of alignment between business, information systems and human resource/organizational strategies inevitably compromised the value of all subsequent IS/IT evaluation effort, to the point of rendering it of marginal utility and, in some cases, even counter-productive. In this respect he reflected the concerns of many authors on the subject (see for example, Earl, 1989; Hares and Royle, 1994; Peters, 1994). A range of already available techniques were detailed for establishing strategic alignment and linking strategy with assessing the feasibility of any IS/IT investment, and these will not be repeated here (for a review see Willcocks, 1992). At the same time the importance of recognizing evaluation as a process imbued with inherent political characteristics and ramifications was emphasized, reflecting a common finding amongst empirical studies (see for example, Currie, 1995; Symons, 1994).

The notion of a systems portfolio implies that IT/IS investment can have a variety of objectives. The practical problem becomes one of prioritization – of resource allocation among the many objectives and projects that are put forward. Several classificatory schemes for achieving this appear in the extant literature (for example Critical Success Factors Analysis in Earl, 1989; the Information Economics Approach in Parker, Benson and Trainor, 1988). Of these the McFarlan and McKenney (1983) IT Strategic Grid is still the most widely quoted, despite now showing its age. Willcocks (1994) and also Butler Cox, 1990; Farbey, Land and Targett, 1992; Hochstrasser, 1994 have suggested classificatory schemes that match business objectives with types of IS/IT project. Thus, on one schema, projects could be divided into six types – efficiency, effectiveness, must-do, architecture, competitive edge, and research and development. The type of project could then be matched to one of the more appropriate evaluation methods available, a critical factor being the degree of tangibility of the costs and benefits being assessed. Costs and benefits need to be sub-classified into, for example, hard/soft, or tangible/intangible, or direct/direct/inferred, and the more appropriate assessment techniques for each type adopted (see Willcocks, 1994 for a detailed discussion). Norris (1996) has provided a useful categorization of types of investments and main aids to evaluation, and a summary is shown in Figure 4.2.

After alignment and prioritization assessment, the feasibility of each IS/IT investment then needs to be examined. All the research studies show that the main weakness here has been the over-reliance on and/or misuse of traditional, finance-based cost-benefit analysis. The contingency approach outlined above and in Figure 4.2 helps to deal with this, but such approaches need to be allied with active involvement of a wider group of stakeholders than those at the moment being identified in the research studies. A fundamental factor to remember at this stage is the importance of a business case being made for an IT/IS investment, rather than any strict following of specific sets of measures. As a matter of experience where detailed measurement has to be carried out to differentiate between specific proposals, it may well be that there is little advantage to be had not just between each, but from any. Measurement contributes to the business case for or against a specific investment but cannot be a substitute for a more fundamental managerial assessment as to whether the investment is strategic and critical for the business, or will merely result in yet another useful IT application.

Following this, Figure 4.1 suggests that evaluation needs to be conducted in a linked manner across systems development and into systems implementation and operational use. The evaluation cycle posits the development of a series of interlinked measures that reflect various aspects of IS/IT performance, and that are applied across systems lifetime. These are tied to processes and people responsible for monitoring performance, improving the evaluation system and also helping to 'flush out' and manage the benefits from the investment. Figure 4.1 suggests, in line with prevailing academic and practitioner thinking by the mid-1990s, that evaluation cannot be based solely or even mainly on technical efficiency criteria. For other criteria there may be debate on how they are to be measured, and this will depend on the specific organizational circumstances.

However, there is no shortage of suggestions here. Taking one of the more difficult, Keen (1991) discusses measuring the cost avoidance impacts of IT/IS. For him these are best tracked in terms of business volume increases compared to number of employees. The assumption here is that IT/IS can increase business volume without increases in personnel. At the strategy level he also suggests that the most meaningful way of tracking IT/IS performance over time is in terms of business performance per employee, for example, revenue per employee, profit per employee, or at a lower level, as one example – transactions per employee.

Kaplan and Norton (1992) were highly useful for popularizing the need for a number of perspectives on evaluation of business performance. Willcocks (1994) showed how the Kaplan and Norton balanced scorecard approach could be adapted fairly easily for the case of assessing IT/IS investments. To add to that picture, most recent research suggests the need for six sets of measures. These would cover the corporate financial perspective (e.g. profit per employee); the systems project (e.g. time, quality, cost); business process (e.g. purchase invoices per employee); the customer/user perspective (e.g. on-time delivery rate); an innovation/learning perspective (e.g rate of cost reduction for IT services); and a technical perspective (e.g. development efficiency, capacity, utilization). Each set of measures

Type of investment	Business benefit	Main formal aids to investment evaluation	Importance of management judgement	Main aspects of management judgement
Mandatory investments as a result of:				
Regulatory requirements	Satisfy minimum legal requirement	Analysis of costs	Low	Fitness of the system for the purpose
Organizational requirements	Facilitate business operations	Analysis of costs	Low	Fitness of the system for the purpose. Best option for variable organizational requirements
Competitive pressure	Keep up with the competition	Analysis of costs to achieve parity with the competition. Marginal cost to differentiate from the competition, providing the opportunity for competitive advantage	Crucial	Competitive need to introduce the system at all. Effect of introducing the system into the marketplace. Commercial risk. Ability to sustain competitive advantage
Investments to improve performance	Reduce costs	Cost/benefit analyses	Medium	Validity of the assumptions behind the case

Figure 4.2   Methods and judgement in evaluating IT investments (Source: adapted from Norris, 1996) (Continued)

Type of investment	Business benefit	Main formal aids to investment evaluation	Importance of management judgement	Main aspects of management judgement
	Increase revenues	Cost/benefit analyses. Assessment of hard-to-quantify benefits. Pilots for high-risk investment	High	Validity of the assumptions behind the case. Real value of hard-to-quantify benefits. Risk involved
Investments to achieve competitive advantage	Achieve a competitive leap	Analysis of costs and risks	Crucial	Competitive aim of the system. Impact on the market and the organization. Risk involved
Infrastructure investment	Enable the benefits of other applications to be realized	Setting of performance standards. Analysis of costs	Crucial	Corporate need and benefit both short and long term
Investment in research	Be prepared for the future	Setting objectives within cost limits	High	Long-term corporate benefit. Amount of money to be allocated

Figure 4.2   Methods and judgement in evaluating IT investments (Source: adapted from Norris, 1996) (Concluded)

would run from strategic to operational levels, each measure being broken down into increasing detail as it is applied to actual organizational performance. For each set of measures the business objectives for IT/IS would be set. Each objective would then be broken down into more detailed measurable components, with a financial value assigned where practicable. An illustration of such a hierarchy, based on work by Norris (1996), is shown in Figure 4.3. Responsibility for tracking these measures, together with regular reviews that relate performance to objectives and targets are highly important elements in delivering benefits from the various IS investments. It should be noted that such measures are seen as helping to inform stakeholder judgements, and not as a substitute for such judgements in the evaluation process.

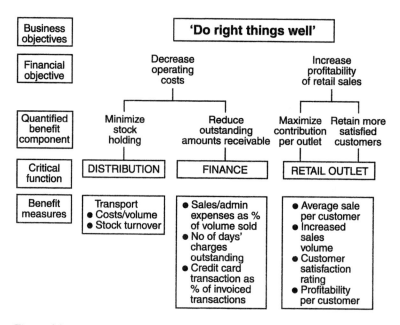

Figure 4.3   Developing metrics from business objectives (Source: adapted from Norris, 1996)

Some detail can be provided on how to put metrics in place, monitor them and ensure benefits are delivered. The following schema is derived from work by Butler Cox, (1990); Grindley, (1995); Peters, (1996); and Willcocks and Lester, (1996). Projects were found to be managed well, (and often over-performed their original appraisal) where a steering group was set up early in a project, was managed by a senior user manager, and represented the key operating functions impacted by the IT/IS. The steering group followed the project to a late stage of implementation with members frequently taking responsibility for delivering benefits from parts of the IT/IS implementation. Project benefits need to be incorporated into business area budgets, and individuals identified for monitoring performance and delivering benefits. Variables impacted by the IT/IS investment were identified and decomposed into a hierarchy based on key operating parameters necessary to deliver the benefit. A framework needs to be established for clearly identifying responsibilities for benefits (see Figure 4.4 for an example). Peters (1996) suggests that the information on responsibilities should be published, and known to relevant parties, and that measures should be developed to monitor benefits at the lowest level of unit performance. We would add that links also need to be made between the individual's performance in the assessment role and his or her own appraisal and reward. The steering group should regularly review the benefits gained, for example, every three months, and also report less frequently to the IT/IS strategy steering group, with flushing out of IT/IS benefits seen as an essential extension of the strategic review process, not least in its capacity to facilitate more effective IT/IS implementation. What is clear in this scheme is that measurement that is business (not solely technical efficiency)-focused plays an important part in evaluation but only in the context of appropriate processes in place operated by a wide range of motivated stakeholders.

Performance variables \ Benefits manager	Sales manager	Purchasing manager	Accts payable supervisor	Warehouse manager	Production scheduler	Production supervisor
Orders/man day	E					
No. of suppliers		E				
Invoices/man day			E			
Finished inventory	S			E	S	
Stock out occurrence	S				E	
Slow movers Lead-time	S					E

E=Executive responsibility   S=Support

Figure 4.4   Assigning responsibility for evaluation (Source: adapted from Peters, 1996*)*

COMPLETING THE CYCLE: EXISTING AND FUTURE INVESTMENTS

One all too often routine phase of review is that of post-implementation (see Figure 4.1). Our own research suggests that this is one of the most neglected, yet one of the more important areas as far as IS evaluation is concerned. An advantage of the above schema, in practice, is that post-implementation evaluation arises naturally out of implementation assessment on an on-going basis, with an already existing set of evaluators in place. This avoids the ritualistic, separated review that usually takes place in the name of post-implementation review (Kumar, 1990; Willcocks and Lester, 1996). A detailed discussion on how to perform an effective post-implementation review cannot be provided here, but see Norris, 1996.

There remains the matter of assessing the on-going systems' portfolio on a regular basis. Notoriously, when it comes to evaluating the existing IS investment, organizations are not good at drop decisions. There may be several related ramifications. The IT inheritance of 'legacy systems' can deter investment in new systems – it can, for example, be all too difficult to take on new work when IT/IS staff are awash in a rising tide of maintenance arising from the existing investment. Existing IT/IS-related activity can also devour the majority of the financial resources available for IS investment (Robson, 1994; Strassmann, 1990; Swanson and Beath, 1988). Very often such failures derive from not having in place, or not operationalizing, a robust assessment approach that enables timely decisions on systems and service divestment, outsourcing, replacement, enhancement, and/or maintenance. Such decisions need to be based on at least two criteria – the technical quality of the system/service, and its business contribution – as well as being related back to the overall strategic direction and objectives of the organization (see Figure 4.1).

Benchmarking

A further element in the assessment of the on-going systems portfolio is the relevance of external comparators. External benchmarking firms, for example RDC and Compass, have already been operating for several years, and offer a range of services that can be drawn upon, but mainly for technical aspects of IT performance. The assessment of data centre performance is now well established among the better benchmarking firms. Depending on the benchmarking database available, a data centre can be assessed against other firms in the the same sector, or of the same generic size in computing terms, and also against outsourcing vendor performance. Benchmarking firms are continually attempting to extend their services, and can provide a useful assessment, if only mainly on the technical efficiency of existing systems. There is, however, a growing demand for external benchmarking services more widely to include business, and other performance measures, many of which could include elements of IT contribution (see above). Indeed Strassmann (1990) and van Nievelt (1997) are but two of the more well known of the growing number of providers of diagnostic benchmarking methodologies that help to locate and reposition IT contribution relative to actual and required business performance. It is worth remarking that external IT benchmarking, like all measures, can serve a range of purposes within an organization. Lacity and Hirschheim (1996) detail from their research how benchmarking services were used to demonstrate to senior executives the usefulness of the IT department. In some cases external benchmarking subsequently led to the rejection of outsourcing proposals from external vendors.

IT outsourcing: assessment issues
This leads into the final point. An increasingly important part of assessing the existing and any future IT/IS investment is the degree to which the external IT services market can provide better business, technical and economic options for an organization. In practice, recent survey and case research by the authors and others found few organizations taking a strategic approach to IT/IS sourcing decisions, though many derived economic and other benefits from incremental, selective, low-risk, as opposed to high-risk 'total' approaches to outsourcing (Lacity, Willcocks and Feeny, 1995; Willcocks and Fitzgerald, 1994). The Yankee Group estimated the 1994 global IT outsourcing market as exceeding US$49.5 billion with an annual 15 per cent growth rate. In 1995 the US market was the biggest, estimated to exceed US$18.2 billion. The UK remained the largest European market in 1996, exceeding £1.3 billion by 1994–5, with an annual growth rate exceeding 10 per cent on average across sectors (ITnet, 1996). Over 50 per cent of UK organizations outsourced some aspect of IT in 1994, and outsourcing represented on average 24 per cent of their IT budgets (Willcocks and Fitzgerald, 1994; see also Chapters 11 and 12).

Given these figures it is clear that evaluation of IT/IS sourcing options, together with assessment of on-going vendor performance in any outsourced part of the IT/IS service, needs to be integrally imbedded into the systems life-cycle approach detailed above. Not least because an external vendor bid, if carefully analysed against one's own detailed in-house assessment of IT performance, can be a highly informative form of benchmarking. Figure 4.1 gives an indication of where sourcing assessment fits within the life-cycle approach, but recent research can give more detail on the criteria that govern successful and less successful sourcing decisions.

In case and survey research Willcocks and Fitzgerald (1994) found six key factors (see Figure 4.5). Three factors are essentially business related. First, as described in Chapter 3, IT can contribute to *differentiate* a business from its competitors, thus providing competitive advantage. Alternatively an IT activity/service may be a commodity, not distinguishing the business from a competitor in business offering and performance terms.

	Tend to outsource	Tend not to outsource
Business:		
● Are future business needs:	Certain ←——→	Uncertain
● Is the potential contribution of this IT service/activity to business positioning a:	Commodity ←——→	Differentiator
● Is the impact of this IT service/activity on the business strategy:	Useful ←——→	Vital
● Is the in-house cost for this IT service/activity compared to the market place:	High ←——→	Low
Technical:		
● Is this IT service/activity:	Discrete ←——→	Integrated
● Is the technological maturity:	High ←——→	Low
● Is the IT capability in-house compared to the market place:	Low ←——→	High

Figure 4.5   Criteria for making sourcing decisions

Secondly, as discussed in the Introduction to this book, IT may be *strategic* in underpinning the firm's achievement of goals, and critical to its present and future strategic direction, or merely useful. Thirdly, the *degree of uncertainty* about future business environment and needs impacts upon longer-term IT needs. High uncertainty suggests in-house sourcing as a better option. As Figure 4.5 suggests, the preferred option where possible is to outsource useful commodities in conditions of certainty about business requirements across the length of the contract. Three technical considerations are also important. It is unwise for an organization to outsource in a situation of *low technology maturity*. This exists where a technology is new and unstable, and/or where there is an existing technology but being applied in a radically new way, and/or where there is little relevant in-house experience with the technology. Next, the *level of IT integration* must influence the sourcing decision. Generally we found it preferable not to outsource

Banker, R., Kauffman, R. and Mahmood, M. (eds.) (1993) *Strategic Information Technology Management: Perspectives on Organizational Growth and Competitive Advantage*, Idea Publishing, Harrisburg.

Barua, A., Kriebel, C. and Mukhopadhyay, T. (1991) *Information Technology and Business Value: an Analytic and Empirical Investigation*. University of Texas Working Paper, Austin, Texas, May.

Brynjolfsson, E. (1993) 'The Productivity Paradox of Information Technology', *Communications of the ACM*, **36**, (12), pp. 67–77.

Brynjolfsson, E., and Hitt, L. (1993) 'Is Information Systems Spending Productive?', *Proceedings of the International Conference in Information Systems*, Orlando, USA, December.

Brynjolfsson, E., and Hitt, L. (1996) 'Paradox Lost? Firm-level Evidence on the Returns to Information Systems Spending', *Management Science*, **42**, (4), pp. 541–558.

Butler Cox Foundation (1990) *Getting Value from Information Technology*, Research Report 75, June, Butler Cox, London.

Cron, W. and Sobol, M. (1983) 'The Relationship between Computerization and Performance: A Strategy for Maximizing the Economic benefits of Computerization', *Journal of Information Management*, **6**, pp. 171–181.

Currie, W. (1989) 'The Art of Justifying New Technology to Top Management', *Omega*, **17**, (5), pp. 409–418.

Currie, W. (1995) *Management Strategy for IT: an International Perspective*, Pitman Publishing, London.

Davenport, H. (1993) *Process Innovation: Reengineering Work through Information Technology*, Harvard Business School Press, Boston, Mass.

Earl, M. (1989) *Management Strategies for Information Technology*, Prentice-Hall, Hemel Hempstead.

Engardio, P. (1994) 'Third World Leapfrog', *Business Week*, June 13, pp. 46–47.

Farbey, B., Land, F. and Targett, D. (1992) 'Evaluating Investments in IT', *Journal of Information Technology*, **7**, (2), pp. 100–112.

Farbey, B., Targett, D. and Land, F. (eds.) (1995) *Hard Money, Soft Outcomes*, Alfred Waller/Unicom, Henley, Oxon.

Gillin, P. (ed.) (1994) 'The Productivity Payoff: The 100 Most Effective Users of Information Technology', Special report in *Computerworld*, September 19, Section 2, pp. 4–55.

Glazer, R. (1993) 'Measuring the Value of Information: The Information-intensive Organization', *IBM Systems Journal*, **32**, (1), pp. 99–110.

Grindley, K. (1995) *Managing IT at Board Level*, (Second edition), Pitman, London.

Hackett, G. (1990) 'Investment in Technology – The Service Sector Sinkhole?', *Sloan Management Review*, Winter, pp. 97–103.

Hammer, M. and Champy, J. (1993) *Reengineering the Corporation: A Manifesto for Business Revolution*, Nicholas Brealey, London.

Hares, J. and Royle, D. (1994) *Measuring the Value of Information Technology*, John Wiley, Chichester.

Harvey, D., Islei, G. and Willcocks, L. (1996) *Measuring the Performance of Corporate Information Technology Services*, Unpublished BI/OXIIM Report, Business Intelligence, London.

Hochstrasser, B. (1994) 'Justifying IT Investments', In Willcocks, L. (ed.) *Information Management: Evaluation of Information Systems Investments*, Chapman and Hall, London.

Hochstrasser, B. and Griffiths, C. (1990) *Regaining Control of IT Investments: Strategy and Management*, Chapman and Hall, London.

ITnet (1996) 'Report on the IT Outsourcing Market, 1995', *Computer Weekly*, February 1, pp. 12.

Keen, P. (1991) *Shaping the Future: Business Design through Information Technology*, Harvard Business Press, Boston, Mass.

Kaplan, R. and Norton, D. (1992) 'The Balanced Scorecard: Measures that Drive Performance', *Harvard Business Review*, January–February, pp. 71–79.

Kew Associates (1995). *User IT Expenditure Survey 1995*, *Computer Weekly*/Kew Associates, London.

Kew Associates/CBI (1996) *Business and IT Strategies in Niche Markets: Trends into the New Millennium* CBI/Kew Associates, London.

Kobler Unit (1987) *Is Information Technology Slowing you Down?* Kobler Unit report, Imperial College, London.

Kumar, K. (1990) 'Post-implementation Evaluation of Computer-based Information Systems: Current Practices', *Communications of the ACM*, **33**, (2), pp. 203–212.

Lacity, M. and Hirschheim, R. (1995) *Beyond the Information Systems Outsourcing Bandwagon*, John Wiley, Chichester.

Lacity, M. and Hirschheim, R. (1996) 'The Role of Benchmarking in Demonstrating IS Performance', In Willcocks, L. (ed.) *Investing in Information Systems: Evaluation and Management*, Chapman and Hall, London.

Lacity, M., Willcocks, L. and Feeny, D. (1995) 'IT Outsourcing: Maximize Flexibility and Control', *Harvard Business Review*, May–June, pp. 84–93.

Landauer, T. (1995) *The Trouble with Computers: Usefulness, Usability and Productivity*, The MIT Press, Cambridge, Mass.

LaPlante, A. (1994) 'No doubt about IT', *Computerworld*, August 15, pp. 79–86.

LaPlante, A. and Alter, A. (1994) 'IT All Adds Up', *Computerworld*, October 31, pp. 76–84.

Loveman, G. (1988) *An Assessment of the Productivity Impact of Information Technologies*, MIT Management In the Nineties Working Paper 88–054, Massachusetts Institute of Technology, Cambridge, Mass.

McFarlan, F. W. and McKenney, J. L. (1983) *Corporate Information Systems Management: The Issues facing Senior Executives*, Dow Jones Irwin, New York.

Moad, J. (1994) 'IS Rises To The Competitiveness Challenge', *Datamation*, January 7, pp. 16–22.

Morrison, C. and Berndt, E. (1990) *Assessing the Productivity of Information Technology*, Equipment in the US Manufacturing Industry, National Bureau of Economic Research Working Paper 3582, Washington, January.

Norris, G. (1996) 'Post-investment Appraisal', In Willcocks, L. (ed.) *Investing in Information Systems: Evaluation and Management*, Chapman and Hall, London.

Parker, M., Benson, R. and Trainor, H. (1988) *Information Economics*. Prentice-Hall, London.

Peters, G. (1994) 'Evaluating your Computer Investment Strategy', In Willcocks, L. (ed.) *Information Management: Evaluation of Information Systems Investments*, Chapman and Hall, London.

Peters, G. (1996) 'From Strategy to Implementation: Identifying and Managing Benefits of IT Investments', In Willcocks, L. (ed.) *Investing in Information Systems: Evaluation and Management*, Chapman and Hall, London.

Price Waterhouse (1994) *Information Technology Review 1994/5*, Price Waterhouse, London.

Quinn, J. and Baily, M. (1994) 'Information Technology: Increasing Productivity in Services', *Academy of Management Executive*, **8,** (3), pp. 28–47.

Roach, S. (1986) *Maco-realities of the Information Economy*, National Academy of Sciences, New York.

Roach, S. (1988) 'Technology and the Services Sector: The Hidden Competitive Challenge', *Technological Forecasting and Social Change*, **34,** pp. 387–403.

Roach, S. (1991) 'Services Under Siege – The Restructuring Imperative', *Harvard Business Review*, September–October, pp. 82–92.

Roach, S. (1994) 'Lessons of the Productivity Paradox', In Gillin, P. (ed.) 'The Productivity Payoff: The 100 Most Effective Users of Information Technology', Special Report in *Computerworld*, September 19, Section 2, pp. 55.

Robson, W. (1994) *Strategic Management and Information Systems,* Pitman Publishing, London.

Sager, I. and Gleckman, H. (1994) 'The Information Revolution', *Business Week,* June 13, pp. 35–39.

Solow, J. (1987) Review of Chen and Zyman's *Manufacturing Matters* in *New York Book Review,* cited by Freeman, C. and Soete, L. in *Structural Change and Economic Dynamics,* **1,** (2) 1990, pp. 225.

Strassmann, P. (1990) *The Business Value of Computers,* Information Economic Press, New Canaan, Connecticut, USA.

Sullivan-Trainor, M. (1994) 'Best of Breed'. In Gillin, P. (ed.) 'The Productivity Payoff: The 100 Most Effective Users of Information Technology', Special Report in *Computerworld,* September 19, Section 2, pp. 8–9.

Swanson, E. and Beath, C. (1988) *Maintaining Information Systems in Organizations,* John Wiley, Chichester.

Symons, V. (1994) 'Evaluation of Information Systems Investments: Towards Multiple Perspectives', In Willcocks, L. (ed.) *Information Management: Evaluation of Information Systems Investments,* Chapman and Hall, London.

Taylor, P. (1995) 'Business Solutions on Every Side', Financial Times Review: *Information Technology,* March 1, pp. 1.

van Nievelt, A. (1992) 'Managing with Information Technology – A Decade of Wasted Money?', *Compact,* Summer, pp. 15–24.

van Nievelt, A. (1997) 'Benchmarking Organizational Performance', in Willcocks, L. and Lester, S. (eds) *Beyond the IT Productivity Paradox – Assessment Issues,* McGraw-Hill, Maidenhead, (forthcoming).

Walsham, G. (1993) *Interpreting Information Systems in Organization,* John Wiley, Chichester.

Ward, J., Taylor, P. and Bond, P. (1995) Presentation of Research at the Second European Conference on IT Evaluation, Henley Management Centre, Henley, Oxon, July.

Weill, P. (1990) *Do Computers Pay Off?,* ICIT Press, Washington.

Willcocks, L. (1992) 'IT Evaluation Managing The Catch-22', *European Management Journal,* **10,** (2), pp. 220–229.

Willcocks, L. (ed.) (1994) *Information Management: Evaluation of Information Systems Investments,* Chapman and Hall, London.

Willcocks, L. (ed.) (1996a) *Investing in Information Systems: Evaluation and Management,* Chapman and Hall, London.

Willcocks, L. (1996b) 'Does IT-enabled BPR Pay Off? Recent Findings on Economics and Impacts', In Willcocks, L. (ed.) *Investing in Information Systems: Evaluation and Management,* Chapman and Hall, London.

Willcocks, L. and Fitzgerald, G. (1994). 'A Business Guide to IT Outsourcing', *Business Intelligence,* London.

Willcocks, L. and Griffiths, C. (1994) 'Predicting Risk of Failure in Large-scale Information Technology Projects', *Technological Forecasting and Social Change*, **47**, (3), pp. 205–228.

Willcocks, L. and Lester, S. (1991) 'Information Systems Investments: Evaluation at the Feasibility Stage of Projects' *Technovation*, **11**, (5) pp. 243–268.

Willcocks, L. and Lester, S. (1996) 'The Evaluation and Management of Information Systems Investments: From Feasibility to Routine Operations', In Willcocks, L. (ed.) *Investing in Information Systems: Evaluation and Management*, Chapman and Hall, London.

Willcocks, L., Currie, W. and Mason, D. (1997) *Information Systems at Work: People Politics and Technology*, McGraw-Hill, Maidenhead, (forthcoming).

CHAPTER FIVE

Decision Support Systems for Strategic Decision-making and Performance Measurements[1]

**GERD ISLEI, GEOFF LOCKETT, BARRY COX, STEVE GISBOURNE
AND MIKE STRATFORD**

INTRODUCTION

Since the 1970s, decision support systems (DSSs) have emerged as a way to apply information technology to help managers make decisions. Such systems have been characterized as 'interactive computer-based systems, which help decision-makers utilize data and models to solve unstructured problems' (Sprague, 1989). Even though this definition has guided much of the research in this area, its realization in the business environment is clearly lacking. Nevertheless several cases have been reported of systems that meet these criteria and were successfully implemented in organizations (Alter, 1980; Gray *et al.*, 1989; Keen and Scott Morton 1978; Turban, 1990). These systems:

- facilitate decision-making processes;
- support rather than replace managerial decision-making; and
- respond to the changing needs of the decision-makers.

However, many applications also testify to a number of important barriers to the wider use of decision support systems in the business environment (Gray *et al.*, 1989; PA Consulting Group, 1990). These

[1]A modified, earlier version of this chapter was published in *Interfaces*, **21**, pp. 4–22, Nov–Dec, 1991.

94

have included:

- incompatible, multi-vendor environments;
- hierarchical and proprietary networks;
- high costs of ownership;
- inability to transfer data between applications and databases, and
- unfriendly user interfaces.

Most DSSs are either large-scale, purpose-built systems that are used to facilitate well-defined and repetitive decision tasks, or else they are small PC-based products offering quick and economic routines to support one-off decisions. Even though the impact of such systems on individual decision-making may be substantial, they have not been adopted by organizations to any degree commensurate with their potential. In many respects few such systems could be presented as 'strategic' in the sense of the term as used in the Introduction to this book. A major reason seems to be that large systems lack the flexibility required to aid unstructured decision tasks (and thus top-level decision-making), whereas small (flexible) systems which are useful for a specific decision-making process are difficult to translate into usable prototypes for different scenarios. Their narrow design also makes them largely incompatible with open systems architectures.

Recent advances in computer technology embracing powerful local area networks, compatible PC environments and a move towards connectability and transferability of models and data could hold the key to flexible decision support in organizations. New systems should emerge which not only are capable of handling large volumes of data, but can also interpret, develop and communicate these data to suit changing organizational requirements. In addition they will be flexible and manageable and remain relevant to their users (i.e. able to support a diversity of models and management styles). To achieve this, system developers must address the whole spectrum of decision-making; in particular, they must develop systems able to accommodate the interdependencies of managerial decision-making.

So far computer systems have had little impact in supporting strategic decision-making, an area in which managers face very unstructured tasks and have to cope with a high degree of uncertainty (Gray et al., 1989; Mallach, 1994; Sprague, 1989; Turban, McLean and Wetherbe, 1996). Such scenarios rely significantly on judgements and the experience of the decision-makers. Therefore we must improve our understanding of the type of support they need for unstructured decision-making and examine the models appropriate for tackling such tasks. To achieve this we have to monitor the progress of suitable systems over extended periods of time and match that progress with appropriate resources.

In this chapter we present a case study where a series of judgemental models were used as the basis for the development of a decision support system in an R&D environment. The purpose of the system is to help management in choosing a portfolio of research projects, monitor project development, and change the allocation of resources if necessary. The system evolved as a result of several years of collaboration between managers at ICI Pharmaceuticals, consultants at ICI Corporate Management Services and researchers at the Manchester Business School. We would argue that the case study shows how a decision support system can be used strategically in support of the specific business to which it is applied, and that the detail of its development, implementation and subsequent use provides the key to understanding how strategic systems can be promoted in organizations.

CASE STUDY IN THE PHARMACEUTICAL INDUSTRY

The DSS environment

In the pharmaceutical industry over the past decades, research has become increasingly competitive. In response to this increased competition, the research-based pharmaceutical companies have tried to develop effective strategies to ensure success. Different organizational structures have been designed to achieve this, ranging from relatively free association of scientists to tightly controlled research environments. The challenge to research management is to create an environment that favours and is conducive to innovative research, but one which, when an innovative discovery is made, permits the company to act efficiently to capitalize on it (Cox, 1989). Typical aims of research-based pharmaceutical company are (De Stevens, 1986; Cox, 1989);

- to discover and produce drugs that make worthwhile contributions to human health by means of research and development;
- to improve or maintain high efficiency to achieve a good competitive position;
- to optimize creativity and scientific debate, and;
- to identify and develop creative young scientists.

In attempting to fulfil these aims, pharmaceutical firms must decide what therapeutic areas to work in and how much of their effort and resources to place in each. The enormous costs of pharmaceutical research and increased development times make decisions concerning research portfolios crucial for maintaining a competitive position. While developing a new drug cost less then $10 million in 1950, it now costs over $120 million. The time consumed in the various stages of developing and marketing a drug are also enormous: five to ten years of research, two to five years in early development, and three to seven years in late development and launch. Research management faces some key issues:

- to maintain and build on the past reputation of certain drugs and to pursue research in new therapeutic areas;
- to take advantage of existing and experienced research expertize and to explore new cultures for developing research initiatives, and;
- to pursue structured research and exploit serendipity.

All these factors and many more influence the selection of a research portfolio and thus determine the organizational design needed to support innovative research activities.

ICI Pharmaceuticals is an international producer of pharmaceutical products. It is part of a much larger group that also produces bulk and fine chemicals as well as fibre and nutrition products. Our case affects the cardiovascular pharmacology section of ICI, the largest of the pharmaceutical research groupings. The company has always placed great importance on managing its R&D, and has often taken innovative approaches. It is not an organization which follows every management fashion, but it constantly strives for excellence and investigates new methods and ideas. The company has explored various ways to improve the management of research portfolios. For example, it provides consultants from a special management services unit to help senior managers develop new approaches. In many cases, they have designed methods that 'measure' the success of the current research. Since typical research projects last well over five years, instantaneous decisions are usually not required. However, the competitive position of the company depends on its ability to produce new drugs on a regular basis: assessing the state of the research projects is vital. Of all management functions, R&D is notoriously the most difficult to manage. Reliable information is in short supply, and the stochastic nature of the process is evident. The research section has therefore used a variety of approaches to assess project worth with varying degrees of success, keeping one method until a better one is proven.

In the past, ICI used methods based on linear programming (Bell and Read, 1970; Gear and Lockett, 1973) to determine their research portfolio and, although they provided valuable insights, for this environment they have not proved sustainable in the long term. They assume project selection as a one-off process, where in fact it is part of a series of interdependent decisions. Another method that has been used successfully is cost/benefit analysis (Gear, Lockett and Muhlemann, 1982; Islei et al., 1991). This approach also points to a key prerequisite for such decision problems: measurement without the constraint of intricate model development. Even though cost/benefit analysis was considered unsatisfactory for appraising research projects, some of its concepts are valuable and have been incorporated in the subsequent developments.

Finally, ICI explored the approach of the Boston Consulting Group (Lockett *et al.*, 1986) throughout the organization but found it not entirely appropriate for this research environment. The data demands were seen as the biggest impediment, and therefore it was not fully implemented. However, the problem remained, and senior management continued to look for a system that would support their task of managing a portfolio of research projects. The managers regularly asked their internal consulting team for advice and thus kept abreast of the developments. They were the driving force for change; any decision support adopted that used up valuable management time would have to offer greater benefits than the system in current use.

CASE STUDY – PROJECT EVOLUTION

A senior manager of the cardiovascular section initiated the first systematic examination of the procedures to support the process of managing pharmaceutical research at ICI. He co-operated with external consultants in assessing how the organization and its methods for evaluating and selecting research topics could be improved. At about the same time, he attended a management course at the Manchester Business School where various MCDM (multicriteria decision-making) techniques were discussed as frameworks for supporting project management in R&D environments. He realized the potential of judgemental models that use computer support for capturing and evaluating basic data, and he thought that such a tool might offer a more transparent and effective method for product profiling than the current approach (Lockett *et al.*, 1986).

When the project with the external consultants was completed, the section manager decided to evaluate the research projects in his area using a more sophisticated computerized technique. He could also compare its outcome with the recommendations from the consultancy project. After some initial discussions among the senior managers, the internal consulting team and researchers from Manchester Business School, we (the authors and researchers) decided to involve the project managers from the cardiovascular section in building a project selection model. Over a period of weeks and several meetings, the group explored the modelling task and clarified the various factors it considered most relevant for assessing project worth. The group members pooled their experience and thoroughly discussed their different assumptions. At all stages, they checked the progression of the model carefully by screening the various options. Finally, they adopted a simple hierarchy of 10 attributes for evaluating projects (Lockett *et al.*, 1986; gives full description of this process).

In total, they intended to assess 10 projects (abbreviated IH, AR, CA, RI, AT, CS, FA, RS, II, CC). Each participant used a computer package based on the Analytic Hierarchy Process (AHP) (Saaty, 1980) to assess these options. However, before participating in this structured evaluation each member ranked the research projects using a simplified version of the Kepner–Tregoe method (Kepner and Tregoe, 1965). We later compared the initial expectations of the participants with the results of the computer-supported assessments (Figure 5.1). As a result of this exercise we changed the project portfolio (Lockett *et al.*, 1986; Islei and Lockett, 1991). Some of the differences between 'intuitive' and 'final' results produced a very thorough discussion of the merits of the decision support system. It was felt that the computer-supported judgemental model allowed a depth of analysis which would otherwise have been difficult to achieve.

Rank position	Project managers												Senior manager	
	1		2		3		4		5		6			
	Bef	Aft	Bef	Aft	Bef	Aft	Bef	Aft	Bef	Aft	Bef	Aft	Bef	Aft
1	CA	CA	RI	IH	AT→AT		AR	AR	RI	RI	RI	IH	CA	CA
2	CC	CS	IH	CA	CA	IH	RS	CA	CA	CA	II/CS		CS	RI
3	II	AT	AR	RI	RI/RI		AT	AT	II	IH	IH	AT	II	IH
4	RI	II	CS	AT	CC/CA		FA	II	IH	CC	CA	RI	RI/CC	
5	IH→IH		CC	CC	IH	CC	CC	RI	AT	II	FA	CA	IH	CS
6	AR	CC	CA	AR	RS	II	CA	IH	FA	AT	CS	II	CC	AR
7	CS	AR	RS	CS	FA	CS	IH	CC	AR	RS	AR	AR	RS	II
8	AT	RI	II	RS	AR	AR	CS	RS	CC	AR	CC	CC	AT	AT
9	RS→RS		AT	FA	II	FA	RI	FA	CS	FA	RS	FA	FA	RS
10	FA	FA	FA	II	CS	RS	II	CS	RS	CS	AT	RS	AR	FA

Figure 5.1   Comparison of participants' expectations with computer-supported assessments. In this comparison of intuitive ranks (Bef) with final choice ranks (Aft), the arrows indicate two changes in rank positions that the participants discussed

The computer-assisted evaluation facilitated the process of quantifying individual preferences and gave scope to an easy exchange and comparison of information. This approach, together with some simple statistical routines, enabled the participants to highlight commonalties in their evaluation and, equally important, to trace crucial differences (Islei and Lockett, 1991). In other words, it made it possible for group members to examine their concepts in the broader context that derived from their colleagues. During the discussion, we realized that the structured evaluation was a valuable aid to justifying preferences and associated decisions. In the end, the team agreed on the selection of a research portfolio. Apart from selecting the portfolio our aims in this initial exercise had been:

- to develop a model that could be used to appraise research projects;
- to involve the team of project managers in formulating and evaluating the model, and;
- to use this exercise to pull the team together.

Overall we saw this fairly simple technique as successful and worth more detailed investigation. In particular, the senior manager thought that on the basis of this experiment a computerized system could be developed to help him monitor the progress of research projects. However, we had several issues to address. First, the software used in the original exercise lacked flexibility and adaptability and needed changes to improve its user interface. Secondly, although we considered the basic judgemental modelling approach valuable, we were critical of some aspects of the Analytic Hierarchy Process (AHP). We noted its data requirements were excessive and the participants did not feel at ease with the pairwise comparison procedure (Islei, 1986; Lockett and Stratford, 1987). Because of this and trials in several other organizations on different decision problems, we developed a computer package based on Geometric Least Squares (Islei and Lockett, 1988). This technique avoids several of the shortcomings of Saaty's AHP methodology while retaining its adaptive format using hierarchical decomposition. The software, called Judgemental Analysis System (JAS), is flexible and user-friendly and has been applied very successfully in a variety of settings (Liddell, 1988; Locket, Naude and Gisbourne, 1991; Islei and Lockett, 1991).

The management team at ICI used this software on a number of occasions to appraise their research portfolio. It also had access to other software packages based on different MCDM methods that were now coming onto the market for PC use. We finally decided to use JAS as the core element in developing a system. It would support the process of assessing criteria weights since it allows the user to examine his preferences and inconsistencies in great detail. Therefore, this component of data collection could be carried out thoroughly. For evaluating project scores, the team at ICI were encouraged by the results of their experiments (Lockett and Stratford, 1987) with a version of Edward's swing weight technique (Von Winterfeld and Edwards, 1986). On the basis of this, they wrote a simple computer programme internally to study project evaluation, but finally decided on a commercial package called VISA (Belton and Vickers, 1989), which could be modified to suit our requirements. The systems development was guided by the habitual decision processing of practising managers and reflected the learning of the management team.

As the users gained experience with the DSS, they developed confidence in the model and its associated output. In consequence, we gradually refined the original attribute structure (Figure 5.2). Although we changed the primary attributes very little, we disaggregated them into several layers of subattributes. Figure 5.3 shows the current structure of the four most important attributes. To facilitate scoring the various projects in terms of these subattributes, we established detailed word-models. Figure 5.4 shows a typical example.

Word-models are simply standard reference frames with explicit anchor points. The user is faced with a series of discrete and well-defined ratings rather than a continuum of choices. Because the data requirements increased considerably as we differentiated the attribute structure, we regarded the use of such word-models as a necessary simplification of the DSS. We also saw this as making assessments more transparent and thus easier to communicate. We made another major modification to the model concerning the attribute technical feasibility. We replaced the original subdivision of this important attribute (Figure 5.2) with a supplementary structure (Figure 5.3) that contains estimates of risk and time as separate components; in other words, the current model differentiates between assessing achievement

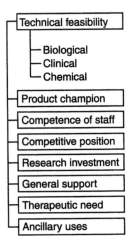

Figure 5.2   Refinement of original attribute structure. The original attribute structure had eight attributes of decreasing importance

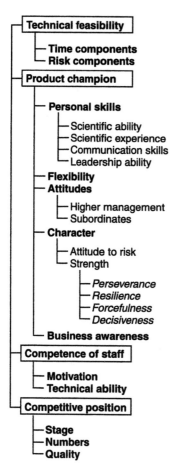

Figure 5.3   Structure of the four most important attributes – technical feasibility, product champion, competence of staff, and competitive position – showing how they were further broken down into subattributes

of technical goals and the time necessary for attaining these goals. To do this, we adopted a distinctive scoring procedure based on the work of Boschi, Balthasar, and Menke, (1979) using probability–time curves (Figure 5.5).

We examined a series of simple judgemental models and implemented them as part of the DSS. Each component can be used separately, but the major benefit comes from their accessibility from within a common shell. Users can store and retrieve data easily and exchange and compare information. Because they share a common shell, the systems components can be used to arbitrate between differing goals or valuations. In the initial exercise, participants found that the DSS helped them to make decisions and enabled them to defend their assessments. The structured evaluation increased the creditability of their judgements.

Leadership ability
Subattribute of product champion/personal skills

100 Sapiential authority, instils enthusiasm and confidence, has drive, initiative plus all positives from below

80 No sapiential authority but instils enthusiasm and confidence, has drive and initiative

60 Encourages team to participate in discussions and has any two of the above at 80

40 Authoritarian, but operates people as a group rather than on a 1:1 basis

20 Authoritarian, operates on a 1:1 basis, does not engender a team spirit

0 'Wally", only issues instructions which may be wrong/confused, inconsistent

---

Figure 5.4   The word model used to assess the subattribute leadership ability

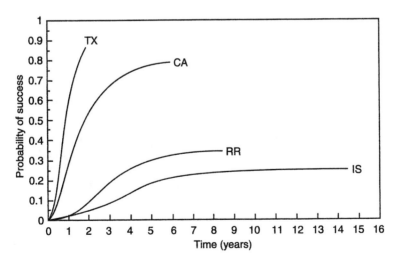

Figure 5.5   The early state of the combined probability versus time curves: IS is seen as a new, risky project whereas TX is near completion

CASE STUDY – PROJECT IMPLEMENTATION

The management team found the initial modelling process extremely valuable: it enabled them to identify and appreciate the differences and commonalties of their judgements. In fact, developing a judgemental model as a group was the basis for their commitment. The structured approach helped to clarify critical issues and provided a basis for informed negotiations. The members felt that using the DSS improved their efficiency and facilitated communication and that it offered access to judgmental data that had either been unavailable or in an unusable form. Our investigation of the actual decision-making process provided the basis for developing several components of the DSS. We have gradually implemented them by prototyping, and then refined them until an agreed procedure evolved. Each component reflects some critical part of the judgemental modelling frame that:

- incorporates important characteristics of the management problem, for example, probability–time curves;
- facilitates data capture, for example, word-models, and;
- offers flexibility to allow users to develop their preferences.

We designed the system in such a way that (1) it was compatible with the way the management team approached its unstructured decision task, and (2) it could be sustained by the team largely unassisted. Even though the systems shell can be used to handle single decision tasks, its main benefit accrues from its ability to support longitudinal decision-making. Unlike most decision-making scenarios that are difficult to replicate, the present case does not concern a one-off problem but affects a process that occurs over a long time horizon with judgemental data serving as the main source of information. In this instance, we could study the impact of computerized decision support on managerial decision-making quite extensively. Although the system changed and evolved, we have enhanced its underlying principles rather than altered it fundamentally. Using judgemental models as the core element of our DSS is firmly established.

The project has now been fully implemented within the largest research section of ICI Pharmaceuticals which uses it regularly to update and monitor the performance of the various research projects (Figure 5.6). By monitoring the progress of research projects the managers are able to determine whether they must change the allocation of effort or take more decisive action, for example terminate a project. The integrated system provides decision support whenever they need to adjust the data base, reallocate resources, or alter the research portfolio. Since previous assessments are stored, they can easily monitor change. The managers assess the various projects every

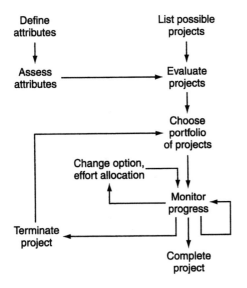

Figure 5.6   A flow chart of the decision-making procedures supported by our DSS shows the entire process from listing possible projects to completing them

three months and if they note problems they can examine the alternatives by simulating appropriate actions; under certain conditions they discontinue research projects. (Subsequently we proceeded to develop an expert system that could help managers decide when to terminate a project (Wilkinson, 1991).)

Each time they use the system, the managers generate new information on the state of the projects. They can do this in a variety of ways across a local area network. The results and estimates, however, can be accessed by all concerned and compared with previous analyses. Gradually, ICI has built up a 'database' of the managers' judgements that it uses to great effect in making decisions. Because of its flexibility and accessibility, the system has helped to promote a participative and open management culture that favours innovative research. Over time it has been carefully implemented and it now provides essential support for a complex and unstructured management task. We will describe two simple examples to show different uses of the decision support components.

Balancing the portfolio

In any industrial research environment, managers must anticipate with reasonable accuracy the productivity of the research section. Using those estimates senior managers can determine the probability of getting successful development candidates in important areas within specified time horizons. The company wants to be able, by monitoring and controlling projects, to hold its research strategy on target. One element in an effective research strategy is maintaining a balanced portfolio of research projects to ensure that projects are completed at an even rate.

We developed a model component for this problem (Islei, Lockett and Stratford, 1991) that uses judgemental data to produce risk and time profiles (probability–time curves) for the research projects. By comparing these curves with 'desirable' profiles the decision-maker can monitor the progress of individual options and also assess the viability of the overall portfolio. If certain indicators signal a need for a corrective action, the manager can simulate the effects of such changes on the portfolio balance. The probability–time curves of an early project portfolio (Figure 5.5) showed the profiles of four projects TX, CA, RR, and IS. Both RR and IS were weak options, and ICI needed a more balanced portfolio. Over time, it altered the research portfolio; Figure 5.7 shows the associated probability–time curves two years later. Some projects were discontinued (RR and IS), several new projects were introduced (SA, TS, RE, AD, CO, HF), and the probability–time curves of others changed (TX and CA). Both TX and CA are nearing successful completion. Clearly the project portfolio in Figure 5.7 is better balanced, and this balance made it possible for the research section to complete projects much more evenly. Gradually, through careful monitoring of projects that passed the various research stages successfully, the manager built up a database that enabled him to improve the accuracy of his forecasts. He was able to enhance the underlying model by including information about actual completion rates.

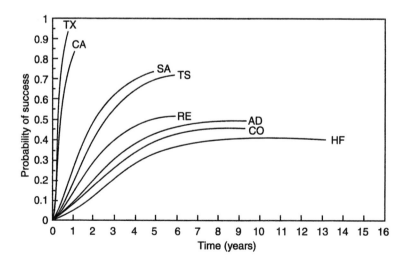

Figure 5.7   The advanced state of the combined probability versus time curves

Attribute profiles

Managers also appraise the performance of the research projects with respect to the other attributes. In each of these cases, capturing data generally involves the use of word-models. By monitoring such information over time, managers become aware of trends that could signal the need for attention. In addition, all these separate assessments can be aggregated, for example by using a simple additive weighted model, to obtain an overall preference structure (Figure 5.8). Most project scores are fairly stable.

When a project is not stable, looking at the disaggregate data allows us to track down the underlying causes. Figure 5.9 shows the scores of project HF for the four most important attributes (technical feasibility,

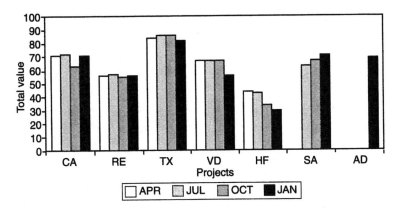

Figure 5.8   Overall project value change over time. Most project scores are relatively stable, with the exception of project HF. It not only underperforms but deteriorates rapidly

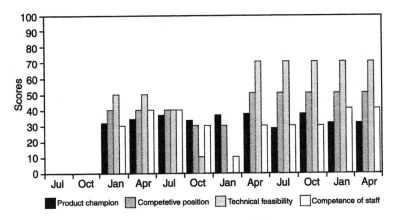

Figure 5.9   Attribute scores for research project HF

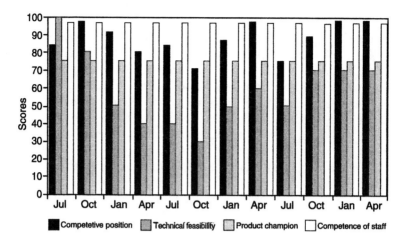

Figure 5.10   Attribute scores for research project CA

product champion, staff competence, and competitive position) over approximately the same time horizon. The manager in charge of the project lacked the personality, skills, and attitude needed to champion a research project to successful completion. Apparently his performance also had a detrimental effect on the research staff working under him. Eventually he was replaced by a different project manager whose performance restored the achievements of the team and improved the competitive position of ICI's product.

It is interesting to compare this development with the performance of project CA (see Figure 5.10) over the same period. CA was a new project with no apparent competing product on the market. This situation changed dramatically when a competitor announced a compound that had very similar properties. The competitive position of ICI's project dropped. But the competing compound, being chemically different, ran into some technical difficulties that enabled ICI's product to gain ground without management action. These two examples show the potential of the DSS and its influence on decision making. By maintaining a knowledge base of subjective data it provides an effective tool for monitoring the perceived progress of research projects and facilitates changes in resource allocation if required.

THE PRESENT DSS – USER VIEWS

So far, we have paid little attention to the most important constituent of the system, the user.

Manager A is a senior R&D manager and visiting professor of

pharmacology at a university. He finds R&D managers typically taking on a variety of research projects that have low probability of success and holding them for too long; they also often eliminate them for a single, possibly inappropriate reason. He considers the following to be the main benefits of the computer-assisted process:

- It formalizes the manager's monitoring process and permits the process to be checked by an outside expert.
- It encourages the manager to look at the whole group of projects regularly to determine the progress of individual projects and the status of the research portfolio.
- It improves the forecasts of project and stage completion times and information on the factors affecting these times.
- It helps to plan resource needs and detect problems.
- It helps identify the types of programmes that are successful and unsuccessful.

One manager who reports to Manager A has worked on developing several components of the system. Although at a different level in the organization, his views are complementary. He observed the following advantages:

- It identifies key work areas required to take a project from the idea to the implementation stage.
- It provides a framework with which to determine whether new ideas are gaining or losing in the early stages of examining potential new projects.
- It clarifies the technical feasibility of new programmes and their impact on resources.
- It offers a structured approach to selling the concept of a new programme and preparing an analysis of the critical issues to be tackled in an ongoing programme.
- It helps to build a team and helps the team to see why one or two programmes are selected from a broad range of potential projects.

The senior consultant from the management services unit, who has been instrumental in producing most of the systems developments and has also advised other sections on implementing management support systems, also offered his views. He has been invaluable in searching for new methods and bringing them to the attention of senior management. He recognized that:

- Both the hierarchical structure of attributes and the word-model definitions helped to reduce ambiguity.
- JAS has been an excellent tool for weighting attributes.
- Managers have found little difficulty with VISA in scoring projects

on each attribute utility scale with the aid of the word-model definitions.

- The systems development has benefited greatly from the use of simple models and our evolutionary approach.

These comments help to put the models in perspective and give a clear idea of their usefulness. With simple hardware and software tools, we created a DSS that has had a fundamental impact on the management of the research department. It is versatile and user friendly (using graphical interfaces that run under Microsoft Windows) and can be accessed easily by the management team for a variety of purposes. It has enabled the team to gradually build up a database that facilitates diagnosis and control of the research portfolio. The managers have instigated most of the developments, and therefore they have a high degree of ownership (see also the Introduction of this book). The system is now largely stand-alone and does not require facilitation by a decision analyst. By using a judgemental model we gave enough structure to the problem to permit transparent decision-making without burdening the decision maker with excessive data requirements. Our analysis of the way the system has been used suggests that the quality of the decisions has improved.

ORGANIZATIONAL LEARNING

It is difficult to be precise about the critical factors that have led to this successful application. Quite clearly effective implementation did not happen overnight but was a long and involved process; confidence in the models had to be earned. One special factor that was very important was top management support. In much of the literature, the involvement and support of senior management is cited as necessary for successful information technology development (see also Chapters 2, 9 and 10). In our case it was of major importance.

In addition, the initial exercise, which ran over several weeks, was very positively received by the whole group of managers. The results gave the participants some idea of the power of this approach that did not require sophisticated and time-consuming techniques. By defining a series of simple attributes, which can be used to measure the various research projects, the managers were able to clarify and improve their process of project appraisal. All the other developments centred around this concept. However, developing a structured model together was essential; all participants were interested in the effort. Inevitably senior management realized that to optimize the likelihood of making worthwhile discoveries, it has to address several issues simultaneously: it must provide the right research environment, it must find technically feasible projects, it must engage competent staff, and it must give capable leaders (product champions) their heads in working on the projects (Cox, 1989). In other words, even though senior management defines the overall target, project leaders have to be left to achieve it their way (Islei and Lockett, 1991; see also Chapter 8). All these factors were constituents of the core model, and putting values to such characteristics gave them a reality that otherwise was elusive. Ultimately it helped management to move project selection from a narrow cost efficiency concept to a more balanced approach, emphasizing the overall effectiveness of the R&D performance appraisal.

Like most innovations, these ideas met with some resistance, however, by using an evolutionary prototyping approach, we gradually overcame that resistance. We did not achieve this with pressure, but by involving the people concerned. They quickly realized the benefits of using an agreed format for evaluating projects. Decision-making became more transparent and therefore managers could focus their attention on critical factors much more easily. Only after several data-collection exercises did the value of the DSS as a monitoring tool become apparent. With increasing user confidence, the credibility and appropriateness of the judgemental data manifested itself, and the knowledge base of the system could be progressively enhanced. The simple software and data structure enabled us to improve the system as the decision-makers' understanding and needs developed. This gradually led to many enhancements of the basic model. Similarly, the systems design was guided by the habitual decision-making of the managers involved and thus underwent various modifications. The present system can be interrogated in an interactive manner and supports attractive dialogue features. Most components of the DSS also enable the user to print the essential results of a dialogue session in a standard format. As users familiarized themselves with the available information and the possible formats, we modified the reporting procedure to reflect the organizational learning. Previously the process of providing information on the progress of research projects was lengthy and fragmented. Usually it was done under time pressure and was generally unreliable. With the present DSS, that problem has been largely overcome. The DSS has imposed a discipline on the research staff that gives them more time for their research and yet enables them to be more confident in their predictions.

ORGANIZATIONAL DIFFUSION

The system has now been used for several years, and its implementation enabled senior management to pursue a research strategy that proved effective and successful. The resultant changes created an open and informative environment that favours innovative research, but that, when a discovery is made, permits ICI to act efficiently to capitalize on it. Other departments of the company have shown interest in the system and emulated several components.

One application took place in a research laboratory producing fine chemicals. Life-cycles are much shorter and research projects take about two years instead of seven to ten years in the pharmaceutical area. The laboratory did not adopt all of the model's characteristics, but it took the core elements of judgemental modelling together with the scoring procedures for quantifying preferences. The attribute structure and the word-models looked very different, reflecting a distinct management problem. In this case, the risk-time assessments proved to be the most effective component for improving performance appraisal. Because the original system was already available, and the time-scale was shorter, the lab could see evidence of benefits much more rapidly than in the pharmaceutical case. The system components have also been used to great effect by the managers of a newly formed division, chemicals and polymers, who had to formulate a new research strategy. Previously, the constituent sections had used a variety of techniques to assess project worth. They believed one unified approach would:

- provide a means for bringing the section heads together to formulate and adopt an organizational structure conducive to research and development;
- make decisions more transparent, and;
- facilitate communication of judgements and preferences.

The original model shell provided them with a framework for communicating differing viewpoints effectively and defusing confrontation. They could include judgements and personal values openly and explicitly in the discussion. For this group the informative application of several system components both stimulated and stabilized organizational changes. They finally adopted the DSS in a slightly modified form (Islei, Lockett and Stratford, 1991).

A further major application involved the marketing departments of two other branches of the company (Islei, Lockett and Gisbourne, 1990). In both cases, the managers wanted to establish suitable strategies for marketing various products. They used the judgemental modelling framework to examine how their products performed compared to those of their major competitors. First, using the DSS they established product profiles internally to assess their competitive positions. Then they employed a researcher to interview major customers throughout Europe using the same procedure to collect comparative data (Lockett, Naude and Gisbourne, 1991). Simple analyses of the data showed how their products were perceived in relation to competing products. The managers could then explore the strengths and weaknesses of their products and their marketing strategies. Senior management was most impressed with 'the speed and uniformity with which strategically relevant data could be collected', (Lockett, Naude and Gisbourne, 1991). The results, although unexpected, were well received within the organization, and the methodology found general acceptance. Subsequently another major marketing study was initiated.

These cases illustrate how computer-supported judgemental models were diffused across the organization. Building on the success within one part of the company, and incorporating managers' experiences has enabled other applications to be achieved within shorter learning cycles. The decision-support system is owned by the users and is not seen as a technical black box. Managers no longer need decision analysts for day-to-day support; they seek advice only for key developments.

CONCLUSION

Our DSS has had major impact in supporting strategic decision-making at ICI Pharmaceuticals. It helps to diagnose problem areas and communicate critical developments. Gradually a knowledge base of judgemental data has been built up. Reasons for its successful implementation are:

- extensive user involvement;
- evolutionary approach to systems development;
- flexibility and simplicity of systems architecture;
- clarity of insights by using judgemental models, and;
- accessibility and transferability of models and data.

Several of these findings reinforce the arguments made earlier (see also Chapters 7 and 8). Managers have aided the diffusion of the ideas to other divisions of the company. They presented the judgemental approach to managing a research portfolio at group meetings, leading to a number of successful applications elsewhere. The company's experience with the original system greatly facilitated the implementation of computerized management support for similar tasks. There has been organizational learning.

This case highlights the advantages of an evolutionary approach that benefited from a close collaboration between practising managers and researchers. It shows how a DSS can be developed that does more than support well-defined management tasks. Our DSS helps managers to form and communicate perceptions, and to manage organizational change.

REFERENCES

Alter, S. L. (1980) *Decision Support Systems – Current Practice and Continuing Challenges*, Addison-Wesley Publishing Company, Reading, Massachusetts.

Belton, V. and Vickers, S. P. (1989) 'V I S A – VIM for MCDA', In Lockett, A. and Islei, G. (eds.), *Improving Decision-making in Organizations, Lecture Notes in Economics and Mathematical Systems*, **335**, Springer, Heidelberg, pp. 287–304.

Bell, D. C. and Read, A. W. (1970) 'The Application of a Research Project Selection Method', *R & D Management*, **1**, (1), pp. 35–42.

Boschi, R. A. A., Balthasar, H. U. and Menke, M. M. (1979) 'Quantifying and Forecasting Exploratory Research Success', *Research Management*, **22**, (5), pp. 14–21.

Cox, B. (1989) 'Strategies for Drug Discovery: Structuring Serendipity', *Pharmaceutical Journal*, **243**, (6551), pp. 329–338.

De Stevens, G. (1986) 'Serendipity and Structured Research in Drug Discovery', *Progress in Drug Research*, **30**, pp. 189–203.

Gear, A. E. and Lockett, A. G. (1973) 'A Dynamic Model of some Multi-stage Aspects of Research and Development Porfolios', *IEEE Transactions on Engineering Management*, **EM-20**, (1), pp. 22–29.

Gear, A. E., Lockett, A. G. and Muhlemann, A. P. (1982) 'A Unified Approach to the Acquisition of Subjective Data in R&D', *IEEE Transactions on Engineering Management*, **EM-29**, (1), pp. 11–19.

Gray, P., King, W. R., McLean, E. R. and Watson, H. J. (1989) *The Management of Information Systems*, The Dryden Press, Chicago.

Islei, G. (1986) 'An Approach to Measuring Consistency of Preference Vector Derivations Using Least Square Distance', In Jahn, J. and Krabs, W, (eds.), *Recent Advances and Historical Development of Vector Optimization, Lecture Notes in Economics and Mathematical Systems*, **294**, Springer Verlag, Heidelberg, pp. 265–284.

Islei, G. and Lockett, A. G. (1988) 'Judgemental Modelling Based on Geometric Least Square', *European Journal of Operational Research*, **36**, (1), pp. 27–35.

Islei, G. and Lockett, A. G. (1991) 'Group Decision-making: Suppositions and Practice', *Socio-Economic Planning Science*, **25**, (1), pp. 67–81.

Islei, G., Lockett, A. G. and Gisbourne, S. (1990) *Judgmental Modelling: An Organizational Perspective*, Paper presented at IXth International Conference on Multiple Criteria Decision-making, at the Interface of Needs in Industry, Business, and Government, Fairfax, USA.

Islei, G., Lockett, A. G. and Stratford, H. (1991) 'Resource Management and Strategic Decision-making in Industrial R&D

Departments', *Engineering Costs and Production Economics*, **20,** (2), pp. 219–229.

Islei, G., Lockett, A. G., Cox, B. and Stratford, H. (1991) 'A Decision Support System Using Judgmental Modelling: A Case of R&D in the Pharmaceutical Industry', *IEEE Transaction on Engineering Management*, **38,** (3) pp. 202–209.

Keen, P. G. W. and Scott Morton, M. S. (1978) *Decision Support Systems.* Addison-Wesley Publishing Company, Reading, Massachusetts.

Kepner, C. H. and Tregoe, B. (1965) *The Rational Manager*, McGraw-Hill, New York.

Liddell, J. (1988) *Decisions, Decisions... Management Topics*, IBM, United Kingdom Ltd, Portsmouth, **31,** pp. 20–23.

Lockett, A. G., Hetherington, B., Yallup, P., Stratford, M. and Cox, B. (1986) 'Modelling a Research Portfolio Using AHP: A Group Decision Process', *R & D Management*, **16,** (2), pp. 151–160.

Lockett, A. G. and Stratford, M. (1987) 'Ranking of Research Projects: Experiments with Two Methods', *OMEGA*, **15,** (5), pp. 395–400.

Lockett, A. G., Naude, P. and Gisbourne, S. (1991) *An Application of Judgmental Modelling to the Vendor Selection Process*, Working Paper 203, Manchester Business School, Manchester, UK.

Mallach, E. G. (1994) *Understanding Decision Support and Expert Systems*, Irwin, Burr Ridge, Ill.

PA Consulting Group (1990) *Information Technology: The Catalyst for Change*, Mercury Books, W. H. Allen, London.

Saaty, T. L. (1980) *The Analytic Hierarchy Process*, McGraw-Hill, New York.

Sprague, R. H. (1989) 'A Framework for the Development of Decision Support Systems', In Gray, P., King, W. R., McLean, E. R. and Watson, H. J. (eds.) *The Management of Information Systems*, The Dryden Press, Chicago, pp. 19–48.

Turban, E. (1990) *Decision Support and Expert Systems: Management Support Systems*, Macmillan Publishing Company, New York.

Turban, E., McLean, E. and Wetherbe, J. (1996) *Information Technology for Management*, John Wiley and Sons, New York.

Von Winterfeld, D. and Edwards, W. (1986) *Decision Analysis and Behavioural Research*, Cambridge University Press, Cambridge, UK.

Wilkinson, A. (1991) 'Developing an Expert System on Project Evaluation', *R&D Management*, **21,** (1), pp. 19–23.

Part Two

Organizing for Development and Delivery

CHAPTER SIX

Configuring the IS Function in Complex Organizations

MICHAEL J. EARL, BRIAN EDWARDS AND DAVID F. FEENY

INTRODUCTION

How to configure the information systems (IS) function in large, complex organizations appears to be an eternal management issue (Dickson *et al.*, 1984, Niederman *et al.*, 1991). This is because it is inherently difficult and because circumstances change. Commonly phrased as a centralization versus decentralization question, it is also often perceived by managers as the issue which most impedes their organization's ability to get value for money from IT.

The two basic arguments are often expressed thus. Centralization of the IS function is necessary to reap economies of scale, ensure the ability to integrate applications or share data and optimize the use of scarce resources. Conversely, decentralization of the IS function is necessary to ensure that IS responds to real business needs, to encourage managers to get involved with IS and often to add control of IS resources to the autonomy that local units possess. These arguments may appear to be no different from the normal tensions of the centralization versus decentralization debate at large (George and King, 1991). However, often there are at least two special characteristics at work. First, information *technology* does raise important questions of scale, infrastructure planning, risk and change (Hodgkinson, 1996). Secondly, information *systems* can often be an emotional issue. Since information is often at the heart of power, arguments about the control of information processing can seem critical in the politics of organizational design. Indeed nowadays information systems are something everybody has a concern about and thus can be guaranteed to stimulate a debate – at least in complex organizations. By complex organizations we mean large, multi-business unit corporation. In the original study in 1987 the authors studied 14 such companies in Europe. We were attracted to studying the configuration of the IS function for three reasons:

1. We had observed that it was a recurring issue in many organizations we knew.
2. Very little empirical research had been reported in the literature – nor has been since.
3. We noted an apparent conundrum. In at least one sector, there were several different configurations in place.

This sector was the automobile sector. In the UK, the then British Leyland group had first made its IS function a separate profit centre and subsidiary, BL Systems, subsequently known as ISTEL (subsequently ISTEL itself was acquired by AT&T). It was then sold off in a management buyout, but supplying information services to Leyland companies and to the marketplace in general. In contrast, General Motors had acquired an IS company, EDS, to provide information services both inside and outside corporation. Ford, however, relied on its own IS function, which was centralized at regional level. Meanwhile, Volvo had recently decentralized much of the IS function from a central bureau to its product divisions.

So one sector displayed at least four IS configurations. So did one major British company. British Petroleum (BP) then had a central IS bureau (ISS) which ran corporate utilities and could bid for divisional IS work. ISS could develop up to 10 per cent of its activity level to external clients. There was also a corporate IS policy-setting group (ISA). BP then owned a software business, Scicon. In addition, each line of business had its own IS function. So if the configuration of the IS function should be aligned with the host organization, the BP example suggested this might be quite a complex matter.

However, other forces seemed to influence the configuration of IS. One was technological change, evidenced by the ever-increasing distribution of hardware, reducing costs of telecommunications and increased availability of software. These trends appeared to increase the feasibility of devoting IS to business units, or sharing and networking information services, or giving more information processing autonomy to end-users. Another, sometimes emotional, force was IS performance. If end-users or business units became disenchanted with a central or corporate IS function, the pressure built up for both decentralization and distribution of information processing. Alternatively, whatever the current configuration, if IS was perceived not to be performing, some change in structure was prescribed. So the research questions were:

1. Is there a preferred way of configuring the IS function?
2. Are there any factors which shape the configuration of IS and give guidance on a preferred solution?

The 1987 study suggested answers to both these questions. It also yielded another insight. However decentralized a company's IS function became, we noticed that end-users often perceived IS to be centralized as they felt remote from, and disenchanted with, the IS specialists. We realized that often past work had confused or conflated two organizational axes of importance in IS (see Figure 6.1). There is the centralization versus decentralization question but also the users versus specialists question. This chapter addresses the first, while Chapter 7 tackles the second.

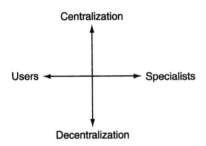

Figure 6.1   The two dimensions of IS configuration

Since 1987, our research has continued, especially in case study mode, because the configuration issue arises in ever new forms. Consider the following examples:

1. A decentralized conglomerate with strong interests in publishing and leisure industries began to wonder if for the first time a group IS presence was required. It was evident that media technologies – important across the group – were converging with other information technologies. Concerns arose about transfer of learning across IS departments and also the ability to pursue new business opportunities based on technological convergence, but which required collaboration or integration between business units.
2. A petrochemical company decentralized most of its IS activities, including downsizing its corporate IS department on a grand scale. As the group IT steering committee ran out of steam and the residual corporate IS group found it difficult either to discover a vision for corporate-wide IS or to pursue IT initiatives, the question arose

whether now to complete the decentralization started two years earlier. However, the CEO worried that possible group synergies might be lost in the long run if no central IS presence was retained.

3. A health care products company found that it had to integrate the selling and distribution of products across five divisions in order to compete effectively with a more centralized, integrated rival and to satisfy the one-stop purchasing habits of its customers. A new IS organization across these five divisions had to be created to meet this challenge.

4. A branded consumer products company created four sectors between head office and its former product divisions. The IS function was asked how it would respond when hitherto there had been both a corporate IS group and divisions IS units (see Earl, 1993).

5. An oil company comprised three regional groupings each with its own IS organization. The CEO was looking for cost savings through rationalization and downsizing. Despite external advice that achieving group-wide economies of scale in information processing rarely worked, the company set up one global IS configuration.

We see in these cases first that continuing technological change can induce new questions about the configuration of IS. Next we see the belief that IS can contribute to synergy even in quite decentralized organizations. We also see that quite often competitive strategies force a rethink of IS organization and that it is not uncommon to see consolidation of information processing, not necessarily at the centre, but at some intermediate level. The consumer brands company reminds us that as new organizational forms evolve, the IS function may have to realign itself. Finally, we see that the increasing demand for more efficient information processing can lead to a rethink of IS configurations. In other words, the policy question of how to configure the IS function is not likely to go away. In this chapter, using our original research, we suggest some organizational design principles which may stand the test of time. We also discuss some trends and experiences evident in more recent cases we have studied.

THEORETICAL FOUNDATIONS

The IS literature

The early information systems literature often related issues of chargeout and responsibility accounting to the question of decentralizing or centralizing the IS function. In those days (Dearden and Nolan, 1983; McFarlan, Nolan and Norton, 1973), the evolution of mainframe computing tended to dictate relative centralization of hardware, but there was some choice on the location of IS development activities and management planning and control of IS. Chargeout was seen as one way of introducing more accountability into centralized mainframe environments and perhaps practices varied with an organization's position on the Gibson and Nolan stage model of EDP growth (Gibson and Nolan, 1974).

When distributed computing became possible, new organization possibilities emerged. Buchanan and Linowes (1980) developed an analytical framework for resolving these configuration choices. They proposed a generic set of IS activities and classified them into operations, development and control, implying choices at each level. They indicated what might be centralized or decentralized but, as has been the tendency since the distributed era, perhaps failed to distinguish between the user-specialist axis and the centralization-decentralization axis in analysing IS configurations. The recognition that IT could be a strategic resource and was beginning to shape competition in certain sectors led McFarlan, McKenney and Pyburn (1983) to propose their strategic grid. This implied that organizations or their segments could be approaching and managing IS differently according to the strategic dependence on, and future importance of, IS. This notion that IS management, and thus configuration, could vary by firm was developed by McFarlan and McKenney (1983a) when they suggested that choices were influenced also by host organization structure, geographical spread and the management control system. Zmud et al., (1986) posited the idea of an 'information economy' in organizations as the IS function's monopoly of IT resources weakened. They observed that responsibility for different technologies and different aspects of IS was migrating to local organizational units and to different specialist groups. This was leading to governance issues and possibly the need for federal approaches to IS configuration.

La Belle and Nyce (1987), reporting on a configuration exercise in Manufacturers Hanover Corporation, described how the tensions between centralization and decentralization of IS had led to such a federal resolution. This exercise had been prompted by Manufacturers Hanover's creation of a new decentralized business sector structure on the one hand and the realization that earlier decentralization of IS had created impediments to information-sharing and applications integration on the other. Contemporaneously, Dearden (1987) had predicted the withering away of the IS function as end-users took over much of their own information processing and many larger-scale utility and development activities were outsourced to third parties. Dearden certainly spotted two key trends, but the iconoclastic scenario he painted had not come to pass by 1992, which was the timescale he predicted. In contrast, Von Simson (1990) three years later claimed that a degree of recentralization of the IS function was happening as firms strove for increasing systems and technological integration, economies of scale and maximizing the use of scarce specialists. He argued for a federal configuration in complex organizations or what he called the 'centrally decentralized' IS organization.

Organization theory
Most of the above contributions have been inductive, interpreting trends and events in the evolution of the IS function. However, the centralization versus decentralization question is not new and more universal insights may be available from the literatures of organization theory and general management.

Lawrence and Lorsch (1967) introduced their language of differentiation and integration to describe how organizations respond to technology and market factors. They pointed out that organizations deal with their external environment by creating units – often 'divisions' – which each seek to master a particular part of the firm's environment (or a particular technology). Lawrence and Lorsch described these units as differentiated because of inevitable differences in 'cognitive and emotional orientations' between them, as well as their contrasting specialist skills. Differentiation, however, leads to a need for integration, in particular collaboration between units in the interests of the organization as a whole. Consequently, as Lawrence and Lorsch found, organizations facing turbulence in their technologies and markets need to achieve high differentiation and high levels of integration simultaneously. This was not likely to be achieved simply by formal organizational hierarchy to resolve conflicts, but more by creation of specific roles, liaison devices and management processes working towards integration. The implications of Lawrence and Lorsch for configuring IS may be these. IT is a core technology for many enterprises today and is also a source of environmental turbulence. The creation of (differentiated) specialist IS units is therefore to be expected. However, IS is unlikely to be effective unless special management processes and organizational devices are created to integrate these units with the host organization. Secondly, if there are differentiated business units with their own IS units, business unit integration may depend partly on information systems. Furthermore, there will be need for some collaboration or integration across the local IS units.

Williamson's (1975, 1996) transaction costs approach to questions of organizational design suggests that any given set of transactions can be conducted internally or externally. Choice depends on which option is more efficient, incurring the lower transaction cost. Organizations exist and grow because not all transactions can be efficiently subcontracted to the market. Williamson's organizational failure framework shows that external contracting can be inefficient when various combinations of environmental and human factors prevail. These include environmental uncertainty combined with Simon's (1955) 'bounded rationality' of organizational decisionmaking; 'small numbers' of bidders combined with supplier or market 'opportunism'; and 'information impactedness' or asymmetry between parties combined with opportunism, small numbers or bounded rationality. Williamson then classifies a number of available organizational forms: Unitary or Functional Enterprise (U-Form), Holding Company (H-Form), Multidivisional (M-Form) and its derivatives (M^1 Form and M Form) and Mixed (X-Form). He concludes that for organizations in complex environments the pure M-Form leads to superior performance: divisions have autonomous responsibility for operations, while corporate management confines itself to giving strategic direction, designing internal controls to achieve congruence between autonomous business unit behaviour and corporate goals, and seeking to optimally manage and allocate cash resources. Interpreting Williamson for IS management, we can posit that organizations will continue to retain at least a partial in-house IS function since the factors which warn against contracting out are often present in abundance for IT. Secondly, for complex (or multi-business unit) organizations, the M-Form structure for the in-house IS function would seem optimal. Such a structure would comprise location of some IS activities within business units plus maintenance of a central IS group concerned with policies in the interests of the organization as a whole.

A related economics perspective on organizational design comes from agency theory (Jensen and Meckling, 1976). This distinguishes principals, often conceived of as shareholders or employers or superiors, from agents, who may be the corresponding managers, employees or subordinates in an agency relationship. The development of agency theory has recognized that the values and interests of the principal and agent can differ, that often agents have informational advantages over principals and that incentives need to be constructed to engineer appropriate behaviour. Also the theory distinguishes between 'decision control' (the ratification and monitoring of decisions by principals) and 'decision management' (implementation of ratified decisions and generation of proposals for resource utilization). Clearly in the centralization versus decentralization debate, the corporate office is the principal and the business unit the agent. This leads into addressing the balance between direction and control and autonomy and responsiveness. In the IS context, agency theory can inform us about the need for reserved powers, for monitoring of risks and for corporate information reporting. It is perhaps interesting that LaBelle and Nyce (1987) talked of the search for an equilibrium point between central control of policy and resources and decentralized ownership of information processing. Such a concept of balance is inherent in federal models of organization as advocated for instance by Drucker (1964) and more recently spelt out in terms of subsidiarity, interdependence, uniform ways of doing things, separation of powers and twin citizenship by Handy (1992). Indeed, we might note that Vancil and Buddrus (1978) even recognize that the decentralized form of organization is a balancing act of 'managerial ambiguity by design'. In other words, federal structures are less likely to be commonplace among complex organizations but will need considerable managing and subtlety in design. IS configuration may follow suit and may never be quite neat and tidy, certainly not permanent and always in need of processes to accompany structure.

To return to Lawrence and Lorsch, their contribution built on the work of Burns and Stalker (1961) and Woodward (1965) in that they were advancing a contingency theory of organizations, namely that different environments, technologies (and other variables) were likely to require different organizational designs. This thinking influenced management control theory and in 1980 Otley (Otley, 1980) proposed a model whereby the firm's environment and perhaps strategy influenced the design of organizational and control arrangements which with other intervening variables (such as managers' abilities), would influence organizational performance. We adapted this framework for our 1987 study (Figure 6.2) as a way of both exploring alternative IS configurations and of seeking whether any particular factors shape a preferred set of arrangements. This underpinned our methodology and is developed in the next section.

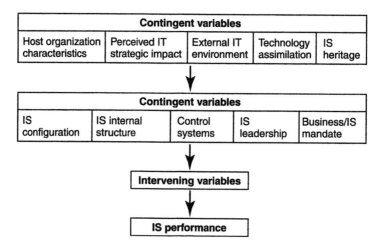

Figure 6.2   A contingency model of IS organization

METHODOLOGY

In 1987, 14 large European organizations were examined from the following sectors: insurance, oil and chemicals, automobiles, food and drink, chemicals and pharmaceuticals, electronics, paper, retailing, aerospace and local government. The investigation comprised field studies, normally interviewing a senior 'IS executive', a senior user manager (and if this was the manager of a local unit, the IS manager) and a senior corporate executive to whom IS reported. Interviews were semi-structured, following a questionnaire, but also encouraging discussion and reflection. Through these interviews and with back-up work, more structured data was collected either of a descriptive nature or in the opinion/satisfaction-rating mode.

Each organization was complex in the sense of comprising multiple business units and large (sales revenue from £1 billion to £27 billion). The 14 organizations represented a continuum of IS configurations from centralized to decentralized; indeed they represented all the forms in Table 6.1 which we discuss later. IS budgets ranged from £13 million to £200 million. Our entry point was through the IS directors and they selected the other interviewees – a possible sample bias. However, we did find that non-IS executives were far from reluctant to take a critical (in the strict sense) view of IS activities and performance. The model in Figure 6.2 drove our data collection. It proposed five independent or contingent variables which might influence what we soon called IS organizational 'arrangements', although configuration, or structure, was our focus and is the emphasis reported here. We did find that, for example, organizational and control choices were interrelated. We were also conscious of the Lawrence and Lorsch observation that processes, policies and personal action as well as structure are involved in resolving the centralization and decentralization debate (or more correctly differentiation and integration). 'Arrangements' became our collective noun for these organizational features. The contingent variables were suggested by the theoretical foundations above. (The instruments used to represent these variables can be found in Feeny, Edwards and Earl, 1987). Host organization characteristics were defined as structure and management style. Respondents were asked to select which of Williamson's (1975) six organizational forms best described their organization's structure. We used an instrument from past IS research to capture interviewees' perceptions of the organization's preferred management style. This was Pyburn's (1983) four categories of planning and control decision behaviour, namely personal informal, personal formal, written formal and written informal.

Respondents were asked to position their firm on the McFarlan, McKenney and Pyburn (1983) strategic grid as a way of capturing the

Table 6.1   Five ways to structure IS

Corporate service   IS is a unified function reporting to corporate management. There may be distributed equipment, but it is under the operational control of central IS. If business units have people whose focus is systems, they are best described as formal IS contact point, or negotiators.

Internal bureau   IS is again unified as described above, but it is run as a business within the organization and reports similarly to other business units. Its business is wholly or largely with other business units in the group, which it charges for its services. Business units may or may not be constrained to use the internal bureau to the exclusion of all other suppliers.

Business venture   Similar to the internal bureau, but there is a clear mission to obtain significant revenue for itself (and ultimately therefore for the group) by selling products or services outside the group as well as inside. Indications of this mode would be published tariffs, marketing literature, dedicated external sales force, some products which are not employed internally at all, or external revenue targets.

Decentralized   IS is a distributed function. Each business unit contains its own IS capability under its own control, or elects to employ commercial data services. There is no central IS unit or responsibility except for the support of corporate headquarters functions. Corporate management review the unit's capital and budget submissions for IS only to the extent required by general financial planning and control procedures.

Federal   IS is a distributed function, with each business unit containing and largely controlling its own IS capability. However, there is, in addition, a central IS unit reporting to corporate management which has responsibility for defined aspects of policy and architecture across the organization, and which may deliver some common or shared services. It may or may not be coincident with the IS unit for corporate HQ.

---

perceived IT strategic impact. The Gibson and Nolan (1974) stage model was used to try and capture technology assimilation. Benchmarks were developed for six categories of IT to help respondents position the firm in one of the four stages of initiation, expansion, formalization and maturity. The external IT environment was assessed by asking respondents to classify the significance of a number of established and emerging technologies. Since some writers argue that technology development has influenced IS configuration, this seemed important. Technologies assessed included personal computers, local area networks, expert systems and mainframe computing.

IS heritage was the fifth independent variable and was more a prejudice of the researchers than a contingency suggested by the literature. In our experience, the history of IS management – particularly traumas and crises – was often stressed by managers when they described the evolution of IS configuration or the latest development. The stage model of Gibson and Nolan (1974) tends to adopt this view when it sees the 'growth curve' being driven by experiential learning. In our study, IS management interviewees were asked to pick out significant successes and failures from the past decade.

Similar types of instrument were used to capture data on the five elements of organization arrangements in Figure 6.2 (see Feeny, Edwards and Earl, 1987). Since IS configuration is our focus here, we should concentrate on this one element. Table 6.1 suggests five idealized IS organizational forms on the centralization-decentralization continuum. These were developed from a consultancy framework previously constructed by one of the authors, Edwards, in his work with IBM. Table 6.1 seemed to contain all the configurational options suggested in the literature. We asked respondents to identify which form they currently adopted and to give an opinion on any future trend.

This contingent model, then, guided our investigation and generated research instruments. However, the model was not intended to be a strait-jacket in our enquiry, just as we do not suggest that it provides a deterministic explanation of IS configuration. The aim was to discover guidelines for the organizational design of the IS function and to capture what were the important lessons and trends in the centralization versus decentralization debate. The expectation was that at least some of the independent variables would appear significant and that exploration of both the dependent and independent variables would demonstrate why they were important and how they could be satisfied. Use of such a multivariate framework and the semi-structured mode of enquiry might lead to largely interpretative results of a propositional nature, but the investigation and analysis were being disciplined by a prior line of argument suggested by the literature and past research. It did seem important to make some assessment of IS performance in assessing different IS configurations and we chose two traditional constructs from management thinking: efficiency and effectiveness. As the specification of these measures became clear during the fieldwork, they are more appropriately explained in the next section.

RESULTS

Trends in configuration

The sample of organizations investigated deliberately represented a spectrum of IS configurations. Figure 6.3 records how many of each ideal form (from Table 6.1) existed in the sample in 1983 and in 1987 when we studied them. It also presents a forecast four years on, based on an interpretation of the respondents' comments on current concerns

IS configuration	Number in sample			
	1983	1987	1991 (outlook)	1993 (actual)
Corporate service	5	2	1	1
Internal bureau/business venture	4	3	0	0
Federal	3	8	9	9
Decentralized	2	1	4	4

Figure 6.3   Trends in IS configuration

and significant trends. We have also added a 1993 column which records the situation (according to our own monitoring) six years after the study. The *federal* form is seen to dominate in recent years. However, (and this will be discussed later), the 1993 version of federal in some cases is more decentralized than in 1987.

In the ideal federal form, the IS function is coordinated from the centre, but IS activities are divided between central and distributed units. Many shades of the federal configuration are possible with different patterns of resource and responsibility distribution. In six of the eight federal structures encountered in 1987, much or all of the operational services was provided from the centre. Each of the federal structures had evolved from a previously centralized form where the initial evolutionary step generally was to install an IS manager and/or user support resources in business units. In this scenario, devolution of development resources may follow, but devolution of operations usually does not because the existing service is generally well regarded. In most cases a strong development capability had been retained centrally in order sometimes to develop common application systems for use across the organization and often to provide a contracting bespoke service. Central development teams, however, seemed to meet with far less success then centralized delivery services.

In the period since 1987 (both forecast and 'actual'), the federal structure looks to be the most stable form as well as the most common in the sample. As Hodgkinson (1996) suggests, it can be adapted to align well with most forms of complex, multi-divisional organization. It perhaps represents a design space in which compromises can be accommodated, balances evolve over time, different types of IS resource get distributed differently and multiple dimensions of most organizational structure serviced. In the two cases where the federal structure was perhaps under threat in 1987, it was because the host organization was moving towards being a clear holding company structure and the need for any IS unit at the corporate level was being questioned. In both cases a reduced corporate IS unit survives, focusing on policy matters and pursuing any remaining economies of scale in information processing (for example, data communications networks). In contrast, the pure corporate service form of IS structure has been waning. Only one instance in the sample has survived, because it sits comfortably within the centralized UK structure of its host organization. Indeed as at 1997, the future of corporate service IS structures is probably only assured within centralized host organizations, as may be found in the retailing sector for example.

Although only a marginal decline in the number of internal bureau or business venture forms was recorded in 1987, they were predicted to decline further in the outlook period, did so, and are judged to be unstable. Internal customers of the sample bureau and business venture structures generally were nervous about relying heavily on market-oriented IS units for important services and were seeking to reduce their dependence on them. They also expressed concern that such units can soon lose touch with, and become less well informed, about their host organization, its units and their needs. In the case of the business venture forms, customers also feared they might allocate their key resources to more lucrative sectors outside, or alternatively use internal customers as 'guinea pigs' for product and staff development. It should be noted, however, that the outlook prediction of decline in business unit or business venture structures does not imply that they will cease to exist. In research on IS outsourcing Willcocks, Fitzgerald and Lacity, (1996) found several examples of these being set up, but also noted difficulties for them competing in a rapidly crowding external market for IT services. Rather, in our view, they will cease to be the dominant structure in an organization's overall mix of IS arrangements. Indeed, they could become one of the sources of supply in a federal IS structure.

The decentralized form in the sample had reduced from two to one. In the company which had rescinded its decentralization of IS, a powerful corporate headquarters wanted to bring in controls over IS in line with its grip in all other areas of activity. However, the decentralized structure would seem to have a good fit in holding companies and it could become the dominant IS form in those organizations. Three host organizations originally were moving in that direction, in addition to the one clear case already within the study sample. The trend was fulfilled by 1993, notably in corporations with a holding company mentality and where the future of component businesses was perpetually uncertain. This analysis suggests that only the centralized, decentralized or federal configurations are likely to survive or be the options that corporations select. A centralized IS function seems to make sense in a purely centralized host organization. Equally, a decentralized IS function seems to fit the structure and spirit of purely decentralized hosts. In more complex organizations, the federal IS configuration seems to offer best fit and be very adaptable. These arguments collectively suggest that host organization characteristics may be a key contingent variable when configuring the IS function. Of course, the bureau or business venture would fit any decentralized or federal host organization in that it becomes a line of business. However, experience seems to show that making a business out of IS is not what organizations should be doing – the rest of the business suffers because integration of the differentiated unit seems to break down or be inhibited.

The contingent factors

Host organization characteristics, then, seem to influence IS configuration. The 1987 study deliberately examined a spectrum of IS configuration. What was not anticipated was the degree of change in *host organizational design and characteristics* most had been recently experiencing. Ten out of 13 organizations had undergone major change in structure and control in the first half of the 1980s. Mostly, there has been a new emphasis on business and business unit definition, usually in terms of product groupings, together with a clearer delineation of responsibility and authority between the centre and the business units, resulting in greater operational autonomy for the business units and often a flatter overall organizational structure. The tendency for management style to be personal rather than written (Figure 6.4) may suggest similar organizational contexts. At the same time formal styles exceed informal, suggesting also clear and felt accountabilities. The stimulus for change was increased external demands for performance in the midst of a fiercely competitive environment.

	Formal	Informal
Personal	69%	28%
Written	3%	0%

Figure 6.4   Management style responses

This trend can be seen to accord with Williamson's (1975) recommendations for the effective structuring of multi-divisional organizations. This business unit structuring also seemed to be facilitating the linking of IS to business strategy, much as suggested by Earl (1989) in his distinction between IS or applications strategies, which are the responsibility of business units, and IT or delivery strategies, which are largely the responsibility of the IS function, often at a higher level in the organization. In short then, redesign of organizations' structure and control seemed to have been commonplace, emphasizing devolution to business units, with possible benefits in IS strategy formulation.

Exploration of IS success and failures to trace *IS heritage* also suggested a clear pattern. The most consistently claimed success was the creation of high quality and professionally managed data centres and networks. Of failures mentioned, more than 50 per cent of organizations mentioned user management hostility or indifference to IT and IS. References to specific major application development projects were made by 11 out of the 13 organizations, but there was near equality between claims of success and verdicts of failure. Interviewees had no difficulty in recalling successes and failures; such assessment seems normal. Indeed in 10 out of 13 organizations a significant review and redefinition of the IS function had occurred sometime in the previous eight years. In seven cases, the resulting configuration included a change of ownership for some or all of the IS resources. In eight cases a crisis of confidence in IS was reported as having reached main board level. Typically the configurational change involved devolution of IS development and/or support resources to the business units. However, the established operations capability – efficiently run data centres and networks – was usually retained intact to provide some or all of the required activity on a service basis. One case was resolved during the period of the fieldwork when three out of four business unit managers told the group executive that they did not want the responsibility of running their own operations facilities. More than once, business executives were heard to say, 'we don't want the hassle of running data centres and networks'. This seems to be justified also by their intuitive reasoning of 'if it ain't broke, don't fix it'. In short, then, IS successes and failures appear to be readily observed and recalled in organizations. More important, serious failures of a crisis of confidence in the IS function seem to lead to significant shifts in configuration of IS (perhaps as common sense would predict).

The proposed independent variable *IT strategic impact* was perceived to be high by most organizations. Two-thirds assessed the strategic impact of current IS to be high, whilst 80 per cent felt that planned IT applications were of strategic importance. Where business managers had a different perception from IS managers, it was the former group who rated IT strategic impact more highly, which is perhaps surprising. Thus most organizations perceived the strategic impact of IT as high, and this may not be a useful distinction in explaining alternative IS configurations. Indeed, subsequent studies by the authors have found that the strategic grid may not be a useful instrument in research. For example, if examining corporations, then each business unit may position itself differently. More recently it seems that most organizations have found themselves to be in this strategic quadrant. Thus perhaps the McFarlan and McKenney (1983b) strategic grid was useful when there were leaders and laggards in recognizing or feeling the strategic impact of IT. In 1993 the diffusion of strategic impact may be widespread. Equally, the 1980s trend towards business unit devolution in host organizations (and the competitive pressures which commonly caused it) may have sharpened up management's attention to, and understanding of, the strategic threats and opportunities of IT. In short, the strategic impact of IT, at least as measured by the McFarlan and McKenney (1983b) strategic grid, does not seem to influence the configuration of IS activities.

All interviewees were able to position themselves on *technology assimilation* curves with ease. A universal picture emerged in 1987 of organizations facing different stages in the stage model for different technologies, with transaction processing, data communication and scientific computing being at more advanced adoption stages than office or physical automation and end-user computing (see Figure 6.5). There were no observable differences in alternative IS configurations. It seemed that all organizations were having concurrently to manage multiple technologies through quite different IS management practices and regimes. This variable may impact the detail and disaggregation of IS management but it does not appear to have a comprehensive or universal impact on overall IS configuration.

The variable *external IT environment*, was less revealing. Interviewees selected an average of 5.5 contemporary technologies or issues from a list of 13 as presenting important threats or opportunities.

| | Assimilation reported: stage 1–4 | | |
Technology	Mean	Median	Inter-quartile range
Business transaction processing	3.1	3	3– to 3+
Data communications	3.0	3	3 to 3+
End-user computing	2.5	2	2 to 3
Office automation	2.1	2	2 to 2+
Scientific computing	3.0	4	2 to 4
Automation of physical/build processes	2.4	3	2 to 3

Figure 6.5   The assimilation of six strands of information technology. When recording responses to this question we found it necessary to qualify a strict numeric response on some occasions. For example, an organization which had manifestly reached and recognized the control stage, but had so far only partially succeeded in establishing controls, would be classified 3 –.

However, no distinguishing trends by technology or organization could be detected. Expert systems were most mentioned and have no obvious implications for structuring the IS function at large. The next three most quoted technologies were telecommunications-based. Rather than point to a preferred structure of the IS function, many observers (for example Keen, 1986) suggest that telecommunications increase the options and allow, for example, decentralization and centralization of both business operations and IS to co-exist. External IT environment was proposed as a contingent variable because certain technologies in the past seem to have influenced the thinking and structuring of IS organizations. To a degree telecommunications may have been one such technology in the 1980s in that where organizations had their own wide area network, it was inevitably under central management. However, some organizations did not have corporate networks or chose to operate through third parties, either group-wide or at business unit level.

We concluded in 1987 that the capability and diversity of available and new technologies perhaps was felt through two of the other contingent variables – IT strategic impact and technology assimilation – which in turn had no influence on IS configuration at the enterprise-wide level. Another interpretation in retrospect is that the external IT environment would be of secondary importance behind the driving variables of host organization structure and IS heritage. (For example, centralized network management is probably not needed in a decentralized organization and not credible if centralized IS groups have a bad reputation, but does appeal in terms of economies of scale and removing the anxiety from business units). A third interpretation is that, as key technologies evolve, the deterministic influence on IS configuration decreases, but that if different technologies are at different stages of evolution, a mixed impact on IS configuration (bringing more pressure for a federal IS function) is likely. In short our 1987 conclusions do not alter. Field studies pointed towards host organization characteristics followed by IS heritage as being the independent factors which most influence the configuration of the IS function. Our measure of strategic impact of IT suggested no relationship. Both technology assimilation and the external IT environment (which may be related) could influence the detail or disaggregation of IS configurations, but not the overall organization design choice. They may have much more to do with the user-specialist axis (see Chapter 7, also Feeny, Earl and Edwards, 1994).

Efficiency and effectiveness
These measures not only allowed us to assess the validity of the contingency relationships, but also to examine what is the key to making them work. Efficiency in the IS context can be seen as the

consistent provision of high quality and low cost IS service. Effectiveness we defined as the successful exploitation of IT in support of business needs. These were partly assessed by asking respondents, especially users, to judge their organization's achievement levels on the criteria in Figure 6.6.

Efficient IS organizations had to score highly on the first two criteria in Figure 6.6. Also, they had to possess a high level of specialist skill in the IS function, be at an advanced stage of assimilation of established technologies, have clear arrangements for tracking and introducing new technologies, and apply sophisticated chargeout procedures. Surprisingly, perhaps, there seemed to be little difference in the levels of efficiency achieved by the sample organizations. It was difficult to distinguish between user satisfaction ratings, other than by role of respondent. All IS sponsors and general managers gave a rating of 'largely satisfactory' (grade 2) whilst all finance directors and controllers opined that service levels had 'some key weaknesses' (grade 3) except one, who conceded a score of 2.5. One technical director gave a 'highly effective' rating of 1.

The researchers' more descriptive evaluation of technology assimilation and the other indicators were no more revealing as discriminants. Furthermore, a subjective overall assessment of each

	Rating	Highly effective – a key asset	Largely satisfactory	Some key weaknesses	Poor or badly exposed
Criteria					
Efficiency	Cost of service provision				
	Quality of service provision				
Effectiveness	Achievement of system benefits				
	Application implementation				
	Relating use of IT to business needs				
	Business management awareness of IT				

Figure 6.6   IS performance ratings

organization suggested little distinction among the organizations. The tentative, bold implication was that the provision of quality IS service at an acceptable cost was no longer a major issue in large corporations. Efficiency in IS apparently can be achieved by any large organization if it is prepared to commit adequate resources to the activity. Perhaps hardware and software products had become so much more reliable, and installation management practice so improved, that efficiency could be expected and was becoming an industry norm. Some users did claim dissatisfaction with IS technical achievement in the area of large application project development. Other respondents claimed success. However, successes and failures were reported in each pattern of IS arrangements. Thus major IS project development may still have been inefficient in several firms, but it was not clear that any particular pattern of IS arrangement would help remedy this deficiency.

The important conclusion drawn was that the operational activities of IS, and many of the development activities, could be located anywhere in an organization – centrally, at sector or regional level, or in business units – if efficiency was the criterion. Since the study, the evidence has not changed, except that we can now say that these activities can be located anywhere inside or potentially outside the organization. There may be relative efficiency differences between internal or external IS rivals, but there is no rule which suggests absolute efficiency in IS, in terms of operations and large-scale applications developments, associated with either centralization or decentralization. If there are historical, economies of scale, or critical mass reasons for having a centralized IS operations and development group, it can work in either a centralized or decentralized host organization. In the latter context, however, the effectiveness analysis adds some other considerations.

Effectiveness was assessed by using the remaining criteria in Figure 6.6 and by recording successes and failures in the following areas: linking IS strategy to business needs, IS contribution to business in comparison with key competitors, achievement of system benefits, and awareness by business managers of IT capability. The views of IS and business interviewees within each organization were checked for consistency. Substantial contrasts in IS effectiveness were identified within the sample organizations and were confirmed by the researchers' subjective impressions formed by the interviews. As the amalgam of effectiveness indicators used focuses on how well the IS function and the business relate to each other, they can also be seen as measuring *integration*, to refer back to Lawrence and Lorsch (1967). Thus this performance data was used to classify the 20 business units assessed across the 14 sample organizations into categories of high, medium and low integration. We examined more than one business unit in some of the more complex organizations. Five situations were classified as showing high integration, ten as medium, and five as low. The 'high' and 'low' were then compared in terms of their IS arrangements and clear distinctions were apparent. The following characteristics of IS arrangements were present in all the high situations and absent in all the low situations:

1. Business unit management perceived that future exploitation of IT was of strategic importance, as indicated by respondents' positioning on the strategic impact grid.
2. An IS executive was established as a full member of the management team or board for the business unit concerned.
3. There was ongoing education for business unit management in the capability and potential of IT. This might be achieved by formal programmes and/or continuous updating from the business unit's own IS executive.
4. There was a top-down planning process in the business unit for linking IS application strategy to business needs. Also the business unit leader was both leading and promoting the exploitation of IT.
5. Some IS development resource was positioned within the business unit, but not necessarily all that was required. The business unit had some capability for systems development and the skill and knowledge base to subcontract development to other internal or external suppliers. Importantly, if a business unit identified an urgent and critical IS requirement, it could propel and develop it with some local resources.
6. The introduction or piloting of new technologies took place at business unit level under business unit control. (Conversely, doubts were often expressed about the effectiveness of central experimental or R&D units for IT). It seems that business evaluation of new technologies is best done by relevant business units who understand their own product-market opportunities.
7. There was a cost centre rather than profit or investment centre control regime for IS within the business. Chargeout procedures were relatively unsophisticated, at levels 6 or below on Allen's (1987) continuum. (A possible explanation of this tendency is that while profit centre management of IS can help focus on efficiency of service, it can also create a transactional relationship between IS and their users, thereby impeding effectiveness). IS resources were not free in cost centre regimes, but pricing did not become an emotional issue.

The discovering of these distinguishing factors suggested that corporate IS management should be concerned primarily with effectiveness. Whereas any set of IS arrangements could, it seems, foster efficiency, there were clear indications that only certain patterns of IS arrangements were conductive to effectiveness. These help clarify which are the significant factors and relationships in our proposed contingency framework. The important recurring feature in the analysis of high integration or effectiveness contexts is that the pattern of IS arrangements is aligned with business units. In particular, IS management and development responsibilities are devolved to business units. We conclude, therefore, that *it is essential that IS arrangements should align with the key characteristics of the host organization.* Whether the host organization in traditional structural parlance is centralized or decentralized, the management of IS and at least some development resources should align with the overall distribution of managerial responsibility and authority. This pattern should then be backed up by IS education, IS planning processes, executive leadership and a cost centre control regime for IS. The business unit and business venture configuration for IS thus are likely to be ineffective because in both structure and process they cannot easily achieve these success factors. It becomes clear that there is no harm in allocating IS management and resources down to business units in decentralized organizations. In centralized organizations, all IS resources can also be centralized with no loss in effectiveness. We could conceive of minimal IS management and development resources being allocated to functions in centralized contexts – functions being the analogues of business units. For federal IS configurations, it is clear that business units should have at least an IS manager and minimal IS development resources and concentrate on the success factors. We still have to suggest what should be done, perhaps minimally at the centre of a federal configuration.

The federal centre

We analysed IS policies in use in the study companies. There was a high incidence of IS policy throughout. Executives running federal IS configurations emphasized policies seeing them as both a need and a rationale of federalization. Ten 'enabling' policies and eight 'restraining' policies were present in more than half the organizations and are listed in descending frequency in Figure 6.7. It appeared from this data and subsequent case study work that group IS goals in federal configurations divide into two:

1. Ensuring good practice and efficiency throughout the corporation.
2. Supporting corporate organizational and business goals.

Using Earl's (1989) taxonomy of strategy questions, the first is to do with information management strategy and often can be expressed as how can we make sure that corporate executives can sleep at night, and that we are running a competent IS function. The second is to do with information systems strategy, and in its wake information technology

Enabling policies	Restraining policies
1. Negotiation of group discounts	1. Technical compatibility standards
2. Shaping IT vendor relationships	2. Defining business units' freedom to procure and run IS
3. Chargeout rules	3. Use of common systems
4. Identifying and orchestrating a group IS 'Guru'	4. Security, disaster recovery, etc.
5. Whether and how to develop common systems	5. Conformance to industry standards
6. Reviewing IS potential in business units	6. IS standards of competence
7. Taking initiatives on asset sharing	7. IS job specifications
8. Legal and tendering procedures	8. Selling IS services externally
9. Managing IS human resources groupwide	
10. Developing centres of excellence in business units	

Figure 6.7   Common groupwide policies

strategy, and is concerned with supporting or enabling group synergies. We can now distil the practices and policies of the organization studied into two sets as in Table 6.2. They become the probable concerns of the federal centre of IS. The pragmatics learnt from case studies of federal configurations are equally important. To achieve the first goal, corporate IS staff must be first class and their expertise maintained. To put it colloquially, head office visitors must be better than the visited. Secondly, processes are required to create, review, monitor and enforce IS policies. To achieve the second goal, the central IS group needs a clear mission backed by corporate officers. They will not receive this support if the corporate business and organizational goals are unclear. These can usually be stated in terms of what value-added benefit does the corporation or group bring to the business units.

The federal balance
If we combine the necessary conditions for effectiveness in IS at business unit level with the responsibilities required at the federal centre and recognize that there are choices on how to configure IS resources for

Table 6.2   Corporate roles in federal IS configurations

Goal One: Ensuring good practice and efficiency throughout the group
- IS education initiatives
- Review of business unit IS strategies
- Standard setting for development and operations
- Audit of quality and security
- Career management of senior staff
- Consultancy report for small business
- Clearing house for technology and application information
- Management of IT vendor support and conditions

Goal Two: Supporting corporate organizational and business goals
- Definition of information infrastructure to support group efficiency, business integration, organizational flexibility and knowledge sharing
- Identifying and commissioning systems which encourage desired co-operation or necessary integration across internal boundaries
- Identifying and commissioning systems which capture distinctive competences and transfer them across business units

---

efficiency, we are able to produce a matrix of guidelines as in Figure 6.8. We see the federal IS configuration as insisting on each business unit being charged with working out and implementing its own IT application needs. The centre oversees the best practice in IS and formulates policies on infrastructure that are required to add value to or provide synergy for the corporation as a whole. Often history, economies of scale, critical mass and removal of worry from business

Local	Central
Essential	
• IS executive in management team	• IT vendor and acquisition policy
• IS strategic planning	• Architectural and technical standards
• IS education of managers	• Technical and quality assurance
• Executive leadership for IT	• Delineation of local responsibilities
• Some IS development capability	• IS human resource development
• Piloting new technologies	• Chargeout and control policies
Possible	
• Some IT operations capability	• IS development consultancy
	• IT operations capability
	• Common systems development
	• Coordinating IS development throughout the function
	• Coordinating IS across business units

Figure 6.8   Federal arrangements

units will lead to some centralization of IT operations. This is not unlike the federal form of IS governance suggested by Zmud *et al.*, (1986).

1987 conclusions

Our conclusions in 1987 have been restated as they emerge in this chapter. They could be summarized thus:

1. The federal IS configuration seems most stable and flexible for complex organizations. We have shown what it might look like.
2. Business unit and business venture IS configurations are not recommended. This is for reasons of effectiveness (and integration) rather than efficiency (or differentiation).
3. Centralized IS configurations suit centralized host organizations. Decentralized IS configurations suit purely decentralized host organizations.
4. A primary contingent factor in configuring the IS function, therefore, is host organization characteristics. We emphasized structure, style and culture may be important too.
5. IS heritage is also influential. Crises and failures do beget, and need, changes in configuration. Indeed they may often be signalling that the IS function is not aligned with the host organization.

We also concluded in 1987 that organizations should avoid drastic 'U-turns' in configuring IS. The cost and disruption are enormous. We see in the next and final section, however, that change, as they say, tends to be constant. However, for complex organizations, which were the primary focus of our study, we suggest that federal IS configurations provide enough design space to adapt to circumstances. They may be difficult to manage, but they are preferred to wide swings of the centralization–decentralization pendulum.

RECENT DEVELOPMENTS

Since the 1987 study, the authors have continued to study the configuration of the IS function. We can detect at least seven trends:

1. The increasing adoption and fine-tuning of the federal configuration.
2. The creation of intermediate levels of the federal configuration, here called consolidation.
3. The construction of IT-based services divisions.
4. The rise in outsourcing.
5. The recognition of new axes of organization.
6. The continued distribution of information processing to end-users.
7. The continuing change in configuration.

Each is addressed briefly below.

Federal sophistication   The variety of options within the federal model was identified earlier. This has turned out to be the practice. We see some firms who have recentralized some of their IS activities, commonly for four reasons:

1. To regain economies of scale or simply to rationalize. A common concern is to introduce control of software standards and centralize buying simply to save costs on software licensing. Another has been rationalizing data centres, given that efficient operations can be run anywhere and the decreasing cost of communications makes some hub and spoke architectures viable.
2. To get control of architecture and thus infrastructure so that cross-functional and cross-business unit application and data integration or connectivity are possible.
3. To facilitate or ensure that processes are in place to share experience and learning about both IT application and IS delivery across the group.
4. To monitor and improve standards of IS performance in all business units and review or coach component businesses on how strategically to exploit IT.

Apart from the first driver, these do not normally involve reconstruction of 'heavy' central IS groups. Sometimes the team is from one to four people. Indeed, some federal configurations have become more decentralized. Four influences are apparent here:

1. The desire to devolve decision-making to business units on what IT applications to develop and how to implement them.
2. The desire to remove corporate headcount and cost either by outsourcing central IS operations centres or distributing them to business units.
3. The unclear added value not only from corporate IS groups, but large chunks of corporate offices in general.
4. The continued decentralization of the host organization.

Finally, some federal configurations are hybrids of the other configurations. Three examples are illustrative:

1. Some operational centres of federal organizations now have a business venture mission to larger or lesser degrees. They sell services outside as well as inside and usually have no monopoly within their host.
2. One company with two divisions has a centralized IS group in one division and a deeply decentralized one in the other. The IS director

of the former looks over the latter and has two consultants to help the smallest segments.

3. One group decentralized all its IS activities including a corporate bureau. Because the group executive wanted peace of mind through monitoring the decentralized activities and believed in providing coaching for local managers, a group CIO was appointed on a part-time basis.

In short, the federal configuration has no standard topology or organization chart.

Consolidation   The federal configuration is not just as in Figure 6.9(a), but can be as Figure 6.9(b). At least four related drivers explain the trend towards consolidation of information processing at intermediate levels of the organization:

1. Where business units are having to collaborate to produce or distribute product families or present a common face to a customer. This happened in one decentralized business who has to compete with a centralized rival who was providing 'one-stop shopping' to its customers. It was too painful, slow and unnecessary to bring decentralized product centres together, but a shared information system centre and distribution function was superimposed over the five business units, to achieve the same results.

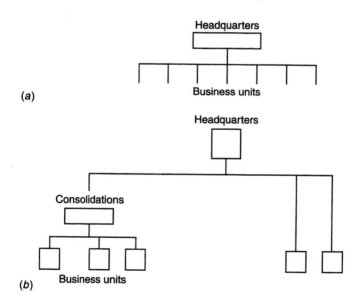

(a)

(b)

Figure 6.9   Federal configurations (a) simple federal, (b) with consolidation

2. As organizations look to take cost out of internal administration, we see information-based activities being consolidated across business units. These showed how service organizations provide economies of scale and may accompany redesign of administrative processes. Common accounting centres are examples.
3. As corporations find themselves competing globally, we observe the need to coordinate IS strategy-making, IS developing and sometimes IT operations across business units and countries in order to support strategies for global efficiency or to transfer knowledge and learning. This requires some intermediate consolidation of IS (see also Chapter 16).
4. There may be simple manageability drivers. Two are becoming popular. One is coping with size or reach by creating, for example, regional data centres to serve whatever business units or functions exist in that region. Another is creating an IS configuration independent of the host organization with the hope of IS becoming less of a roadblock to organizational change. The theory is that operations and development centres are created (almost as bureaux) to serve a set of business units wherever located and however impermanent. If a unit changes its position in the organization chart or merges or splinters, there is not an IS impediment because IS activities and assets are not located within and owned by the business unit, they are corporate but central utilities.

All these consolidated forms can fit within the federal model.

Service organizations Apart from shared service centres, some corporations are now adding information-based functions or businesses to IS to create a bureau or business venture. This could be seen at Barclays Bank in the mid-1990s where credit card processing, money transmission services, global custody and the like were joined with information services as a line of business providing sources inside or outside the host organization. However, they are not necessarily the only IS unit in the group. Responsibility for IS development and management at Barclays, for example, was devolved to business units. The latter could also buy IS services from the marketplace. Again this is one form of the federal configuration. One should note that Barclays in the mid-1990s also provides us with an example of an IS structure that is continually being reviewed in the light of business and IS exigencies (see the section 'Continual change' below).

Outsourcing The growth of the third-party marketplace and organizations' desire to reduce information processing costs has encouraged outsourcing. This may or may not be a good idea (Earl, 1996b; Lacity, Willcocks and Feeny, 1996; see also Chapters 11 and 12), but reminds us that IS configurations now extend beyond the traditional boundaries of the host organization. Outsourcing of operations and developments is an option available to all five ideal IS configurations. However, what seems to be emerging is that outsourcing is just one partial answer to information services supply and rarely totally displaces the whole IS function (see also Chapter 17). It certainly does not remove the need for managing either efficiency or effectiveness of IS and so, although outsourcing may lead to downsizing of the IS function, it does not necessarily alter the centralization versus decentralization axis of IS configuration.

New axes   However, new axes are appearing. The most contemporary one is 'business process'. Where firms are engaged in business process redesign, not only may business operations and management be reallocated to key processes, but process-oriented (often cross-functional) systems are required too. We are then seeing IS management positions and development teams being allocated to these business processes and reporting to the business process sponsor or executive. These could prove to be temporary units, but currently they introduce a new axis at any level of the host organization (Earl, 1996a; see also Chapter 10). They may increase the 'federal' proportion of information resources in essentially decentralized or functional organizations.

End-users   Particularly the distribution of computing, combined with networking, client–server architectures and the like are not only putting more power and application capability into the hands of users, they are increasing the technological experience and knowledge of users. So at any level of the centralization–decentralization axis, we see a shift in responsibility towards end-users (see also Chapters 7 and 8). Indeed, over 50 per cent or more of IT resources may now be located outside the IS function. This has at least three implications. We do have to reanalyse the specialist–user axis. Secondly, the authority given to distributed users has to be considered carefully. This explains why infrastructural responsibility and reserved powers are being relocated to the centre in some organizations and reinforcing the good sense of federal configurations. Such a move also is reflecting the need to control costs.

Continual change   We have tracked substantial organizational change in five of the original field study companies. It thus seems unlikely that IS configurations can or should remain static for long. Curiously, however, none of these can be reclassified on our continuum in Table 6.1. We could suggest that the outline configuration of IS in complex organizations is settling down, but the detail is always changing. One federal configuration is now more decentralized because the host has become deeply decentralized. Another federal configuration has intermediate or consolidated levels now because business units are combining into product groups. One federal configuration has coped with a merger which has introduced regional units for global manageability reasons. In contrast, another federal configuration has split into two federal patterns because of a de-merger. Finally, a group which was becoming decentralized after a business venture phase is now more decentralized because it was acquired by a conglomerate. It is notable that host organization characteristics seem to be very influential.

CONCLUSION

Six years on, our principal propositions had not been revised. Subsequent developments in the mid-1990s have done little to impinge on the central thrust of our position. There seem to be five ideal forms of IS configuration, of which three seem more viable than the others. The federal configuration seems the best fit with most complex organizations. It is varied in form and, as we suggested, seems to be very flexible and adaptive. As we had tracked organizations over the 1987–93 period, the federal configuration had been able to accommodate some recentralization or deeper decentralization or consolidation.

Host organization characteristics certainly appear to drive IS configuration. The most significant influence pre- and post-1987 seemed to have been wider organizational change. Of course this may have been driven by business strategy as much as preferred management theory. However, adjustments within one of our archetype configurations – particularly the federal structure – may have been due also to technological change and assimilation, the economics of information processing and the requirements of IS strategy. IS heritage may have remained a mediating influence, but as firms' IS management experience grows, perhaps we can expect fewer major crises resulting in configurational revolutions.

Outsourcing alongside other aspects of downsizing now appears to be affecting the size of the IS function, but not dramatically affecting configuration, at least in most cases (Lacity, Willcocks and Feeny, 1996). However, the total scale of IS activities seems likely to grow further, partly as more capability is put into the hands of end-users and partly as other, newer technologies, particularly media and image technologies, converge with what was conceived of as IT in the 1980s.

We therefore should not expect the issue of configuring the IS function and IS activities at large to go away.

REFERENCES

Allen, B. (1987) 'Making Information Services Pay its Way', *Harvard Business Review*, January–February.

Buchanan, J. and Linowes, R. (1980) 'Making Distributed Data Processing Work', *Harvard Business Review*, September–October.

Burns, T. and Stalker, G. (1961) *The Management of Innovation*, Tavistock Publications, London.

Dearden, J. (1987) 'The Withering Away of the IS Organization', *Sloan Management Review*, Summer.

Dearden, J. and Nolan, R. (1973) 'How to Control the Computer Resource', *Harvard Business Review*, November–December.

Dickson, G., Leitheiser, R. and Wetherbe, J. (1984) 'Key Information Systems Issues for the 1980s', *MIS Quarterly*, September.

Drucker, P. (1964) *The Concept of Corporation*, John Day & Co Inc, New York.

Earl, M. (1989) *Management Strategies for Information Technology*, Prentice-Hall, London.

Earl, M. (1993) *Grand Metropolitan PLC*, Centre For Research In Information Management, CS 93/1, London Business School, London.

Earl, M. (ed.). (1996a) *Information Management: The Organizational Dimension*, Oxford University Press, Oxford.

Earl, M. (1996b) 'The Risks Of IT Outsourcing', *Sloan Management Review*, **37**, (3).

Feeny, D., Earl, M. and Edwards, B. (1994) *Organizational Arrangements for IS Roles of Users and IS Specialists*. Research and Discussion Paper RPD 94/6, Oxford Institute of Information Management, Templeton College, Oxford.

Feeny, D., Edwards, B. and Earl, M. (1987) *Complex Organizations and the Information Systems Function: A Research Study*, Research and Discussion Paper RDP 87/7, Oxford Institute of Information Management, Templeton College, Oxford.

Gibson, C. and Nolan, R. (1974) 'Managing the Four Stages of EDP Growth', *Harvard Business Review*, January–February.

George, J. and King, J. (1991) 'Examining The Computing and Centralization Debate', *Communications Of The ACM*, **34**, (7), 63–72.

Handy, C. (1992) 'Balancing Corporate Power: A New Federalist Paper', *Harvard Business Review*, November–December.

Hodgkinson, S. (1996) 'The Role of the Corporate IT Function in the Federal IT Organization', In Earl, M. (ed.). *Information Management: The Organizational Dimension*, Oxford University Press, Oxford.

Jensen, M. and Meckling, W. (1976) 'Theory of the Firm, Managerial Costs and Ownership Structure', *Journal of Financial Economics*, October.

Keen, P. (1986) *Competing in Time: Using Telecommunications for Competitive Advantage*, Ballinger Press, Cambridge, Mass.

LaBelle, A. and Nyce, H. (1987) 'Whither the IT Organization?', *Sloan Management Review*, Summer.

Lacity, M., Willcocks, L. and Feeny, D. (1996) 'The Value of Selective IT Sourcing', *Sloan Management Review*, **37**, (3), pp. 13–24.

Lawrence, P. and Lorsch, J. (1967) *Organization and Environment: Managing Differentiation and Integration*, Division of Research, Graduate School of Business Administration, Harvard University, Boston, Mass.

McFarlan, F. W. and McKenney, J. L. (1983a) 'The Information Archipelago – Governing the New World', *Harvard Business Review*, July – August.

McFarlan, F. W. and McKenney, J. L. (1983b) *Corporate Information Systems Management: The Issues Facing Senior Executives*, Dow Jones Irwin, New York.

McFarlan, F. W., McKenney, J. and Pyburn, P. (1983) 'The Information Archipelago – Plotting a Course', *Harvard Business Review*, January–February.

McFarlan, F. W., Nolan, R. and Norton, D. (1973) *Information Systems Administration*, Holt, Rinehart and Winston, New York.

Niederman, F., Brancheau, J. and Wetherbe, J. (1991) 'Information Systems Management Issues for the 1990s', *MIS Quarterly*, **15**, (4) December.

Otley, D. (1980) 'The Contingency Theory of Management Accounting: Achievement and Prognosis', *Accounting Organizations and Society*, **5**, (4).

Pyburn, P. (1983) 'Linking the MIS Plan with Corporate Strategy: An Exploratory Study'. *MIS Quarterly*, June.

Simon, H. (1955) 'The Behavioural Model of Rational Choice', *Quarterly Journal of Economics*, February.

Willcocks, L., Fitzgerald, G. and Lacity, M. (1996) 'To Outsource IT or not? Recent Findings on Economics and Evaluation Practice', *European Journal of Information Systems*, **5**, pp. 143–160.

Williamson, O. (1975) *Markets and Hierarchies*, Free Press, New York.

Williamson, O. (1996) *The Mechanism of Governance*, Oxford

University Press, Oxford.

Woodward, J. (1965) *Industrial Organization: Theory and Practice*, Oxford University Press, Oxford.

Vancil, R. and Buddrus, L. (1978) *Decentralization: Managerial Ambiguity by Design*, Dow Jones Irwin, Homewood, Ill.

Von Simson, E. (1990) 'The "Centrally Decentralized" IS Organization', *Harvard Business Review*, July–August.

Zmud, R., Boynton, A. and Jacobs, G. (1986) 'The Information Economy: A New Perspective for Effective Information Systems Management', *Data Base*, Fall.

CHAPTER SEVEN

Information Systems Organization: The Roles of Users and Specialists

DAVID F. FEENY, MICHAEL J. EARL AND BRIAN EDWARDS

INTRODUCTION

The most immediately visible component of any organizational design is usually the 'structure' or vertical component – the definition of organizational units, the reporting relationships for each of them, and the distribution of responsibilities and authority. A second component, which may be less well defined in the design or its operation, is the 'process' or horizontal component – the way in which different organizational units work with each other when necessary to achieve organizational objectives. When organizational arrangements for IS are being considered, this second component takes on a particular importance because of the well-documented difficulties experienced between IS professionals and representatives of other parts of the organization. Problematic relationships are seen to arise regardless of choice of IS structure. Corporations which demolish a central 'ivory tower' IS function by devolving resources into business-based IS units regularly find they have created a series of smaller ivory towers. In this chapter we consider how organizational arrangements can foster effective working relationships between IS specialists and the 'users' they serve, irrespective of their positioning within a structural framework.

USERS, IS SPECIALISTS AND INTEGRATION

A starting point is to recognize that IS professionals typically possess – or at least are perceived to possess – particular personal characteristics

151

which inhibit their working relationships with other members of the organization. Couger and Zawacki (1980) reported that IS specialists consistently demonstrated a higher need for constant challenge ('growth need strength') but a lower need for interpersonal relationships ('social need strength') than other professional groupings. Their findings have since been the subject of some academic debate (for example, Ferratt and Short, 1986, 1988, 1990; Inmon and Hartman, 1990). But among practitioners the perception of differences remains: in a survey of IS directors by Grindley (1995), 46 per cent reported that a 'culture gap' between IS professionals and business counterparts represented their most important challenge. The culture gap was demonstrated by contrasting approaches to tasks and problem solving, which inhibited effective working relationships. The description remains consistent with the earlier findings of authors such as Edstrom (1977), Gingras and McLean (1979), Zmud and Cox (1979) when they reported on the distinctive cognitive styles of IS professionals.

The importance attached to the culture gap by the IS directors may be readily understood when one considers how the literature of information management is permeated with appeals for the 'involvement', 'commitment' and even 'ownership' of those who are the intended beneficiaries of IT investments. The challenge is further underlined when Barki and Hartwick (1989) define the necessary 'involvement' as a 'subjective psychological state, reflecting importance and personal relevance'; it must be distinguished from mere 'participation' by users in IS-related activity. In the language of contingency theorists such as Lawrence and Lorsch (1967), we are seeking a high degree of 'integration' between groups (of users and IS specialists) who exhibit significant 'differentiation' in terms of personal attributes. The work of Lawrence and Lorsch reminds us that distinctive personal characteristics may be expected to be consistently associated with the ability to master a set of fast-changing technologies. A group of IS professionals who are selected to be less 'differentiated' and easier to 'integrate' may lack the necessary technical proficiency. To address the challenge of integration Lawrence and Lorsch (1967), and later Galbraith (1977), suggested a range of integrating mechanisms. Many of these can be recognized in the various prescriptions proposed for the IS field over the years. These include integrative process designs, such as Mumford's (1983) ETHICS model for systems development; and the use of particular individuals as integrators, such as the 'hybrid managers' investigated by Earl and Skyrme (1990). More recently, in the context of systems development, the research of Taylor-Cummings (1993) (see Chapter 8), has highlighted the importance to integration of contextual arrangements – users and specialists reporting to the same project manager, shared physical space, shared goals and incentives, etc.

Taylor-Cummings found a strong consensus on a set of 'goal' arrangements for IS development, but the practice of the organizations researched generally fell well short of their aspirations. There would seem to be two major reasons why organizations struggle to implement the integration arrangements they see to be most appropriate:

- First these arrangements are seen to be expensive and demanding of scarce resources. There is a strong temptation to compromise and settle for the 'practical' rather than the 'ideal'.
- Second, the 'ideal' arrangements may challenge the existing culture of the organization and/or the IS function. The arrangements may therefore be resisted or subverted (see, for example, Davidson's (1993) study of organizational attempts to introduce joint application development workshops).

These difficulties may be diminished by a more targeted and selective implementation of such integrating mechanisms than is generally espoused. We propose a contingency approach, arguing that appropriate integration mechanisms are a function of the IS activity being addressed, and the maturity of the technology on which it is based. We argue that 'expensive' integration mechanisms based on teamworking are only required when uncertainty is high. As a technology and its application become familiar, then simpler, more contractual, arrangements are not only adequate, they are actually superior.

In the remainder of this chapter we introduce a contingency model for managing relationships between users and IS specialists, and explore its implications. Our proposals are based on analysis of the organizational experiences we encountered during the Earl, Edwards and Feeny study described in Chapter 6, illuminated by the findings of other authors.

THE CONCEPT OF TECHNOLOGICAL MATURITY

The first proposition of our model is that integration mechanisms should vary with the maturity of the technology in question. The idea that information management processes should be a function of the relative maturity of the technology is not of course a new one. The stage theory of Gibson and Nolan (1974) suggested a pattern of practices for the management of computing, dependent on positioning relative to an S-shaped expenditure curve which serves as a proxy for organizational learning. Although Gibson and Nolan were at the time describing the evolution of the 'EDP department', the department in 1974 was synonymous with the exploitation of a single broad strand of technology for business data processing. Gibson and Nolan themselves predicted that there would be 'more S-shaped curves as new EDP technologies emerge'. Subsequently McFarlan and McKenney (1982) detected the same pattern of assimilation for office automation, and other new technology capabilities; and Raho, Belchlav and Fielder (1987) pointed to a conceptual fit with the broader work on technology diffusion by Rogers (1962) and others. Henderson and Treacy (1986) used the McFarlan and McKenney model to suggest IS management perspectives appropriate to each phase of the assimilation of end-user computing. Our own model therefore follows well-established precedents in proposing that *user–specialist relationships must be planned and managed separately for each distinctive technology, in the light of the relative maturity of that technology.*

The phrases 'distinctive technology' and 'relative maturity' elude precise definition, but our experience is that they do represent meaningful and helpful concepts in practice. In our field study of 1987 we distinguished between six areas of technology which we called business transaction processing, data communications, end-user computing, office automation, scientific computing, and automation of physical/build processes. For each area we proposed benchmarks to denote an organization's position in relation to a four-phase model of assimilation. None of our interviewees had any difficulty with our methodology, either conceptually or pragmatically in terms of being able to locate their organization relative to our benchmarks. They readily accepted the implication that they could be, and often were, at different states of assimilation across these six technologies. They also anticipated that further distinctive technologies would emerge and require their own separate but similar patterns of learning, assimilation, and diffusion.

The 'relative maturity' of a technology can be considered with reference to the technology *per se*; to the application which the technology is being used to support; and to the organization which is using the technology. For example, a technology is classified as having 'low' maturity if it exhibits a high rate of change in terms of function provided, technical specification, and performance; as function and specification stabilize it moves towards a classification of 'high' maturity even though price/performance may continue to improve. On the other hand, there is a real sense in which maturity is 'low' when a well-established technology is used to implement a radically new application, or when the implementing organization has little prior experience of the application or technology (even though both have been successfully exploited elsewhere). As we shall describe, the model can be used to suggest appropriate integration arrangements in each of these different contexts.

From user to specialist focus

The second proposition of our model is that integration mechanisms should vary: to engender teamworking between users and IS specialists when technology maturity is low; to coordinate the separate contributions of users and IS specialists when technology maturity is high. We describe this as a migration from a 'user focus' to a 'specialist focus'. In the 'user focus' domain (see Figure 7.1) the overriding objective is to identify and deliver the potential benefits of new technology, to search out 'instrumental effectiveness' (Thompson, 1967). With high technological uncertainty it is inappropriate to closely specify tasks for individuals. Effective integration mechanisms will be of the type identified by Taylor-Cummings (1993), fostering collective effort towards a single shared goal expressed in terms of business benefits. While the goal may be a fixture, tactics and plans will change frequently as learning is achieved and uncertainty resolved; the team culture provides the flexibility to respond to such changes. The management style is consultative, to benefit from the perspective of each individual. But the leadership is effectively (and probably formally) invested on the user side, because the key question is 'Can this type of technology bring business benefits?', not 'Which product/supplier is the leader in this technology?'

	User focus	Specialist focus
Principal concern	Business benefits	Professional excellence
Operating style	Teamworking	Individual roles
Performance appraisal	Shared goal	Contractual responsibility
Leadership	User	Specialist

Figure 7.1   Contrasting modes of integration

By contrast, in the 'specialist focus' domain the concern is to achieve IS professional excellence, the 'economic efficiency' which Thompson (1967) defines as performance of the specified task at minimum cost. The assimilation of the technology is sufficiently advanced for the 'demand' side of the equation to be clear. Hence users can be expected and obliged to state clearly their requirements; IS specialists can be charged with selecting and delivering the most appropriate technical responses. Rather than teamworking and a sense of communal responsibility, the emphasis is on defining individual responsibilities and the boundaries and interfaces between them. These are enshrined in a contract of service between users and IS specialists, which is the principal integration mechanism and may be the basis for formal chargeout of IS activity. Leadership passes to the IS specialist in the sense that the key question has become 'What is the best choice of technology (to meet a well-defined need)?'

Integration by IS activity
The third and final proposition of our model is that the transition from 'user' to 'specialist' focus should occur at different times for each main area of IS activity. Four such areas of IS activity are identified:

1. *Delivery* refers to the physical provision of IS service, the operations function. It encompasses both direct service activities and also those activities which are required to sustain such a service – equipment planning and provision, fallback/recovery procedures, systems programming, etc.
2. *Support* covers the assistance provided by the IS function to consumers of IS services. Activities include education, general advice and guidance, troubleshooting or user problems.
3. *Development* reflects standard IS terminology for the activity required to produce the hardware and more especially the software for planned applications.
4. *Strategy* refers to the activities involved in determining the portfolio of applications which should be undertaken. The tasks in this area include identification of new application opportunities, evaluation of opportunities compared to business needs, financial assessment of proposals, resource management in the light of priorities.

In each of these areas the IS function needs to interact with the user community, and may do so with the equivalent of either user focus or specialist focus. For example, in the 'delivery' activity IS can provide qualified operators to work in a user-based team working on a departmental computer; or alternatively IS can respond to a user-prepared service level agreement request, basing its response on whatever technical platform it believes represents the best price/performance option. At the 'strategy' level, Earl (1993) has identified five different approaches from his field research. The 'organizational' approach, in which IS is part of the team pursuing a nominated business theme, is clearly equivalent to user focus; the 'business led' approach, in which IS attempts to identify IS investments based on top managements' statement of business strategy, qualifies as a form of specialist focus.

As depicted in Figure 7.2, we suggest that for each distinctive technology the transition from user to specialist focus follows the same sequence: starting with delivery, followed by support, and then

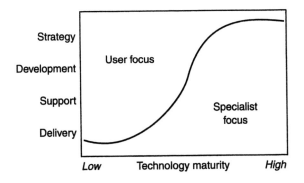

Figure 7.2   Contingency model of user–specialist integration

development. The assumption that this is the sequence in which learning takes place and uncertainty is resolved is supported by Curley and Pyburn (1982). These authors suggest that in contrast to earlier hard-wired technologies, information technologies require a relatively short period of 'Type A' learning (how to operate the technology) followed by a much more substantial period of 'Type B' learning (how to exploit the technology). Curley and Pyburn's emphasis on the prolonged nature of Type B learning can be related to the S-shaped boundary between the user focus and specialist focus domains: the transition from user to specialist focus can be expected to be fairly rapid in the case of delivery; a much more gradual transition is likely to be appropriate in the development phase as relatively familiar technologies can still be the platform for fundamentally new applications, involving high levels of uncertainty.

INTERPRETING THE MODEL

To illustrate more clearly the potential contribution of the model, consider a particular technology at three points in time within its lifecycle.

In the *early* phase of the life-cycle, when maturity is low, users are confronted with a new and uncertain capability and the technology is characterized by rapid change. The model suggests that all areas of IS activity should be guided by a user focus. The expectation is that a mixed team of business and IS people is seeking to determine the potential value of the new technology. Problems are addressed and resolved by face-to-face meetings within each team, requiring excellent communication between team members. Indeed Lockett (1987) suggests from his research that each team must comprise a continuous spectrum of understandings between the business and the technology to ensure that misunderstandings do not occur. Each team will be led by a project champion from the user side (Runge, 1985; Lockett, 1987) who is directing and driving the project towards the valued business goal. The reputation at stake is that of the project champion and therefore, with or without due debate within the team, the ultimate authority is his or hers – whether the decision involves the application area to be tackled, the project design, or the equipment to be used. In achieving successful innovation, such champions are not constrained by established business or IS procedures in arriving at decisions. Most decisions are dominated by considerations of effectiveness, speed, quality, risk minimization, rather than cost efficiency.

In the *middle* phase of the life-cycle, some of the emphasis has changed as the delivery and support activities migrate to the specialist focus domain. The potential of the technology has been demonstrated, and early benefits are being achieved. It is time to ensure that those benefits are not jeopardized by system failure, loss of databases, inferior service. Since the direction of development of the technology is by now more clear, as is its role within the business, it is also time to devise formal standards which will relate to its use. While the user still drives the application or 'IS' strategy, the specialist's insight is used to develop an 'IT' strategy or technical architecture which will allow the consistent and efficient exploitation of the technology across the business. The specialist also accepts clear management responsibility for the delivery and support activities, contracting to provide whatever level of service is required (and can be afforded) by users who are now well informed of their needs in relation to established IS activity. However, the development activity remains within the user focus domain. The potential for further learning about how to use the technology requires a continuing emphasis on teamwork between users and specialist, supported by the use of interactive development processes such as prototyping. The development 'contract' remains a soft one, with a sense of shared purpose to achieve a successful system, and no refusals to make specification changes, no litigious disputes.

Finally in the *mature* phase of the life-cycle, all IS activity except strategy has migrated to the specialist focus domain. Strategy remains in the user focus domain because it is still essential that IS is informed of and responsive to the changing needs of the business. However, once the strategy is clear, the users are now sufficiently sophisticated in relation to this mature technology to be able (and to be required) to make a precise statement of their needs for new systems. These specifications are used to negotiate a formal development contract with an internal or external supply source, enforced with financial penalty clauses applying when either side deviates from contract. We have reached a point where development, support and delivery are all contracted to the specialist. Formal charging procedures apply to all three areas – but the user is well able to exercise judgements about value for money, and an efficient market mechanism for further exploitation of that technology is in place.

Organization versus technology maturity
There may be occasions when the technology maturity is relatively high in the general marketplace, but a particular organization is seeking to exploit that technology for the first time. In these cases, the model can be used to provide a number of alternative prescriptions:

1. The organization concerned may properly ignore the fact that maturity is high in the marketplace, and proceed on the basis that maturity is low in its own case. It will therefore adopt a 'user focus' in all spheres of IS activity.
2. Alternatively the organization may seek to by-pass the inefficiencies of a 'user focus' regime by buying in from the marketplace experienced IT management and staff. This may enable them to move immediately to 'specialist focus' in the delivery activity; however, 'user focus' will be required in the support, delivery and strategy areas because of the inexperience of the user personnel. One of the companies in our field study of 1987 had adopted this combination for a major new project with conspicuous success.
3. In some cases the organization concerned may perceive that the application required is well established in the general marketplace, in addition to the technology on which it is based; there may be a 'package' solution available. Nevertheless, our model should be interpreted as counselling *against* moving directly to a 'specialist focus' in the development area. Our experience is that high uncertainty surrounds the implementation of even a package when the user is inexperienced. Only if experienced/'mature' *users* are brought into the relevant area of the organization can a rapid transition to 'specialist focus' in the delivery activity be planned with confidence.

Prescription versus practice
Our model provides guidance on what we believe to be effective arrangements for integrating the efforts of users and IS specialists. It is a prescriptive not a descriptive model. Hence it may be instructive to contrast the prescriptions of the model with generally reported experience of the assimilation of technologies.

Data processing tended to spend its early days inside the controller's department, from the standpoint of both reporting line and applications emphasis. Integration between users and specialists was relatively straightforward within the department's boundaries. However, during the 1960s and 1970s the application portfolio broadened – with systems being developed for the use of many other departments – and reports of dissatisfaction accumulated. In 1970, Zani (Zani, 1970) claimed that 'no tool has proved so disappointing in use'. As Bostrom and Heinen (1977) reported, attempts to explain the shortcomings consistently stressed behavioural rather than technical problems. Failure was associated with ineffective communications between users and developers (Edstrom, 1977); and the dominant power of specialists who 'consciously or unconsciously directed the development and use of computing' (Bostrom and Heinen, 1977). By contrast, success was associated with user rather than specialist origination of projects (Powers and Dickson, 1973); a priori involvement of users (Zmud's (1979) summary of previous research); and a fluid, iterative design process, characterized by collaboration between users and developers (Bostrom and Heinen, 1977). In the language of our model, these are descriptions of failure stemming from development under specialist focus while maturity is far too low; and prescriptions for success consistent with development under user focus. The welcome for prototyping techniques (Earl, 1978, Naumann and Jenkins, 1982) confirms the contemporary need for user focus. But prototyping is not a permanent panacea for all development activity – it is unlikely for example to be the right tool for development of a replacement payroll system. When a relatively mature technology is applied to a well-understood application area, development under specialist focus is entirely appropriate.

The literature reporting on *end-user computing* represents a sharp contrast to that on data processing. The introduction of personal computers (PCs) is seen to be characterized by an extreme form of user focus, with the specialist frequently absent from the partnership. Benson (1983) found that in only eight of 20 organizations surveyed did the IS department have a stated policy towards PCs; and in only two was there any planned support for their users. But the issues to which Benson and others drew attention are not resulting failures of application development. On the contrary, Benson refers to user 'euphoria' and the development of further applications as familiarity with the technology increases; Gerrity and Rockart (1986) write of the critical importance of end-user computing, and refer to widely publicized benefits. The concerns that are highlighted relate to the other three areas of activity – delivery, support and strategy – and can be seen to arise from the absence of well-directed IS involvement. For the delivery activity, the recommendations made (Benson, 1983; Rockart and Flannery, 1983; Gerrity and Rockart, 1986) amount to a call for a specialist focus regime: there are critical issues of data provision and security, and a lack of documentation; standards are needed to enable efficiencies to be achieved in purchasing, operations and support. On the other hand, support apparently should remain a while longer under user focus: distributed out to the users (Rockart and Flannery, 1983); with an emphasis on end-use rather than technology knowledge, plus strong inter-personal skills (Gerrity and Rockart, 1986). Finally, the strategy activity has been overlooked. There is a critical need (Benson, 1983) for IS to persuade senior business management of the need for 'top-level planning' to ensure that the 'bottom up' movement does not lead to disruption and chaos. Gerrity and Rockart (1986) similarly highlight the need for a stated end-user strategy, and the proactive targeting of critical applications. In short, end-user computing was typically introduced under a user focus regime and suffered few birth-pangs; the model highlights where and how action needed to be taken as the technology matured.

The successful introduction of office automation can also be associated with the prescriptions of the model. For example, Meyer (1983) reporting on a study of 35 organizations, listed success factors which correlate closely with the definition of a user focus regime: an office automation pilot should be clearly targeted at the solution of an important business problem; implemented by a team which includes business, administrative and IS staff, with an emphasis on collaboration and interpersonal skills; IS specialists should be seen as 'facilitators' rather than 'experts'. Interestingly, Meyer also concluded that IS rather than user control over equipment selection was not worth fighting for 'at this stage'. Such control was not associated with successful introduction, and could be counter productive in alienating users. Curley (1984) also emphasized the importance of linking the introduction of office automation to an achievable and desirable corporate goal; and of allowing for/planning for user experimentation and learning rather than attempting early formalization of applications. By contrast, Hirschheim and Feeny (1986) suggested that the 20 office automation pilots funded by the UK government were largely unsuccessful because of a focus on specific technologies and applications rather than business problems – tantamount to operating from the start under a specialist focus.

There are two other established strands of information technology on which it is difficult to comment because of the lack of research literature. A general view of *scientific computing,* consistently supported by anecdotal evidence, would be that it was introduced under a user focus regime and has only slowly migrated any activity areas to specialist focus. As a result, scientific computing tends to be rated highly in terms of effectiveness, at least as measured by user satisfaction. In our own study of 1987, it was noticeable that the assimilation of scientific computing through the four-stage model was on average further advanced than any of the other five referenced areas of information technology. And yet scientific computing never featured among the 'war stories' revealed when we asked about the company's history and heritage of IT. However, the efficiency of the scientific computing activity could be strongly questioned, with evidence of some organizations operating hundreds of lightly loaded minicomputers, representing so many different architectures that acquisition and maintenance costs were extremely high.

The case of data communications is intriguing since for many businesses in the late 1980s it represented an unfamiliar technology despite quite a lengthy history in the overall marketplace. The prescriptions of the model would therefore be to buy in specialist skills and operate delivery under specialist focus; while maintaining a user focus regime for support, development and direction. In practice this could be seen to have been an appropriate prescription in the UK life insurance industry (Feeny and Knott, 1988). Three network provider companies targeted this sector and promoted the concept of links between insurance companies and intermediaries (distribution channels). Two of the three – IBM and British Telecom – were large companies offering technically sophisticated networks; but with preconceived ideas of how they should be used. Neither won significant business. The successful company – ISTEL – was very small by comparison and offered a relatively unsophisticated network based on viewdata; but they went beyond the network to provide an application service which they had jointly developed with the largest intermediary to address the key business requirement.

The model and sourcing strategy

A further application of the model can be to provide input to decisions on the sourcing of IS activity. Lacity and Hirschheim (1993) and Willcocks and Fitzgerald (1994) have warned of the dangers of contracting out the entire IS function. Our model, adapted as in Figure 7.3, can help to guide a more selective use of the external market for IS services, taking advantage of its abilities without incurring unacceptable risks.

Wherever the model suggests that specialist focus is appropriate for a particular activity/technology combination, there is potential for what is normally called outsourcing. Since the business is sufficiently clear of its requirements to operate in specialist focus mode, it may reasonably choose to contract with an external rather than internal provider. The contract will specify performance of a well-defined task to required standards. Facilities management of data centres (delivery activities)

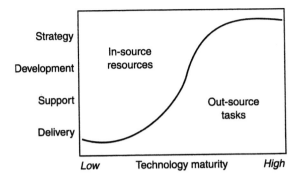

Figure 7.3   Sourcing strategy

are well established examples; contracts to provide the support activity for the population of PCs are also becoming common.

On the other hand when the model prescribes a user focus regime, the implication is that outsourcing will not be appropriate. There will be insufficient organizational learning in place for a robustly specified performance contract to be developed, and the buyer will face the problems identified in the classic work of Williamson (1975) – information impactedness, opportunist suppliers, future uncertainty, high switching costs. This does not mean that the external market should not be used at all. But the contract should now focus on needed resource rather than required task, and the resource acquired will be under internal rather than external management. 'Insourcing' is one way of describing such a use of the market. One familiar example would be to bring in from a software house a technical specialist to join the in-house development project team. Such a resource should be acquired on a daily rate basis, ideally with an incentive payment geared to achievement of the in-house team's own business goal. The objective is to maintain the teamwork culture of the user focus regime. The notion of using this model for IT sourcing strategy is further developed, based on empirical work, in Chapter 11.

CONCLUSIONS

We have presented a model whose purpose is to guide the management of new information technologies. It differs from one of the best known models – Nolan's (1979) six stages of assimilation – in a number of ways, but largely in taking each distinctive technology as a unit of analysis, whereas Nolan is concerned with the management of IS resources overall. The prescriptions of Allen (1987) for charging out IS services, and those of Dearden (1987) for contracting out, are also targeted at the IS function as a whole – mistakenly in our view. Allen's goal of 'functional pricing' and Dearden's of market contracting we see to be very appropriate to a mature technology – but only to a mature technology. Yet there is little to indicate that information technology in general can be treated as mature for decades to come.

Our model is more comparable with the original Gibson and Nolan (1974) stage model (for data processing); or with McFarlan and McKenney's generalized four-stage model. However, neither is a very close match. The Gibson and Nolan model has little to say about users rather than specialists until stage 3 when they recommend that analysts are devolved to user areas to act as conduits between users and programmers. Nolan (1979) did add a set of user awareness benchmarks to his expanded six-stage model, but continues to place far less emphasis than we do on user–specialist integration; users are relatively insignificant figures until stage 4. Our own stronger emphasis on integration receives some support from the empirical testing of Nolan's stages by Drury (1983). Drury found that development of user awareness – alone of Nolan's five benchmark variables – was consistently and significantly associated with progress towards effective and efficient exploitation of data processing.

McFarlan and McKenney's model is closer to our own, but with two major differences. First, McFarlan and McKenney (1982) are describing four phases *in the early life* of a technology; our model is attempting to prescribe throughout the life. Secondly, McFarlan and McKenney do not distinguish as we do between delivery, support, development and direction. Thus, in their phase 3 an apparently complete transition takes place from an entrepreneurial to a control-oriented group. Our categorization of IS activity into four areas allows for the prescription of the most appropriate form of management for each activity area, according to the status of technology maturity.

Other stages of growth models continue to be proposed: for example, Mills (1983), Summer (1985), and Magal *et al.*, (1988) all subscribe to such a model for the development of information centre management. Galliers and Sutherland (1994) have produced a revised model developed out of Gibson and Nolan (1974). It seems that the basic idea is a consistently powerful one for those who study the assimilation of new technology, despite consistent problems in establishing empirical support. Our own model is probably a particularly difficult one in terms of any formal validation. It sets out to be prescriptive, and its application clearly requires judgements to be made – what is a distinctive technology?, what level of maturity has been reached?, where exactly is the boundary line between user focus and specialists domains? Yet its prescriptions do seem to be consistent with research-based findings. Of particular note is the support it receives in recent research into sourcing decisions and their outcomes (Lacity, Willcocks and Feeny, 1996; see also Chapter 11).

Finally, we have found since 1987 that managers in organizations – both from IS and the business side – consistently confirm that the ideals of the model relate to their experience and provide insights. These managers are confronted with more and more strands of technology to manage, and an increasing variety of options in terms of where to obtain resources and how to deploy them. The purpose of the model is to prompt managers into asking critical questions about the management of each IS activity, and to provide them with first-level guidance on which management options are likely to be appropriate given the nature of that activity.

REFERENCES

Allen, B. (1987) 'Making Information Services Pay its Way', *Harvard Business Review*, Jan–Feb, pp. 57–63.

Barki, H. and Hartwick, J. (1989) 'Rethinking the Concept of User Involvement', *MIS Quarterly*, March, pp. 53–63.

Benson, D. (1983) 'A Field Study of End User Computing: Findings and Issues', *MIS Quarterly*, December, pp. 35–45.

Bostrom, R. and Heinen, J. (1977) 'MIS Problems and Failures: A Socio-Technical Perspective', *MIS Quarterly*, September, pp. 17–32.

Couger, J. and Zawacki, R. (1980) *Motivating and Managing Computer Personnel*, Wiley, New York.

Curley, K. and Pyburn, P. (1982) 'Intellectual Technologies: The Key to Improving White Collar Productivity', *Sloan Management Review*, Fall, pp. 31–39.

Curley, K. (1984) 'Are There Any Real Benefits from Office Automation?', *Business Horizons*, July–August pp. 37–42.

Davidson, E. (1993) 'An Exploratory Study of Joint Application Design (JAD) in Information Systems Delivery', *Proceedings of the 14th International Conference on Information Systems*, December, pp. 271–283.

Dearden, J. (1987) 'The Withering Away of the IS Organization', *Sloan Management Review*, Summer, pp. 87–91.

Drury, D. (1983) 'An Empirical Assessment of the Stages of DP Growth', *MIS Quarterly*, June, pp. 59–70.

Earl, M. (1993) 'Experiences in Strategic Information Systems Planning', *MIS Quarterly*, March, pp. 1–20.

Earl, M. (1978) 'Prototype Systems for Accounting, Information and Control', *Accounting Organizations and Society*, March, pp. 161–170.

Earl, M. and Skyrme, D. (1990) *Hybrid Managers. What Do We Know About Them?*, Oxford Institute of Information Management, Research and Discussion Paper 90/6, Templeton College, Oxford.

Edstrom, A. (1977) 'User Influence and the Success of MIS Projects: A Contingency Approach', *Human Relations*, **30**, (7), pp. 589–607.

Feeny, D. and Knott, P. (1988) *Information Technology and Marketing in the UK Life Insurance Industry*, Oxford Institute of Information Management, Research and Discussion Paper 88/5, Templeton College, Oxford.

Ferratt, T. W. and Short, L. (1986) 'Are Information Systems People Different: An Investigation of Motivational Differences', *MIS Quarterly*, Dec, pp. 377–387.

Ferratt, T. W. and Short, L. (1988) 'Are Information Systems People Different: An Investigation of How They Are and Should Be Managed', *MIS Quarterly*, Sept, pp. 427–443.

Ferratt, T. W. and Short, L. (1990) 'Patterns of Motivation: Beyond Differences Between IS and Non-IS People', *MIS Quarterly, Issues and Opinions*, March, pp. 3–6.

Galbraith, J. (1977) *Designing Complex Organizations*, Addison-Wesley, Reading, Mass.

Galliers, R. and Sutherland, A. (1994) 'Information Systems Management and Strategy Formulation: The "Stages of Growth" Model Revisited', in Galliers, R. and Baker, B. (eds.) *Strategic Information Management*, Butterworth-Heinemann, London.

Gerrity, T. and Rockart, J. (1986) 'End User Computing: Are you a Leader of a Laggard?', *Sloan Management Review*, Summer, pp. 25–34.

Gibson, C. and Nolan, R. (1974) 'Managing the Four Stages of EDP Growth', *Harvard Business Review*, Jan–Feb, pp. 76–88.

Gingras, L. and McLean, E. (1979) *A Study of Users and Designers of Information Systems,* IS Working Paper 2–79, Graduate School of Management, UCLA, Los Angeles.

Grindley, K. (1995) *Managing IT at Board Level*, Price Waterhouse/Pitman, London.

Henderson, J. and Treacy, M. (1986) 'Managing End User Computing For Competitive Advantage', *Sloan Management Review*, Winter, pp. 3–14.

Hirschheim, R. and Feeny, D. (1986) 'Experiences with Office Automation: Some Lessons and Recommendations', *Journal of General Management*, Winter, pp. 25–40.

Inmon, J. and Hartman, S. (1990) 'Rethinking the Issue of whether IS People are Different from Non-IS People: Issues and Opinions', *MIS Quarterly*, March, pp. 1–2.

Lacity, M. and Hirschheim, R. (1993) 'The Information Systems

Outsourcing Bandwagon', *Sloan Management Review*, Fall, pp. 73–86.

Lacity, M., Willcocks, L. and Feeny, D. (1996) 'The Value of Selective IT Sourcing', *Sloan Management Review*, **37**, (3), pp. 13–25.

Lawrence, P. and Lorsch, J. (1967) *Organization and Environment: Managing Differentiation and Integration*, Division of Research, Graduate School of Business Administration. Harvard Business School, Cambridge, Mass.

Lockett, M. (1987) *The Factors Behind Successful IT Innovation*, Oxford Institute of Information Management, Research and Discussion Paper 87/9, Templeton College, Oxford.

Magal, S., Carr, H. and Watson, H. (1988) 'Critical Success Factors for Information Center Managers', *MIS Quarterly*, September, pp. 413–425.

McFarlan, F. and McKenney, J. (1982) 'The Information Archipelago: Maps and Bridges', *Harvard Business Review*, Sept–Oct, pp. 109–119.

Meyer, N. (1983) 'The Office Automation Cookbook: Management Stategies for Getting Office Automation Moving', *Sloan Management Review*, Winter, pp. 51–60.

Mills, C. (1983) 'The Information Center', *DRS Journal*, Spring, pp. 42–46.

Mumford, E. (1983) *Designing Human Systems for New Technology: The ETHICS Method*, Manchester Business School, Manchester.

Naumann, J. and Jenkins, A. (1982) 'Prototyping: The New Paradigm for Systems Development', *MIS Quarterly*, September, pp. 29–44.

Nolan, R. (1979) Managing the Crisis in Data Processing, *Harvard Business Review*, March–April, pp. 115–126.

Powers, R. and Dickson, G. (1973) 'MIS Project Management: Myths, Opinions and Reality', *California Management Review*, Spring, pp. 147–156.

Raho, L., Belchlav, J. and Fiedler, K. (1987) 'Assimilating New Technology into the Organization: An Assessment of McFarlan and McKenney's Model', *MIS Quarterly*, March, pp. 47–57.

Rockart, J. and Flannery, L. (1983) 'The Management of End User Computing', *Communications of the ACM*, October, pp. 776–784.

Rogers, E. (1962) *The Diffusion of Innovations*, Free Press, New York.

Runge, D. (1985) *Using Telecommunications for Competitive Advantage*, Doctoral Dissertation, Oxford University, Oxford.

Summer, M. (1985) 'Organization and Management of the Information Center', *Journal of Systems Management*, November, pp. 10–15.

Taylor-Cummings, A. (1993) *Bridging the User–IS Gap*, Oxford University Doctoral Dissertation.

Thompson, J. (1967) *Organizations in Action*, McGraw-Hill, New York.

Willcocks, L. and Fitzgerald, G. (1994), *A Business Guide to Outsourcing IT*, Business Intelligence, London.

Williamson, O. (1975) *Markets and Hierarchies*, Free Press, New York.

Zani, W. (1970) 'Blueprint for MIS', *Harvard Business Review*, Nov–Dec, pp. 95–100.

Zmud, R. (1979) 'Individual Differences and MIS Success: A Review of the Empirical Literature', *Management Science*, October, pp. 966–979.

Zmud, R. and Cox, J. (1979) 'The Implementation Process: A Change Approach', *MIS Quarterly*, **3**, (2), pp. 35–43.

Part Three

Managing Strategic
Technology Projects

CHAPTER EIGHT

The Development and Implementation of Systems: Bridging the User–IS Gap

ANDREA TAYLOR-CUMMINGS AND DAVID F. FEENY

INTRODUCTION

A 'culture gap' between IS professionals and their business counterparts has been blamed for many of the systems development problems and failures that have occurred over the last four decades. The concept persists unquestioned, becoming embedded in the language used to describe user–IS interaction, despite the lack of precise definition about what it actually is. 'Definitions' used are merely examples or symptoms of its existence, but the term is so widely accepted that knowledge has perhaps been acquired through osmosis. What is suggested, however, is that the costs of the existence of a culture gap between these two groups is escalating to phenomenal proportions. A 1991 Price Waterhouse (1991, 1992) survey of IT directors in the UK found that 47 per cent of IT directors stated their main problem was the culture gap existing between IT and business professionals, and 56 per cent believed that the culture gap was losing or seriously delaying IT opportunities for their company to gain competitive advantage. The difficulty is that despite the elusive nature, the origins and sources of the destructive forces involved must be identified before the issue can be adequately addressed. The persistence of the symptoms strongly suggest that previous methods have not been conclusively successful.

The research described in this chapter sought to address the issue of the culture gap on the premise that the destructive effects stemmed from negative attitudes and preconceptions developed and perfected

171

over time. This approach contrasts with the prevailing belief that the problem results from fundamental differences between the two groups. The research borrowed perspectives from literature on organizational behaviour, in an effort to develop a richer understanding of the issue. By viewing organizations based on two metaphors – organizations as cultural systems, and organizations as political systems (Morgan, 1986) – a definition of the problem was developed based on concepts of cultures and subcultures, diverse interests, conflict and power. A research model of user–IS integration, based on the concept of shared values through socialization processes was proposed. The model was tested primarily through the use of case studies, and secondarily through the administration of a large-scale questionnaire survey.

EXISTING PERSPECTIVES

Before describing the research and its findings, let us consider the antecedents of the research project. Problematic relationships between IS specialists and their business counterparts have been a recurrent theme in the IS literature since the application of computers to business problems in the 1950s. Several attempts at improving the effectiveness of user–IS relationships have been made over the years. Among the first of such attempts was the introduction of the systems development life cycle (SDLC) in which well-defined phases of development provided a basis for management and control (Davis and Olson, 1985). Later, influenced by the prevailing systems theory, attempts to address the 'technical competence but social incompetence' (Mumford et al., 1978) of such structured methods led to the emergence of the concept of user participation, with notable contributions on the subject from Mumford et al., (1978), Land (1982), Mumford (1983) and Mumford (1985).

Various system design methodologies (for example the socio-technical system (STS) approach, (Bostrom and Heinen, 1977), soft systems methodology (Checkland, 1981), joint application design (JAD, developed by IBM in 1977) and ETHICS (Mumford, 1987)) were developed to incorporate ideas of user participation based on a paradigm of learning. Other techniques emerging from this idea include the use of:

- *prototypes* (Earl, 1978; Naumann and Jenkins, 1982; Robey and Markus, 1984; Mahmood, 1987);
- *multidisciplinary project teams* (Lockett, 1987);
- *steering committees* (Gibson and Nolan, 1974; Lucas, 1975; Robey and Markus, 1984; Lockett, 1987);
- *facilitators* (Mumford, 1987);

- *third-party intervention* (DeBrabander and Edstrom, 1977; DeBrabander and Thiers, 1984);
- *user project managers, champions and sponsors* (Lucas, 1975; Runge, 1985; Lockett, 1987; Earl *et al.*, 1988).

Education, the suggested long-term solution to improved relationships (Mumford *et al.*, 1978), has been given consistent emphasis over time. Based on marketing concepts, and the drive to 'get close to the customer' (Peters and Waterman, 1982), new IS structures like decentralization, federal arrangements and the use of account managers have been adopted. Consistent with the emphasis on new structures to forge better relationships is the drive to elevate the status of the head of IS to board level, or at least to the level of top management team (Feeny *et al.*, 1992). *Partnerships* (Henderson, 1990) and *hybrids* (Palmer and Ottley, 1990; Skyrme, 1992) represent the latest proposed solutions to the problem of poor relationships between IS specialists and their business counterparts.

The assumptions
In surveying the integrating mechanisms proposed to date, two key observations are made. The first is that a premium has been placed on communication as a means of improving user–IS relationships. Despite the ambitious intentions of the concept of user participation, all the mechanisms seem to address negative attitudes and preconceptions indirectly through increased communications rather than directly as an issue in its own right. With few exceptions, notably Lucas (1975), most research embracing the relevance of user attitudes primarily investigated attitude towards the information system being developed and the changes imposed, rather than attitudes towards and perceptions of IS personnel (see for example, Schewe, 1976; Robey, 1979; Ginzberg, 1981). This suggests that the culture gap has been interpreted consistently as 'communication gap', with the implicit assumption that improved communication and understanding will alleviate the problem.

By comparison with the concept of integration, these solutions merely attempt to improve the *translation* of business requirements into system features by supposedly facilitating better communication. However, more communication is not always the answer to poor communication. Rather, more communication may increase the number of opportunities to *demonstrate* that a problem exists, thereby aggravating the situation with no attempt at resolving it. Further, by emphasizing the need to have 'middle men', the suggestions have perpetuated the 'them and us' attitude. The second, perhaps more fundamental observation is the underlying commitment to an oversimplified, rational model of human nature. The techniques described all represent rational attempts at improving the effectiveness of user–IS interaction, with little consideration for inevitable, emotive behaviour. As Argyris (1971) highlighted, systems development is an emotional as well as a rational process. This emphasis on rationality reflects the underlying functionalist assumptions which characterize much of the developments in the field of IS in particular (Hirschheim and Klein, 1986) and organizational and management theory in general (Pondy et al., 1983). As Hirschheim and Klein (1986) indicated, functionalism has not been a particularly successful paradigm for understanding organizational and societal life, as the object of study, people, does not lend itself to study through positivistic means. It is no surprise therefore, that the integration mechanisms suggested so far in the IS literature underwhelm the problem.

Towards a richer model
Unfortunately, paradigmatic changes are difficult to accomplish in practice and attempts to cross boundaries usually result in shifts towards the extremes of the same paradigm (Burrell and Morgan, 1979). Given the persistence of problematic user–IS relationships, despite the notable cadre of academics that have sought to address the problem, the promise of a complete shift across paradigms might be foolhardy. Even if such a shift were possible, the approaches may be so alien and far removed from current practice that implementation would be significantly delayed – if the concepts were incorporated at all.

While such a theoretical breakthrough may be an ultimate goal, a more modest goal was set for this research. The primary aim was to generate richer understanding of the culture gap and how it can be addressed, by borrowing perspectives which use more complex models of human nature. As Pondy et al., (1983) suggest, attention to more complex patterns of human activity within the functionalist framework can facilitate the development of more enriched concepts and techniques, representing a move towards greater understanding of organizations. In so doing, significant contribution to knowledge may derive from shifts which represent movement closer to the ideal.

THEORETICAL FOUNDATION

This research sought to address the issue of the culture gap on the premise that the destructive effects stemmed from negative attitudes and preconceptions developed and perfected over time, rather than resulting from fundamental differences between the two groups. The research borrowed perspectives from literature on organizational behaviour, in an effort to develop a richer understanding of the issue.

By viewing organizations based on two metaphors – organizations as cultural systems, and organizations as political systems (Morgan, 1986) – a definition of the problem was developed based on concepts of cultures and subcultures, diverse interests, conflict and power. The relevance of these two metaphors to the study of IS has been emerging as a consistent theme in the literature (for example, Lucas, 1973; Robey and Markus, 1984; Willcocks and Mason, 1987; Willcocks, 1991; Galliers *et al.*, 1992).

By studying organizations as cultures, attention is drawn towards another means of creating organized activity: by influencing the language, norms, folklore, ceremonies and other social practices that communicate the key ideologies, values and beliefs guiding action. Viewing organizations as political systems encourages focus on concepts of interests, conflict and power, concepts which are generally discouraged when assumptions of rationality prevail (Morgan, 1986). While other metaphors may also be useful, the cultural and political metaphors offer familiar language and concepts, and share a commonality in their recognition of different interests and possible means of addressing such differences. Specifically, the concept of co-operation through ideology can be successfully applied to organizations when viewed using the cultural and political metaphors. Recent approaches to conflict resolution emphasize the use of 'softer' ideas like shared values and superordinate goals (Handy, 1985; Prahalad and Doz, 1987; Bartlett and Ghoshal, 1989; Orton and Weick, 1990; Pascale, 1990; Mintzberg, 1991; Pinto and Pinto, 1991) rather than 'harder' approaches based on structure and formal procedures. Socialization, a well-developed concept in sociology is an effective means of developing and reinforcing a distinct organizational ideology. By using these metaphors, a more complex model of human nature was incorporated, representing an attempt to address the criticisms of oversimplified, rational models used in previous IS approaches. A research model of user-IS integration, based on the concept of shared values through socialization processes (for example, recruitment procedures, performance evaluation and reward systems and organizational folklore), was developed and tested, based primarily on case studies, and augmented by a large-scale questionnaire survey. The results suggest that socialization makes positive contributions to overcoming the user–IS culture gap.

THE RESEARCH MODEL

For the purposes of the research, integration was defined in terms of the perceived quality of relationships existing between users and IS specialists, consistent with the definition offered by Lawrence and Lorsch (1967). Figure 8.1 suggests that there are three variables through which the combined set of socialization processes are operationalized. Essentially this model has separated the 'hard' or tangible processes which are easier to access from the 'soft' or less tangible processes, while recognizing that the process may operate at organizational level in a distinctly different way from how they operate at group level.

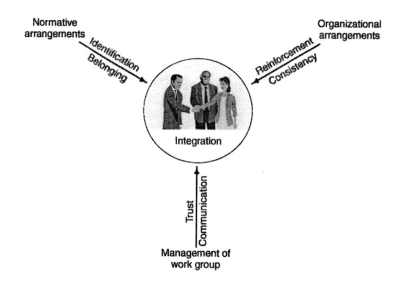

Figure 8.1   Model of IT integration

Normative Arrangements encompass all processes through which the softer issues of staff characteristics, management style and shared values are transferred and implemented, establishing identity with and a sense of belonging to the organization. It includes the selection criteria used in recruiting IS development staff, induction processes and career/personal development training. Organizational arrangements cover strategy, and its consistent translation into structure and systems, which together provide a mutually reinforcing environment. This includes issues like the physical location of IS development staff relative to their users, and performance evaluation criteria. Management of the work group describes the other two processes as they occur at project level. Arrangements at this level include team member selection criteria, the process of allocation of roles and responsibilities and the use of team building processes. The sub-elements of the research variables are

Table 8.1   IT integration model: sub-elements of research variables

Normative	Organizational	Work group
N1 – Corporate culture	O1 – Alignment	W1 – Team selection
N2 – Selection criteria	O2 – Physical location	W2 – Team building
N3 – Induction exposure	O3 – Career path	W3 – Conflict resolution
N4 – Personal/career	O4 – Reward systems	W4 – Team accessibility
development		W5 – Project management
N5 – Career policy		W6 – Project manager
		W7 – Superordinate goals

shown in Table 8.1 and detailed in the appendix to this chapter (page 198). Three research propositions were identified:

1. Normative arrangements shared by IS specialists and members from other parts of the organization improves integration.
2. Organizational arrangements, and principles and practices governing the management of work groups also contribute to integration.
3. Poor implementation of one of the three variables may be compensated for by good implementation of the other two.

THE RESEARCH DESIGN

Given that the primary aim of this research was to explore the relevance and potential contribution of socialization to user–IS integration, case studies provided the primary research methodology (Yin, 1981; Benbasat *et al.*, 1987). The fieldwork was divided into three phases. The first phase, aimed at increasing learning, involved an investigation of three pilot case studies, one of which provided a longitudinal dimension to the current study based on previous research in this organization.

The second phase consisted of case studies of 10 leading edge companies who were major operators in their industries, and provided the bulk of the research data. Leading edge companies were targeted in the hope that investigating their successful project developments would shed real light on effective methods for user–IS integration. The 10 companies investigated consisted of five of the largest high street retailers and five major operators in the electronics field. The company names and sizes (in turnover) are shown in Table 8.2 below. In two of the retail companies, Marks and Spencer and J Sainsbury, permission to investigate two projects which were relevant to the research was granted. As a result, a total of 12 projects (seven retail and five electronics) were investigated and included in the study.

Table 8.2 Companies involved in user–IS integration study

Company names	Turnover (£'000 000)
Retail:	
B&Q Plc	1 019
J Sainsbury Plc	10 270
Marks and Spencer Plc	5 793
Safeway Plc	4 411
Tesco Plc	7 582
Electronics:	
3M (UK)	488
Digital (UK)	800
IBM (UK)	3 750
Philips Components (UK)	908
Philips Consumer Electronics (UK)	126

These case studies involved in-depth, semi-structured interviews with at least six people in each organization, interviews lasting about 45 minutes. The IS director was interviewed to gain an understanding of the background, culture and structure of the organization and the IS department. An outcome of this interview was the identification of a project group to be researched. In each project group, interviews were held with the sponsoring business director, the project manager, the top user/IS specialist (whichever the project manager was not), a lower-level user and a lower-level IS specialist. Each project group member was asked about their recruitment, induction and socialization experience, and about their perception of the relationships existing between users and IS specialists in the organization in general, as well as among members of their project group. Where possible, personnel managers responsible for IS staff were also interviewed, to gain information on existing policies versus the practices described. On several occasions, other members of the organization who became familiar with the research volunteered to discuss issues and further explain the organizational context. These discussions were frequently held informally, and contributed to a richer understanding as well as validating the data received in the 'official' interviews. Documentation in the form of company reports, appraisal forms and any other relevant publication also provided triangulation.

The interviews followed a consistent set of guidelines, and culminated in a set of structured questions which provided a rough measure of perceived user–IS integration (18 questions) and perceived project effectiveness (eight questions) based on responses to a five-point Likert scale. There were a total of 85 interviews conducted over a three-month period, resulting in about ninety 90-minute cassettes. At the end of each interview, a log of impressions and emerging ideas was updated, and follow-up questions for the next interview with that company recorded (Eisenhardt, 1989). The third phase of the fieldwork involved the administration of a large-scale questionnaire survey developed based on the experiences of the case study companies, and refined through a piloting process. Using a combination of addresses from *The Times* 1000 companies and the list of IS directors held at Templeton College, a total of 742 questionnaires were sent out, addressed mainly to IS directors. This yielded a response rate of 38 per cent overall and 36 per cent (265 usable responses) in terms of valid questionnaires.

RESEARCH RESULTS: CASE STUDIES

The measure of integration calculated from the structured questionnaires used in the interviews, though crude, provided a convenient overview of the positioning of the case study projects in terms of relative degrees of integration and effectiveness. Two key observations provided a context for making sense of a potentially overwhelming mass of data. The first was that user–IS integration and effectiveness on all the project teams were 'good', although two projects were distinctly better than others. Companies were allowed to identify the project(s) to be investigated, and without fail each offered the one(s) which reflected the latest state of thinking about IS projects, management and organization. In each case, the decision on 'best practice' was arrived at through a painful process of trial and error, reflected in the comments about previous 'bad' experiences and the improvements derived from current arrangements. This led to the second observation, which is that the projects seemed to have achieved integration and effectiveness through different means.

Against this background, the qualitative data was analysed first by using the tapes to develop detailed case studies of each project (Eisenhardt, 1989) and then by using the model elements to facilitate cross-comparisons between projects. In conducting cross-comparisons, patterns of similarities and differences, exceptions and extremes were identified and the findings evaluated against explanations offered by the model. From this process three points of significance emerged. First, the descriptive data suggested a need for refinements to the model elements; secondly, a pattern of desired and undesired practices became evident, and provided support for the proposed model of integration; and thirdly, certain factors were consistently identified as keys to the degree of integration and effectiveness achieved. These are discussed in the following subsections.

Refinements to the model

With the exception of 'conflict resolution' (W3), all the model elements were considered relevant to user–IS integration. 'Conflict resolution' did not feature as an element in its own right, but seemed more appropriate as part of the management style of the project manager. As such, it has been removed from the list of model elements. The model element 'corporate culture' (N1) had to be unpacked into two sub-elements which emerged as important to integration: 'Bureaucracy' (N1-a) and 'IS commitment' (N1-b).

'Bureaucracy' is used to describe corporate culture in terms of the amount of inflexibility in an organization. This determined the ease with which organizational members from different functions and with different levels of seniority could function in the same team. In other words, the presence of bureaucracy at an organizational level had a direct impact on the effectiveness of relationships at team level. 'IS commitment' examines the nature of any overall goals/values collectively recognized by members of the IS function. One of the main reasons for seeing IS people as 'different' was the perception among the users that IS staff were removed from business concerns. Conversely, it seemed that the more committed to business objectives the IS function was seen to be, the better the relationship that existed between IS and the user community. This element was distinct from the presence or otherwise of a mission statement. The model element 'project management' (W5) also had to be unpacked into 'methodology' (W5-a) describing the use or otherwise of formal methodologies, and 'project structure' (W5-b) describing the reporting line for users and IS staff involved in the project team. A final modification to the model resulted from the recognized influence of the status of the head of IS (O1-b). This emerged as a significant influence on user-IS relationships in terms of the extent to which the head of IS was included in top management discussions and the credibility gained among business colleagues based on perceived commitment to business objectives.

Desirable and undesirable practices

A sense of desirable ('goal') and undesirable ('unhelpful') practices for each of the model elements emerged, along with a sense of movement in the direction of desirable practices. For example, inclusion of IS development staff on induction processes which involved recruits from other departments, visits to stores/plants that lasted for weeks rather than days ('intensive' induction) were considered very effective in enhancing user–IS integration. Conversely, the lack of IS involvement in induction processes, or the presence of induction processes which were for IS staff only were considered unhelpful. Similarity, locating the IS development function close to users (for example, on the same floor, or on different floors of the same building but strategically locating photocopiers and coffee machines to encourage casual contact between the two groups) improved user–IS integration. This is contrasted with arrangements in which physical distance caused interaction to be limited to a work-only basis. Discussions also revealed the existence of 'transitional' practices which were not seen to be ideal but which represented a workable compromise between the ideal and what was feasible given the organizational context. Table 8.3 provides a summary of the final set of model elements, the categories used to describe the range of experiences and the suggested usefulness of these states (referred to as 'goal', 'transitional' and 'unhelpful') in improving user–IS integration. The definition of each of these categories is given in the appendix to this chapter (see page 198).

The profile of the projects in terms of the amount of goal, transitional and unhelpful practices in place provided consistent explanation of the

Table 8.3   Categorization of model element states

SOCIALIZATION	'Goal'	'Transitional'	'Unhelpful'
Normative:			
Bureaucracy	Project-based	Adaptable	Mechanistic
IS commitment	Business	Re-orienting	Diffuse
Selection criteria	Relevant	Business, balance	Technical
Induction	Continuous, intensive	Basic	None
Training	Standard	Discretionary	IS only
Hybrid policy	Choice	Barriers	Isolated
Organizational:			
Alignment	Process	Function	Technology
Status of head	Board, team	'Get involved'	Distant
Location	Integrated	Accessible	Remote
Career paths	Multiple paths	Business analyst	IT professional
Reward systems criteria	Specific objectives	Range of criteria	Technical
Work group:			
Team selection	Right blend	Compatibility	Skills
Team building	Team process	Training policy, social events	None
Accessibility	Hot house, shared space	Accessible	Isolated
Methodology	DIY	Prototype	Proprietary
Structure	Multidisciplinary	Separate teams, intermediaries	IS only
Project manager	Credible	User, joint	IS
Superordinate goals	Business benefit short delivery	User satisfaction	Time budget

relative degree of integration and project effectiveness, and supported the initial observation that integration and effectiveness were achieved through different routes. The proposition that poor implementation of one of the three variables may be compensated for by good implementation of the other two was therefore also supported. Perhaps more importantly, the case study data suggests that the model elements do provide an explanation of the degree of user–IS integration and project effectiveness, and that there are positive associations between 'goal' states and improved perceptions of relationships and project success.

Key factors
The concept of 'goal' states in particular was sharpened by the identification of certain factors that interviewees considered key in achieving the degree of integration that existed. These factors included the use of multidisciplinary teams (versus the use of intermediaries or separate user/IS teams); the credibility and management style of the project manager; the presence, formally or informally, of an account manager; the 'right' mix of skills on the team (as opposed to in any given individual); co-location of team members; the use of social events; delivery of functionality to the business in short (6–9 months) timescales. These findings are consistent with the theoretical framework developed, as well as suggestions in the IS, organizational behaviour and project management literature. However, further attempts at unravelling the characteristics which render these factors particularly useful to integration and effectiveness revealed one significant commonality; each of the factors had the inherent ability to challenge preconceptions and create new attitudes among IS, the business community, or both. In other words, each of the key factors identified has both an instrumental and an expressive role (Daft, 1983) in improving user IS integration. The expressive role is evidenced by improved perceptions and attitudes resulting from increased visibility and the resultant credibility facilitated by the various arrangements. For example, multidisciplinary teams and close physical proximity provide the occasions for preconceptions to be challenged (visibility), while simultaneously encouraging effective communication, immediate access to relevant expertise and speedy resolution of issues. Delivering business benefits in short timescales provides tangible evidence of IS abilities and commitments (credibility), while simultaneously enabling the business to respond effectively to environmental challenges.

RESEARCH RESULTS: SURVEY

A large-scale survey was developed from the case study findings with three specific objectives in mind:

1. to gain empirical evidence about where organizations are in relation to the model elements;
2. to test how closely organizations 'fit' with the profiles of 'goal', 'transition' and 'unhelpful' states, that is, empirical support for the model of transition;
3. to discover if the trends emerging, in terms of the suggested goal states, as well as the direction of those trends, were supported by data based on a larger sample.

The questionnaire solicited response for three time periods: arrangements that previously existed, current arrangements and plans for the future. Perceived success/satisfaction with systems development provided a surrogate measure of the effectiveness of user–IS relationships.

Current practice

Table 8.4 provides a summary of responses under 'unhelpful', 'transition' and 'goal' states for each of the time periods: PAST (P), NOW (N) and FUTURE (F). Currently, respondents are seen to be mostly in 'transition' states for normative arrangements, 'unhelpful' states for work group arrangements, and a mixture for organizational arrangements. The predominance of FUTURE responses which correspond to 'goal' states suggests growing appreciation of the relevance of these arrangements individually, but not necessarily as a coherent whole.

While it was immediately apparent that the survey data did not support any suggestion that 'unhelpful', 'transition' and 'goal' states represented three holistic 'stages', the basic concept of movement through the states is supported in a number of ways. The incidence of goal/unhelpful/transition states was plotted against the PAST/NOW/FUTURE choices of respondents. The adoption of 'goal' states, was demonstrated by the median increasing from (PAST) zero to (NOW) 8 to (FUTURE) 11. The choice of 'unhelpful' states correspondingly decreases, with the median falling from (PAST) 8 to (NOW) 3 to (FUTURE) zero. On the other hand the median for 'transition' states remains roughly constant, from (PAST) 5 to (NOW) 7 to (FUTURE) 5, supporting the contention that transition states are not considered to be final arrangements. Reference to Table 8.4 provides further support: of the six 'transition' states which were predominant PAST choices, only one (basic induction) retains its popularity in FUTURE plans. By contrast, the seven 'goal' states which are predominant choices NOW remain predominant FUTURE choices.

Table 8.4 *Questionnaire responses (Continues)*

Socialization	'Unhelpful'	P(%)	N(%)	F(%)	'Transitional'	P(%)	N(%)	F(%)	'Goal'	P(%)	N(%)	F(%)
Normative:												
Bureaucracy	Mechanistic	79°	57°	33	Adaptable	15	29	25	Project-based	5	12	40°
IS commitment	Boffins	62°	9	0	Support	33	54°	20	Core/strategic	5	35	79°
Selection criteria	Technical	62°	18	11	Business	6	18	19	Relevant	27	58°	67°
Induction	None	35	21	10	Basic	47°	46°	45°	Intensive	6	6	15
					IS only	7	13	19				
					Hands-on	5	14	11				
Training	None	31°	18	9	Discretionary	30	39°	30	Standard	21	28	47°
					IS only	16	12	10				
Hybrid policy	Isolated	5	2	2	Policy	2	6	28	Choice	39	57°	56°
					Barriers	53°	35	14				
Organizational:												
Alignment	Technology	50°	19	12	Functional	32	48	36°	Process	5	13	36°
Status of head	Distant	52°	20	14	(Not tested)				Board	18	28	39
									Team	28	50°	45°
Location	Remote	37	14	8	Accessible	44°	52	38	Integrated	14	24	46°
Career/rewards	Technical	54°	11	8	Business	8	27	33	Relevant	33	58°	56°

Table 8.4 *Questionnaire responses (Concluded)*

Socialization	'Unhelpful'	P(%)	N(%)	F(%)	'Transitional'	P(%)	N(%)	F(%)	'Goal'	P(%)	N(%)	F(%)
Work group:												
Team selection	Availability	46°	13	8	Compatibility	13	30	49	Right blend	5	10	9
	Skills	35	47°	33								
Team building	None	65°	40°	28	Training policy	15	21	23	Team process	2	12	26
					Social events	17	27	23				
Accessibility	Isolated	38	16	16	Accessible	46°	53	41	Shared space	14	30	43°
Methodology	Proprietary	44°	42°	28	Prototype	5	16	43°	DIY	44°	26	11
Structure:												
User/IS contact	(Not tested)				Separate teams	27	14	6	Multidisciplinary	21	60°	74°
					Intermediaries	45°	19	14				
Programming resource	Contract-out	8	6	17	Contract-in	14	29	26	In-house staff	72°	51°	43°
Project manager	IS	79°	40°	20	User	11	33	21	Credible	7	16	36°
					Hybrid	2	9	21				
Superordinate goals:												
Success	Time/budget	38	23	7	User satisfaction	43°	23	10	Business benefits	18	54°	83°
Timescales	Lengthy	81	48°	27	(Not tested)				Short	11	39	56°

Support for goal states

The identification of 'goal' states is supported firstly by reference to the FUTURE choices of respondents. For 14 of 19 model elements, the identified 'goal' state was the predominant FUTURE choice (Table 8.4); for another element it was an equal first choice. Only in the 'induction', team selection, 'team building' and 'methodology' elements were the 'goal' states predicted from the case study analysis not recognized by the survey data. 'Goal' states were particularly strongly favoured for the model elements 'IS commitment' (77 per cent) 'selection criteria' (67 per cent), 'project structure: user/IS contact' (74 per cent) and 'superordinate goals: success criteria' (83 per cent). In other words, respondents were most consistent about the future, and in line with prescribed 'goal' states, in their plans to implement/accomplish perceptions of IS staff in providing a core/strategic function to the business, recruitment criteria based on relevant skills, multidisciplinary system development teams and success criteria based on delivering business benefits.

To further test the power of 'goal' states, respondents' expressed current satisfaction with systems development was regressed against the number of matches between their current arrangement (NOW responses) and 'goal' states. A positive and significant ($P = 0.0001$) correlation was found between the number of 'goal' states and expressed satisfaction. Similar regressions of satisfaction against the number of 'unhelpful' and 'transition' states showed negative, but not significant, associations in both instances. Although the survey was designed for a different purpose, analysis of the survey data also highlighted predictors of satisfaction which were consistent with key factors identified by case study interviewees. Two responses to perception of the IS function emerged as significant determinants of satisfaction with systems development. The perception of the IS function as a strategic/core function whose people understand and contribute towards the key objectives of the business appeared as the first determinant, which was strongly and positively related to satisfaction with systems development. The perception of the IS function as 'boffins' was strongly, negatively correlated with satisfaction. 'Delivering business benefits' and 'short delivery timescales' also emerged as significant predictors of satisfaction. Additionally, success criteria based on time and budget deadlines and lengthy development timescales emerged as strong, negative predictors of satisfaction.

The use of multidisciplinary teams did not emerge as a significant predictor in any of the regressions, but the use of separate user/IS teams was found to be negatively correlated with satisfaction. Intermediaries emerged as positively correlated with current satisfaction, when satisfaction was regressed against the number of unhelpful states. However, although this is contrary to the model propositions, it might reflect the period in which the use of intermediaries improves the effectiveness of user–IS relationships for a while, even though, based on the experiences of case study projects, such structures then become dysfunctional. The results were confirmed by cluster analysis, in which one cluster in particular was characterized by the presence of each of the responses positively associated with satisfaction. The other two clusters were less clear, except that they were characterized by a predominance of 'transition' and 'unhelpful' states rather than 'goal' states.

One point of caution must be made in discussing the results. In all regressions reported, the adjusted R^2 was no more than 0.12. Despite the fact that the regression models themselves are significant, the amount of variation explained is very low. There could be a number of explanations for this. First, there may well be other variables contributing to a measure as generalized as 'satisfaction with systems development'. Secondly, the responses did not discriminate widely on a five-point scale. Thirdly, all respondents were IS staff who might not be expected to be the most objective assessors of organizational satisfaction with IS development. Nevertheless, the significance of the regression models and the predictors of satisfaction identified are consistent with case study findings and therefore are included in the discussion.

Analysis of change

A further proposition embedded in the transitional model is that the direction of change in systems development arrangements can be predicted. Cross tabulation in conjunction with the McNemar test for change were used to identify the direction and significance of movement occurring between the time periods PAST to NOW, NOW to FUTURE, and PAST to FUTURE. *Chi-square* was not considered relevant because calculations would have included respondents who were already in certain states rather than focusing on only those actually moving. Except for induction, hybrid policy and project methodology, any significant movement ($p < 0.05$) occurred in the direction predicted. Although there is a growing appreciation of the need for IS induction processes, there is a movement from no induction or basic induction programmes to IS-only programmes. Based on the case study evidence, this represents a backward step in terms of integration because induction processes are more effective in terms of integration if they are shared with non-IS members of the organization. Over half the organizations already encourage cross-functional moves, without having a job-rotation policy, but the trend is towards implementing such a policy. This may be a direct reflection of current thinking, but is contrary to the suggestion of the model. Based on the case study experiences it is better to allow opportunities for individuals to move based on choice, as there are IS individuals who do not desire rotation, or who believe that cross-functional project teams are a more effective means of accomplishing the same end. Formal project methodology was considered a hindrance to speedy development in the case study experiences. The survey data reveals that this is still a dominant practice, although the trend is towards the use of more prototyping approaches. Changes to arrangements in two specific areas – delivery timescales and perceptions of the IS function – emerged as individually significant predictors of improved satisfaction with systems development success.

DISCUSSION

Both the case study data and the survey results support the relevance of socialization to user–IS integration, and provide evidence which upholds the research propositions made. Normative, organizational and work group arrangements all make positive contributions to user–IS integration, and poor implementation of one of these arrangements is compensated for by good implementation of the other two.

The concept of 'goal' states was also endorsed by the survey results, and in most cases the survey respondents supported the arrangements defined as 'goal' states based on the case studies. In addition to the individual contributions made by each 'goal' state, the results suggest that a collective power is accrued when a number of 'goal' states exist simultaneously. This mutually reinforcing nature of the integration arrangements is supported by Skyrme (1992). The research therefore provides practical suggestions on arrangements which improve user–IS integration. Against the background, the discussion following is aimed at teasing out issues that stand out from the research model and need to be addressed directly. Specifically, discussion focuses on:

- findings which challenge current thinking and practice;
- an emergent order of implementation of the model elements;
- limitations and implications for future research; and
- contribution of the research.

Challenges to current thinking and practice
The results of the survey indicate that the research could make significant contribution to the *practice* of IS by providing suggestions about 'best practice' where induction and team building processes are concerned. Additionally, the research findings raise some questions which challenge current IS *thinking*.

Based on the theoretical foundation developed, and the supporting evidence provided by the case studies, induction processes shared between IS and non-IS recruits, involving exposure to the main operations of the business and encouraging group activity (for example, project assignments) are most effective in forging good user–IS relationships. However, some organizations are moving from shared basic orientation programmes to IS only programmes. One possible explanation for the predominance of basic orientation programmes for IS staff (rather than intensive) might be that the organizations surveyed only have basic orientation procedures for all employees, whether IS or not. This would suggest the lack of a strong corporate culture (Pascale, 1985).

The implications of the research model developed is that formal team-building sessions in a newly formed team makes greater contribution to developing effective user–IS relationships than does the development of team skills through personal/career development training. Team skills possessed by particular individuals may allow mutual adjustment and promotion of team spirit to occur faster, but they do not make direct contributions to the process itself, whereas formal team-building sessions do. Team social events are also more effective for the same reason. Awareness of the processes facilitated, and the importance of such processes to effective user–IS relationships can provide guidance on practices to implement in the future.

The first challenge to current IS thinking concerns the emphasis on hybrids. The research suggests that having the right 'blend' of people is more important than having business and IS skills embodied in a single individual. Skyrme (1992) also reported a dispute about the need for hybrids on cross-functional teams versus having a 'hybrid team' whose overall composition has a wide representation and a full complement of skills. Additionally, the trend towards implementing hybrid policies is questioned, the implication being that cross-fertilization experience for IS staff should be based on individual choice. The issue of re-entry to the host function and loss of currency has already been recognized (for example, Skyrme, 1992), but still poses a constraint on implementing cross-fertilization processes in practice. The wisdom of contracting out rather than including contractors (if necessary) on an in-house development team is also challenged by the research, based on the need for close proximity and informal communication. However, this challenge must be tempered by reference to project context. The case study projects were, by definition, projects which involved significant organizational change, and it is in this context that the task of integration becomes more critical, as well as more complex. It may be that contracting out is a feasible arrangement for other project contexts.

Implementing the model of integration

The consistency with which key factors emerge as significant determinants of satisfaction suggest an order of implementation of the model elements. It could be argued that these factors are not necessarily more significant than other model elements, but are easier to implement because of the level at which they are introduced. Each of these factors is either local to the IS department or to project teams and therefore represent integration arrangements which can be immediately and effectively implemented in organizations. Multidisciplinary teams, for example, are local to the IS and user departments involved, and have a direct impact on the attitudes and perceptions of those working on the team. This may in turn have a knock-on effect, influencing the attitudes and preconceptions of the host departments to which the team members belong. In so doing, they lay the foundation for successful implementation of other integration arrangements.

However, while these new attitudes may filter to other members of the respective departments, the absence of additional methods at organizational level may create a distinction between those on the team and their respective departments, as was observed in some of the case studies. Thus, while these factors may be useful for explaining team relationships and project effectiveness, they do not provide sufficient explanation for the general user–IS relationships that were found to exist in the case study organizations. This suggests that the key factors may be a starting point, but certainly do not represent the end of the journey. The fact that key predictors of satisfaction primarily occur at work group level, may therefore be a reflection of a general lack of attention to factors at the corporate level, especially where normative arrangements are concerned. This suggestion is supported by the survey finding that most respondents are predominantly in the 'transitional' states for current normative arrangements.

On this basis, it may be more useful to visually represent the model elements in terms of the level at which they predominantly operate. Figure 8.2 offers an alternative view of the model elements, grouped simultaneously according to their ease of implementation and the level at which they operate. Concentric circles are used to visually suggest the locus of the influences in relation to the organization as a whole, and the potential for the influence to be confined to that domain. The solid arrows represent the outward influence from project group arrangements to the organization as a whole, and the dotted arrows represent the reinforcing nature of an appropriate organizational context. The figure is used to suggest a dynamic interplay and mutually supportive relationship among the various arrangements. The implication is that attention first be directed at work group arrangements, as these will assist in creating an environment conducive

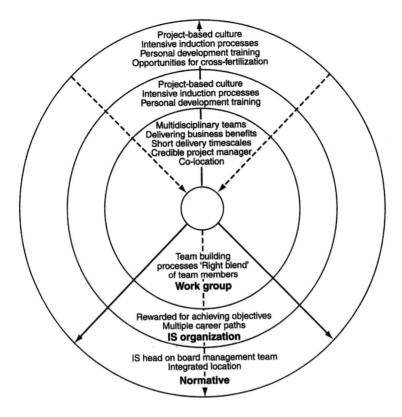

Figure 8.2   A proposed order of implementation

to more lasting arrangements. For example, the credibility gained from successful delivery of business benefits may lay the foundation for including the IS director on the company board. Intuitively, a time-lag will exist between the implementation of the arrangements and experiencing the effect. The main point, however, is that efforts to achieve user–IS integration should be consistent and holistic in approach. It should be noted that there is no significance to the ordering of the arrangements within each circle.

Limitations and implications for future research

Selection of case study companies was deliberately biased towards large successful corporations implementing projects involving significant organizational change. The bias towards larger organizations was translated into the survey sample by the choice of databases used for the company addresses. The effect, therefore, is that the findings are probably biased towards medium to large corporations. Firm size, in terms of the number of employees may affect several organizational processes crucial to the research (Attewell and Rule, 1991). Specifically, socialization may occur differently in small firms. It may be that the emphasis on challenging preconceptions and attitudes renders the concept just as relevant but perhaps easier to implement in small organizations. For example, visibility based on close proximity and increased opportunity for casual contact may be a natural process in small organizations.

Emphasis on projects involving significant organizational change potentially limits the applicability of the findings to such project contexts. Since each additional integration arrangement incurs extra costs (Lawrence and Lorsch, 1967; Thompson, 1967), it may be that the suggested 'goal' states are unnecessary luxuries for other project contexts. However, given the current urgency among researchers and practitioners alike to discover ways in which IT can be used to gain significant and sustainable competitive advantage, the key systems being developed will by definition involve significant organizational change. It is in this context that the task of integration is more critical as well as more complex, hence it is in this context that the integration arrangements suggested by the research are most relevant.

The emerging trend towards outsourcing raises potential concerns about the applicability of the research. The findings suggest that in-house development is the preferred arrangement for the project context investigated, and that where contractors are used, they should be brought in to the organization as part of the development team. This may be a biased finding, given that only in-house development teams were investigated. However, there is currently no significant research suggesting how such projects would fare if outsourced. This is one obvious area for future research. Another possible area for future exploration emerging from this research is the question of whether or not socialization can alleviate 'boffin' characteristics. In other words, did IS specialists develop characteristics of poor communication and lack of interest in/commitment to the business as a result of the way they have been managed, or because of innate, inherent characteristics of the individuals concerned? Essentially this means introducing the nature versus nurture debate into the IS arena. The potential impact of more 'user-friendly' development tools, (for example CASE and object-oriented design) and off-the-shelf packages has not been considered in this research. It could be argued that with such tools and packages, the need for very technically competent IS staff, and associated 'boffin' tendencies is removed, with a concomitant decrease in, if not alleviation of, the problem of the culture gap.

One final point about the applicability of the research relates to timing. If the culture gap is the result of a generation gap, then the more positive attitudes of later generations brought up in this IT era will eventually erode the effects of the culture gap. However, given the significance of current development efforts, the problem cannot be left to time. Also, preconceptions may continue to be handed down from generation to generation if measures are not taken to challenge the relevance of the stories and myths that perpetuate them.

CONTRIBUTIONS OF THE RESEARCH

The unique contributions of this research derive from the distinctive approach taken to tackle the issue of the user–IS culture gap. Based on the proposition that the destructive effects of the culture gap resulted from deep-seated attitudes and preconceptions that have remained unaddressed over the years, the research sought to identify integration mechanisms that were successful in effecting positive attitudinal changes, and improved user–IS relationships. Unlike previous approaches which have emphasized rationality, the issue of the culture gap was viewed using a more complex model of human beings and organizational life, embracing concepts of culture, interests, conflict and power. This facilitated the development of a richer model of integration which has been supported and endorsed by the findings of the study. The specific contributions of the research are threefold. It provides:

- *A challenge*

to confront the culture gap. Rather than accepting the suggested inevitability of poor user–IS relationships based on individual differences, the attitudes and preconceptions should be confronted directly, with the expectation that the negative effects will be removed. Indeed, the very appropriateness of the term 'culture gap' should be questioned. The research suggests that 'culture gap' should be replaced by a term reflecting what it really is – an excuse for, rather than the cause of ineffective working relationships.

- *A context*

for implementing previously suggested integration mechanisms. By focusing attention on the symbolic, expressive function of integration arrangements as well as the instrumental function, the research provides a context for understanding why previous methods have and have not worked. For example, a historic neglect of the social context provides some explanation for the low level of user participation which other researchers have found. Attention to the expressive role of certain arrangements also cautions against the assumption that the mere appointment of project champions, sponsors and account managers is sufficient to accomplish the desired integration. By addressing the psychological climate and social context of development project teams, the research therefore provides a foundation for the effective implementation of other integration mechanisms previously proposed.

- *A course*

of action, giving practical suggestions for the future. This research provides empirical evidence of the relationship between socialization practices and improved user–IS integration, and gives practical suggestions on overcoming the user–IS culture gap and achieving effective relationships. By identifying 'goal' arrangements and synergistic effects, the research provides a course of action and a direction for the future. Using Schwartz and Davis's (1981) terminology, this research provides a means of adjusting the culture to reduce the amount of risk associated with developing systems involving significant organizational change. Additionally, it offers practical suggestions on how to move to later, mature stages of proposed growth models by strengthening bridges between users and IS (Gibson and Nolan, 1974) and achieving integrated harmonious relationships (Galliers and Sutherland, 1991). For practitioners, the specific implications are:

- confront the culture gap;
- implement key factors immediately;
- engender a commitment to business objectives among IS staff;
- treat IS staff as 'one of us', particularly with respect to induction, training, and reward systems

This research has suggested that if attention is given to the areas identified in the list of model elements, and inconsistent efforts towards achieving suggested 'goal' states made, the destructive effects of the user–IS culture gap can become a thing of the past.

REFERENCES

Attewell, P. and Rule, J. B. (1991) 'Survey and Other Research Methodologies Applied to IT IMPACT Research: Experiences from a Comparative Study of Business Computing', in Kraemer, K. L. (ed), *The Information Systems Research Challenge: Survey Research Methods*, Harvard Business School Research Colloquium, **3**, pp. 299–315.

Argyris, C. (1971) 'Management Information Systems: The Challenge to Rationality and Emotionality', *Management Science*, **17**, (6), February, pp. 275–292.

Bartlett, C. A. and Ghoshal, S. (1989) *Managing Across Borders: The Transnational Solution*, Hutchinson, Boston, Mass.

Benbasat, I., Goldstein, D. K. and Mead, M. (1987) 'The Case Research Strategy in Studies of Information Systems–Advice to Researchers who wish to use the Case Study Method', *MIS Quarterly*, **11**, (3), September, pp. 369–385.

Bostrom, R. P. and Heinen, J. S. (1977) 'MIS Problems and Failures: A Socio-Technical Perspective PART 1: The Causes', *MIS Quarterly*, September, pp. 17–32.

Burrell, G. and Morgan, G. (1979) *Sociological Paradigms and Organizational Analysis*, Heinemann Educational Books, London.

Checkland, P. B. (1981) *Systems Thinking, Systems Practice*, Wiley, Chichester.

Daft, R. L. (1983) 'Symbols in Organizations: A Dual-Content Framework for Analysis', in Pondy, L. R., Louis, R. Frost, P. J. Morgan, G. and Dandridge, T. C. (eds) *Organizational Symbolism*, pp. 199–206, JAI Press, Greenwich, Connecticut.

Davis, G. B. and Olson, M. H. (1985) *Management Information Systems: Conceptual Foundations, Structures and Development*, (2nd edition), McGraw-Hill, New York.

DeBrabander, B. and Edstrom, A. (1977) 'Successful Information Systems Development Projects', *Management Science*, **24**, (2), October, pp. 191–199.

DeBrabander, B. and Thiers, G. (1984) 'Successful Information System Development in Relation to Situational Factors which Affect Effective Communication between MIS-Users and EDP-Specialists', *Management Science*, **30**, (2), February, pp. 137–155.

Earl, M. J. (1978) 'Prototype Systems for Accounting Information and Control', *Accounting Organizations and Society*, **3**, (2), pp. 161–170.

Earl, M. J., Feeny, D., Lockett, M. and Runge, D. (1988) *IT, Competitive Advantage and Innovation: Maxims for Senior Managers*, Oxford Institute of Information Management Research and Discussion Papers, RDP 88/2, Templeton College, Oxford.

Eisenhardt, K. M. (1989) 'Building Theories from Case Study Research', *Academy of Management Review*, **14**, (4), pp. 532–550.

Feeny, D. F., Edwards, B. R. and Simpson, K. M. 'Understanding the CEO/CIO Relationship', *MIS Quarterly*, **16**, pp. 435–448.

Galliers, R. D., Reponen, T., Pattison, L. and Ruohenen, M. (1992) 'Four Viewpoints to Information Strategy', *15th Informations Systems Research Seminars in Scandinavia*, 9–12, August.

Galliers, R. D. and Sutherland, A. R. (1991) 'Information Systems Management and Strategy Formulation: the 'stages of growth' model revisited', *Journal of Information Systems*, **1**, pp. 89–114.

Gibson, C. E. and Nolan, R. L. (1974) 'Managing the Four Stages of

EDP Growth', *Harvard Business Review*, January–February, pp. 76–88.

Ginzberg, M. J. (1981) 'Early Diagnosis of MIS Implementation Failure: Promising Results and Unanswered Questions', *Management Science*, **27**, (4), April, pp. 459–478.

Handy, C. (1985) *Understanding Organizations*, 3rd edition, Penguin Books, London.

Henderson, J. C. (1990) 'Plugging into Strategic Partnerships: The Critical IS Connection', *Sloan Management Review*, Spring, pp. 7–27.

Hirschheim, R. and Klein, H. (1986) *The Emergence of Pluralism in Information Systems Development: Stories, Consequences and Implications for the Legitimation of Systems Objectives*, Oxford Institute of Information Management Research and Discussion Papers, RDP 86/15, Templeton College, Oxford.

Land, F. (1982) 'Notes on Participation', *Computer Journal*, **25**, (2).

Lawrence, P. R. and Lorsch, J. W. (1967) *Organization and Environment*, Harvard Graduate School of Business Administration.

Lockett, M. (1987) *The Factors Behind Successful IT Innovation*, Oxford Institute of Information Management Research and Discussion Papers, RDP 87/9, Templeton College, Oxford.

Lucas, H. C. Jr (1973) 'A Descriptive Model of Information Systems in the Context of the Organization', *Database*, Winter, pp. 27–39.

Lucas, H. C. Jr. (1975) *Why Information Systems Fail*, Columbia University Press.

Mahmood, M. A. (1987) 'Systems Development Methods – A Comparative Investigation', *MIS Quarterly*, September, pp. 293–307.

Mintzberg, H. (1991) 'The Effective Organization: Forces and Forms', *Sloan Management Review*, Winter, pp. 54–67.

Morgan, G. (1986) *Images of Organization*, Sage Publications, London.

Mumford, E., Land, F. and Hawgood, J. (1978) 'A Participative Approach to the Design of Computer Systems', *Impact of Science on Society*, **28**, (3), pp. 253–256.

Mumford, E. (1983) *Designing Human Systems for New Technology: The Ethics Method*, Manchester Business School.

Mumford, E. (1985) *Socio-technical Systems Design – Evolving Theory and Practice*, Manchester Business School, WP 100.

Mumford, E. (1987) *Participation in Systems Design: What Can it Offer?* Manchester Business School, WP 140.

Naumann, J. D. and Jenkins, A. M. (1982) 'Prototyping: The New Paradigm for Systems Development', *MIS Quarterly*, **6**, (3), September, pp. 29–44.

Orton, D. J. and Weick, K. E. (1990) 'Loosely Coupled Systems: A Reconceptualization', *Academy of Management Review*, **15**, (2), pp. 203–223.

Palmer, C. and Ottley, S. (1990) *From Potential to Reality: Hybrids – A Critical Force in the Application of Information Technology in the 1990s*, January, The British Computer Society, London.

Pascale, R. (1985) 'The Paradox of "Corporate Culture": Reconciling Ourselves to Socialization', *California Management Review*, **27**, (2), pp. 26–41.

Pascale, R. (1990) *Managing on the Edge: How Successful Companies Use Conflict to Stay Ahead*, Penguin, London.

Pinto, M. B. and Pinto, J. K. (1991) 'Determinants of Cross-functional Cooperation in the Project Implementation Process', *Project Management Journal*, **XXII**, (2), June, pp. 13–19.

Peters, T. J. and Waterman, R. H. (1982) *In Search of Excellence*, Harper Row, New York.

Pondy, L. R., Louis, R. Frost, P. J. Morgan, G. and Dandridge, T. C. (1983) *Organizational Symbolism*, JAI Press, Greenwich, Connecticut.

Prahalad, C. K. and Doz, Y. L. (1987) *The Multinational Mission: Balancing Local Demands and Global Vision*, Free Press, New York.

Price Waterhouse (1991, 1992) 'The Culture Gap', *Information Technology Review*, London, pp. 16–19.

Robey, D. (1979) 'User Attitudes and Management Information Systems Use', *Academy of Management Journal*, **22**, (3), pp. 527–538.

Robey, D. and Markus, M. L. (1984) 'Rituals in Information System Design', *MIS Quarterly*, March, pp. 5–15.

Runge, D. A. (1985) *Winning with Telecommunications: An Approach for Corporate Strategists*, International Centre for Information Technology, Washington DC.

Schewe, C. D. (1976) 'The Management Information System User: An Exploratory Behavioural Analysis', *Academy of Management Journal*, **19**, (4), December, pp. 577–590.

Schwartz, H. and Davis, S. M. (1981) 'Matching Corporate Culture and Business Strategy', *Organizational Dynamics*, Summer, pp. 30–48.

Skyrme, D. J. (1992) *From Hybrids to Bridge Building*, Oxford Institute of Information Management, Research and Discussion Papers, RDP92/1, Templeton College, Oxford.

Thompson, J. D. (1967) *Organizations in Action*, McGraw-Hill, Chicago.

Willcocks, L. and Mason, D. (1987) *Computerising Work: People, Systems, Design and Workplace Relations*, Paradigm Publishing, London.

Willcocks, L. (1991) *Information Systems in the 1990s: Toward a New Agenda for Management Education*, City University Business School Working Paper Series, March, No. 107.

Yin, R. (1981) 'The Case Study Crisis: Some Answers', *Administrative Science Quarterly*, **26**, March, pp. 28–65.

APPENDIX TO CHAPTER 8: DEFINITIONS USED TO CATEGORIZE CASE STUDY FINDINGS

'Bureaucracy'

Project-based Cross-functional team approach to tasks is commonplace.

Adaptable Project team/task groups not commonplace, but their occasional introduction seems reasonably painless.

Mechanistic Issues of status and reporting lines create serious problems in team integration.

'IS Commitment'

Business IS departments in which the members have all bought in to the fact that unless they deliver benefits to the business, they serve no useful purpose.

Re-orienting IS director is totally oriented towards meeting business objectives and is actively trying to transfer this to the department in a process of re-orientation.

Diffuse IS departments in which there was no distinguishable commitment, either to the business or technology.

'Selection criteria'

Technical Selection based purely on technical skills and requirements.

Business Selection based primarily on business acumen and interpersonal skills.

Balance Both technical and business acumen/interpersonal skills given equal consideration in recruitment.

Relevant Both sets of skills varied, and recruitment could occur based on technical and/or business and interpersonal skills.

'Induction'

Intensive Induction into the company involves working at the sharp end of the business – for example, in retail companies this would mean actually working in the stores and depots – for at least one week, usually one month. This includes the use of cross-functional teams who work on a project for a few months and do a presentation to senior management.

Continuous Not only is there an intensive induction programme, but exposure to the sharp end of the business is a continuous process occurring alongside day-to-day tasks. This includes revisiting stores on a regular basis, sharing customer service duties and so on.

Basic Short (maximum of two days) session of familiarization with the core business operations.

None No opportunities for exposure/interaction outside of specific work assignments. No company orientation programmes attended by IS.

'Personal/career development training'

Standard There is an organizational policy towards a general career/personal development training as a natural outcome of a standard performance evaluation procedure.

Discretionary IS staff are sent by exception, based on management discretion.

IS only Personal/career development training may or may not result from a formalized process, but courses are run for and attended by IS staff only.

'Hybrid policy'

Choice Individuals are encouraged to seize opportunities to move across functions, and are potentially rewarded for their experience.

Barriers Individual choice to move is hindered by organizational red tape and a reluctance by the recipient department to accept that real benefits can accrue from gaining a new perspective. Included here also are the difficulties presented by the differential in compensation that exists between IS and the counterpart business positions.

Isolated IS function is isolated from the rest of the business and there is no movement nor potential for movement across functions.

'Alignment'

Technology IS development function has subdivided itself based on technology specialisms e.g. mainframe versus micros versus minis and therefore seeks to develop technical specialists in each area.

Function IS development function mirrors the functional subdivisions of the organization e.g. there is an IS subdivision looking after accounts, another in charge of distribution, another manufacturing and so on.

Process IS development function is aligned with business processes e.g. supply chain, strategic planning.

'Status of the head of IS'

Board   Head of IS is a member of the board of directors of the organization.

Management team   Head of IS is not a board member, but is otherwise seen to be an active and valid part of the operating management team.

Distant   Head of IS is not a board member and has no direct input in the running of the organization.

'Location of IS development staff'

Remote   IS development resources are isolated from the rest of the business.

Accessible   IS development staff and users are easily accessible to each other, for example across the road or on another floor of the same building, but traffic between the two is limited to interaction on a work-related, professional basis only.

Integrated   The physical location may be on the same or separate floors, but siting of coffee machines, photocopiers, lounges, lunch rooms, creates the occasion for casual, informal contacts as well as work-related interaction.

'Career paths for IS development staff'

IT professional   Career progression follows the traditional hierarchical sequence (trainee programmer, programmer, programmer analyst, analyst, project leader, systems manager).

Business analyst   Situations in which organizations have gone to the other extreme: IS career 'progression' is essentially increased seniority/salary for performing the same business analyst role.

Multiple paths   More than one career path within the IS function is available to IS personnel.

'Reward systems for IS development staff'

Technical criteria   IS staff are rewarded mainly for their technical skills and qualifications.

Range of criteria   IS staff are rewarded for technical skills as well as interpersonal/communication and business skills.

Specific objectives   Appraisal system is based on objectives set for individuals, where these objectives may be a mix of technical, business and/or interpersonal skills. Reward is according to the level of achievement of objectives.

'Team selection criteria'

Professional skills Selection is based on the necessary business/technical skills, perhaps including considerations of availability.

Compatibility Selection is primarily based on interpersonal/communication skills and whether or not a person would 'get on' with others in the team.

Right blend High levels of knowledge and good interpersonal skills are not expected to be resident in a single individual. Selection is aimed at getting the necessary set of skills together, frequently referred to as the 'right mix' or 'blend' of people.

'Team-building processes'

Training policy Team-building is a formalized part of personal/career development training programmes, as a result of which all employees, including IS, are sent on team building courses at some time during their career.

Team process Team members undergo team building processes together as a means of creating effective working relationships on a newly formed team.

Social events Social events – visits to pubs, dinners, games – either planned or impromptu were considered effective in building cohesion among team members.

None Situations in which no team-building occurred outside that resulting from formal project work.

'Team accessibility'

Hot house The entire team is together and physically separated from the rest of the business.

Shared space The entire team is located in the same area, for example on the same floor, but may not necessarily be sitting side by side.

Accessible The team is not necessarily located in the same general area, but contact is frequent and members are readily available to one another.

Isolated Team members are in separate locations and may either be isolated due to geographic distance or a perceived difficulty in accessing each other.

'Project methodology'

Proprietary Formal, named project methodology used to control the systems development process.

DIY   Formal methodologies not rigidly adhered to, but the underlying principles used to guide the process of systems development. Frequently included the use of prototypes.

'Project structure'

IS only   No user membership in the project work group.

Separate teams   Both users and IS involved in the system development, but each report to their own management.

Intermediates   Only contact IS and end users had with each other was through a group of 'interpreters' in the middle.

Multidisciplinary   Project team had representatives from areas affected by the development brought together under a single project manager.

'Project manager'

IS   Project manager, by appointment of default, is from a purely IS background.

User   Organizational policy or practice dictates that a user should always head systems development.

Joint   Projects are managed by both an IS person and a user either throughout the length of the project, or with changeovers of responsibility occurring at certain stages.

Credible   A user with experience in IS, or an IS person with business experience and/or credibility among the users is selected as the project manager.

'Superordinate goals'

Time/budget   Most important criterion for judging success is delivering the system on time and perhaps within budget.

User satisfaction   Most important criterion for judging success is whether target users are satisfied.

Business benefit   Delivering agreed benefits to the business is the main determinant of the success of the system.

Short delivery   Emphasis was on delivering functionality in rapid succession – usually every three or six months – in order of criticality to business operations.

CHAPTER NINE

Management and Risk in Major Information Technology Projects

LESLIE P. WILLCOCKS AND CATHERINE GRIFFITHS

INTRODUCTION

The conclusion to be drawn from reviewing the main research studies on risk is that major projects commonly experience overruns, are often over budget, do not perform in the way expected, involve severe strain on participating institutions, or are cancelled prior to their completion after the expenditure of considerable sums of money (See for example, Appleton, 1991; Collingridge, 1992; Davidson and Huot, 1991; Morris and Hough, 1987). These studies suggest that these problems relate essentially to issues of size, complexity, long time-span, uncertainty, governance and management peculiar to larger-scale projects. The resulting management challenges are compounded when the additional factor of technological innovation integral to the project is added. This is precisely the case in major information technology (IT) projects; indeed a range of studies show that the IT component adds a different dimension of risk which all too often can tip the balance towards project failure, rather than toward project success. Disregarding scale for the moment, recent studies (see for example, Bessant, 1991; Griffiths and Newman, 1996; Mitev, 1996; Willcocks and Margetts, 1994a,b) show the following typical problems in IT-based projects:

- lack of strategic framework, or conflicts over strategy;
- lack of organizational adaptation to complement technological change;
- IT supplier problems and general immaturity of the supply side;

203

- poor management of change, with particular neglect for its implications for organizational and project structure, processes and culture;
- too much faith in the 'technical fix';
- a love of technology for its own sake or for its novelty value, with resulting inappropriate applications – too often IT has been solutions looking for problems, and there has not been a major demand for the resulting product/service;
- lack of skills to support implementation; and lack of exploration of a wide range of options, resulting in the exclusion of lower technology alternatives.

Many of these issues can be read into the case histories described below. The particularly critical factors are the newness of the technology, and its centrality to a major project. Working with new technology always introduces heightened levels of risk, which in turn affect the timing, costs and delivery deadlines (Hochstrasser and Griffiths, 1991; Willcocks, 1994). Delays due to research and development, as well as experimentation, may also result in unexpected or unwanted results. These factors can cause original projects to be sidetracked and initial objectives to be changed, with insufficient appreciation of the wider implications. More often time pressure results in experimentation passing into fully-fledged implementation before a sufficient testing phase, with sub-optimal consequences when the technology is operationalized, and large on-going 'maintenance' costs. As Collingridge (1992) has shown, when the dimension of scale is added, all too many technology-based projects fail, or at least sub-optimize, because the technology has been too experimental for the scope of what is being undertaken. As will be seen, this may particularly be the case where governments sponsor major projects and where there are national aspirations inherent in equating technological innovation with economic progress (Eglizeau, Frey and Newman, 1996; Madon, 1992).

We argue in this chapter that risk assessment and management provide highly useful keys to the management and control of large-scale IT projects. Indeed the risk profile of a major project needs to set the parameters for what is realistically possible, what risks need to be reduced, and how their management can be pursued. In the light of risk frameworks and research findings, we investigate seven major IT projects, with a view to further identifying the reasons for varying experiences of success and failure. The focus moves from the Singapore TradeNet system and the French, British and German promotion of Videotex as bases for an information economy, through the Indian CRISP project to use IT for improved coordination of alleviation of rural poverty, to the on-going 17 year (1982–99) plan to computerize the UK Department of Social Security, and the major London Stock Exchange TAURUS project that was finally abandoned in 1993. But before we look at and derive lessons from the case studies it is useful to assess what studies have identified so far as the main risks in IT-based projects, and how they can be diagnosed and managed. The case studies will then add the dimension of scale and some new evidence to assess. Throughout IT and IS (information systems) are used as largely interchangeable terms, though a distinction can be made between IT as hardware, software and communications technologies – essentially equipment – and attendant techniques, and IS as a wider concept referring to how designed information flows attempt to meet the defined information requirements of an organization.

IT-BASED SYSTEMS AS RISK

Risk in computer-based IS projects is surprisingly under-managed. The surprise comes when the large size of information technology (IT) expenditure, and the history of disappointed expectations is considered (Keen, 1991; Hochstrasser and Griffiths, 1991; Willcocks, 1994; 1996). Surveys regularly report IT introduction and usage as a high-risk, hidden cost process. As one example, a 1992 survey, in reviewing IT projects over the previous 10 years in 200 organizations, found that for projects over £660 000, 90 per cent were over budget, 98 per cent had changed specification, 60 per cent were over time, and 20 per cent were inappropriate (OTR Group, 1992). Despite this, significant omissions occured at investment appraisal stage, with only 30 per cent of the companies surveyed applying any risk analysis. Indeed there is a lack of managerial use of risk analysis in capital budgeting decisions generally, with one study finding managers lacking the required understanding to apply formal approaches and/or unable to find an approach that is systematic, easy to apply and cost-effective (Pike and Ho, 1991).

Such under-analysis of risk is also not untypical in major IT projects, despite the higher risks being undergone. One example has been the development and implementation of SOCRATE, the French railways' new computerized reservation system. In 1989 the French railway company SNCF bought a version of the airline reservation system SABRE for FF1.3 billion. After customizing and testing it was introduced in April 1993. One short-term economic result was that SNCF experienced a decrease in sales of up to 10 per cent in the first six months (Eglizeau, Frey and Newman, 1996). The causes could be traced to technical malfunctions, lack of user friendliness in the designs, user resistance by SNCF employees, poor project management, and time pressures set by government and senior management. But most significantly, despite its huge size, complex technology and multiple stakeholders – making it a high risk project from the beginning – no meaningful risk analysis was ever undertaken (Eglizeau, Frey and Newman, 1996; Mitev, 1996).

In fact, risk is involved in all IT projects. Here risk is taken to be a negative outcome that has a known or estimated probability of occurrence based on experience or some theory (Charette, 1991; Stringer, 1992; Warner *et al.*, 1992). Risk of a negative outcome only becomes a salient problem when the outcome is relevant to stakeholder concerns and interests. Different settings and stakeholders will see different outcomes as salient (Douglas and Wildavsky, 1983). For example, for the governments promoting the CRISP and Videotex systems described below, the policy impact of the systems, as well as their administrative efficiency, and so the risk of negative outcomes on this further dimension, all may well be deemed significant. Risk is taken on a broad definition here. A range of risk factors may contribute to negative outcomes of varying degree. Emerging from the research studies reviewed below, in terms of factors there are those that appear inherently risky, for example, risk increases with size and complexity of project; those that are inherent in contextual factors about which project managers and many stakeholders can do little, for example time limits set by government or a holding company; and those shading in varying degrees into mistake and/or inadequate action. The purpose here is to examine all such risk factors as they emerge in the research and case studies.

Risk frameworks
A number of frameworks have been generated from research and experience to assist risk assessment at the feasibility stage of IT projects. The Cash, McFarlan and McKenney (1992) framework suggests that there are at least three important project dimensions that influence the inherent implementation risk. These are: project size (staffing levels, elapsed time, cost, number of departments affected), experience with the technology, and project structure (a highly structured project with fixed, certain outputs not subject to change during the lifetime of the project experiences less risk). A version of how these factors relate to one another, and engender different levels of risk, is shown in Figure 9.1. This provides a simple and useful starting point for analysing risk, and serves to highlight why large-scale IT projects are inherently risky, though the framework does omit many factors identified as potentially significant by the research work reported below.

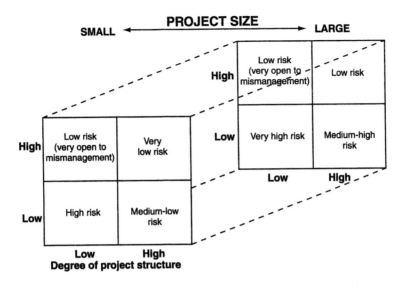

Figure 9.1   Risks in project implementation (Source: adapted from Cash *et al.,* 1992 in Willcocks and Griffiths (1994))

The framework developed by Parker, Benson and Trainor (1988) suggests that five major risks need to be assessed:

- *Organizational risk* – looking at how equipped an organization is to implement the project in terms of personnel, skills and experience.
- *IS infrastructure risk* – assessing how far the entire IS organization needs and is prepared to support the project.
- *Definitional uncertainty* – assessing the degree to which the requirements and/or the specifications of the project are known. Also assessed are the complexity of the area and the probability of non-routine changes.
- *Competitive response* – assessing the degree of corporate risk associated with not undertaking the project; (for major projects the risk may be to many organizations and even perceived as a national one).
- *Technical uncertainty* – evaluating a project's dependence on new or untried technologies.

Corder (1989) suggests high-risk factors as project size, project definition, user commitment and stability, project time, and number of systems interfaces. Medium-risk factors include functional complexity, number of user departments, newness of technology/vendor, user experience of computers, the project team's experience of the user area, newness of technology to the organization, number of vendors/

contractors. Low-risk factors include number of geographical sites, functional newness and number of project phases.

Research studies

More detailed research tends to support these frameworks as representing the major risk factors, while also indicating a range of other factors significantly different from project to project. One comprehensive review of the literature found 12 groups of reasons for information systems failure – lack of sophisticated technology; lack of fit of the IS to user capabilities or to the organization or organizational operating environment; deficiencies in the IS development process relating to lack of adequate and powerful methods, or lack of sufficient attention to types of decision supported, nature of work, contingency factors, organizational implementation or to the fact of biased or wrong assumptions driving development; and finally insufficient skills and capabilities on the part of IS professionals and/or users (Lyytinen and Hirschheim, 1987). More recent research tends to focus on limited sections of this listing, but also supports generally the finding that the major risks and reasons for failure tend to be through organizational, social and political, rather than technical factors (Beath and Ives, 1989; Kearney, 1990; Scott Morton, 1991; see also Chapter 10). Another way of assessing risk is through utilizing innovation theory. Thus Harrow and Willcocks (1992) adapt Rogers and Kim (1985) and point to five attributes of innovations that affect adoption rates in various contexts. In terms of IS projects, innovations with:

- greater relative advantage (over preceding practices);
- more compatibility (with potential adopters needs and values);
- less complexity;
- more 'trial-ability' (testing possible on a limited basis);
- more observability (results visible to others)

are more readily and rapidly adoptable than others. There is considerable support in the research literature, particularly for the first three factors as major determinants of IS success or failure defined typically in terms of IS usage and/or user satisfaction with the system. As will be seen relative advantage and compatibility factors emerge particularly strongly in the TradeNet and Videotex case studies discussed below. However, a range of support factors probably need to be incorporated into innovation theory if robust risk frameworks are to be developed. Thus, in the public sector, a recent study found that even situations diagnosed as low risk, that is where many of these innovation factors tend to support IT adoption, risk can be reintroduced by financial and time constraints imposed by central government that do not reflect the realities of project managing robust, usable systems into operation (Willcocks and Margetts, 1994b). This is a particularly important point to make, given that many major IT projects, because of their high likely impact, have direct government involvement, as can be seen in the SOCRATE case and in the cases of Videotex, TradeNet, CRISP and the DSS operational strategies detailed below.

Risk and reward

A fundamental part of risk assessment is to identify the risk in terms of its probability and impact, then evaluate what might be the acceptable trade-offs between risk and reward. It is useful to support the risk assessment process with a number of now widely available financial estimates and statistical techniques (Hull, 1990; Post and Dilz, 1986; Williams, 1990). But if such techniques are under-used in risk assessment, they also come in the 'necessary but insufficient' category. One problem is that decisions on the risk–reward trade-off are invariably arrived at through what has been called a 'formal–rational' analysis. This assumes a high degree of objectivity in the calculations; moreover the appearance of objectivity can be enhanced by expressing the calculations and results in numerical form. However the influence of perception, politics, culture and attitude to risk cut across all such analyses and decision-making in quite fundamental ways. Formal–rational analysis frequently has a strong ritualistic element, often acting as a symbolic expression of a belief in rational management rather than a reliable aid to decision-making (Kumar, 1990; Walsham, 1993). Different stakeholders in different sectors will perceive IS issues, and value the attendant risks in different ways. There are varying attitudes to risk in the oil, insurance and health services sectors, for example. Specific organizations develop their own risk cultures. An illuminating major technology project example is that of the US Space Agency NASA and the space shuttle program. In fact NASA built into its culture the belief that risk was not minimized by quantitative risk analysis but by improving the reliability and quality of design (Shenhar, 1992). The proportion of rocket launch failures was driven down from 1958–86, contributing to a culture of increasing success. When a safety board suggested they should be working on figures of failure as 1 in 1000, NASA recommended 1 in 10 000, 'due to unique improvements in design and manufacture of solid rocket fuel boosters (SRBs)', (Charette, 1991). For political reasons, and partly to maintain government funding, risk was downplayed; as one example, the space shuttle was designed as an airliner, suggesting similar reliability. An SRB failed on the 25th space shuttle launch, in 1986, killing all the crew. NASA now applies quantitative risk analysis together with its quality design approach and uses a 1 in 78 failure rate for its SRB launches. Clearly attitudinal, cultural and political issues can greatly influence risk perception (Douglas and Wildavsky, (1983), Willcocks, Currie and Mason, 1997). One conclusion must be that these aspects themselves are neglected risk factors that need inclusion in analyses and evaluation of risks to be managed.

Developing the analysis

The research work reviewed so far provides a number of guidelines for identifying the risks to be managed in IT projects. To focus the issue on scale, these will be developed further in conjunction with a more detailed, processual and longitudinal analysis using case histories of seven large-scale IT projects. We will suggest that more comprehensive frameworks for risk assessment are needed to complement the all too frequently encountered truncated forms of assessment developed from the project management, operational research and financial management fields. Risk needs to be interpreted operationally as not just inherent in certain structural features of the environment or of a project, but also arising as a result of distinctive human and organizational practices and patterns of belief and action. This leads on to the need to develop a more process-oriented and organization studies-based framework for risk analysis and management for major IT projects. An attempt will be made at developing such a framework out of the findings from the research studies cited above and from an analysis of the case studies that now follow.

SINGAPORE TRADENET: TOWARD AN INFORMATION ECONOMY

Background

The application of IT in the Singapore TradeNet system has been portrayed as a major success story (Cooke, 1994; Donovan, 1993; King and Konsynski, 1990(a) and (b); Sisodia, 1992). What made the project so effective? One major aspect was that by 1985 Singapore's pre-eminent trading position was being threatened by the prospect of severe recession combined with an escalation of Far East competition, notably from Hong Kong. The scale of the threat concentrated the minds of a high-level committee that subsequently defined two areas for achieving competitive advantage through expanding external trade. The quality of trade could be improved through streamlining all pertinent legal, financial and documentation processes. Secondly, cost containment could provide an attractive fee and port charge pricing structure. The project began with the critical acceptance that investment in IT was an integral part of achieving these objectives (King and Konsynski, 1990a). The absence of such an acceptance, and the lack of high-level support and finance so obviously present in the Singapore example, have been contributory factors to failure in many other major IT projects. However their presence provides a platform for, not the delivery of, success.

Detail

In the TradeNet case a further contributory factor was the groundwork set in place in the 1970s. The government had established a Committee on National Computerization (CNC) to define how Singapore could harness the power of IT. The CNC reported that, as a first step, a massive education process was needed because at least 10 000 IT professionals would be required by 1990. The education programme and the introduction of computers into government departments was well underway by the time of the 1985 economic crisis. It was also appreciated at an early stage that commitment and agreement would be needed from a number of important interest groups, in order to change any aspect of the process of trade. A series of discussions between the Economic Development Board, National Computer Board and Trade Development Board (TDB) ensued, the main focus being the simplifications and streamlining of documentation integral to the trading process. The TDB was given the task of mobilizing key organizations such as the Civil Aviation, Port of Singapore Authority and Customs and Excise to gain their commitment to create a trade-oriented Electronic Data Interchange (EDI) system. This system was to be called 'TradeNet'.

A major risk in IT projects relates to definitional uncertainty about information requirements (Iliff, 1994). In the TradeNet case this was first tackled by developing a detailed understanding of what existing trade procedures were being followed. To cope with the detail, and also the sensitivity of commercial and political issues, a sophisticated structure of committees was established so that every interest could be represented. The TradeNet Steering Committee (TNSC), set up to oversee and verify all procedures, was split into three sub-committees representing maritime, air and government agencies/statutory institutions. These met regularly and produced a series of reports on current procedures, resulting in a final definitive report on trade activities and related documentation. This revealed that replication of the existing complex, multi-form procedures into electronic form would not achieve quality improvement and cost containment. Only a massive simplification process could achieve this. The TNSC therefore decided to have designed a single form in use for trade agreements as a basis for a computer specification.

In parallel the TDB began testing a prototype on-line system called Trade-Dial-Up which allowed traders to complete forms on-line. The fact that this worked in controlled circumstances introduced the idea of developing this system into the EDI system being sought by Singapore. However, moving from concept to build, and ensuring that IT in the diverse range of companies and agencies that needed to be part of a successful trade networking system were integrated, this presented a massive technological problem, typical of many major IT projects. It was realized that the existing skills base and experience within Singapore were not sufficient. Management and coordination of the project were necessary, and the TNSC made the decision to seek outside assistance.

The process of selecting from an invited shortlist of companies was assisted by the clear terms of reference and information requirements already generated through the committee process. Tendering companies all had experience in dealing with large-scale IT projects. Feasibility studies were undertaken and similar systems investigated in other countries. A new management structure that established clear ownership was created for the next project stage. The TDB, Port of Singapore, Civil Aviation Authority and Singapore Telecoms established a separate company whose aim was to operate the TradeNet system for profit. This company awarded to IBM the contract to establish systems integration and have responsibility for all systems aspects except software. The latter contract was awarded to Computer Systems Advisers, Pte. Ltd. of Singapore. Many of the problems engendered on multi-supplier IT projects were minimized by clear delineation of responsibility for every aspect of implementation. Parameters were set out for a comprehensive implementation of the project according to well-defined and detailed specifications. In practice, especially over long-timescales, it is well known that user needs change as expectations and knowledge develop (De Greene, 1991; Strassman, 1985; see also Chapter 7). It was therefore decided, by the project manager, that rigorous change procedures would operate, analysing the time, impact and cost of proposals before any changes could be contemplated. Objectives were therefore always maintained, and implementation held very firmly on track.

In January 1989 TradeNet was officially declared operational. Direct capital cost was S$20 million, the project stuck to agreed timescales, and the two overriding objectives were achieved. The quality of interaction with outside customers had improved. As one example, turnaround time for trade documentation had been reduced from a maximum of four days to 10–15 minutes. As another, some freight forwarders were reporting cost savings of between 25–30 per cent. TradeNet also opened up further business possibilities as more and more companies decided to subscribe. The system also represented a core system as pressure came to take electronic communications further into providing funds transfer, banking and even healthcare through EDI systems, with the possibility of linking into TradeNet (Sisodia, 1992).

There were solid reasons for these outcomes, not least the effective management of risks in such a large-scale project. Objectives for undertaking TradeNet were focused, explicit, and understood and accepted by all interest groups involved in project preparation and implementation. The objectives were not changed; the price of failing to achieve them was high enough for the objectives not to be re-examined and argued over continuously. Fundamental control procedures did not change and were not disrupted. The drive to achieve objectives was maintained at the most senior levels. Communication both vertically and horizontally was facilitated by a willingness to include all interested parties and to compromise on certain aspects to achieve the end results. A skills infrastructure was in place to ensure take-up of new systems. The objectives fitted into the long-term objectives of the government, and it was realistic to expect companies to adapt to the new systems and processes that were inevitably part of the introduction of IT. The implementation of such a major project was not hampered by lack of knowledge and familiarity of the relevant technologies.

There was a remarkable willingness to bring in outside expertise once project scale and complexity were fully realized. This undoubtedly saved time and ensured that Singapore personnel could be introduced to a major project implementation through working alongside more experienced IT staff. Innovative technology was not introduced into the main project until it had been fully tested in controlled circumstances. Only when these conditions could be replicated on the main project were decisions made to include new technologies. This caution and strict management approach undoubtedly prevented the TradeNet project collapsing due to technological weaknesses or limitations. Moreover, human and cultural factors were attended to. The project developed in such a way that all parties, including users, traders, government, suppliers and customers could see benefits from taking part in it. The objective of securing Singapore as a preferred trading centre was achieved. An important element in this success, was the wider and long-term development of a knowledge and skills culture supportive of IT developments. This has resulted in the institutionalization, as opposed to the mere installation of the TradeNet system, into the administrative, commercial, and social life of the country.

THE UK DSS OPERATIONAL STRATEGY: RISKS IN A MAJOR PROJECT

Background

The Operational Strategy (OS), the project to fully automate the Department of Social Security (DSS) in the UK, provides a comparable example of computerization and risk on a major scale. As at 1994 the

DSS was one of the largest government departments, consuming 30 per cent of public spending and employing around 10 per cent of central government staff. The OS was a plan involving the construction of large-scale computer systems and the installation of 40 000 terminals in 1000 local offices and unemployment offices. It was claimed to be the largest programme of computerization ever undertaken in Europe, on 1992 figures costing in excess of £2 billion, with originally planned £700 million savings on DSS operating costs by 1995 as a result of computerization (Margetts, 1991; Willcocks and Margetts, 1994b).

Work carried out on the OS fell into three stages. The planning and design phase lasted from 1982 until June 1985. In 1985 the Government announced its plans for the reform of social security in a two-volume Green Paper. This had far-reaching implications for the systems in the strategy and new plans had to be made to account for the subsequent restructuring of benefits. The third stage started in 1987 when it became clear that many of the projects had slipped behind their original target dates. The speed of implementation after 1987 was fast and furious, and subsequent target dates for individual projects were largely met. More detailed descriptions of the history of the OS, and the risks engendered in the project, appear elsewhere (Margetts, 1991; Willcocks and Margetts, 1994b; Willcocks and Mason, 1987b). Therein we question the extent to which the original objectives of cost savings, system robustness, increased job satisfaction for staff and improved quality of service have been, and can be met. Nor is this surprising when the risks undergone are examined.

Detail

Within the overall context of high risk due to large size, high complexity, large number of divisions being computerized and length of time for project completion (from 1982–99), a number of additional risks can be demonstrated in the DSS case, some of them distinctive to the public sector (see Figure 9.2).

---

1. Large number of divisions
2. Length of time for completion
3. Separation of IT management from policy-making
4. Large size
5. Difficulties aligning business/IT organizational strategies
6. Insufficient IT expertise
7. Industrial relations risk
8. High complexity
9. Environmental turbulence/pressures
10. Isolation of IT in development phases
11. Newness of, and changing, technologies

Figure 9.2   Risk factors in the DSS Operational Strategy

The history of a soured industrial relations climate, flowing in part from a seven-month 'pensions' strike at Newcastle computer centre in the mid–1980s caused difficulties in securing employee commitment to the project, while the strike itself caused significant disruption to project timings (Willcocks and Mason, 1987b). Overall a major risk was that of costs rising out of control. In fact these rose from the original estimate of £700 million to over £2.6 billion by 1993. According to a 1989 report even by that date it seemed unlikely that any of the cost savings, estimated then at £175 million, would be achieved (National Audit Office, 1989). The OS also underwent risks associated with the organization not possessing sufficient IT expertise. In fact the OS struggled with IT staff turnover rates of 45 per cent. In practice, the DSS dealt with the problems of skills shortages almost exclusively via the use of consultants. In 1986–87, they employed around 150 consultants at a cost of £12.1 million, thus making real the risk of spiralling costs. After 1987 the number of consultants used on the project increased significantly. Half the internal programmers working on the OS project were moved to other areas because they were seen as a strike risk. The number of consultants employed in 1987–88 was 235, at a cost of £22 million, nearly five times the cost of equivalent in-house staff (National Audit Office, 1989).

Further risks were inherent in the separation of IT management from policy-making. As contextual factors, social security reforms between 1985–88 had far-reaching effects on the project. Little development work had taken place on the main projects at the time the social security reforms were introduced, but the changes meant that project plans had to be altered within a relatively brief period of two years up to April 1988. According to many sources, those involved in planning the OS were not consulted until the Green Paper was published. The speed demanded for modification of supplementary benefit software to income support software in time for the introduction of the new benefit created considerable problems. Many of the smaller projects, largely those designed to improve quality of service, were dropped from the plans. While those in charge of administration appeared unconcerned with policy issues, it also seems that politicians were reluctant to equip themselves with an understanding of information technology. There were considerable risks inherent in the isolation of IT in the DSS. All the problems encountered seem to point to this one major feature. While succeeding in bringing the computers themselves to the heart of the organization, all expertise in IT had been kept largely on the periphery. While much of the design and specification of the system was carried out by consultants, those with experience of actually using the DSS administrative systems were relatively excluded.

Using the frameworks in Figures 9.4 and 9.5 (see later), a range of risk factors come strikingly together in the history of the DSS Operational Strategy. In terms of outer context, government pressure, imposed deadlines, and the many legislative changes in the 1980–92 period all created a riskier climate for the delivery of robust IS. Additionally, historically, the organization lacked relevant IS experience and skills. Reward systems in the organization created labour market problems and exacerbated IS skills shortages; in a soured industrial relations climate, against tight deadlines, the policy became to cut off staff participation in systems development and pull in external consultants. This put pressure on cost targets, left systems design largely to IS professionals, and put at risk stated objectives on job satisfaction and systems quality. At the same time a number of inherently risky factors feature in the OS, in particular the large size, high complexity, large number of units being computerized, a high degree of technical and definitional uncertainty, and the 17-year time-span for project completion. Furthermore the processes of change saw little user commitment and training to 1990, mainly due to tightening deadlines, management decision and the perceived high cost of further delay. Much of the case evidence indicates that the major risks and reasons for sub-optimization are as much due to organizational, social and political, as inherently risky or merely technical factors. The complex nature of risks in large IS projects are well exemplified in the DSS case, with the public sector setting also bringing distinctive outer and inner contextual factors to bear.

THE CRISP PROJECT IN INDIA: A CULTURAL SHOCK

Background
In the 1970s it was recognized that significant sections of the Indian population were not sharing in the benefits of the expanding economy. The biggest losers were the rural poor who often had no saleable product or service to market, and no income-generating skill to provide them with employment. They were entirely dependent on aid or government grants. Under these circumstances the process of alleviating poverty was self defeating because most grant recipients were left as helpless after funding had finished as they were beforehand. In order to provide a more consistent policy of aid which raised living standards, and facilitated employment, the government set up the Integrated Rural Development Programme (IRDP) in 1978. This programme established a process of grants and subsidies to selected poor families to purchase their first assets. A heavy IT investment programme at national level was seen as necessary to support this

initiative. It could facilitate the coordination of data from the regions and provide local representatives with a helpful decision-support tool. The end result would be more effective targeting of the most vulnerable, and the alleviation of endemic poverty.

Detail

The IRDP was established as a national programme for the alleviation of poverty in rural areas. The large scope of the project meant that massive amounts of detailed information about rural communities was collected locally, but because most of the processes were manually based this information could not be integrated or coordinated nationally. Computers were seen as the most effective means of supporting the IRDP nationally allowing the effective resource allocation to the most needy, and providing local areas with a decision-support tool to assist in programme administration. The Computerized Rural Information Systems Project (CRISP) received the full backing of the Indian government, and finance was made available for its installation nationally. The CRISP system consisted of microcomputers running a range of standard report generating packages. Its specific objectives were:

- to facilitate the generation of reports required by local and national government;
- to create records of beneficiaries;
- to collect village information for planning.

Once relevant information about rural families was generated, this was passed from the blocks (the lowest administrative unit) to the districts and to central government. The aim was to evolve an integrated series of reports for villages, that could be developed into block, district and state level reports and eventually into an All-India IRDP plan.

The decision to invest in the CRISP system was based upon a successful implementation of this technology in the Karwar district of Karnataka, in southern India (Banerji and Ghosh, 1989). In Karwar, an effective management approach had ensured that systems design and development for the IRDP application had the active participation of users. Specific skills training was given and clerks were shown how the system could help them to work more productively. As a result, the district was able to make better planning decisions, to access data more quickly, coordinate local efforts more effectively, and to arrange more field visits. All of these benefits were seen as critical to ensuring the IRDP's success nationally (Patel, 1987). Once the decision had been taken to establish CRISP nationally there was little further direction or support from the centre about how to manage the technology locally. It was left to individual state governments to allocate funding, purchase equipment, and agree contracts. Some states floated their own tenders, and so kept the contracts within their own political influence. Many contracts were given to unqualified individuals or agencies. Power failures, technical problems and poor maintenance support characterized implementation in all districts. These problems, often encountered at the implementation and use stages of the initiative, resulted in lowered expectations and negative attitudes among staff.

In practice CRISP has not resulted in the massive alleviation of poverty in India, or even in the effective coordination of information for better central planning (Madon, 1991). In many states CRISP was never fully utilized, and is now a redundant system. Four main barriers have been identified as accounting for CRISP's lack of success. Firstly, computerization was imposed in a top-down manner, which did not take account of local requirements, practices or processes. Local administrators were neither consulted about the approach nor included in the decisions about speed and scope of implementation. The policy of making technology available to even the poorest in the community could not ensure a successful project on its own. Secondly, and ironically, the aim of decentralizing rural development by allocating computers to the local level was interpreted as a threatening form of centralization of information. Local officials perceived computerization as undermining their influence; consequently they were not eager to make it effective. In many instances it was also found that informal covert systems were at work subverting the original objectives of the formal IRDP initiative. Thirdly, education and training were not provided throughout the country. There was no formalized approach to covering specific skills training linked to broader education on the implications of IT. Many unskilled people were expected to operate computers for the first time without adequate support. Finally, installation and maintenance support were sporadic, and often insufficient to keep CRISP to the operational level that was technically achievable.

In the original implementation of CRISP in the Kanwar district these four barriers were not encountered because a close involvement by users and beneficiaries was an essential part of the whole process. When CRISP was expanded to become a country-wide implementation new technical problems were introduced as a result of increased size and complexity, but many of the neglected risk factors related to human, cultural, political and managerial issues rather than technical ones (Madon, 1991, 1992). Additionally many short-cuts were taken. The result was that a previous small-scale success developed into a large-scale failure of a major IT project.

VIDEOTEX: KEY TO THE FUTURE?

Background

In the 1970s and 1980s several European governments were particularly interested in technologies that offered the possibility of creating the 'information society' (Ciborra, 1993; Feenberg, 1995). Major breakthroughs in microelectronics' research made new forms of communication possible, with considerable implications for national broadcasting and communication standards. Furthermore, instead of being limited to telephone, telegraph and telex, information could suddenly be exchanged through facsimile, electronic mail and other data transmission systems. Links between users meant that systems could be interactive, and include the conveyance of graphics and text as well as voice. Videotex grew out of a combination of these developments. It used familar business technology such as computers, and it offered potential mass market appeal because the systems could be linked through existing telephone networks. Three countries in particular, France, Britain and Germany, saw videotex as a worthwhile technology to promote and support nationally. In all three countries it was perceived as offering the most immediate means of introducing a national 'nervous system' of communication. Two distinct approaches were adopted to the management of these country-wide initiatives, and help to explain the differing outcomes in these countries.

The French Minitel system – a prestige project

The French government was very attracted to a major national prestige technology project and proved willing to provide major technological and financial support to the videotex initiative known as Minitel (Rapaport, 1992). In 1978 the French government expressed its intention to replace paper-based and operator dependent telephone directories with an electronic one. To ensure the day-to-day management of the initiative from design to implementation, control was handed to DGT, the state-owned telecommunications company. Two test sites were established at Rennes and Velizy to explore how the videotex technology would work and cope with demand. After successful initial results from the uptake of the telephone directory service, the system was made available throughout France.

In order to persudade potential subscribers to acquire the system, standard terminals called Minitels were distributed free by DGT together with a copy of the directory. The expectation was that savings would still eventually come through as a result of not printing the conventional paper directories. In addition it was found that specialist information services were also interested in linking into the system once potential accessibility could be verified. In effect, costs could be further recouped by charging information providers. The system evolved as a collection of information providers and subscribers linked through the public packet-switching network accessed through the telephone system. The charging of customers was coordinated through DGT who passed a proportion of the funds collected to the service providers. Importantly, Minitel did not seek to become a centralized database system that aimed to control all its information. By 1990 Minitel had more than 4 million terminals in use. Through the network it was possible to access over 15 000 services; customers were from both domestic and business sectors. The system has been upgraded and is expandable to meet any rise in demand from services and customers. Minitel's long-term future, however, is not guaranteed and will depend on its ability to maintain its attraction particularly when confronted by newer multi-media technologies.

British Prestel and German BTX systems – great hopes

As with the French DGT, other national post, telephone and telegraph organizations, including BT in Britain and DBP in Germany, were keen to promote exploitation of their telephone network infrastructure to facilitate videotex use. These companies could not, however, rely on their governments to provide the same level of technological or financial backing that the French government had done with Minitel. Selective government backing focused on publicity and government endorsement of the projects and their applications. Control of the technology was left to the marketplace as it was expected that television companies would provide the necessary terminals to subscribers of the systems. Both governments expected that any extension of the technology and support for it should be consumer led. For this reason, the governments aimed to create a solid demand in the marketplace before major investments were advocated in the technology itself. However, the 1979 launch of Prestel in the UK proved premature. It had been rushed due to false fears about overseas competitors utilizing the technology successfully to gain a stranglehold on information provision in the UK. In reality the technology was not ready for the market, and user uptake was very limited despite widespread awareness of the services being offered.

The German videotex system was finally introduced in 1983. Like the British system it failed to gain the commercial threshold that was necessary to make it either operationally or financially viable. Consequently both versions lapsed into providing small specialist groups with limited information of particular importance to individual industries. In the UK the highest users of Prestel are travel agents and particular financial groups within the City of London. The German system shifted its emphasis from the domestic to the commercial market in 1985 after failing to gain sufficient backers and subscribers to its systems. As in the UK, the system has failed to gain the national profile and support anticipated.

Outcomes

In all three countries videotex technology failed to become the centrepiece of a national IT infrastructure along the lines originally envisaged. Videotex did not provide a sufficient impetus to transform these countries into strategically networked nations along the lines of, for example, Singapore. In France alone videotex implementation acquired a significant role. There are a number of distinct reasons for this, accounted for by the different approach that France took to its management of the project.

First, the French government had already established a broad framework for planning to encourage the uptake of new technology. The concerns the French had about their ability to handle new technological developments had been publicly voiced. Consequently the French government was actively seeking a likely project for official endorsement and support. Videotex fitted in well with this longer-term policy because it held out the possibility of being a truly national project. Secondly, the backing of the government and its commitment to provide resources reduced the risks attached to marketing the technology. As a result no single company was disproportionately burdened at the very early experimental stages of the project. Thirdly, the distance-independent cost structure encouraged a geographic diffusion of information providers. This meant that it was possible to provide a market that was not limited to one or two regions. The system could therefore have national appeal. Fourthly the monopolistic control exercised by the French DGT ensured that management, design and implementation were firmly coordinated by one organization. Every aspect of the project design and implementation was monitored carefully, and particular standards were rigidly enforced. DGT had control of all aspects of the technology from the decisions about the specification for the terminals to the communication standards to be enforced. Fifthly, the government's focus on a tangible requirement, that is the electronic telephone directory, provided the necessary impetus at an early stage. The deliverables were clearly defined, understood and tested in a controlled study. This built up consensus, and some experience for handling the new IT.

The British and German approaches, by contrast, were too generalist and broadly based. Although both governments were actively encouraging the use of new IT, often this was promotional effort rather than linked to developing particular applications. The poor control that was provided over the design of equipment, and lack of standards to enforce delivery, budgets and performance caused critical delays in implementation (Collingridge, 1992). In addition, videotex became perceived by many to be a solution looking for a problem to solve; and no single organization was prepared to risk becoming a main stakeholder in such an ill-defined implementation, with so few perceived real returns.

However, the costs of introducing videotex have been high in all three cases. None of the systems produced have repaid the initial outlays. The German and British governments have lost massive amounts of money due to the projects beind reduced in scale at an early stage. The French government has continued to subsidize its system heavily, partly because of the prestige it draws from implementing a nationally networked system. By the mid–1990s it was still exploring how it might possibly incorporate other more strategic requirements into the videotex system in order to be able to convert it into the originally sought, national communications system. In practice, even Minitel failed to become consumer led, and if the French government subsidy was withdrawn it was expected that system use would contract severely. This indicates that one of the major problems with introducing national videotex systems has been lack of demand for the technology, as much as problems with how it has been managed and introduced.

TAURUS IN THE UK: A RUNAWAY PROJECT

Background

The London Stock Exchange's first experience of a large-scale IT project had been the comprehensive implementation of electronic dealings known euphemistically as the 'Big Bang' of 1986. Effectively this had removed the need for face-to-face meetings between what were called jobbers and stockbrokers, as the whole process of share dealing became automated. The TAURUS (Transfer and Automated Registration of Uncertified Stock) project was conceived in the early 1980s as the next phase of automation, ultimately leading to a paperless dealing and contractual system for shares. The aim was that all share certificates would be scrapped, and share transfers would be handled by book entry on a computer. The main impetus for TAURUS came in 1987 with a crisis in settlements stemming from back office, mainly paper-based, support systems failing to keep track of the massive number of share dealings and related transactions. Many of the international banks that had become owners of the main stockbroking firms exerted pressure on their subsidiaries to develop better systems. As an industry familiar with mass processing of routine financial data, the banks were keen to automate as much as possible as quickly as possible. There was, however, widespread and strong resistance to extending automation. Vested interests, such as registrars who would be put out of business if share certificates were abandoned, fought against further use of technology. This presented a major dilemma for the Stock Exchange. On the one hand it could not allow its international reputation to suffer through inefficient dealing; on the other it was aware of the need to maintain the support and confidence of all City interests.

Detail
The Bank of England appointed the Siscott Committee with terms of reference to provide a compromise that would leave no group in the securities industry worse off than before. The idea of developing a computer system remained at the heart of the solution the City was seeking. The focus of the committee, therefore, turned to what this system should provide. Inevitably with each compromise, expectations and systems design grew exponentially, as did the complexity of what was being sought. Although the Siscott Committee spearheaded the investigation, it did not enjoy the support of the main interest groups (Waters and Cane, 1993). Additionally, the Department of Trade and Industry (DTI) began to add restrictions, such as technological, financial and legal constraints to protect investors. The main focus was lost and decisions regularly swung from developing a massively-centralized computer system to the provision of an integrated network of computer databases, with the Stock Exchange acting as the 'hub'.

A complex series of committees were formed, disbanded and reformed to include major stakeholders in the City, including the banks. There were at various times the Exchange's Settlements Board Committee, The TAURUS Monitoring Group, The TAURUS Review Committee, as well as a range of different external consultants involved in the management of the project. Due to in-fighting and lack of clear objectives, the project developed a momentum of its own. Meetings often failed to decide central issues, and communication between committees or project managers was inconsistent or non-existent. Many business aspects concerning the data to be input were not satisfactorily resolved, so further delays and legal worries developed. Despite these drawbacks, however, a decision was made to start implementation of TAURUS. A project team was appointed and given the go-ahead to buy a £1 million software package from Vista Concepts of New Jersey for the core system. Work commenced on adapting the package to the London securities market, but in fact so much customization was needed that a further estimated £14 million was spent on rewriting the software. This process was never finished. All of these decisions were made despite there being no central design for the full system, and no planned operating architecture. Subsequently it was found that large parts of critical processes, such as overnight reconciliation, had been omitted or labelled non-urgent. Quality control was weak, and project management slack. Changes to requirements were introduced regularly on an *ad hoc* basis. Delays became a familiar characteristic of the project. Five years after starting, with direct project costs probably exceeding £50 million, TAURUS was finally abandoned in 1993.

TAURUS was a project that quickly grew out of control, and its history can be usefully compared to those of other major projects described in this chapter. The initial decision to design the system was flawed (Currie, 1995). There were no clear objectives. A crisis situation had brought together a wide, diverse group of interests which were, under the circumstances, unlikely to be conciliatory or looking for a wider, best solution for the City as a whole. No clear thinking or vision emerged from a series of committee structures, all of which failed to realize the extent of the scope and complexity of the project (Waters, 1993). Communication between these groups was inconsistent and intermittent. As a result, the number of individuals who were involved but not able or willing to act grew as the timescales became more protracted. Communication at all levels appears to have been poor, but this is particularly true of the channels established between the supervisory committees and project managers. Control was not linked sufficiently to a project-wide process of evaluation and accountability operating on a regular basis at several levels.

The lack of consensus about what the computer system was to provide ensured that the implementation process would be very slow. Without a design blueprint for the system it was difficult to know at the outset what problems were likely to arise, and how the system could be designed to maximize user friendliness. The lack of design also left open the option of changing aspects of the project at short notice, perhaps often without understanding the possible consequences and implications. Although in principle standards were issued, in practice they appear not to have been followed. TAURUS was being developed broadly using the guidelines set out in the SSADM methodology specified by the UK government for the implementation of large computer projects. In fact many of the central guidelines were not adhered to; for example testing of the system was being undertaken before the operational requirements had been specified. This lack of adherence to procedure was another cause of delays in systems delivery.

The lack of accountability that characterized the project meant that quality control both managerially and technically was weakened (Griffiths, 1994). Consultants were hired and changed without adequate consideration for what was being delivered or needed. Decisions were not scrutinized sufficiently, and as a result both time and cost targets were regularly missed. There are well-documented dangers in introducing untried or innovative technologies into major projects when they have been insufficiently tested (Bessant, 1991; De Greene, 1991). The decision to select Vista's high-priced global custody system was inappropriate; the core package needed so much customization that a huge learning process was required on the part of the technologists employed to adapt it. It would have been more appropriate to consider a bespoke system, though its development would also have probably run into considerable problems in the circumstances prevailing.

The TAURUS project was characterized by a series of fatal flaws that major projects need to avoid individually, let alone in combination. Many of the fundamental mistakes made throughout the project could have been avoided through learning from major project experiences of other organizations. At the beginning of 1994, while the settlements crisis had temporarily passed, the Stock Exchange was no nearer to addressing the core issues highlighted in the TAURUS project. The City was still in need of a mechanism for resolving complex inter-company issues which affected the stability of the financial services and securities sectors. The next, more limited computerization project was already being planned, though no new management or control structures had been announced, while firms and interest groups were as diverse in opinion and as strong on limited personal goals as ever. From 1994 to 1996 CREST, a more limited settlement system, was under active development, in the expectation that learning from TAURUS could be passed on into the new project.

MANAGING SCALE IN IT PROJECTS: TOWARD A RISK FRAMEWORK

In this section we will analyse the case studies further with a view to establishing learning points on the management of major projects, and developing a framework for risk profiling. A summary of the conditions for success and failure in each of the case studies appears in Figure 9.3. A review of the case studies points to several fundamental points on which effective management of these large-scale IT projects appeared to hinge.

Governance
The concept of governance here refers to how the major stakeholders organize themselves to establish objectives, allocate resources and make decisions. As such governance can be differentiated from project

Major issues	TradeNet	Operational strategy	CRISP	Videotex (France)	Videotex (UK & Germany)	TAURUS
Strategic framework	Clear and stable	Fluctuated with government policy and industrial relations problems	Control dispersed to regions	Strong fit with government planning	Control and development left to marketplace	Ill-defined and changing
Role of government	Interventionist; supportive	Isolation of IT; financial support	Financial backing	Financial and technical support; coordination	Publicity and endorsement only	'Hands-off'; legislative restrictions
Organizational adaption	Trade operations and jobs redefined	Coercive rather than through participation	Stakeholder resistance	New customer–supplier relationships	Little adaption; small take-up	Manual processes automated: resistance
IT supplier problems	Clear terms of reference; strong management	Some, created by time pressure and changing requirements	Poor contracting; variable standards	Run by state-owned company	Suppliers demotivated by lack of demand	Unclear terms of reference; poor management arrangements
Change management	Supportive cultural context; strong project disciplines	High use of consultants to circumvent internal resistance	Lack of user participation	Well coordinated	Lack of demand meant no real problems	Lacked coordination and control focuses

Figure 9.3   Conditions for success and failure in seven major IT projects (Continued)

226

Major issues	TradeNet	Operational strategy	CRISP	Videotex (France)	Videotex (UK & Germany)	TAURUS
Faith in technical fix	Business needs first	Technology driven	Underplayed human and social factors	Evolutionary: see how used	Over-optimistic about its usefulness	Technology-driven
Market and economic demand	Seen as economic survival issue	Mainly to cut administrative costs	Distributive mechanism	High take-up (at subsidized rates)	Limited to specialist groups	Demand fluctuated; stakeholder ambivalence
Skills to support implementation	Educational infrastructure; additional skills imported	External technical skills used	Skills not available	Available and used	Available but not widely used	Largely bought-in
Exploration of wider options	Comprehensive review combined with proto-typing approach	'Technical fix' updated by time pressure and IR issues	Options not explored	Yes, through evolutionary development	Technology as solution	Only after 1993 failure

Figure 9.3   Conditions for success and failure in seven major IT projects (Concluded)

management, which is here characterized as the critical, but lower level management of the set of activities delivering on decisions arrived at through governance. The case studies reveal that governance sets the critical parameters in which effective project management can take place. On large-scale projects governance is revealed as particularly difficult because of the involvement of multiple and powerful stakeholders, including governments (Collingridge, 1992). The TradeNet case is notable for the high intervention of the Singapore government and the high degree of coordination between interest groups permitting the developing of clear objectives, strategy and information requirements. This can be contrasted most significantly with the TAURUS arrangements, marked by poor coordination within the governance structure. The French government gave clear leads in governance in their videotex project, unlike in the ill-fated German and British videotex initiatives. In the Indian CRISP project the governance structure tended to be dysfunctional where regional implementation was required. The governance arrangements influenced the clarity of objectives, the direction and momentum of these major projects in different and crucial ways.

Project management: balancing top-down and bottom-up
A major issue faced in all major projects is the degree to which objectives and decisions set at the top are followed through at lower levels. We see in the case studies examples of displacement of objectives, in particular in the CRISP and TAURUS projects, in the latter case because of lack of clear objectives and signals emerging from the governance structure. While it is inherently difficult to prevent these displacement effects, this seems to have been largely achieved in the TradeNet case through balancing defined top-down parameters together with more local involvement in deciding information requirements and project delivery. The DSS Operational Strategy in fact had little bottom-up involvement, time constraints being one of the determining parameters of this approach, and suffered on a number of objectives as a result.

Market need/economic survival
The success of a project was critically influenced by the degree to which there was really a market need for what it was delivering, and/or whether economic survival was at stake. This helps to explain the planning and energy driving the TradeNet system to success; stakeholders were brought together by a clear overriding, salient set of objectives. CRISP lost its way in regional issues and, like the more successful DSS Operational Strategy, was a distributive system rather than one delivering on market need or economic survival. In the

TAURUS case it is not clear that stakeholders perceived the IT project as determining their economic survival in a significant way, especially once the settlements crisis subsided. In the videotex cases the systems demonstrated no great market need in Germany and Britain, but there was a greater need in France, though mainly supported by government subsidy.

Learning

From the cases there would seem to be two aspects of learning that are particularly significant: learning from experience, and learning something new. The history of IT experience has not been one of evolutionary learning. On the contrary, it has been one of not learning lessons well enough to avoid repeating previous mistakes (Bessant, 1991; Hochstrasser and Griffiths, 1991; see also Chapter 18). This weakness, linked to that fact that major IT projects are often synonymous with charting new learning territory, make them high-risk ventures. Under these circumstances, the difficulties of building up appropriate teams with the most relevant experience and skills cannot be underestimated, and were clearly not avoided in several of the case studies under review. Collingridge (1992) makes the further point that major projects are too often over-ambitious and over-designed at the front end, looking to deliver a completed design fast using a 'big bang' strategy (see also Chapters 7 and 10). This would seem particularly risky with technological innovations and the alternative approach he suggests is one of incremental innovation, not least because it allows learning. From this perspective the DSS Operational Strategy and TAURUS would seem to have been over-ambitious, and seemed to have placed strong restrictions on both types of learning. In fact in both cases the initial designs had to be radically recast on the long road to implementation. In the TradeNet case the supportive educational environment mentioned in several studies (King and Konsynski 1990(a) and (b); also Singapore Bulletin, 1993), and the early prototyping approach, were clear factors in using experience and promoting learning within the project.

In the context of these factors a further, more comprehensive framework can be put forward for risk profiling of major IT projects. This is based on reviewing research studies, frameworks and the cases detailed earlier in this chapter. The framework shown in Figure 9.4 represents a development from earlier work (Pettigrew and Whipp, 1991; Pettigrew, Ferlie and McKee, 1992; Willcocks and Margetts, 1994b), and is put forward to complement rather than to replace other methods for risk analysis. However, a major advantage of carrying out this additional, deeper analysis is to enrich the degree to which risk analysis informs and enables the subsequent task of risk management.

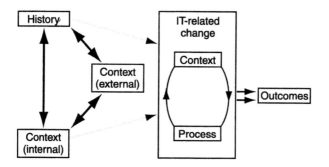

Figure 9.4   A framework for risk analysis

Major factors that seem to bear critical study during IS development, implementation and usage are summarized in Figure 9.5. For clarificatory purposes we will discuss illustrative examples of these factors; however, these examples from the case studies receive considerable support from the other evidence detailed in this chapter.

A *history* of information systems success or failure seems to have a bearing on subsequent risks experienced. TradeNet could draw upon a supportive educational infrastructure and prior computerization in government departments. In the DSS case the Operational Strategy followed on a previously failed, high-profile project in the department; ironically in the CRISP case there was a history of success on a regional project that could not be repeated when the national scale of the project introduced new risk dimensions and management requirements (Madon, 1991, 1992). A lack of relevant IS experience at the DSS, and in the TAURUS case, contributed to subsequent risk development in each case. Organizational history of industrial relations problems directly impinged upon creating risks to computerization in the DSS case.

The way in which *external contextual* factors contribute to the 'riskiness' of computerization is demonstrated in the DSS case (government deadlines and the speed of new legislation). The differing levels of government support influenced the outcomes in all seven cases; the manner of government involvement was also influential, in the case of TAURUS government was involved but not in particularly helpful ways. The 'newness of technology' factor operated in all cases, but was more appropriately handled in some cases than others. Often this factor led organizations to expose themselves to the vagaries of the consultancy/supplier markets; this was better handled for TradeNet than, for example, TAURUS and to a lesser extent the DSS, but represented a significant risk to be managed in every case. We have already commented on how over-anticipation of market demand can

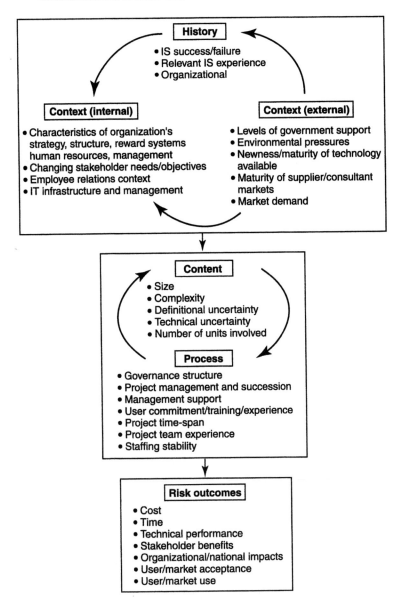

Figure 9.5   Risk profiling – major factors

lead on to lack of take-up when the project has been delivered. The risk here resides in adhering to a belief in the inherent attractiveness of new 'technology' to the market, as in the videotex cases.

Internal contextual factors also have a critical bearing on levels and types of risk engendered. As examples: the degree to which organizations possesses relevant IS experience can influence the risks subsequently undergone, as was clearly the case with CRISP. Managerial, cultural, human resource and evaluation and reward systems issues can feed into the degree of risk experienced in computerization. Misfits between organizational and IS structure/ infrastructure can cause problems (Hochstrasser and Griffiths, 1991). These issues can be seen most clearly in the DSS and TAURUS cases. The DSS case also illustrates the impact of the industrial relations climate on project risk. Changing stakeholder and business needs, all too typical on large projects over long time-spans, can also greatly affect the riskiness inherent in IS development and introduction. The need here is to control for such changes, as in the TradeNet example, rather than allow them to happen in an *ad hoc* manner, as was all too typical in the TAURUS case.

The *content* issues in IT-related change listed in Figure 9.5 emerge strongly from all studies, but particularly clearly from the DSS and TAURUS cases, each high in terms of size and complexity and number of units being computerized, and both illustrating the risks inherent in 'definitional' and 'technical uncertainty' (see the Parker, Benson and Trainor (1988) framework above). It is instructive to contrast the different outcome in the TradeNet case, resulting from more active risk management. The organizational/project risks associated with *process* issues also flow through all the cases but are particularly clear in the TAURUS and DSS cases. A further point relates to the study of desirable *outcomes* in computerization. Typical outcomes pursued in the cases we have detailed are summarized in Figure 9.5. This listing does not exhaust the possibilities, of course.

What becomes important in analysing preferred IS outcomes is discovering whose perceptions and vested interests these represent. If defined outcomes are not representative of the desired objectives of salient stakeholders who can affect the course of computerization, then this may decrease the achievability of those outcomes. Clearly a detailed stakeholder analysis can assist in defining the type, size of impact and probability of risks becoming real here (examples of ways to carry out such a stakeholder analysis appear in Willcocks and Mason, 1987a). However, the dominant point that must emerge from our analyses and this discussion must be that it is the relationships between all the factors detailed in Figure 9.5, the way in which they interconnect to engender risk, that deserve analysis. The study of such interrelationships receives too little attention in other risk analysis approaches, and the present framework can provide a useful, complementary, heuristic tool.

CONCLUSION

We have argued that major IT projects are inherently very high risk. All IT projects bear risks that need analysis and management, though, in practice, formal risk analysis seems to be distinctly a minority pursuit. However, new technology in combination with large scale adds dimensions of risk that necessitate an explicit concern for risk profiling to set the risk parameters in which project management can be conducted. We have used case studies of large-scale IT projects together with findings from other research studies on computerization to delineate the critical risk factors that emerge and that need reduction, control and management.

We have attempted to go beyond restricted definitions of risk and have applied a study framework that sees risk not just inherent in certain structural features of the environment or of a project, but also arising over time from their interconnection with history, process and external and internal context as a result of distinctive human and organizational practices and patterns of belief and action. It is certainly clear that certain features are inherently more risky than others. However we have also sought to develop the notion of risk to take into account factors which shade into mistakes and inadequate action by stakeholders and participants in IT-related change processes. This is to begin to suggest coherent alternatives to the all too frequently encountered truncated forms of risk assessment used, or to the situations where little formal assessment of risk is carried out at all. Risk in large-scale IT projects is high, multi-dimensional and can arise from unanticipated combinations of factors. This argues for less spurious accuracy in risk measurement, for broader definitions of what constitutes risk in practice, and more comprehensive risk frameworks able to catch where and how risks arise. This can then lead on to risk management, a core critical activity in the management of large-scale IT projects.

REFERENCES

Appleton, D. (1991) 'Very Large Projects', *Datamation*, January 15, pp. 63–70.

Banerji, S. and Ghosh, D. (1989) 'Information Technology and Rural Development: A New Harvest', *PC World India*, May, pp. 15–26.

Beath, C. and Ives, B. (1989) *The Information Technology Champion: Aiding and Abetting, Care and Feeding*, Oxford Institute of Information Management Research and Discussion Papers RPD89/2, Templeton College, Oxford.

Bessant, J. (1991) *Managing Advanced Manufacturing Technology: The Challenge of the Fifth Wave*, NCC-Blackwell, Manchester.

Cash, J., McFarlan, W. and McKenney, J. (1992) *Corporate Information Systems Management*, Irwin, Boston.

Charette, R. (1991) *Application Strategies for Risk Analysis*, McGraw-Hill, New York.

Ciborra, C. (1993) *Teams, Markets and Systems*, Cambridge University Press, Cambridge.

Collingridge, D. (1992) *The Management of Scale*, Routledge, London.

Cooke, K. (1994) 'Singapore Finds Quay To Success', *The Financial Times*, 13th January.

Corder, C. (1989) *Taming your Company Computer*, McGraw-Hill, London.

Currie, W. (1995) *Management Strategy for IT*, Pitman, London.

Davidson, F. and Huot, J-C. (1991). 'Large-scale Projects: Management Trends for Major Projects', *Cost Engineering*, **33**, (2), pp. 15–23.

De Greene, K. (1991) 'Large Technology-based Systems and the Need for a Paradigm Shift', *Technological Forecasting and Social Change*, **9**, pp. 349–362.

Donovan, L. (1993) 'Wired for Trade in Singapore', *The Financial Times*, 20th July.

Douglas, M. and Wildavsky, A. (1983) *Risk and Culture: An Essay on the Selection of Technological and Environmental Dangers*, California University Press, Los Angeles.

Eglizeau, C., Frey, O. and Newman, M. (1996) 'SOCRATE: An Implementation Debacle', In Coehlo, J., Jelassi, T., Krcmar, H., O'Callaghan, R. and Saaksjarvi, M. (eds.), *Proceedings of the Fourth European Conference on Information Systems,* Lisbon, July 2–4.

Feenberg, A. (1995) *Alternative Modernity: The Technical Turn in Philosophy and Social Theory,* University of California Press, Berkeley.

Griffiths, C. (1994) 'Responsibility for IT: A Grey Area of Management', In Willcocks, L. (ed), *Information Management: The Evaluation of Information Systems Investments*, Chapman and Hall, London.

Griffiths, C. and Newman, M. (eds.) (1996) 'Theme Issue: Management and Risk In Information Technology Projects', *Journal Of Information Technology*, **11**, (4).

Harrow, J. and Willcocks, L. (1992) 'Management, Innovation and Organizational Learning', in Willcocks, L. and Harrow, J. (eds.), *Rediscovering Public Services Management*, McGraw-Hill, London.

Hochstrasser, B. and Griffiths, C. (1991) *Controlling IT Investments: Strategy and Management*, Chapman and Hall, London.

Hull, J. (1990) 'Application of Risk Analysis Techniques in Proposal Assessment', *Project Management*, **8**, (3), pp. 152–157.

Iliff, M. (1994) 'The Real Value of Strategy Formulation for Information Technology', In Willcocks, L. (ed), *Information Management: The Evaluation of Information Systems Investments*, Chapman and Hall, London.

Kearney, A. T. (1990) *Breaking the Barriers: IT Effectiveness in Great Britain and Ireland*, AT Kearney/CIMA, London.

Keen, P. (1991) *Shaping the Future*, Harvard Business Press, Boston.

King, J. and Konsynski, B. (1990a) *Singapore TradeNet (A): A Tale of One City*, Harvard Business Case Studies, Ref: 9–191–009, Harvard Business Press, Boston.

King, J. and Konsynski, B. (1990b) *Singapore Leadership (B): A Tale of One City*, Harvard Business Case Studies, Ref: 9–191–025, Harvard Business Press, Boston.

Kumar, K. (1990) 'Post Implementation Evaluation of Computer-based IS: Current Practices', *Communications of the ACM*, **33**, (2) pp. 203–212.

Lyytinen, K. and Hirschheim, R. (1987) 'Information Systems Failures – A Survey and Classification of the Empirical Literature', In Zorkoczy, P. (ed.). *Oxford Surveys of Information Technology*, **4**, pp. 257–309, Oxford University Press, Oxford.

Madon, S. (1991) *The Impact of Computer-based Information Systems on Rural Development Administration: A Case Study in India*, PHD thesis, Imperial College, London.

Madon, S. (1992) 'Computer-based Information Systems for Decentralised Rural Development Administration', *Journal of Information Technology*, **7**, (1), March, pp. 60–74.

Margetts, H. (1991) 'The Computerization of Social Security: The Way Forward or a Step Backwards?, *Public Administration*, **69**, (3), pp. 325–343.

Mitev, N. (1996) 'Social, Organizational and Political Aspects of Information Systems Failures: The Computerised Reservation Systems At French Railways', In Coehlo, J., Jelassi, T., Krcmar, H., O'Callaghan, R. and Saaksjarvi, M. (eds.), *Proceedings of the Fourth European Conference on Information Systems*, Lisbon, July 2–4.

Morris, P. and Hough, G. (1987) *The Anatomy of Major Projects*, John Wiley and Sons, Chichester.

National Audit Office, (1989) *Department of Social Security Operational Strategy*, Report by the Comptroller and Auditor General, HMSO, London.

OTR Group, (1992) 'Report on Risk in IT Projects', *Computer Weekly*, December 12, p. 12.

Parker, M., Benson, R. and Trainor, E. (1988) *Information Economics:*

Linking Business Performance to Information Technology, Prentice-Hall, Englewood Cliffs, New Jersey.

Patel, N. (1987) 'The Impact of Technology on Governmental Systems. County Study in India on Searching For A Paddle', *Trends in IT Applications in Asian Government Systems*, **3**, APDC, Kuala Lumpur, Malaysia.

Pettigrew, A., and Whipp, R. (1991) *Managing Change for Competitive Success*, Basil Blackwell, Oxford.

Pettigrew, A., Ferlie, E. and McKee, L. (1992) *Shaping Strategic Change*, Sage, London.

Pike, R. and Ho, S. (1991) 'Risk Analysis in Capital Budgeting: Barriers and Benefits', *Omega*, **19**, (4), pp. 235–245.

Post, G. and Dilz, D. (1986) 'A Stochastic Dominance Approach to Risk Analysis of Computer Systems', *MIS Quarterly*, December, pp. 362–375.

Rapaport, I. (1992) *The Technology of the Minitel System*, Harvard Business Case Studies, Ref: 693–006–1, Harvard Business Press, Boston.

Rogers, E. and Kim, J. (1985) 'Diffusion of Innovations in Public Organizations', In Merritt, R. and Merritt, A. (eds.), *Innovation in the Public Sector*, Sage, Beverly Hills.

Scott Morton, M. (ed.) (1991) *The Corporation of the 1990s*, Oxford University Press, Oxford.

Shenhar, A. (1992) 'Project Management Style And The Space Shuttle Program (Part 2): A Retrospective Look', *Project Management Journal*, **23**, (1), pp. 32–37.

Singapore Bulletin, (1993) 'Tradenet', *Singapore Bulletin*, **27**, (7), July.

Sisodia, R. (1992) 'Singapore Invests in the Nation–Corporation', *Harvard Business Review*, May–June, pp. 40–50.

Strassman, P. (1985) *Information Payoff: The Transformation of Work in the Electronic Office*, Collier MacMillan, New York.

Stringer, J. (1992) 'Risk in Large Projects', In Mortimer, M. (ed.), *Operational Research Tutorial Papers*, Operational Research Society, London.

Walsham, G. (1993) *Interpreting Information Systems in Organizations*, John Wiley and Sons, Chichester.

Warner, F. *et al.* (1992) *Risk: Analysis, Perception and Management*, The Royal Society, London.

Waters, R. (1993) 'The Plan that Fell to Earth', *The Financial Times*, 12 March.

Waters, R. and Cane, A. (1993) 'Sudden Death of a Runaway Bull', *The Financial Times*, 19 March.

Willcocks, L. (ed.) (1994) *Information Management: The Evaluation of Information Systems Investments*, Chapman and Hall, London.

Willcocks, L. (ed.) (1996) *Investing in Information Systems: Evaluation And Management*, Chapman and Hall, London.

Willcocks, L., Currie, W. and Mason, D. (1997) *Information Systems At Work: People, Politics and Technology*, McGraw-Hill, Maidenhead, (forthcoming).

Willcocks, L. P. and Griffiths, C. (1994) 'Risk of Failure in Large-scale Information Technology Projects'. *Technological Forecasting and Social Change*, **47**, (2), pp. 205–208.

Willcocks, L. and Margetts, H. (1994a) 'Information in Public Sector Organizations: Distinctive or Common Risks?', *Informatization and the Public Sector*, **3**, (1), pp. 1–19.

Willcocks, L. and Margetts, H. (1994b) 'Risk Assessment and Information Systems', *European Journal of Information Systems*, **4**, (1), pp. 1–12.

Willcocks, L. and Mason, D. (1987a) *Computerising Work: People, Systems Design and Workplace Relations*, Paradigm, London.

Willcocks, L. and Mason, D. (1987b) *The DHSS Operational Strategy, 1975–1986, In-Business Case File in Information Technology*, Van Nostrand Reinhold, London.

Williams, T. (1990) 'Risk Analysis Using an Embedded CPA Package', *Project Management*, **8**, (2), pp. 84–88.

CHAPTER TEN

Does Radical Reengineering Really Work? Emerging Issues in Strategic Projects

LESLIE P. WILLCOCKS AND WENDY CURRIE

INTRODUCTION

In Chapter 9 we saw how many factors, in combination, can contribute to high risk in major IT projects. But what happens where IT is part of a much larger organizational change project? This is particularly the case with reengineering, or business process reengineering (BPR), described by Hammer and Stanton (1995) as the fundamental rethinking and radical redesign of business processes to bring about dramatic improvements in performance. A key element is a focus on process – a structured, measured set of activities designed to produce a specified output for a particular customer or market (Davenport, 1993a). The BPR activity described in the literature varies in the scale and type of change contemplated (Heygate, 1993; Morris and Brandon, 1993). Central to BPR practice, according to most sources, is a holistic approach to strategy, structure, process, people and technology (see for example, Galliers, 1994; Hammer and Stanton, 1995; Johannson et al., 1993).

BPR as an analysis, a set of prescriptions for management, and as practice can be assessed in several ways and at several different levels. A major concern must be to compare the exhortations against what is actually being achieved in BPR programmes. A major issue that arises from surveys, case study research, and also more anecdotal evidence is why, despite the large sums being spent on reengineering by some high profile organizations, and a deluge of prescriptive management literature and consultancy activity, BPR so often seems to fail to live up to expectations. Hammer and Champy (1993) estimated a 70 per cent failure rate for the radical reengineering efforts they had observed, though this figure was not rigorously arrived at, and 'implied nothing about the expected rate of success or failure of subsequent reengineering efforts,' (Hammer and Stanton, 1994). Two US studies show most reengineering projects consistently falling well short of their expected benefits (Hall *et al.*, 1993; Moad, 1993). In the UK case study research found dramatic improvements in some companies, but documents these examples as few and far between (Bartram, 1992; Harvey, 1995).

Findings from a 1995 UK survey add to this picture. High risk, radical BPR approaches were generally not being undertaken. One indication of this was the low size of spend with 43 per cent of medium and large organizations each incurring BPR related expenditures of under £1 million. Many of the processes being reengineered seemed to be existing ones to which improvements were being sought rather than those identified as a result of a radical rethink of how the organization needed to be reconfigured and managed. Radical BPR is portrayed as achieving sizeable job losses yet we found that for all completed BPR projects and all types of process, staff redundancies averaged less than 5 per cent of total BPR costs (Willcocks, 1995a). Generally, whatever the process being reengineered, organizations did not seem to be aiming high when they looked for improvements from BPR. There may well be a cause and effect here, with organizations 'aiming low and hitting low', because the actual improvements being achieved were also relatively low.

The best performance on actual improvements were found to be with core processes. Support, management and cross-boundary process reengineering produced consistently lower improvements than these. Very few organizations were achieving what could be called 'breakthrough' results. Thus, of the organizations that had completed BPR programmes, if a relatively conservative benchmark of significance of 20 per cent profitability gain, 20 per cent revenue gain and 10 per cent decrease in costs of doing business is used, only 18 per cent of organizations had achieved significant financial benefits from BPR on all three measures. Organizations were achieving, and in most cases aiming for, tangible improvements rather than radical change. The picture of discontinuous change represented in the BPR literature is not clearly underscored in BPR practice.

We have argued elsewhere, with others, that such less radical approaches, or the way in which espoused radical aims become emergent – incremental improvements – may be related to the difficulties inherent in actually implementing BPR programmes (Craig and Yetton, 1994; Currie, 1995; Davenport, 1993b; Grint and

Willcocks, 1995; Smith and Willcocks, 1995). One issue only just emerging, is the extent to which BPR efforts fail to link closely with business strategy and with effective organizational processes for strategy formulation. This is a feature also of a number of texts, ironically those ostensibly concerned with securing the business strategy–BPR linkage (see for example, Belmonte and Murray, 1993; Hammer and Champy, 1993; Johannson *et al.*, 1993; Morris and Brandon, 1993). This has led some to posit the need to go beyond BPR and focus on business systems engineering (Galliers, 1994; Watson, 1995). Further, a prime question raised by the multidisciplinary holism at the heart of BPR study and practice, is whether there are robust methodologies and tools available to facilitate the outcomes required from BPR activities. The conclusion has been that there are many approaches, methodologies and tools more or less useful, but that bringing together the offerings from such diverse fields has so far proved difficult, and adds up to an immaturity and a lack of integration on the methodological front (Earl and Khan, 1994; Klein, 1994).

In case study research in four organizations we found that the methodologies adopted were often partial, and handled some aspects of what should be a holistic approach better than others (Willcocks and Smith, 1995). Frequently IT-based change actvities have utilized methodologies that focus on information flows and processes, and are based on systems analysis techniques, but in such a way as to marginalize human, social and political processes and issues (Clegg, Waterson and Carey, 1994; Walsham, 1993). Our own UK survey found such predilections often flowing into how IT-enabled, or IT-driven BPR projects were being handled (Willcocks, 1995b). Indeed, what emerges from the BPR literature itself is the frequency with which failure is related, among other reasons, to mismanagement of human, social and political issues and processes (for examples only see Belmonte and Murray, 1993; Buday, 1992; Moad, 1993; Oram and Wellins, 1995; Thackray, 1993. A more detailed commentary on the political aspects and difficulties experienced in BPR can be found in Grint, Case and Willcocks, 1995).

A long stream of research suggests that these risks and difficulties are compounded where, as is usually the case, IT is added to BPR projects and is seen as a critical enabler in the design phase of BPR and in supporting redesigned processes. Recent UK research found that IT expenditure regularly fell between 22 per cent and 36 per cent of total costs on BPR projects, and that a majority of respondent organizations saw IT as a critical enabler of BPR efforts (Willcocks, 1995a; Currie and Seddon, 1995). As Chapter 9 also revealed, such risks are also related significantly to both the size of the project and the 'maturity' or newness of the technology being utilized relative to the organization's experience with that technology (Stringer, 1992; Willcocks and Griffiths, 1994). Faced with this confusing set of findings, arrived at through studies conducted by a range of stakeholders for various purposes and with varying degrees of rigour, it is clear that further research is needed, particularly in the area of radical reengineering projects. If the majority of organizations have been found to be conducting process improvement, albeit dressed in radical clothes and vocabulary, and if, despite high-profile successes declared in the trade literature, most radical reengineering disappoints, one needs to investigate in detail the distinctive conditions under which radical reengineering projects are being carried out. The purpose of this chapter is to investigate and analyse in detail three such projects, but before doing so we detail the methodological considerations that informed and were operationalized in the research process.

RESEARCH METHODOLOGY

The research objective was to develop academically-researched cases that provided some counterpoint to the many under-researched cases found in the literature, all too often prematurely declared by interested stakeholders as examples of success. The aim was not to provide examples of successful or unsuccessful BPR, but rather to investigate in depth the issues that emerged during the course of large-scale reengineering projects. The research objectives break down into several aspects. First, we were interested to elicit data from stakeholders on how specific organizations would set about reengineering key business processes. Second, the research was focused on some of the critical implementation issues in reengineering programmes and how these related to the original strategic vision in each case. Thirdly, the researchers were keen to develop a longitudinal perspective on large-scale BPR change programmes and compare the findings with some of the claims of those who advocate reengineering as *the way forward* for contemporary businesses (Hammer and Champy, 1993; Champy, 1995; Johansson *et al.*, 1993). For example, the notion that senior managers can engage in a process of 'collective forgetting' (Grint, Case and Willcocks, 1995) and are thus able to redesign the business from a starting point of a *blank sheet of paper*. In addition, the espoused view that reengineering can transform human relations to the extent that power is shifted from superordinate to subordinate; supervisors to coaches; scorekeepers' to leaders; and a shift from concern for the boss to concern for the customer (see Hammer and Champy, 1993 and a critique in Grint, 1993). While much of the management literature suggests that the human resource issues in the process and as the endpoint of change are critical, recent survey research discussed later, however, shows how these issues are often overlooked by those in charge of implementing BPR (Willcocks, 1995b; see also Peltu and Clegg, 1996). We wished to investigate whether detailed case research substantiated this finding.

Fourthly, the cases chosen were to have a strong IT-enabling aspect to the BPR activity being investigated. This was partly to reflect, and enable the investigation of, the strong correlation posited in the literature between BPR 'newness'/effectiveness and the development of appropriate information systems (see Davenport, 1993a; Hammer and Stanton, 1995; O'Hara and Watson, 1995). This selection also enabled us to examine the degree to which IS can have a leadership role in BPR, and at what point this may need to be relinquished, as suggested for example by Davenport and Stoddard (1994). In-depth case studies also enabled investigation of risk issues associated with major IT projects. Finally, in all three cases the BPR projects at commencement were also explicitly recognized by senior management to be a) strategic, that is underpinning the organization's business strategy, b) radical, in terms of the organizational and technical innovations embraced by the project, and c) large-scale, in terms of the financial and resource implications for the specific organization. This enabled investigation of the claims made in the management literature for how radical reengineering might be conducted, and what it could achieve.

The research adopted a range of qualitative techniques to investigate and construct the case histories. These were systematically applied to each case study to provide a consistent base for analysis. One element was regular participant observation in the events as they occurred. A second was semi-structured interviews, each of between one and one and a half hours in length, with stakeholders from different levels in the organization and with different roles in the BPR process being undertaken. For example, in the Columbus case personnel interviewed ranged from senior and middle managers from the business units and technology division, project managers controlling various elements of the Columbus project, analyst/programmers (permanent and contract) and other associated personnel (database administrators, testing/support personnel and contractors from supplier organizations). The objective throughout was to achieve at least a triangulation of viewpoints on events as they developed. A third element was to focus on the process of change over periods ranging from two to three years, rather than take an aprocessual 'snapshot' of events at a particular moment in time. A fourth element was to utilize detailed internal documentation available in the organizations studied in order to enrich the accounts and explanations arrived at.

To avoid the ahistorical, aprocessual and acontextual character of much research on organizational change data gathering, techniques were also focused on organizational history and context, as well as the content, process, and emergent outcomes of change. This approach built on that of Pettigrew, (1985) Pettigrew and Whipp (1991) and Pettigrew et al., (1992), adopted for the study of major organizational change, and by the authors for parallel studies of risk in major IT projects (see Currie, 1994; Willcocks and Griffiths, 1994). Finally, for the purposes of analysis the research utilized a framework developed from studying parallel case and survey research (Willcocks, 1995(a) and (b); Smith and Willcocks, 1995), from reflecting on the case experiences and from reviewing the extensive literature on BPR and change management. Outcomes seemed to relate to five significant factors:

- pressure to act;
- locus of support;
- levers for change (intervention points from which to initiate activity);
- themes (focal messages in the rhetoric of change);
- approach (types of technique, degree of participation).

In what follows the three case histories are detailed, as arrived at through applying the research techniques described above. The five-factor framework is then used to develop a comparative analysis. We then relate the findings to those from parallel survey and case research on BPR practice and risk factors in major IT projects.

CASE 1 – REENGINEERING INSURANCE: NATIONAL VULCAN

Context

In 1990 National Vulcan (NV), an autonomous subsidiary of composite insurer Sun Alliance, (now Royal Sun Alliance) was the largest UK insurer in engineering, with a 23 per cent share of a £390 million market. However, after a decade of healthy profits, these reduced to £6.1 million in 1990, and the company recorded its first loss – of £6.3 million – in 1991. The appointment of a new chief executive from a non-engineering subsidiary of Sun Alliance in June 1990 brought an external perspective to long-term operational problems exposed by the recessionary climate for which the organization was clearly unprepared. Loss of major customers, including the major defence contractor British Aerospace in this period added to the sense of crisis within the company.

The company had two main types of product. First, it sold more than

100 different types of insurance policy. By 1991 some 75 000 annually renewable policies had been issued to customers, providing 60 per cent of the company's revenue. The policies covered engineering risks such as explosion of boilers, physical injury and damage to third-party property. NV also sold policies covering clients' computer installation risks. Sales were through the Sun Alliance sales network, its own 24 branches and professional broking intermediaries specializing in the engineering sector. Secondly, NV provided a site safety inspection service, available separately, but more often tied in with an NV insurance policy. Here many customers also required annual safety certification to meet statutory safety regulations on items such as electrical equipment, elevators, boilers and heavy machinery. A wide range of customers included most of the UK's nuclear power stations, several multinationals, and also medium-size companies and their offices, retail outlets and factories. Some 2.5 million inspections a year resulted in the creation and issuing to clients of nearly 0.5 million written reports.

Internal reviews of the company commissioned by the new chief executive, Ken Sinfield, revealed lack of significant investment, under-developed computer-based systems, departments operating in isolation from one another, over-elaborate bureaucratic procedures, and staff operating through 55 job grades. A commissioned survey on customer service relative to its competitors revealed NV as bottom. While inspection engineers were rated as best in the sector, and the inspection service contributed 40 per cent of NV revenue, its cost structure was far too high and typically a report took two months to deliver to the client. The insurance business was more open to the fluctuating risk of claims, but on the more controllable cost side was highly inefficient. Issuing a new policy, for example, passed through 43 steps, 20 members of staff and 10 departments. An even more serious problem identified in the review was the lack of a sense of crisis among the workforce. From the chief executive Ken Sinfield's perspective:

> One hundred and thirty years as market leader had bred complacency and introversion . . . people did not have a sense of imminent death . . . we had become a prisoner of our own history (of) technical excellence . . . when it was put to a group of managers that we were in a crisis one perplexed reply was 'I don't know what has changed, we haven't'.

Identifying core processes and the role of IT

Sinfield determined on a top-down approach incorporating stretch goals for changes in performance. A thorough analysis, by consultants and internal management, of the company's operations and its relations with its customers detailed significant weaknesses. Across all operations little was completed within a three-month cycle. Typically however, an item was worked on for only three days of the cycle and only three hours of that time provided what Sinfield came to call 'the valuable difference—that is, added value for the customer'. It also became clear that the company was over-dependent on paper-based manual operations, many of which were ripe for automation.

In more detail, in the inspection service one or more of the 521 inspection engineers would be assigned to a particular client order. The time taken on subsequent administrative procedures, and the engineers' high involvement in these, was identified as troubling. Engineers used one of 400 available forms to produce a typed report with seven carbon copies. These would be batched twice a week and sent to the Manchester head office where each report was checked by an acceptance engineer, a task that took only a few minutes. However, a backlog of several months had developed; moreover if a report had inaccuracies it had to be returned to the inspection engineer for further checking. In the insurance policy area, each insurance policy passed through 30 different checks in 10 departments before insurance cover was authorized. These checks applied to all policies regardless of value and complexity. Despite this level of detail NV could not produce accurate data to identify the profitable and loss-making product lines and clients. Lack of management information could be partly explained by limited experience with IT. The only significant operational IT was the plant database held on an IBM mainframe shared with other Sun Alliance operating companies and based remotely at Bristol. The NV database contained 1.7 million items. The procedure for updating information was elaborate, there was high staff turnover and wide use of temporary staff, all of which contributed to a high level of data inaccuracy. Finally, NV had too many sales offices for a company its size. Moreover, many were too small to carry out the many different functions ranging from sales generation, handling customer enquiries, policy issuing and service, and debtor control.

A top management team redeveloped the business strategy in early 1991. The mission was to restore profitability and customer confidence through becoming 'the highest-quality, lowest-cost operator in the UK engineering sector' (internal document). A key aspect was radical process redesign. The underlying approach to activity analysis is summarized in Figure 10.1.

Beyond this three key processes and actions were identified. These were:

1. Streamlining the insurance process involving the branch offices and policy administration.
2. Upgrading the plant database process involving responding to

customer enquiry, updating the database, and scheduling field inspections.
3. Simplifying and improving the speed and quality of the report process involving engineers carrying out inspections and making reports, and report delivery to customers.

Type of activity		Action/sourcing
1. 'Idle time'	⟶	Eliminate
2. Unnecessary	⟶	Eliminate
3. Necessary	⟶	IT-enabled/packages and outsourced
4. Added value	⟶	Insourced

Figure 10.1   Identifying added-value activities at National Vulcan

The management team identified IT as a critical enabler of process redesign. The IT manager supported these developments. He had spent some three years at NV with a mandate to improve IT but, in a cost-cutting culture, had not received appropriate support from either the wider Sun Alliance IT community or NV senior management. The new management asked for and received from its loss-making holding company scope for an IT development budget of £6.5 million over two years, on top of an on-going annual operating budget of £2 million. However, IT was to follow rather than lead:

First we had to define very clear business goals. Then we defined the processes that flowed from them . . . only then did we go anywhere near IT.

IT manager

Making change the priority
From a senior management perspective, an important means for pushing through change was the setting of 'stretch' performance goals. A 24-hour target for the key activity areas was insisted on, whether the activity be policy issue, database update or report despatch. Moreover, whenever a customer contacted the organization only one NV person would be responsible for processing the subsequent transaction. Both goals were counter-cultural and widely perceived among middle management and staff to be too difficult to achieve. Senior management responded by heading up some project teams with more junior staff

who were supportive of changes. Moreover project teams were forced to think radically and produce radical solutions by the continuous insistence on getting key processes down to the 24-hour target. The other factor designed to speed progress, maintain enthusiasm and focus effort was the timescale set for change. To keep this to a minimum the three IT-enabled process reengineering projects were to run in parallel not sequentially. In the first six months, and despite lack of in-house development expertise senior management made the decision to bypass readily available and stable IT and go with emerging client–server technologies, enabling the company to follow rapid but evolutionary development skills.

Short timescales were explicitly applied for restructuring the sales network. Sales branches were reduced from 26 to nine, and in a nine-week period 138 key people were relocated to a central service unit (CSU) in Manchester. Under a former sales manager from Liverpool branch office, by 1992 the CSU consisted of 300 staff, including 80 from outside the company. Lower-level staff in closed branches were made redundant but the key staff, including branch managers, were assigned to Manchester to retain local knowledge and customer contact. Throughout this process customer service levels actually improved and existing business was retained. Three major IT-related projects were set up, with a tight nine-month timescale set for each. The existing two-person computing unit was supplemented by consultants and new full-time IT staff, and business managers were put in control of the projects. One major project was to develop systems based on Sun workstations and Ingres software to support the insurance administration process. This was achieved in nine months by a nine-person development team, despite software delivery problems, due to the supplier experiencing financial difficulties. (Difficulties at NV were also experienced with Wang equipment delivery, for similar reasons). Ultimately the integrated system enabled a single person at a branch to quote, follow all steps through on a single screen, and issue a policy within 24 hours (see Figure 10.2). Details would then be transmitted overnight to the CSU for subsequent administration, including printing and mailing of policies.

A second nine-person team developed, and transferred the existing records onto a new Wang-based plant database. The design reduced the updating procedure to two steps, the process became paperless and the previously high levels of labour turnover among plant database operating staff were greatly reduced (see Figure 10.2). A further project saw inspection engineers issued with notebook computers supported by software that formatted data automatically and offered flexible layouts and proforma facilities. This was backed by four days training in notebook use for every inspection engineer. Reports could be

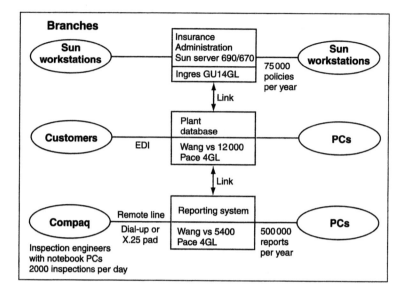

Figure 10.2   IT-enabled reengineering at National Vulcan

dispatched nightly to the Manchester CSU via modem link, while engineers also had access to the plant database. Only one in 20 reports now needed checking, and this was done on screen, rather than manually. By 1995 any dialogue with the inspection engineers was achieved electronically and nearly all reports sent to customers within 24 hours. CSU staffing of the area was reduced from 140 to 12, and inspection engineer productivity was enhanced, and also, for the first time, was monitored accurately.

Subsequent developments

These reengineering activities experienced a number of difficulties. Some of the systems identified as necessary but not adding customer value (see Figure 10.1) had been outsourced to suppliers, including the business analysis and consultancy aspects of systems development. However, vendors proved too responsive to every user request resulting in expensive systems overfunctionality and the business analysis and consultancy functions were brought back in-house. As the CSU became increasingly IT-driven, new processes required older ex-branch personnel to replace their old skills of dealing with brokers and clients with those of team management, a set of skills for which they were ill-equipped. Branches were reducing their numbers by half at a time when Manchester CSU was also reducing staff from 300 to 155 by summer

1993 (and to 75 by mid-1994). Tensions and staff reductions put the 24-hour turnaround target at risk. In early 1993 the CSU was reorganized into a key account team dealing with the top 2000 policies in terms of financial value, and regional teams each dealing with specific branches. However, tensions continued between the CSU and branches, with the latter believing the CSU was too remote from customer service. In the CSU morale fell in the face of all these changes, particularly among older staff confronted with rising skill demands. Turnaround times fell to three days for a period as greater loads fell on the CSU staff from the downsized branches. Among the inspection engineers some frustration was felt at lack of ongoing IT training, and role isolation. By winter 1993 inspection engineers were being grouped into teams of 10 under a senior engineer responsible for appraising performance and training needs. Subsequently NV has undertaken more widespread training for software packages and PC use among CSU staff as well as for inspection engineers. In addition, NV have moved much more towards performance-related pay in their reward system, higher accountability among staff and wider adoption of performance appraisal.

Many of these dips in morale could be explained by transition problems, the huge cultural and skills shifts required, and the challenges presented through the lack of IT experience throughout the company. From a chief executive perspective middle management in particular represented the major barrier to the changes envisaged:

> I am under no illusion about middle management problems . . . it will take us years . . . I have great sympathy with middle management, but they have got to get in the lifeboat and row with us or we've got a problem.
>
> Ken Sinfield, quoted in Harvey, 1995

In this statement one can gain some insight into the political and cultural issues prevalent in this reengineering programme, but also, in the language, a sense of the crisis the chief executive attempted to communicate to the NV workforce.

Despite these difficulties National Vulcan reported a £5.4 million profit in 1993, rising to £9 million in 1994. By mid-1995 its staff had been reduced by 25 per cent from its 1991 figure of 1341. This had been mainly achieved through early retirement and voluntary redundancy. Customer complaints were negligible, productivity of inspection engineers had doubled. As at mid-1995 the company was developing its strategy for the next six years. According to senior management, future changes would have wider staff involvement than in the top-down approach adopted throughout the BPR programme from 1991.

CASE 2 – REENGINEERING IN HEALTHCARE: THE JOHN RADCLIFFE HOSPITAL

Context

This case is set in the 1990–94 period in a major acute hospital, the John Radcliffe (JRH), in the UK's National Health Service (NHS). From the mid–1980s the NHS was the subject of radical management and organizational reforms prompted by central government. One major feature was the introduction of general managers, and private sector management practice, into hierarchically-based administrative structures replete with occupational and professional groupings. Relatedly a resource management initiative sought to introduce mechanisms to identify and improve performance in this area. Government also increased pressures to control NHS spending, and sought to develop an internal market in healthcare. This involved devolution of responsibility for service delivery and increased competition among service providers, for example hospitals. These reforms came together in the implementation of a purchaser–provider split across the NHS, accompanied by radical changes in the basis of allocation of finance to purchasers. Henceforth cash-constrained purchasers would seek the most cost-effective healthcare whether from NHS or private sector providers.

The NHS reforms made sound financial performance a critical issue for hospitals such as the JRH. A number of critical success factors were identified for operating in the new NHS environment, for example, financial net income had to be maximized. This made efficiency in resource management, together with accurate costing and activity information crucial. At the same time hospital reputation, standards of care and staff morale had to be maintained, a broad case-mix was necessary for teaching hospital purposes, and there needed to be timely and detailed clinical and audit information to maintain and improve clinical performance.

Earlier top-down reforms of the structure, breaking hierarchically-based administration into clinical directorates, only partially worked. It was recognized that a bottom-up approach was needed. The response in late 1990 was to begin a pilot BPR project, facilitated by external consultants. A lead clinician was identified in each of six pilot areas, for example radiology and cardiac services. Each clinician then led a multi-disciplinary team to identify the core clinical processes in its own area. In each case there were identified up to 20 processes with a definable start and finish, and for which resources – own and bought-in – could be defined and measured. The pilot study proved successful and BPR concepts, together with the pilot way of working, were then applied to the whole hospital.

Process reengineering and the SDU concept

The essence of the changes were described by a leading clinician as 'a move from separate, vertical hierarchies for doctors, nurses and managers toward a more horizontally-oriented multi-disciplinary team culture'. The main elements were: describing hospital work in process terms; producing an organizational structure enabling management of those processes and related resources; and developing IS supportive of the new arrangements. Using process analysis, and an incremental bottom-up approach, nearly 70 service delivery units (SDU) or service areas were identified. An example of an SDU is shown in Figure 10.3. Though no rigid model was developed, typically each SDU became responsible for delivering a defined set of services to patients or other SDUs, and consumed resources that it owned or bought in from other units. Typically, a senior clinician and nursing manager would lead a SDU and develop and manage its service plan. SDUs became responsible for delivering services and managing their own resources. SDUs were grouped into service centres (SC) of related medical specialties or support services, each with, typically, a clinical consultant chairman and full-time service manager. These would be responsible for interfacing with senior hospital management. SC chairmen would meet senior management monthly as the hospital strategy and policy board; SC managers and senior management fortnightly as the hospital operational board. Essentially the approach pushed down responsibility and accountability to the SDU level, and

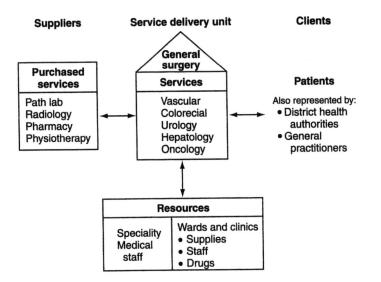

Figure 10.3   Example of a service delivery unit (SDU)

gave professional staff, such as clinicians and senior nursing staff, critical roles in management.

Information and IS would provide vital underpinning to the new organizational arrangements. In the period under study existing IT-based systems were widely judged inadequate even for the previous ways of working. An information strategy steering committee (ISSC) of senior managers, clinicians and IT specialists involved a wide range of hospital staff in a number of task groups for developing ways forward. Early on it was commonly recognized that not only eliciting the information requirements, but also developing and implementing the information systems needed would have to be an incremental and highly participative process. Some reasons for this are suggested by the following comment:

> We're finding the hospital a very complex place in which to develop information systems. We're taking an evolutionary approach, and supporting the process changes. Even in low level jobs, there are major differences in the way one secretary does the same job to another one. The technical problems are small; it's defining what's needed and getting the agreement and buy-in that's taking the time.
>
> IT Consultant

Moreover, systems had to be developed to meet not just clinician needs but also underpin SDU operations, budgeting and management, together with meeting higher-level hospital requirements. A range of interest groups pulled in several different directions at once, not least clinicians with considerable power:

> The hospital will demand data from me in my management role, but if they insist on a data collection through a system unfriendly to us at the operational end – in how we do our jobs – then they will get data but it will not be accurate. These sorts of issues mean that we (doctors) need to be fully involved in the management of implementation.
>
> Senior Clinician

Clearly, it was not just the complexity of the environment and the difficulties in identifying information requirements that led to an evolutionary, bottom-up approach, but also the political dimensions inherent in the situation.

Extended implementation 1992–95

Throughout 1991–92 a new hospital information system was protyped based on client–server architecture and open systems. Different SDUs would share the same data held on a patient data server, essentially a hospital-wide database of data collected mostly by the SDUs. The database would hold all details relating to patients treated at the hospital. This data could be used in different ways in a range of activities, including contract and case-mix management, financial management, SDU work and for clinical support. Additionally SDUs would develop their 'private' information needed exclusively to support their own activities. Both the common and 'private' data would be available through new user-friendly clinical workstations; these would be linked to the patient data server, and also to each other where required.

By 1993 the new process-based structure was in place and working. On the whole, clinicians were positive about running their own service groups. Operationally the new arrangements were held to be more efficient, despite rising pressure, financial constraint, and unprecedented demand in terms of patient numbers. Forward planning had also become more accurate. Throughout 1993–95 the information systems were being rolled out slowly. Politically and culturally this approach was acknowledged as a wise one, as illustrated in the following comment from a nursing manager in trauma services:

> The way that the IT-systems are lagging behind is quite positive. In devolved management, unless you have got a team used to and wanting to work together and take responsibility you can have all the IT systems you like but it's not going to work. This way we also are becoming much more clear about the systems and information we really need.

Even so a number of respondents suggested that implementation plans were not being well communicated even to immediately affected stakeholders. Also many nurses still remained cautious to sceptical about the usefulness of information systems in their work. Additionally, in the more advanced implementations in the critical care SDUs, there were potential problems arising as a result of lack of experience within the SDUs of rolling out information systems. Funding issues were also being raised – in particular about getting enough terminals and operators for data entry, and getting sufficient IT support staff. There was also emerging a shortage of time and resources, human and financial, to support the IT/IS training required in each SDU. A senior clinician summarized the implementation problems in the following way:

> End-games are difficult in the NHS. Government or the Department of Health, for example, move the goal posts, staff move on, outside support in the form of consultants and software suppliers starts working then funding runs out. You also get political opposition, given the range of professional groups and stakeholders. In information systems there are many interests to look after. Not only must it be a patient-centred system that also produces management information; critically it needs to be a user-centred system as well.
>
> Member of ISSC

CASE 3 – THE COLUMBUS BPR PROJECT AT THE ROYAL BANK OF SCOTLAND

Context

As a consequence of intense competition in the financial services industry, Royal Bank of Scotland (RBS) embarked upon a major change programme in the form of the Columbus project in 1992. As an exercise in radical BPR, the change programme was conceptualized as a company-wide solution to growing competition, not just from other banks but also from building societies and insurance companies. Senior managers at the bank conceded that 'lifetime customer loyalty is no longer a guarantee'. Indeed, customers were increasingly aware of the range of financial services offered by competitors, and were therefore fickle in their choice of financial institutions. With Columbus, the bank hoped to become in senior managements' words, 'the best retail bank in the UK by 1997'. This would be achieved by implementing major changes to structures, products, services, job titles and roles, training policies, technology and marketing/sales. The major characteristics of the Columbus programme are summarized in Figure 10.4.

- Branch banking division (BBD) to be organized around three customer streams – retail, commercial and corporate

- New managerial roles introduced network-wide during 1995

- Each branch to have ready access to specialist centres and knowledge without having to house all the traditional back office functions

- Five branches to test the new branch design;

- Over £100 million committed to developing new technology

- HR policies and processes designed to reflect the new organization

---

Figure 10.4   Columbus 1992–1995: IT-enabled reengineering in financial services

Developing the Columbus project 'vision'

A Columbus project team was set up to identify major elements of the change programme. According to senior managers, it was crucial that line management were the focus for building the 'new bank'. This was reflected in other comments made by senior managers in both the business units and technology division, who stressed that in spite of millions of pounds being spent on technology, Columbus was more than simply an IT project. Rather, it was a major change programme which had been conceptualized and planned at the most senior levels with the aim to revolutionize the entire bank. For them the success or otherwise of Columbus depended on six key interrelated issues being addressed.

First, for senior management the most important challenge of Columbus involved changing peoples' attitudes to encourage them to embrace 'new philosophies' of work organization. Banks were renowned for being highly bureaucratic and regimented and senior managers were aware that some customers were intimidated by this image. It was pointed out that the old emphasis on 'geographical splits' was no longer appropriate and this had given way to a different structure which established three distinct but interrelated businesses – retail (for personal and business customers), commercial and corporate. To facilitate this structural change, new managerial roles were required which clearly distinguished between sales and service responsibilities. Indeed, corporate customers required a different service level from personal customers.

Secondly, new technology was seen as an enabling factor in transforming the vision of reengineering into practice. With over £100 million invested in new technology the bank was hoping to achieve a 'seamless service'. Irrespective of the type of services required by customers, technology would integrate one service with another across the network. However, according to senior managers:

> Technology is a key component of our change programme but we have not fallen into the trap of seeing technology as an end in itself. Rather it is being used as a means of improving business performance and of producing that essential seamless service.

A key element of IT-enabled BPR was to achieve consistent levels of services where entire transactions would be conducted in front of the customer. In addition, senior managers were hoping to reduce the risk of fraudulent transactions by improving ways of identifying their customers. The 'new branch' PC-based system would have three main components: customer service, cashier/teller and account opening. In the past, technology was perceived in a senior manager's words as 'not always delivering appropriate technical solutions to particular business problems'. As a result, technology developments would no longer be planned in isolation. Communication between project sponsors/users (those who commission IT systems) and project managers and analyst/programmers (those who manage and design IT systems) would need to improve. According to one project manager, 'technology developments should not be left to the technology division alone, but ... (involve) ... business users as well'. IT-enabled reengineering would therefore seek improvements in three areas: proposed technology developments would be user friendly; staff would feel confident about using the new system, and equally, customers would wish to use the technology.

Thirdly, facilitated by the technical developments, changes to the retail outlets would also enable branch staff to become more directly involved in serving their customers. The new branch design was being tested in five different prototypes:

(The design is to) . . . create more flexible surroundings for staff to work in and a welcoming environment for customers to conduct business . . . Gone are the forbidding exteriors, regimented queuing zones and glass screens. Instead, a more welcoming layout invites customers to feel comfortable.

Senior RBS manager

According to one senior manager, BPR should not be perceived only in terms of how it changes bureaucratic or technical systems of the banking business. It is also about changing customer perceptions of the bank. Customers should not feel intimidated when they enter a bank, nor should they be faced with long queues. An important activity was to monitor customer perceptions about the *new look* of the bank. Thus the physical appearance of the new branches was another element of the BPR change programme and though it was accepted that some customers would not like the new set-up and withdraw their custom, the net result was expected to be the winning of new customers.

Fourthly, Columbus would mean major changes to the network. The traditional set-up where each branch was a 'mini-bank in its own right' was gradually being phased out. Instead, each branch would have access to specialist centres and knowledge without having to house all the traditional back office functions. New specialist centres would be set up such as a mortgage centre serving the whole network, and UK-wide mortgage shops. Some 18 corporate centres housing 'specially selected' relationship managers were planned where these individuals would develop close links with corporate customers. In addition, 15 service centres strategically located throughout the UK would deal with traditional back office functions. At the time of interviews, centralized cheque returns would initially be handled by the service centres, but ultimately outsourced to EDS (a major outsourcing supplier). Part of the rationale for these changes was to facilitate a situation where customers would become customers of the bank and not of a branch. These changes were described by respondents as 'a total reeengineering of current practices', where many services would move from a traditional manual-based approach, 'with all its inevitable inconsistencies' to a computer-based system. Fifthly, credit processes were further being reengineered, primarily to achieve efficiency gains and consistency in credit policies and lending decisions. Technology was essential for this goal to speed up processes and automate administration. Thus, 'our credit process will comprise an effective team-lending approach between relationship manager, analyst and sanctioner'. The final element of the Columbus programme concerned major changes in human resource policies and practices. It was stressed that:

> None of our planned improvements are possible without the support of our staff. It is only through our people that we can hope to reach our goal of becoming the best bank in the UK by 1997.
>
> Senior manager, RBS

People changes would encourage staff 'taking charge of their own careers', in that promotion would no longer be based upon 'keeping your nose clean' but on achievement and ability. In a document obtained from the bank it was observed that:

> No industry or sector is immune from market forces. Banking is no exception. The current competitive situation calls for different skills and much more flexible working practices. In a world where technological improvements can be copied, it is the people element which is often the only true differentiator . . . We believe that it is through our staff that true change will occur'.

It is to these human resource issues we now turn in our examination of the implementation of BPR in the technology division at the bank.

Implementation: emerging issues

Much has been written about strategic visioning in reengineering, albeit fewer empirical studies exist concerning its implementation. Senior management seemed sensitive to the risks in large-scale IT-related change. Thus in a document published by the bank at the outset of Columbus, the head of the technology division stated that too many large-scale IT projects had been unsuccessful, in spite of successive increases in the annual IT spend. As a result, he felt there had been no correlation between IT spend and IT project success. Nevertheless, the bank had now invested over £100 million in IT to transform the Columbus strategic vision into a practical reality. Moreover, Columbus was not simply a large-scale IT project but a radical reengineering change programme designed to 'revolutionize existing business processes'.

The disappointing results from many of the bank's previous large-scale IT projects had not been on the same level as the TAURUS fiasco which beset the City of London in 1993 (see Currie, 1994; Willcocks and Griffiths, 1994). However, senior managers at the bank adopted the position that previous disappointing results from IT were in part due to a failure to align IT with the corporate strategic vision. Furthermore, in the bank, as elsewhere, users often complained they were given information systems they could not use, and technologists complained that since users changed their minds so frequently about what it was they actually required, the initial functional and technical specifications became irrelevant. Several previous IT projects had experienced escalating costs, difficulties in meeting delivery dates, and low morale among users and the technical team. Typically these results were attributed to the technical team, poor project management, and/or confusion among users. According to senior managers at the bank, the Columbus programme would be different from other large-scale IT-enabled projects since it was 'company-wide' and would affect 'all bank personnel'. As a result, all bank staff were expected to participate in its development and implementation.

Tracking the development of the new branch IT project over a two-year period highlighted some interesting issues and problems relating to IT-enabled reengineering. By far the most important related to human, political and cultural issues rather than technical factors. However technical considerations, for example the process of systems development, could also be described in political terms. Thus technology development carried with it the values and priorities not only of senior managers and business users, but also the technical teams charged with their development. At the wider organizational level, the vision for the Columbus programme, with all its complex and interrelated elements, was highly dependent upon the design and implementation of effective technical systems. With planned job losses of 3500 over the duration of the five-year change programme (2000 jobs had already been shed in the 1992–95 period), the role of IT was becoming even more political. In fact, many of the job losses had been middle management positions where traditional skills were perceived to be redundant in the 'new bank' environment.

As recently as 1994, the bank had hired a firm of consultants to develop and administer 'core competency' tests to its senior and middle management. Some 44 managerial jobs were shed as a result with some cynical comments that the 'hit list' had been drawn up before the tests were conducted. Notwithstanding this issue, interviews carried out with managers and technical staff suggested that against a backdrop of job losses, the bank was suffering from serious skills shortages, particularly those associated with both managing and developing newer technologies such as client–server. This issue was highly contentious as people with traditional skills acquired in previous decades were somewhat threatened by the new technological environment. This was felt by some technical personnel to apply, for example, to project managers with mainframe skills. Two issues seem relevant here. First, technical personnel at the sharp end of systems development were usually critical of the nature of the project management role. Common complaints suggested that project managers had abandoned their technical skills in favour of managerial work. Relatedly, there existed a wide gulf between managerial and technical staff. Many technical personnel (particularly analyst/programmers) indicated that they worked autonomously by setting their own performance targets even though project managers tried to give the appearance of being in control. According to one senior analyst/programmer.

> My project manager usually asks me to set my own deadlines. He doesn't really understand what it is I do, even though he is responsible for my performance.

Evidence to support this was found by examining the nature of client–server systems development work. Here, technical staff were responsible for writing systems for the new branch project. Since they were working with new tools, formal project management methodologies were not entirely relevant, and much of the technical work was the product of trial and error. In spite of the bank's statement that technology was not an end in itself, but a means of achieving improvements in business performance, the skills shortages of project managers and some technical personnel, as well as the limitations of the technology, were important factors inhibiting reengineering progress. This was compounded by senior managers' lack of appreciation of the significance of technical issues in such a large-scale change programme. As one team member commented:

> They (senior management) . . . might understand what the business requires, but they don't understand how it can be achieved technically. They seem to think that technical solutions are just a matter of pressing a few buttons on a keyboard.

As one example, interviews with technical personnel, especially analyst/programmers highlighted the problem of interfacing new technology (client–server) with old technology (the mainframe). Analyst/programmers, many hired in on contract, pointed out that new programs written in fourth generation languages (4GLs) could not easily interface with those written years before in COBOL for the mainframe. Furthermore, the new branch vision embraced by senior managers was that the system would become customer based. Staff would be able to call up all the customers accounts on one screen to carry out funds transfers and monitor transactions, and this could be done at any branch to speed up processing time. To deliver this, many new programs written in SQLWindows would be needed to interface with the legacy (mainframe) system. However, technical staff encountered numerous obstacles in the development process, the main one being that the mainframe was essentially account based and could not easily be changed. When the technical team were unable to develop a customer-based system within the set timescale and budget, senior and project managers were faced with the dilemma of either developing a less ambitious account-based system within time and budgetary constraints, or pursuing the expensive option of developing a full customer-based system. In the end senior management decided to follow the first route, given that it would satisfactorily meet time and budget deadlines. However, it was generally felt among the technical team that such an option was against the reengineering vision outlined in the new branch documentation.

CASE ANALYSIS AND DISCUSSION

In this section a comparative analysis of the cases is presented utilizing a five-factor framework (see Figure 10.5). The analysis is then developed further through a comparison of the case study findings against those from parallel studies by the authors and others on issues and risks in major BPR and IT projects.

Only in the case of National Vulcan (NV) could the BPR programme be considered largely complete by the end of 1995. At both the John Radcliffe Hospital (JRH) and Royal Bank of Scotland (RBS) senior management had opted for a longer time-span for completion. In itself this could become a significant risk factor. Survey respondents and commentators typically stress the need for rapid completion of core process reengineering, preferably within 12 months. Otherwise loss of focus and momentum occur coupled with loss of enthusiasm and commitment from top management (Hammer and Stanton, 1995; Heygate, 1993; Willcocks, 1995b). Our own survey of completed BPR programmes found core process reengineering averaging 11.4 months. However, the reengineering activity tended to be smaller in scale than in these three cases. Here, the scale of activity in the cases presented was in itself a further risk element and also contributed to risk by elongating timescales.

In the case of NV respondents were generally agreed that BPR had been, in business terms, largely successful. In the JRH case respondents generally felt that in a changing NHS environment the hospital was a complex organization in which to attempt reengineering; that steady progress had been made, but that the activity was at least two difficult years from its end-point. In the RBS case senior management felt they

	National Vulcan – insurance	John Radcliffe – Healthcare	Royal Bank of Scotland – banking
Pressure to act	Poor financial performance, loss of major customer. New chief executive appointed by holding company.	Government imposed reforms. Development of internal healthcare Market. Pressure to measure and improve performance. Budgetary constraints.	Intensive competition; deregulation; changing customer requirements.
Locus of support	Senior management team and IT director. Promotion into project roles of those supporting changes.	Grown over time, rolled out through management, clinical and nursing groups in each SDU. Senior clinicians supported process of change.	Top-management. Projects with high business-user involvement. External consultants.
Change levers	Wide use of consultants/suppliers. IT identified as key enabler. Sustained focus on radical change throughout the company.	Careful use of external consultants. Methods not imposed. Facilitation of mutual incremental learning. Need to respond to external pressures.	Staff and line management involvement 'company-wide'. Over £100 million investment in IT. Widespread use of contractors.
Themes	'The valuable difference'. 24-hour turnaround for customer service; best quality, lowest-cost provider.	Improved measurement and control. Devolved responsibility. Empowerment of service staff. IS in a support role.	'New bank' vision. Flexible banking; seamless service new work practices; 'empowerment'; flexible working; achievement culture.
Approach	Top-down. Identify key processes. Three project teams operate simultaneously. Nine-month time constraint. Continuous open communication about 'the new world'. Business managers in control of projects.	Bottom-up. Get clinicians involved. Use of consultants to develop incremental learning. Representative steering committees. Service delivery staff responsible for changes.	Top-down. Business-focused team building for projects. IT-enabled change.
Outcomes	Return to profit within two years. 25% reduction in job numbers. £6.2 million IT development spend. Negligible customer complaints. HO – branch tensions. Skills issues. Reduced management layers.	Painstaking, evolutionary roll-out across service delivery units within severe budgetary and resource constraints.	£100 million profit improvement in three years. 200 job reductions; more to come. Leading-edge technology e.g. OS2. New services targeted at profitable customers. Range of application development problems.

Figure 10.5   Five-factor analysis of three strategic BPR projects

were on course to achieving the ambitious objectives they had set. At the time of interview in 1994, a statement obtained from the bank stressed that:

> Already, significant improvements have been introduced which have resulted in much better business results. In 1992, our aim was to achieve £200 million profit improvement within five years. We are half-way there already.

Interviewees closer to the implementation process tended to stress more the problems and displacement of goals occurring in such a large programme of change.

National Vulcan

In the case of NV, BPR was initially driven by the declining competitive position manifested in poor financial performance. A new chief executive signalled change, and forcefully communicated a sense of crisis and urgency throughout the BPR programme. Part of the rhetoric of change created by senior management included the 'valuable difference', '24-hour turnaround' and 'best for less' concepts. These were used to focus daily attention and underpin and communicate the longer-term vision of the reengineered company. A top-down approach saw a small group of senior managers together with three business-led project teams push through IT systems development and implementation, aided by consultants, newly-hired systems staff and suppliers. The high age profile of the existing labour force made early retirement a major option to ease 25 per cent reductions in job numbers enabled by large-scale application of new technologies. The setting of tight timescales, for example nine months for completion of all the major systems development, appeared to focus effort and attention, including that of senior management.

The significant factors enabling senior management to achieve their reengineering objectives would seem to include: the ability of the senior executive to create what was called a 'burning platform' equating radical change with business survival, relatedly, the poor state the company was in made dramatic improvements more easy to achieve; the ability to deliver workable technological solutions quickly to underpin the reengineered processes; and continuous, focused senior management drive and attention. A further set of factors would also appear significant, namely clear key processes, and an identifiable strategic business unit with clear objectives and relatively straightforward, easily monitored performance criteria, including its financial results. Several parallel studies support the finding that radical reengineering appears easier to achieve in such organizations (Harvey, 1995; Willcocks, 1995b). An interesting contrast is the more problematical reengineering experienced in the complex JRH environment (70 SDUs identified) and in the RBS – an even more complex and much larger-scale organization.

John Radcliffe Hospital

In the JRH case there was also clear and demanding external pressure to act due to radical reforms imposed by government. However it was clear that little could be achieved unless the diverse professional and occupational groupings of hospital staff actively supported change. The locus of support was throughout management, clinical and nursing echelons, but this had to be grown over time through the incremental, participative approach adopted. BPR provided a mode of addressing fundamental and intractable problems that previous attempts had failed to resolve. The pilot studies enabled basic problems to be addressed, established workable alternatives, and also released the energy needed for change. The careful use of consultants also provided levers for change; methods were not imposed, but rather both BPR and IS consultants facilitated incremental learning both by themselves and by key stakeholders. A strong point favouring the new BPR activity was that much had been learnt from past experiences in the organization about how *not* to introduce large-scale change and information systems into the organization.

What proved particularly important was the choice to relegate the development and implementation of IS to a support role – after processes had been reengineered, and while the working arrangements were being refined. The political and human issues surrounding IS development and implementation were well understood, and explicitly managed through adoption of an incremental, prototyping, user-led approach, rolling out the information systems a SDU at a time and carefully eliciting the different information requirements and IT/IS demands of each service unit. The approach adopted involved all salient stakeholders and, in terms of our earlier review of BPR, tended to be suitably multidisciplinary and holistic in its operationalization.

However, the case does demonstrate the long time period it requires to roll out an effective BPR programme within a large organization such as an acute NHS hospital. Though begun in 1991, the BPR activity in question was likely to continue into 1997, especially where delivering information systems to service units was concerned. This raises the question of whether there is a catch-22 in BPR: effective large-scale BPR may take many years to implement, but can organizations wait that long for the effects to come through, and can energy, attention and resources continue to be focused sufficiently to maintain momentum?

Royal Bank of Scotland

At RBS the 'new bank' vision arose from top management analysis of an increasingly difficult competitive position, and the need to address changing customer requirements. However, in practice, unlike in the NV case, the bank was already profitable, and change could not be communicated clearly as a survival issue. Not surprisingly, this created a range of political issues for the BPR activity, given also the extant 'rules/procedures' culture, the espoused heavy reliance on line management and staff to deliver the changes, and the radical cultural overhaul BPR and Columbus represented. These issues are discussed in more detail below. Aware of skills shortages RBS employed a large number of consultants and short-term contractors to help lever the changes. There was also concern to ensure that the critical technology projects were business-focused with high user involvement. IT was also seen by senior management as fundamental to BPR, both levering change and underpinning reengineered processes. All three levers both facilitated change but also created additional tensions.

Nevertheless, RBS continued to increase profits in the 1992–95 period, only partly through large-scale reductions in job numbers (3500 by 1997). It continued to experience a range of IT applications development difficulties (the reasons are discussed below) but also had built itself as a major site of leading technologies, for example one of the largest in Europe for OS2, though the benefits of this were open to contention among some of our respondents. The wider question for RBS perhaps, remains whether the strategic vision will be delivered on too late to match the intense competition from not just other banks but from other financial service companies, including building societies.

Risk in major BPR projects

The case findings can be related to earlier empirical work on profiling risks in major IT-enabled change projects (Willcocks and Griffiths, 1994; Willcocks and Margetts, 1994; see also Chapter 9). A central finding there was that risk of failure correlated strongly to a drive into the technology resulting in a loss of focus on the business purpose to be achieved, and neglect of the fundamental organizational and behavioural changes implicated in and fundamental to the delivery of espoused objectives. In all three cases IT was utilized as a critical enabler of reengineering. NV was interested in reinventing itself technically, and gained advantage firstly (and ironically), from starting from a low technical base, and secondly, from carrying out the IT aspects quickly and in a prototyping fashion with mixed project teams. JRH sought to mitigate risk by pursuing a more evolutionary, high involvement path technically. This proved successful up to 1995 but was placing a strain on limited financial and human resources, and raising doubts about the sustainability of the approach. At RBS senior managers were sensitive to the need to avoid technology-driven projects, and introduced countervailing measures but risks were increased by the size, complexity, and time span of projects and the 'newness' of the technologies to the organization.

In Chapter 9 risk of failure in major IT-enabled projects was also related to factors relating to history, external and internal contexts, content and process of change. On *history*, the record of previous IT disappointments in the three cases did cause new ways of working on IT projects. In NV and JRH the lack of relevant IT experience meant greater emphasis on organizational learning and education/training in systems development. Both also bought in technical expertise to mitigate risk but, of the three organizations RBS seemed to rely more heavily on this approach, partly because it had more complex technical issues on a larger scale. On *external context*, environmental pressures for change seemed less obvious to many of the workforce in the RBS case, and this created tensions and problems during reengineering activity. Supplier problems could also create risks as most clearly seen in the NV case where Wang and Ingres ran into financial/market problems, but difficulties could also arise from newness of the technology and consequent skills shortages in the market, as in the RBS case. On *internal context*, in all three organizations radical reengineering, by definition, meant wholesale change in structure, strategy, reward systems, skills, culture, management styles and levels and types of teamwork. This inevitably implied the generation of major political and cultural issues which, in practice represented the major risks in all three cases.

In terms of *process*, this prompted different responses. NV took a 'big bang', open communication approach on a relatively short timescale to push through changes. In JRH a more evolutionary approach was taken in recognition of the difficulties inherent in winning over a complex set of occupational and professional groups that made up the workforce. The RBS approach seemed less convincing to many respondents because it appeared to embody mixed messages – full staff involvement on the one hand, large job reductions and senior management 'pushing through' changes on the other. However, the *content* of change largely helps to explain the greater degree of risk prevalent in the RBS case. In looking at BPR and the related IT projects, the major risk factors we have identified elsewhere in major change projects – size complexity, number of units involved technical uncertainty (because of new technologies), and definitional uncertainty (lack of clarity on business requirements) – these factors are all at their greatest in the RBS case.

BPR and the technological imperative

In all three cases reengineering core processes were to be heavily dependent on IT to deliver the anticipated dramatic performance improvements. In this respect they reflect in practice a central theme of most of the management literature. It is useful therefore to analyse further the contrasting ways in which technology was to be delivered to the three organizations.

In all three cases business goals and the processes to be reengineered were defined before IT requirements were arrived at. This avoided many of the problems associated with being too IT-led. NV's approach of fast systems development in time-constrained projects led by business managers achieved several stretch objectives, and provided considerable organizational learning on IT, despite numerous mistakes being made and a range of problems with suppliers. The development and management of 'low value' systems was outsourced, but this resulted in costly systems overfunctionality. Subsequently the business analysis and consultancy aspects of these systems was brought back in-house. BPR was enabled by a rapid build-up of skills through bringing in full-time staff and contractors organized into four teams. Intensive and on-going training of user staff supported the widespread use of IT from a previously low technical base in NV. The company had an advantage over JRH and RBS in having few 'legacy' systems/technical skills. This factor, allied with the development approach and high levels of staff development for IT should have enabled fast application of client–server technologies. In practice many of the technical issues proved more difficult to deliver on than envisaged. By early 1996 the IT budget was twice as high as planned, due to maintenance and unresolved development work. In IT terms the main success had been in improving the report process. However, the plant database and administration process were still quite dependent on the old technology platform, and only some headway had been made in streamlining data entry.

In JRH there were relatively few technical problems once the information requirements had been defined. The evolutionary user-led approach was proving successful, if difficult to sustain. The major problems stemmed from finding time and resources for user training, and securing technical support once systems had been implemented in a SDU. RBS experienced the biggest difficulties technically because of the relative size and complexity of the technical projects, the 'newness' of the technologies, lack of relevant technical experience within RBS, and the problems of interfacing legacy mainframes with, for example, client–server technologies.

Of the three examples, RBS provides the most obvious test case of a complex organization with low technological maturity. 'Maturity' refers to where an organization is dealing with a radically new/unstable technology, an existing technology in a radically new application and/or where in-house staff lack the relevant IT experience (Feeny *et al.*, 1989; see also Chapter 7). All these factors prevailed in some degree at RBS. Following Feeny *et al.*, in Chapter 7, this made necessary a user-focused, as opposed to a specialist-led approach to systems development. This was attempted but it became clear from respondents that project managers selected for their dual business and technical background and skills frequently became out of touch with the technology, and sometimes found it difficult to understand what their technical staff were doing. A shortage of project management and technical skills and the newness of the technologies also contributed to delays and compromises in delivering, for example, the full customer-based account system. The general sense was one of lack of understanding of the technical issues at senior management levels together with their underestimation of the complexities and difficulties inherent in developing and exploiting the 'new' technologies chosen. Early reliance on existing project management approaches and methodologies revealed these as not always appropriate. In practice, systems development relied as much on trial and error as formal methodology. RBS was described by some respondents as a good training ground for technologists, where there was a willingness to spend a lot of money, some of it less wisely, on technology.

Human, cultural and political issues
In the three cases it is worth highlighting that management respondents deeming BPR as relatively successful all cited management of human resources, cultural and political issues as playing the really key role in that success. This finding is strikingly supported in our survey work. Here respondents identified the top five most persistent barriers to BPR programmes as: middle and line management resistance; loss of commitment/non-enthusiasic support from the top; prevailing culture and political structure; and lower-level employee fear and resistance (Willcocks, 1995b).

In each case the new technical environment in itself had considerable political and human resource implications and impacts. In NV and RBS new technology could be equated with large reductions in job numbers for all but technical people. Even so, in RBS it threatened the traditional skills held by existing IT staff. In RBS, and to a lesser extent in NV, the large influx of technical staff and contractors signalled new working practices and types of contract, and that banking (or insurance) was no longer a job for life. In both NV and RBS the new technological environment symbolized the 'new organization' in a positive sense i.e., progress and investment, and so could be tied in with politics as the management of meaning (Pettigrew, 1985; Willcocks, Currie and Mason, 1997). Simultaneously it symbolized a threat to existing work practices, the distribution of power and resources, 'the way things were'. This symbolic ambivalence had considerable political ramifications in NV and RBS, but much less so in JRH where the wider changes relating to introducing the internal market in healthcare had much greater symbolic significance.

More broadly, it could be seen that senior managers in each organization chose specific strategies for working through the political, cultural and human resource aspects of radical change. In NV it was specifically top-down with change pushed through by constant senior management pressure and attention. In a larger organization with much more extensive change envisaged, RBS senior management had to lever change through lower levels of management, project management and widespread use of contractors. This inevitably dissipated focus. Moreover the 'new bank' vision, in its human resources implications, could be perceived as threatening interests and change at all levels. Not surprisingly, we found more evidence of emergent protectionist strategies among the workforce in RBS than in NV, while in JRH the explicit political strategy of those managing the BPR activity was to go with the existing culture and ways of working in order to win over the entrenched interest groups without whom the reengineering could not go ahead. Moreover, reengineering at JRH did not have the large job losses so explicitly associated with radical change in the other two cases. Also, although departments and processes were being reconstituted at JRH as at NV and RBS, in the hospital there was less breakdown of the traditional skills base, and a lesser degree of retraining and multi-skilling inherent in the changes.

CONCLUSION

Of the three cases, the NV experience is perhaps the most typical of radical reengineering as put forward by Hammer (1990), and Hammer and Champy, (1993). We have pointed out elsewhere, as has Davenport and Stoddard (1994), the contradiction represented in the violence inherent in their approach to human resources issues against their stress on the vital role people play in the reengineered world of empowerment, teamwork, achievement culture and devolved responsibility. In a later book the stress on imposing change quickly, and rooting out resistance can be contrasted with one of the top ten ways of failing at reengineering being listed as 'ignore the concerns of your people' (Hammer and Stanton, (1995). At NV the human resource and political problems inherent in radical reengineering were ameliorated by the ease with which job reductions could be made through early retirement and voluntary redundancy; through constant top management attention to the political and human resources issues; because of an open communications policy and due to the dramatic improvements that could be made from the low start point of the organization in performance terms.

It was also clear that radical reengineering on the Hammer and Champy (1993) model was more possible in a definable business unit like NV with relatively simple structures, clear objectives and where performance and improvement is easily measured. These characteristics were not prevalent in the hospital and bank cases, and it is significant that the JRH did not attempt radical reengineering along Hammer and Champy lines, while at RBS organizational complexity and scale frequently pushed reengineering activity into other directions.

The cases also reveal that the notion that senior managers can simply begin process innovation anew starting from a blank sheet of paper is somewhat naïve, at least in most cases, particularly as traditional practices and procedures both influence and inhibit the reengineering activity. More broadly, in all three cases the human, cultural and political issues pointed up the degree to which continuity as well as change needed to be considered as part of reengineering activity. For example, even in the NV case the most valuable part of the organization (which was duly preserved) was the skill base of the inspection engineers. The case studies also reveal that Hammer (1990), Hammer and Champy (1993), Hammer and Stanton (1995) all too easily adopt a unitary, largely senior management, perspective on the organization, and as a result relegate politics and the pursuit of other stakeholder perspectives and interests as aberrant behaviour characterized as 'resistance to change'. Human resources are treated largely in mechanistic terms, passive recipients of (ironically) senior management 'empowerment'. The notion of organizations as complex, socio-cultural institutions with histories is seen largely, and largely rhetorically, in negative terms. Radical reengineering offers senior management the opportunity to forget the past and to dismiss any responsibility for dealing with its residues (Grint, Case and Willcocks, 1995). The cases help to illustrate that complexities of organization, the importance of continuity as a basis for change, the political and cultural difficulties radical reengineering stores up for itself by taking the 'don't automate, obliterate' route, are all too easily lost in the attractive rhetoric of transformation through simplification. In all these aspects, of course radical reengineering is revealed as essentially political. Artefacts, in the form of reengineered processes underpinned by technology, are powerful means for achieving objectives. The cases reveal that pursuing such objectives and means will invariably generate a range of human political and cultural issues central not marginal to radical reengineering.

In earlier research we found very few organizations pursuing the radical reengineering route, and only 18 per cent of organizations achieving what could be called 'breakthrough' performances as a result of reengineering (Willcocks, 1995(a) and (b)). While the cases described here reveal what radical reengineering can entail, they may also serve to indicate why many of the organizations we surveyed seemed to adopt a more low-risk process improvement approach that in the long term could achieve substantial, even similar levels of performance gains. Finally, against Hammer and several other commentators, it remains a moot point, of course, whether in practice, on a case by case basis every organization is the 'burning platform' that make radical reengineering so (rhetorically) necessary.

REFERENCES

Bartram, P. (1992) *Business Reengineering: The Use of Process Redesign and IT to Transform Corporate Performance*, Business Intelligence, London.

Belmonte, R. and Murray, R. (1993) 'Getting Ready for Strategic Change: Surviving Business Process Redesign', *Information Systems Management*, Summer, pp. 23–29.

Buday, R. (1992) 'Forging a New Culture at Capital Holding's Direct Response Group', *Insights Quarterly*, **4**, pp. 38–49.

Champy, J. (1995) *Reengineering Management*, Nicholas Brearley, London.

Clegg, C., Waterson, P. and Carey, N. (1994) 'Computer Supported Collaborative Working: Lessons From Elsewhere', *Journal of Information Technology*, **9**, (2), pp. 72–86.

Craig, J. and Yetton, P. (1994) *The Dual And Strategic Role of IT: A Critique of Business Process Reengineering*, Working Paper 94-002, Australian Graduate School of Management, University of New South Wales, Kensington.

Currie, W. (1994) 'The Strategic Management of Large-scale IT Projects in the Financial Services Sector', *New Technology Work and Employment*, **9**, (1), pp. 19–29.

Currie, W. (1995) *Management Strategy For IT: An International Perspective*, Pitman Publishing, London.

Currie, W. and Seddon, J. J. M. (1995) *Reengineering and Process Innovation at a UK Bank: A Case Study on the Development of a Branch Banking System*, British Academy of Management Conference, 11–13 September.

Davenport, H. (1993a) *Process Innovation: Reengineering Work through Information Technology*, Harvard Business Press, Boston, Mass.

Davenport, H. (1993b) 'Book Review of 'Reengineering the Corporation'', *Sloan Management Review*, Fall, pp. 103–104.

Davenport, T. and Stoddard, D. (1994), 'Reengineering: Business Change of Mythic Proportions?', *MIS Quarterly*, **18**, (2), pp. 121–127.

Earl, M. and Khan, B. (1994) 'How New is Business Process Redesign?', *European Management Journal*, Spring, **12**, (1), pp. 20–30.

Feeny, D., Earl, M. and Edwards, B. (1989) *IS Arrangements to Suit Complex Organizations 2 – Integrating the Efforts of Users and Specialists*, RDP 89/5. Templeton College. Oxford.

Galliers, R. (1994) *Information Technology and Organisational Change: Where Does BPR Fit In?* Paper at the Conference: 'Information Technology and Organisational Change: The Changing Role Of IT and Business', Nijenrode University, Breukelen, The Netherlands, 28–29 April.

Grint, K. (1993) *Reengineering History: An Analysis of Business Process Reengineering*, Management Research Paper 93/20, Templeton College, Oxford.

Grint, K. and Willcocks, L. (1995) Business Process Reengineering in Theory and Practice: Business Paradise Regained? *New Technology Work and Employment*, Autumn, **10**, (2), 99–109.

Grint, K., Case, P. and Willcocks, L. (1995) 'Business Process Reengineering: The Politics and Technology of Forgetting, *Proceedings of the IFIP WG 8.2 Conference Information Technology and Changes in Organisational Work*, University of Cambridge, United Kingdom, 7–9 December.

Hall, G., Rosenthal, J. and Wade, J. (1993) 'How To Make Re-engineering Really Work', *Harvard Business Review*, November–December, pp. 119–131.

Hammer, M. (1990) 'Reengineering Work: Don't Automate, Obliterate', *Harvard Business Review*, **90**, pp. 104–112, July–August.

Hammer, M. and Champy, J. (1993) *Reengineering the Corporation: A Manifesto for Business Revolution*, Nicholas Brearley Publishing, London.

Hammer, M. and Stanton, S. (1994) 'No Need For Excuses', *The Financial Times*, 5 October, p. 20.

Hammer, M. and Stanton, S. (1995) *The Reengineering Revolution*, Harper Collins, New York.

Harvey, D. (1995) *Reengineering: The Critical Success Factors*, Business Intelligence, London.

Heygate, R. (1993) 'Immoderate Redesign', *The McKinsey Quarterly*, Spring, **1**, pp. 73–87.

Johannsson, H., McHugh, P., Pendlebury, A. and Wheeler, W. (1993) *Business Process Reengineering: Breakpoint Strategies for Market Dominance*, John Wiley, Chichester.

Klein, M. (1994) 'Reengineering Methodologies And Tools', *Information Systems Management*, Spring, pp. 31–35.

Moad, J. (1993) 'Does Reengineering Really Work?', *Datamation* August 1, pp. 22–28.

Morris, D. and Brandon, J. (1993) *Reengineering Your Business*, McGraw-Hill, London.

O'Hara, M. and Watson, R. (1995) 'Automation, Business process reengineering and Client Server Technology: A Three Stage Model of Organizational Change', In Grover, V. and Kettinger, W. (eds.), *Business Process Change: Reengineering Concepts, Methods and Technologies*, Idea Group Publishing, Harrisburg.

Oram, M. and Wellins, R. (1995) *Reengineering's Missing Ingredient: The Human Factor*, Institute of Personnel Development, London.

Peltu, M. and Clegg, C. (eds.) (1996) 'Business Process Reengineering: The Human Issues', *Proceedings of Business Process Reengineering Forum 4 ESRC/IWP*, Coventry.

Pettigrew, A. (1985) *The Awakening Giant: Continuity and Change at ICI*, Blackwell, Oxford.

Pettigrew, A. and Whipp, R. (1991) *Managing Change for Competitive Success*, Blackwell, Oxford.

Pettigrew, A., Ferlie, E. and McKee, L. (1992) *Shaping Strategic Change*, Sage, London.

Smith, G. and Willcocks, L. (1995) 'Business Process Reengineering, Politics and Management: From Methodologies to Processes', In Grover, V. and Kettinger, W. (eds.) *Business Process Change: Reengineering Concepts, Methods and Technologies*, Idea Group Publishing, Harrisburg.

Stringer, J. (1992) 'Risks in Large Projects', In Mortimer, M. (ed.), *Operational Research Tutorial Papers*, Operational Research Society, London.

Thackray, J. (1993) 'Fads, Fixes and Fictions', *Management Today*, June, pp. 41–43.

Walsham, G. (1993) *Interpreting Information Systems in Organizations*, John Wiley, Chichester.

Watson, G. (1995) *Business Systems Engineering*, John Wiley and Sons, New York.

Willcocks, L. (1992) 'The Manager As Technologist?', In Willcocks, L. and Harrow, J. (eds.), *Rediscovering Public Services Management*, McGraw-Hill, Maidenhead.

Willcocks, L. (1995a) 'False Promise or Delivering the Goods? Recent Findings on the Economics and Impact of Business Process Reengineering', *Proceedings of the Second European Conference in IT Evaluation*, Henley Management College, Henley, UK, July.

Willcocks, L. (1995b) 'A Survey of Current BPR Practice' In Harvey, D., *Reengineering: The Critical Success Factors*, Business Intelligence, London.

Willcocks, L., Currie, W. and Mason, D. (1997) *Information Systems At Work: People, Politics and Technology*, McGraw-Hill, London.

Willcocks, L. and Griffiths, C. (1994) 'Predicting the Risk of Failure in Major Information Technology Projects', *Technological Forecasting and Technological Change*, **47**, (2), pp. 205–228.

Willcocks, L. and Margetts, H. (1994) 'Risk and Information Systems: Developing the Analysis' In Willcocks, L. (ed.), *Information Management: The Evaluation Of Information Systems Investments*, Chapman and Hall, London.

Willcocks, L. and Smith, G. (1995) 'IT-enabled Business Process Reengineering: Organizational and Human Resource Dimensions', *Journal of Strategic Information Systems*, **4**, (3), pp. 279–301.

Part Four

Sourcing Information Technology

CHAPTER ELEVEN

The Value of Selective IT Sourcing

MARY C. LACITY, LESLIE P. WILLCOCKS AND DAVID F. FEENY

INTRODUCTION

Information technology (IT) outsourcing is defined here as the third-party management of IT assets, people and/or activities to required performance levels. The IT outsourcing market has grown dramatically throughout the 1990s. When Eastman Kodak turned over the bulk of its IT operations to three outsourcing partners in 1989 IT outsourcing was a US$4 billion a year business (Applegate and Monteleagre, 1991; Loh and Venkatraman, 1992; Willcocks and Fitzgerald, 1994). According to some estimates, by end of 1994 global revenues exceeded US$49.5 billion, would exceed US$70 billion by the end of 1998 and on some accounts reach US$121 billion in the year 2000 (IDC, 1992; IDC, 1996 reported on May 20, http://www.outsourcing.com; Willcocks and Fitzgerald, 1994). By 1996 the European market was about US$8 billion, with the UK the largest at £1.7 billion revenues and an estimated growth rate of 24 per cent (Holway, 1996; see also Chapter 12). Following Kodak, companies from various industries such as Continental Bank, General Dynamics, Continental Airlines, and National Car Rental have opted to dismantle internal IT departments by transferrring IT employees, facilities, hardware leases, and software licenses to third-party vendors for seven to ten year periods (Ambrosio, 1991; Anthes, 1991, Hamilton, 1989, Hopper, 1990). But while such high-profile deals continue to be reported – including in the mid-1990s Xerox, Delta, Sears, Rolls-Royce and British Aerospace – another, different, more typical pattern has also been developing. The growth of IT outsourcing is increasingly based on what we call 'selective sourcing' deals, characterized by short-term contracts (under four to five years) for specific activities. As we discuss in this chapter, selective sourcing serves to meet customers' needs while minimizing the risks associated with total sourcing approaches.

IT is outsourced for many reasons, ranging from a bandwagon effect from the subject's high profile to cost pressures due to competition and economic recession (Lacity, Hirschheim and Willcocks, 1994; see also Chapter 12). However, industry watchers attribute the growth of the IT outsourcing market to two main phenomena. First, interest in IT outsourcing is largely a consequence of a shift in business strategy. On this account, many companies have recently abandoned their diversification strategies, once pursued to mediate risk, to focus on core competencies. Senior executives have come to believe that the most important sustainable competitive advantage is concentrating on what an organization does better than anyone else and outsourcing the rest (Pralahad and Hamel, 1991). As a result of the focus strategy, IT came under scrutiny: is IT a competitive weapon or merely a utility? Senior executives frequently view the entire IT function as a non-core activity, and reason that IT service vendors possess economies of scale and technical expertise to provide IT services more efficiently than internal IT departments (Lacity and Hirschheim, 1993; 1995).

The second reason for the growth in outsourcing is uncertainty about the value delivered by IT. In many companies, senior executives perceive that IT failed to deliver the promise of competitive advantage propagated in the 1980s (Kettinger et al., 1994, also see Chapter 3 for the promise, and Chapter 4 for the uncertainty of IT). Consequently, many senior executives view IT as a necessary cost to be minimized. The CEO of an American conglomerate of petroleum, natural gas, and chemicals expressed to us his frustration with IT:

> All we see is this amount of money that we have to write a check for every year. Where is the benefit? IS says, 'Well, we process data faster than we did last year.' So what? Where have you increased revenue? All you do is increase costs, year after year and I am sick of it. All I get are these esoteric benefits and a bunch of baloney on how much technology had advanced. Show me where you put one more dollar on the income statement.

These two phenomena – refocus to core competencies and the perception of IT as a cost burden – prompt many senior executives to sign outsourcing 'mega-deals' for the provision of all IT services (Mehler, 1992). When such deals are first signed, companies publicly announce anticipated benefits of outsourcing, such as refocusing resources on core activities, reducing IT costs by 10 to 50 per cent, and increasing IT service levels (Krass, 1990, Rochester and Douglas, 1990). The vendor is often heralded as a 'strategic partner' who will provide access to new technologies and technical expertise during the course of the relationship. In the seven years that have passed since the surge of outsourcing interest prompted by Kodak, companies that followed suit have had time to evaluate whether their expectations have been realized.

During 1991–1996, we investigated whether IT outsourcing has delivered its promise by studying 62 IT sourcing decisions made in 40 US and European organizations (the most updated version of the research is to be found in Lacity and Willcocks, 1996). Because most organizations made their outsourcing decisions prior to this period, enough time has elapsed to evaluate the consequences. In general, we found that organizations engaging in total outsourcing experienced significant difficulties a few years into the contract. Among the problems were increased IT costs and poor service levels due to ill-defined 'relational' contracts, and inflexibility in adapting to both business and technical changes. The latter problem stems from treating the entire IT function as a homogeneous commodity. Thus many IT activities that should have remained in-house were handed over to vendors. Equally troublesome were companies that exclusively used their internal IT departments to provide IT products and services. By ignoring the external services market altogether, senior executives unwittingly created an environment of complacency and erected organizational barriers against continuous improvement in IT costs and services.

Most of the successful experiences were associated with a reasoned, incremental, and selective approach to outsourcing, which is increasingly reflected in the structure of the market. This case study-based finding is supported by a survey we conducted in 1993. Of the 162 large European companies that responded, just under half had IT outsourcing contracts (Willcocks and Fitzgerald, 1994). These contracts represent on average 24 per cent of their IT budgets, predicted to increase to 36 per cent by 1998. These numbers reduce to 13 per cent of current IT budgets and 25 per cent of predicted 1998 budgets when the total outsourcing deals are excluded from the analysis. The survey further revealed that very few total outsourcing deals had been signed, despite their high profile in the media. The practice of outsourcing select IT applications to vendors while retaining other IT applications in-house has been variously referred to as 'smartsourcing' and 'rightsourcing'. This practice eschews the all-or-nothing approach to outsourcing in favour of a more flexible and modular approach. But while selective outsourcing provides managers with a greater array of options, it is also more confusing – managers may make wrong decisions about what IT services to outsource and what services to retain in-house, neglect the technical issues involved in outsourcing, and miscalculate the long-term economic consequences. Based on the successful (as well as unsuccessful) experiences of our case companies, we have developed a selective sourcing framework for working through the complex issues and assumptions associated with information technology sourcing decisions.

RESEARCH METHOD

In order to develop an in-depth understanding of IT sourcing decisions, we adopted a multiple case study approach (Yin, 1984). This approach was deemed most appropriate because it was not possible to tightly control the research variables nor the interactions between them; different stakeholders within organizations were likely to have different views of the evaluation process; historical antecedents needed to be taken into account to appreciate the decision context; and key actors needed to be available to be interviewed. We based the selection of cases upon the notion of 'theoretical sampling' in which researchers select a number of cases representing polar extremes to enable comparison across important aspects of the decision domain (Applegate, 1994; Pettigrew, 1987). The polar extremes we focused on were: (a) scope of the sourcing decision and (b) financial outcome of the sourcing decision.

Sourcing decisions – scope

The cases represent a variety of sourcing decisions, with many options ranging from ten-year contracts for the provision of all IT services to providing almost all IT services through the internal IT staff. In addition to 'outsourcing' contracts, there were many examples of 'insourcing', where companies were using external staff and resources within IT activities that remained under in-house management. For the purpose of analysis we grouped the decisions of our case study participants into four categories:

Total outsourcing   The decision to transfer IT assets, leases, staff, and management responsibility for delivery of IT services from internal IT functions to third-party vendors which represents at least 80 per cent of the IT budget.

Total insourcing   The decision to retain the *management* and *provision* of at least 80 per cent of the IT budget internally after evaluating the IT services market. Included in our definition of insourcing is the buying-in of vendor resources to meet a temporary resource need, such as the need for programmers in the latter stages of a new development project or the use of management consultants to facilitate a strategic planning process. In these cases, the customer retains responsibility for the delivery of IT services, vendor resources are brought in to supplement internally-managed teams.

Selective sourcing   The decision to source selected IT functions from external providers while still providing between 20 and 80 per cent (typically 24 per cent) of the IT budget. The vendor becomes responsible for delivering the result of the selectively outsourced IT activities, while the customer remains responsible for delivering the result of the insourced IT activities.

De facto insourcing   The exclusive use of internal IT departments to provide IT products and services which arise from historical precedent, rather than a reasoned evaluation of the IT services market.

Using these definitions, the 62 sourcing decisions made in the 40 organizations we studied were classified as follows: 14 decisions resulted in total outsourcing, 15 decisions resulted in total insourcing, and 33 decisions resulted in selective sourcing, (see Table 11.1, Chapter 12 extends the research findings and Table 12.1 provides detailed case profiles). The common element of all 62 decisions is that participants went through an evaluation of the external IT services market before making a sourcing decision. As we will discuss, the evaluations were often prompted by the failure of *de facto* insourcing.

Table 11.1   Sourcing scope and financial outcome of 62 sourcing decisions

	Cost savings met or exceeded	No cost savings achieved or estimated	Failure to meet expected cost savings	Unable to determine financial outcome	Total
Total outsourcing	2	1	5	6	14
Total insourcing	10	5	0	0	15
Selective sourcing	23	3	4	3	33
Total	35	9	9	9	62

Sourcing – financial outcomes

Some participants consider their sourcing decisions successes, while others consider them failures. The criteria for success vary from organization to organization, and in some cases perceptions of success vary within an organization. However, to generalize, the criteria included the following: (1) targeted cost savings achieved or better than anticipated; (2) service levels maintained or improved; (3) user management satisfaction; (4) low levels of client–vendor dispute; (5) vendor responsiveness and attention; (6) generally favourable comparisons between objectives and outcomes; and (7) decision to renew the contract.

Although characterizations of 'success' or 'failure' varied across firms, we targeted 'achieving anticipated cost savings' as a major indicator of success for two reasons. First, 85 per cent of the participants cited cost savings as a major reason for conducting a sourcing evaluation. Secondly, cost savings was the easiest surrogate measure of success to determine – in 53 of the 62 sourcing decisions, participants had clear indications of financial outcomes. (In the remaining nine cases it was too soon for participants to judge the financial outcome, particularly for long-term total outsourcing decisions).

Case study participants
We interviewed 145 participants. At each case site, we conducted face-to-face interviews with individuals directly involved in the outsourcing decision on behalf of the organization or outsourcing vendor. Each interview lasted from one to three hours. Interviewees included senior business executives and chief information officers (or equivalent title) who initiated the sourcing evaluations, consultants hired to assist contract negotiations, and vendor account managers responsible for the execution of the resulting contract. We also interviewed IT personnel responsible for gathering technical and financial information. All interviews were conducted in person at the company site, tape-recorded, and transcribed into a 1120 page, single-spaced volume.

Interviews followed the same protocol, proceeding from an unstructured to a structured format. During the unstructured portion, participants were asked to tell their insourcing or outsourcing story. The unstructured format allowed the participants free rein to convey their interpretations. After participants completed their stories, they were asked to provide specific evidence to support their viewpoint. The evidence consisted of anecdotes as well as documentation such as benchmarking reports, IT budgets, and outsourcing bids. Participants were also asked specific questions about their company and IT department. Pertaining to their company, participants described the organizational structure, the major products and services produced, competition in their industry, their financial situation, corporate goals, business successes and failures. Pertaining to IT, participants described their IT activity in terms of the number of MIPs (millions of instructions processed per second), headcount, budget, chargeback system, user satisfaction, challenges, goals, and reputation. After they completed their stories, participants were asked semi-structured questions designed to solicit information on specific insourcing/outsourcing issues that may have been absent from their previous recollections. All participants were assured of anonymity. The organizations studied represent a wide spectrum of industries, venues, sizes, sourcing decisions, and financial outcomes. Of the 36 private companies 32 are characterized as large (as designated by their existence in the *Fortune* 500 or *The Financial Times* European 1000), while four of the 36 private companies are characterized as small. Four organizations were medium to large public sector bodies.

THE PROBLEMS WITH ALL-OR-NOTHING OUTSOURCING

The first insight from our study is that total outsourcing, characterized by long-term mega-deals, can lead to trouble a few years into the contract, as we witnessed in five of the 14 total outsourcing cases. (Note: it was too soon to definitively determine the financial outcome of seven of the total outsourcing decisions, although participants reported unexpected excess fees and hidden costs; only two total outsourcing decisions were reported as successes). After the initial honeymoon period, these companies complained of a loss of alignment between business strategy and IT, failed promises to access new technologies, and contractual costs which were significantly greater than current market prices. Although several of the companies in our study involved in mega-deals wished to terminate their contracts, senior executives often found it prohibitively expensive to switch vendors or bring IT back in-house when 'strategic partnerships' fail. Only two companies have bitten the bullet and actually brought IT back in-house.

Case example: US chemical company

The experiences of this company, which are by no means atypical, challenge the concept of total outsourcing. Here the senior executives who signed a seven-year, total outsourcing contract saw the entire IT function as a commodity. They selected a particular vendor partly because its representatives promised access to the industry-specific systems that other chemical customers used. Because the representatives presented themselves as 'partners', senior executives from the chemicals company neglected contract negotiations and hastily signed the vendor's generic contract. They failed to analyse the economics of the deal or question how the vendor would cut costs or whether the internal IT department could implement practices to reduce costs on its own. They merely assumed that the vendor was more efficient because of its size.

After the first month, the vendor's excess charges for items missing from the contract exceeded the fixed monthly price. As time went on, promises of access to additional software disappeared, and, instead, the chemical company paid the vendor to build new systems. When these systems were late and over-priced, users purchased cheaper PC-based solutions, funded by discretionary money. Rather than continue the partnership with the outsourcing vendor, senior executives paid a stiff penalty to terminate the contract, purchased hardware and software, and hired a new IT staff of 40 people. Despite the undisclosed expenditure, which the IT director characterized as 'embarrassing', senior management believes IT costs will be lower in the long run.

Total insourcing

Although such total outsourcing 'war stories' rightfully discourage total outsourcing, they do not suggest that exclusive sourcing by an internal IT department is the answer. Our research strongly indicates that internal IT 'monopolies' promote complacency and erect organizational obstacles against continuous improvement. Many IT managers in our study exploited total outsourcing failures and have adamantly refused to deal with outsourcing vendors. These IT managers have met personal misfortune when their own organizations have failed to demonstrate value for money. For example, the vice president of IS at a waste management company tried to deflect his CEO's interest in outsourcing by producing a white paper highlighting outsourcing failures. His CEO eventually dismissed the white paper and signed an outsourcing contract for all applications development and support.

More commonly, _de facto_ policies of exclusive insourcing create organizational obstacles against improvement because internal users resist cost reduction tactics proposed by IT managers. Because IT typically lacks the clout to implement the unpopular tactics practised by outsourcing vendors, such as data centre consolidation or software standardization, unbridled users can significantly drive up IT costs. For example, at an American food manufacturer, users resisted the IT director's attempts to cut costs by standardizing software. Despite the IT department's efforts, users insisted on their own operating systems, utilities, report generators, statistical packages, spreadsheets, and electronic mail. It was not until senior executives threatened the organization with outsourcing that the IT director was empowered to behave like an outsourcing vendor. Users agreed to allow him to standardize software rather than have an external vendor do it for them. IT costs subsequently dropped by 45 per cent. We saw similar results with nine other insourcing decisions – insourcing led to lower costs _after_ formal evaluation of market capabilities enable internal IT managers to behave like vendors.

The distinctiveness of IT

We believe the problems with all-or-nothing outsourcing stem from the distinctive nature of IT. Although many senior executives approach IT outsourcing like any other make or buy decision, this can be a mistake. Unlike other functions, such as mailrooms, cafeterias, legal departments, manufacturing, distribution, and advertising, IT cannot be easily handed over to a vendor. IT is different in a number of ways.

Information technology is not a homogeneous function, but comprises a wide variety of IT activities

Some IT applications enable business operations and management processes in a unique way. Other IT activities, such as accounting systems, may appear less critical, but closer scrutiny often reveals that the value of such systems lies in the cross-functional integration of business processes. In many organizations, information technology integrates product design, material purchases, manufacturing processes, sales, and customer service. The ubiquitous penetration of many IT applications across business functions hinders outsourcing because IT cannot easily be isolated, unlike other commonly outsourced functions such as legal departments. Outsourcing such activities can hinder business performance because vendors lack an understanding of the implications IT has for other business processes. For example, a UK food manufacturer outsourced the development of its factory automation system, only to discover that the vendor did not understand the critical interfaces with other business units such as purchasing and inventory control. The system was delivered two years late and was twice as expensive as the company expected. This and other examples strongly suggest the need for a selective rationale for outsourcing – while some activities can be outsourced, many others require management's attention, protection, and nurturing to ensure current and future business success.

IT capabilities continue to evolve at a dizzying pace; thus, predicting IT needs past a three-year horizon is wrought with uncertainty

Although companies initially perceived that vendors would provide access to new technologies, mega-deals are usually contracted around current technologies with only vague references to future technologies. Most companies find that by the third year into an outsourcing deal, the original contract actually hinders their adoption of new technologies. For example, a US petrochemical company signed a ten-year total outsourcing contract in 1988. At that time, the majority of the company's sytems were running on mainframe technology. With the advent of client–server technology, the company wanted to migrate to the smaller platform, but found their outsourcing contract erected significant obstacles. In the end, business unit managers were forced to use discretionary funds to build client–server systems, while still meeting their contractual obligations for the increasingly obsolescent mainframe.

There is no simple basis for gauging the economics of IT activity
Although price/performance improvements occur in every industry, in few industries do the underlying economics shift as fast as in IT. A unit of processing power that cost $1 million in 1965 costed less than $30 000 by the early 1990s (Benjamin and Blunt, 1992). Today's computing resources may well cost 20 to 30 per cent less next year. The rapid change in the underlying economics makes it extremely difficult for senior executives to evaluate the long-term costs of outsourcing. While a 20 per cent reduction of current IT costs for the next ten years may be appealing to a senior executive today, a few years into the contract he or she may be paying the vendor above-market prices for computer resources.

Economic efficiency has more to do with IT practices than inherent economies of scale
Although there are indeed economies of scale in some aspects of IT, they occur at a size achievable by many medium-sized and most large-sized companies. For example, small development teams are markedly more productive and successful than larger ones. In the area of data centre operations, convincing evidence states that economies of scale are achieved at 150 MIPs (processing power equivalent to one large mainframe) (Barron, 1992). Because many companies operate IT functions large enough to achieve economies of scale, how do vendors propose to cut costs? Our research suggests that vendor bids are based more on management practices than inherent economies of scale. For example, vendors may cut costs through chargeout mechanisms which motivate business users to manage demand, by consolidating data centres from multiple sites to one site, or by standardizing software. From our experiences, IT managers can duplicate these cost reduction tactics if empowered by senior executives to overcome user resistance. For example, IT costs at an American shoe manufacturer/retailer were high because users refused to let IT managers consolidate their data centres. Once senior management threatened users by inviting outsourcing bids, users acquiesced and agreed to let IT managers consolidate. IT costs subsequently dropped by 54 per cent.

Most distinctively of all, large switching costs are associated with IT sourcing decisions
In most business operations, management can protect itself against poor sourcing decisions in a number of ways, for example by dual

sourcing of component supply or annual reviews of an advertising agency contract. These techniques are often inapplicable or ineffective for IT outsourcing, particularly when a total outsourcing approach is taken. The CFO from a US airline who signed a ten-year total outsourcing contract in 1991, perceives that switching costs poses a major risk:

> Once you sign with a vendor, you have no options other than onerous contract terms, so when you get into that situation it's a lose/lose for both parties. What are you going to do? Sue them? Fire them? Stop buying services? There is nobody else, in a short period of time, who you can buy services from.

Those who approach outsourcing in all-or-nothing terms either incur the great risks involved in total outsourcing or forego the potentially considerable benefits of selective sourcing by committing to a policy of total insourcing.

BEYOND ALL-OR-NOTHING: SELECTIVE OUTSOURCING

We believe that the debate about all-or-nothing outsourcing has obscured the real issue. The key question is not, 'Should we outsource or insource IT?', but rather 'Where and how can we take advantage of the developing market for IT services?' Based upon our research, successful organizations carefully select which IT activities to outsource, rigorously evaluate vendors, tailor the terms of the contract, and carefully manage the vendor. From the rich variety of case experiences studied we have been able to build a set of frameworks for thinking through sourcing decisions. These frameworks embody a logic of firstly clarifying the sourcing options, then considering the critical business, economic and technical factors influencing the effectiveness of sourcing decisions.

IT sourcing options

A first stage is to clarify the different ways in which IT can be delivered to the business. Our case study organizations expressed some frustrations over the terms 'outsourcing' and 'insourcing'. In many ways 'outsourcing' is not a new concept. External providers such as service bureaux, facilities management companies, contract programmers and consulting firms have been used since the early days of data processing. Equally confusing was the term 'insourcing' which was used to describe a variety of sourcing options, such as managing and delivering IT services solely through the in-house function, bringing previously outsourced activities back in-house, or buying in vendor resources but managing them internally. Figure 11.1 provides a consistent set of concepts for thinking through the IT sourcing options. It suggests that a wide variety of contracting strategies can be used to manage vendors, from buying in resources as part of an in-house team, to contracting out the entire delivery of an IT activity. In general, participants' contracts can be categorized based on two dimensions: purchasing style and purchasing focus. We identify two purchasing styles: transaction or relationship. The transaction style involves one-off contracts with enough detail to serve as the original reference document. The relationship style involves less detailed, incentive-based contracts based on the expectation that customer and vendor will do business over many years.

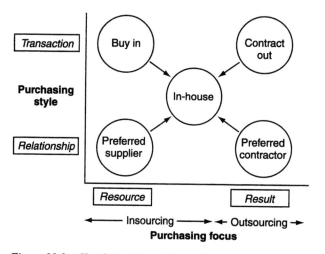

Figure 11.1   Clarifying IT sourcing options

We identify two purchasing focus options: resource or result. With a resource option, companies buy in vendor resources, such as hardware, software, or expertise, but self-manage the delivery of the IT activity. With a result option, vendors manage the delivery of the IT activity to provide the company with the specified results. Combining purchasing style and focus, four distinct ways of using the external IT market emerge, which we label 'buy in', 'contract out', 'preferred supplier', and 'preferred contractor'.

1. With a buy in strategy, companies buy vendor resources to meet a temporary resource need, such as the need for programmers in the latter stages of a new development project. In these cases, companies are often unsure of the exact hours needed to complete the coding, so they sign contracts that specify the skills required and per day cost per person.

2. With a contract out strategy, the vendor becomes responsible for

delivering the result of the IT activity. This strategy is most successful when the companies can clearly define their needs in an airtight contract. The contract must be complete because it will serve as the original reference to manage the vendor. For example, companies often use a contract out strategy to outsource data centre operations. In these contracts, precise service levels, escalation procedures for missed measures, cash penalties for non-performance, adjustments for volume increases or decreases, and termination clauses, are specified.

3. With a preferred supplier strategy, companies intend to develop a close relationship with a vendor in order to access their resources for on-going IT activities. The relationship is managed with an incentive-based contract that defines complementary goals. For example, one company engaged a preferred supplier to provide contract programmers whenever they were needed. The contract ensured complementary goals, the participant received a volume discount in exchange for not going out to tender when programmers were needed. The vendor was motivated to perform because they relied on a steady stream of revenue.

4. With a preferred contractor strategy, companies intend to engage in a relationship with a vendor to help mediate risk. The vendor is responsible for the management and delivery of an IT activity. To ensure vendor performance, the company tries to construct an incentive-based contract that ensures shared goals. For example, when one company decided to reduce costs by outsourcing data centre operations and support of existing, they mediated risk by entering into a joint venture with a software house. By establishing a jointly-owned company they created shared goals and prevented vendor opportunism.

There remains, in Figure 11.1, the in-house arrangement. We found this option having a critical role to play even when organizations were spending over 80 per cent of the IT budget on contracting out or on preferred contractors. All forms of contract run larger risks if certain capabilities are not retained in-house (see also Chapter 17):

- ability to track, assess, and interpret changing IT capability, and relate this to the needs of the organization;
- ability to work with business management to define the IT requirements successfully over time;
- ability to identify the appropriate ways to use the market, to help specify and manage IT sourcing and to monitor and manage contractual relations.

We refer to the 'buy in', 'preferred supplier' and 'in-house' options collectively as 'insourcing' options because in all of them in-house management retains full visibility, and control of the IT activity. We refer to the 'contract out' and 'preferred contractor' options as 'outsourcing' options because in each of them in-house management pass control of the IT activity to the external vendor.

Having clarified the sourcing options we now present a decision matrix for each of the key sets of business, economic and technical factors. These matrices seek to capture the key learning from our research case studies. They aim to represent a structure for management discussion and decision, not a mechanistic methodology. In practice managers will need to choose between a range of trade-offs that will arise during the debate. Political issues and interests will also be integral to the decision-making process. However, we have found that where business and IT executives can agree how to map their IT activities onto these matrices, the frameworks will provide a strong guide towards an effective strategy.

BEING SELECTIVE: BUSINESS CONSIDERATIONS

Selecting which IT activities to outsource and which to retain in-house requires treating IT as a portfolio. Successful sourcing begins with an analysis of the business contribution of various IT activities. Conventional wisdom has it that 'commodity' IT functions, such as payroll or data centre operations, are potential outsourcing fodder, while 'strategic' functions, such as on-line reservation systems, should be retained in-house (McFarlan and Nolan, 1995). Our study indicates that this delineation is too simplistic for two reasons. First, generalizations about which IT activities are 'commodities' or 'strategic' are often fallacious. For some companies, alleged IT commodities such as payroll, accounting systems and data centre operations actually serve to critically differentiate them from competitors. For example, in one security guard firm, payroll is a strategic application because on-time payment attracts a better quality of staff, leading to superior customer service. Also, applications often migrate from 'strategic' to 'commodity' within each industry as competition ebbs and flows. For example, while early adoption of automated teller machines (ATMs) once represented a strategic advantage by attracting more customers, universal adoption has delegated ATMs to mere commodities, as we found in our banking cases. Thus, each company must analyse the delineation of IT activities in its own business context, rather than accept generalities.

Secondly, many companies do not operate highly visible competitive systems, so senior executives may mistakenly classify all

IT activities as commodities. In many cases, the business contribution of IT may be masked by accounting for IT as an overhead, which serves to highlight only the costs of IT. In a US petroleum company the CEO continually asked his CIO why IT costs were rising when other departments had managed to cut costs. The CIO explained that other departments primarily reduced costs through IT. Transportation costs were cut when IT automated 16 truck terminals, and market costs were reduced when IT implemented a new credit card system. By abandoning the view of IT as a cost to be minimized, this CEO realized IT's business contribution and he subsequently rejected an outsourcing vendor's request to bid.

We have found that companies that consistently succeed in their selection of what can be outsourced to advantage use a richer vocabulary. They distinguish between the contribution that an IT activity makes to business operations, and its impact on competitive positioning. These dimensions, which are depicted in Figure 11.2, are further explored below.

Some IT activities can differentiate a company from its competitors while other IT activities merely provide necessary functions. Some well-publicized examples of IT products that have successfully differentiated companies from their competitors include American Airline's SABRE, American Hospital Supply's Order Entry System (subsequently acquired by Baxter), and Merrill Lynch's Cash Management System (Clemons and Row, 1988; Copeland and McKenney, 1988; Venkatraman and Short, 1990). These systems created barriers to entry, increased switching costs, and changed the

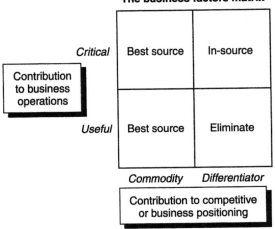

Figure 11.2   Selecting IT outsourcing candidates

nature of competition. Most IT activities, however, are viewed as commodities. Although IT commodities do not distinguish a company from its competitors in business offering and performance terms, these types of activities need to be performed competently. Examples of IT commodities, depending on the specific company, may include IT products such as accounting systems or IT services such as data processing centres.

Some IT activities are viewed as critical contributors to business operations, whereas other IT activities are viewed as merely useful because they only make incremental contributions to the bottom line. For example, a US petrol refiner views an information system which monitors the refining process as a critical contributor because it prevents fires and ensures product quality. Conversely, the company views an employee scheduling system as a useful contributor to business operations, but not a critical contributor.

After mapping an IT activity's contribution to business positioning and business operations, four categories of potential outsourcing candidates emerge:

1. 'Critical differentiators' – IT activities which are not only critical to business operations, but also help to distinguish the business from its competitors. In 1994 a European ferry company considered its reservation and check-in systems to be 'critical differentiators'. The company had ships similar to those of its main rival, and operated them from the same major ports across the Channel between Britain and France. Its competitive strategy was to differentiate through service, including the speed and ease with which passengers and their cars completed the boarding process. It is constantly making innovations in this respect, and the systems are instrumental in achieving this. As at 1996 while the company outsources a number of its IT activities, the reservation and check-in systems are retained in-house. This protects their ideas, expertise, and continuing ability to rapidly innovate.

As three examples, we found similar 'critical differentiators' in a comprehensive customer management system at a UK insurance company, a product development support system at a UK chemical manufacturer, and a foreign exchange system in a US commercial bank. Although such systems should be managed internally, we have seen organizations boost their in-house IT capability by bringing in specialists from an external vendor. However, these outsiders work alongside in-house people, under the company's own management.

2. 'Critical commodities' – IT activities that are critical to business operations but fail to distinguish the business from its competitors. A major British airline views its IT systems which support aircraft

maintenance as critical commodities. Like its rivals, the airline must obviously maintain its fleet to specification or face very serious consequences. However, the maintenance activity and supporting systems respond to the mandated requirements of the manufacturers and regulatory authorities. There is no benefit from over-performance. Although the airline has not yet outsourced these systems, it is in principle prepared to do so. Because of the risks involved for the business, such a decision would be based on clear evidence that an external vendor could meet stringent requirements for quality and responsiveness, as well as offer a low price. The policy is 'best source', not 'cheapest source'. A more standard critical commodity – the provision of an emergency/standby computer centre – is commonly outsourced by businesses because a number of high-quality vendors is available.

3. *'Useful commodities' – the myriad IT activities that provide incremental benefits to the business, but fail to distinguish it from its competitors.* In our experience, payroll, benefit, and accounting systems are the first examples of useful commodities volunteered by most businesses. But sweeping generalizations cannot be made, even within industries, as we have noted with the security guard firm. Useful commodities are the prime candidates for outsourcing. We found many such examples in the cases, such as personal computer support at a US chemical manufacturer, accounting services at a UK oil company, and mainframe operations at a US commercial bank. External vendors are likely to have achieved low costs and prices through standardization. The business makes further gains if it can free up internal management time to focus on more critical activities. But the expectation of outsourcing must be validated through analysis of economic considerations.

4. *'Useful differentiators' – IT activities that differentiate the business from its competitors, but in a way that is not critical to business success.* Useful differentiators should not exist, but we have found that they frequently do. One reason is that the IT function is sometimes relatively isolated from the business and subsequently pursues its own agenda. For example, the IT department at a European paint manufacturer created a system that precisely matched a paint formulation to a customer's colour sample. IT managers envisaged that the system would create competitive advantage by meeting customers' wishes that paint should match their home furnishings. However, senior management had established the company's strategy as colour innovation. They failed to market the system because it ran counter to their strategy, and the system became an expensive and ineffective distraction which was eventually eliminated.

A more common reason for the creation of useful differentiators is that a potential commodity has been extensively reworked to reflect 'how we are different' or to incorporate the 'nice-to-haves'. This was an extensive phenomenon at a Dutch electronics company, resulting in very problematic and high-cost software maintenance. The CIO of the company has now implemented a policy requiring that all needs for useful systems be met through standard software packages, with strict limits to customization. Useful differentiators need to be eliminated from or migrated within an IT portfolio, but never outsourced merely to reduce their costs.

In summary, treating IT as a portfolio helps to identify outsourcing candidates by analysing not only an IT activity's contribution to competitive strategy, but also its contribution to business operations. Through these two dimensions, senior executives more easily identify the value of IT. In addition to business contribution, economic considerations, which are often prematurely assumed to favour the vendor, are an important consideration in confirming the viability of IT outsourcing candidates.

ECONOMIC ISSUES: COMPARING VENDOR OFFERINGS WITH IN-HOUSE CAPABILITIES

Many senior executives may assume that a vendor can reduce their IT costs because vendors possess inherent economies of scale that elude internal IT departments. But we have noted that a distinctive feature of IT is that economies of scale occur at a size achievable by many medium to large organizations. If this is true, how can a vendor under-bid current IT costs? Often, the answer is that vendors implement efficient managerial practices that may be replicated by internal IT departments if empowered to do so. Successful companies we studied compare vendor bids not against current IT offerings, but against a newly-submitted bid prepared by internal IT managers.

As previously noted, many IT managers possess a plethora of ideas to reduce costs, but internal user resistance, or even outright user sabotage, may have hindered their efforts in the past. The problem stems from stakeholders within organizations who have different performance expectations for IT. Senior executives, who typically write the cheque for IT every year, often set cost minimization as the performance expectation for IT. Business units and users who actually consume computer resources often demand service excellence as their primary performance expectation. These expectations are in conflict because service excellence drives up IT costs. For example, users perceive software customization, local data centres, fast response time, and 24-hour help-lines as elements of service excellence – practices that drive up IT costs. IT managers are left to resolve the dilemma: provide a Rolls-Royce service at a Chevrolet price.

Senior management's threat of outsourcing often serves to align IT performance expectations, typically with the cost minimization agenda. IT managers are then free to prepare bids which include cost reduction tactics practised by vendors. These practices include chargeback systems to curtail user demand, employee empowerment to reduce supervision costs, consolidation of data centres to one physical site, standardization of software, automation of data centre operations, and archival of inactive data. Users understand that if their internal IT managers, who are at least familiar to them, do not implement these practices, a hoard of vendor employees will.

We studied a number of turnaround cases where previous attempts by IT managers to reduce costs failed until senior management invited external and internal bids. To ensure fair play, internal bid teams are removed from the organization – in the case of a US petrochemicals company from its Tulsa offices to a Dallas bunker – and treated with the same formality as vendors. For example, all bidders submit questions in writing and responses are distributed to all parties. In these companies, the internal bids not only beat current IT costs, but significantly beat vendor bids. After insourcing, IT managers from a US food manufacturer reduced costs by 45 per cent through software standardization. A US university reduced costs by 20 per cent by re-organizing the IT department and eliminating redundant staff. A US petroleum company reduced costs by 43 per cent by consolidating three data centres into one.

Case example: the outsourcing threat
Prior to the outsourcing threat, users in all these companies had resisted cost reduction practices. At a US telecommunications company, however, an outsourcing threat served to mobilize a more formidable opponent than users, namely an IT trade union. Senior executives decided to outsource after reading about Kodak's success. They rightfully perceived that the internal IT department was not cost competitive due to a strong IT labour union that promoted inefficient work practices. In particular, the union specified narrow job descriptions that created excessive staffing. For example, it forbade data centre managers to touch the hardware and software, required a union manager on every shift, and called for both a manager and a worker in emergencies. Although the IT manager had tried many times to negotiate better terms, the strong labour union resisted. Only after the request for proposal attracted two external bids did the labour union agree to allow the internal IT department to include revised union rules

in their internal bid. The union had to either succumb or risk losing the entire work site. The internal IT department subsequently reduced headcount by 45 per cent.

Decision-making matrix

We have incorporated these two economic considerations – in-house economies of scale and adoption of leading practices – into a matrix to guide senior executives through these issues (See Figure 11.3). If the internal IT department has reached critical mass and had adopted leading management practices, it is unlikely a vendor will be able to reduce costs further because vendors have to earn a 15 to 20 per cent profit, whereas internal IT departments merely need to cover costs. If the in-house IT department possesses theoretical economies of scale but has failed to implement efficient managerial practices, senior executives should allow internal IT managers to compete against vendor bids. As we have seen in the previous cases, competition serves to empower IT managers to overcome user resistance to the idea of reducing costs. If the internal IT department is of sub-critical mass but has adopted efficient practices, it is quite possible that a vendor's size advantage may be negated by their need to generate a profit. We recommend best source in these cases, that is, test the market to determine the economic validity of outsourcing. Finally, if the internal IT department is of sub-critical mass and has failed to adopt efficient practices, there is a strong economic justification for outsourcing. But even companies that fall in this quadrant may wish to empower IT to implement what practices they can before outsourcing to avoid giving the vendor the large share of easy savings.

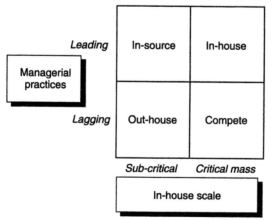

Figure 11.3   Comparing vendor offerings and in-house capabilities

But what happens when external vendor bids beat internal bids? Prudent managers question where and how the vendor proposes to earn a profit while still meeting the bid. In the most desirable scenario, vendors clearly out-bid internal IT departments based on a number of valid reasons: superior management practices which could not be replicated by the internal staff; inherent economies of scale; or superior technical expertise. But in many cases, vendor bids may be based on 'voodoo' economics, i.e. customers are offered long-term, fixed prices which are attractive in year one but will be out of step with price/performance improvements a few years into the contract. Or the vendor may be trying to buy market share in a fiercely competitive market. Once the contract is signed, the vendor may recoup losses by charging exorbitant excess fees for any change, realizing that the customers are captive. Vendor bids may contain hidden costs. For example, a US commercial bank failed to question a software transfer fee license clause that ended up costing the bank half a million dollars.

Of particular note, some companies may actually seek a purely economic package based on financial manipulations rather than inherent best practices or efficiency. Two of our case studies, a US transportation company and a US aerospace company, used outsourcing to escape financial peril. The CFO from the transportation company signed a ten-year outsourcing contract when his company went bankrupt. Senior executives from the aerospace company signed a ten-year contract after several years of negative profits. These arrangements brought in multi-million dollar cash infusions when the vendor purchased IT assets, transferred 2000 employees in one case and 1600 employees in the other to a more stable vendor, and postponed fixed fees until the latter portion of the contract.

TECHNICAL CONSIDERATIONS: SELECTING AN APPROPRIATE CONTRACT

Regardless of the impetus for outsourcing, once senior executives are convinced of the validity of vendor bids, the process continues by selecting appropriate contracting options. In practice, appropriate contracting depends on several important technical considerations. The danger in ignoring technical considerations is that senior executives may sign flimsy contracts which strongly favour vendors. Vendors negotiate many deals each month and understand the technical implications of contracting, while the customer company may have little or no experience with outsourcing. To counter-balance vendor negotiating power, senior executives must have a sound understanding of the specific service requirements associated with the outsourced technology. We have determined from our research that the degree of technology maturity and the degree of technology integration are two key technical considerations.

Technical maturity

The degree of technical maturity determines a company's ability to precisely define their requirements to vendors. As discussed in Chapter 7, we describe an IT activity as having low technology maturity when the technology itself is new and unstable, when the business has little experience with a technology that may be better established elsewhere, and/or when the business is embarking on a radically new use of a familiar technology. Examples include an organization's first venture into imaging or client–server technologies, or the development of a major network to support a new business direction of globalization. In these instances, all that senior executives know for sure is that requirements will change over time, based on experience and the availability of new options.

Outsourcing technically immature activities engenders significant risk. Ironically, these are precisely the IT activities many senior executives wish to outsource. For example, many companies choose to outsource their first client–server application, reasoning that vendors possess the technical expertise lacking in-house. This practice often proves disastrous because companies are in no position to negotiate sound contracts. In addition, such companies lose a valuable learning opportunity which leaves them dependent on the vendor after implementation.

Consider the experiences of a US rubber and plastics equipment manufacturer, in which outsourcing the delivery of new technology led to failure. Here senior executives outsourced the conversion from one mainframe environment to another. They reasoned that vendor could better perform the conversion and provide continued management after installation because of its vast expertise with the new environment. They soon discovered that it was unwise to outsource what they did not understand; they could not evaluate the vendor's performance. For four years senior management questioned the vendor about the escalating costs of IT. When it provided justifications for the expense, internal IT managers lacked the technical knowledge to evaluate them. When IT costs rose to four per cent of sales, they terminated the contract early and brought the environment back in-house. After a painful adjustment and conquering the learning curve, IT costs subsequently dropped to 1.5 per cent of sales.

The important lesson from this case history is that the company was in no position to write a detailed contract because of technical immaturity. On the other hand, companies in this position may well benefit from an injection of external expertise to support their voyage of discovery. The recommendation is to 'buy in' this expertise, but to integrate external resources into an internally-managed team. The business retains full management control and visibility of the project, capturing as much learning as possible about the technology and its application. A US petroleum company used this pattern to develop its first expert system application, a system designed to calculate sales tax for material transfers to and from pipe and wellhead warehouses. A specialist expert systems vendor seconded resources to the in-house team, which retained management of the project. The project was completed successfully, and the in-house IT staff now had the capability to take full charge of the on-going support and development of the system.

In contrast to the risks of outsourcing low technology maturity, there is significantly less risk in outsourcing activities characterized as technically mature. We can describe an IT activity as having high technology maturity when it represents well-established use of familiar technology. Mainframe-based data centre operations and accounting systems were highly mature activities for many of our case companies. In these cases, the business has conquered the learning curve and reached a point where its requirements are well-specified and reasonably stable.

Outsourcing technically mature activities provides less risk to organizations because they can precisely define their requirements. For example, a US commercial bank outsourced its mainframe operations to a vendor. The CIO was able to negotiate an airtight contract because of her experience and understanding of the requirements and costs of her mainframe operations. In the contract, she fully specified the service levels required, such as response time and availability, service level measures, cash penalties for non-performance, and adjustments to changes in business volumes. Three years into the contract she achieved the anticipated savings of ten per cent.

Degree of integration

A second important technical consideration is the degree of integration with other business processes. In the simplest case, an IT activity is easily separated out and handed over to vendors. For example, a US chemicals company successfully contracted out support for PCs. At that time, in the late 1980s, users operated standalone PCs which ran word processors and electronic spreadsheets. The CIO wanted to outsource because the growing adoption of PCs forced him into regular and poorly received requests for additional headcount. Through his two-year outsourcing contract, he reduced costs and avoided further requests for staffing.

In cases where technical integration with other business processes is high, the risks of outsourcing increase. For example, when a UK food manufacturer outsourced the development of factory automation, managers soon realized that the new system had profound implications for almost every business unit in the company. Although the vendor was an expert in factory automation software, it lacked an understanding of business interfaces. The system took four years to develop instead of two. In contrast, one financial services company, outside our research but widely documented, successfully outsourced the development of a highly integrated system using a preferred supplier model. This company invested in imaging technology to replace paper records (such as customer letters) with an electronic file. The company first explored the technology through a discrete R&D project. Senior executives reached a point at which they were convinced of the benefits of large-scale adoption but realized that many of their existing systems would now be affected. At this stage, the company turned to its preferred IT supplier, a vendor with a very broad product line, with whom it had worked for many years. Resisting the vendor's instinct to develop a detailed fixed-price agreement, the company set up an enabling, resource-based contract. The project was completed successfully, providing competitive advantage for both the business and its supplier, which had established a reference site for its own imaging products.

Technical considerations – the degree of technical maturity and degree of integration – strongly suggest the need to limit the length of contracts. A typical respondent view from our research is that three years is the maximum period for which one could assume requirements would be stable. Returning to the case of the outsourced PCs, the CIO was wise to limit the contract to two years because the company subsequently integrated the PCs onto a client–server network. Thus, the degree of integration and degree of maturity were only stable for two years. After that time, new management and possibly new outsourcing arrangements were required.

Making technical decisions
We have mapped the two technical considerations, technology maturity and integration, in Figure 11.4. Of particular note is the absence of the term 'strategic partnership' from the contracting options. The strategic partnership contracting model has been widely recommended as the preferred governor of outsourcing contracts (Henderson, 1990; McFarlan and Nolan, 1995). But we have seen the rhetoric of strategic partnership used as an excuse to sign poorly constructed contracts and lead to failure in five of our total outsourcing cases. We argue that strategic partnerships require shared, or at least complementary, risks

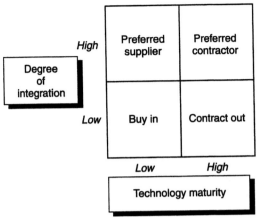

Figure 11.4   Selecting an appropriate contract

and rewards. In the five total outsourcing failures, this requirement was missing. Instead, every dollar out of the customer's pocket in terms of excess fees or hidden contractual costs went directly into the vendor's pocket.

Instead of the term 'strategic partnership', we have labelled relationships based on shared or complementary goals as 'preferred contractors'. With a preferred contractor strategy, companies engage in a relationship with the vendor to help mediate risk. This strategy worked best for technically mature and highly integrated IT activities. Because of technical maturity, companies can negotiate a detailed contract in which the vendor is responsible for the management and delivery of an IT activity. Because of the high integration with other business processes, companies must develop a close relationship to maintain the integrity of interfaces. To ensure vendor performance, the company tries to construct an incentive-based contract that ensures shared goals. For example, when a Dutch electronics company decided to reduce costs by outsourcing data center operations and support of existing systems, it mediated risk by entering into a joint venture with a software house. By establishing a jointly-owned company, it created shared goals that prevented vendor opportunism. In another example, a large UK clothing and household products company set up such an arrangement with one of the biggest outsourcing vendors. In a ten-year deal, the vendor will provide almost all the company's IT services. In addition, the retailer and the vendor will share profits from exploitation elsewhere of the retailer's existing and future systems. For example, the vendor has already proposed to market the retailer's data models, which will generate profits for both parties. In the words of one of the directors of the retail business, 'We believe, as they do, that we are working together to make the profit pie bigger rather than just arguing over who gets the biggest piece.' The success of the deal depends on these attitudes being maintained, and on achieving a bigger profit pie.

CONCLUSIONS

The frameworks we have described have a number of strengths. They are empirically derived, focus attention on the critical factors, and provide usable tools for a variety of decision-making processes. To our knowledge, 11 major corporations have actively employed these frameworks in arriving at an effective IT sourcing strategy. For example, Grand Metropolitan, a US$14 billion global corporation, that manufactures and markets branded foods and drinks, used the decision-making framework to review its IT sourcing strategy. The analysis structured IT into ten major activities. Of these, five were potential candidates for outsourcing. The company determined that the market was not yet sufficiently mature for two other functions; it is waiting to outsource those, while improving current in-house performance. It benchmarked the three remaining activities. The process resulted in clear identification of the candidates for outsourcing together with a planned programme of formal benchmarking to assess the ongoing in-house performance against opportunities in the IT services market. The director of IS planning, Berwick Mitchell, commented, 'The frameworks and process allowed us to clearly identify and assess the factors that were most important for GrandMet in making IS sourcing decisions. We were able to involve both senior business executives and technical staff in the review process in a structured way, and were able to reach rational conclusions that now have support across the organization'.

Such experiences, and those of our case study organizations, suggest a number of final points. The outsourcing market is changing in the customer's favour. Once dominated by a few big players – EDS, Andersen, CSC, and IBM – the IT outsourcing market has fragmented into many niche services. As competition in the outsourcing market increases, companies have more power to bargain for shorter contracts, more select services, and better financial packages. Also in the customer's favour is a growing experience base with IT outsourcing, which allows customers to intelligently evaluate and negotiate outsourcing deals. In fact many of our respondent companies adopted incremental outsourcing precisely to mitigate risk and develop in-house learning from outsourcing over time. Our evidence points to long-term total outsourcing as a possible option only for those highly experienced in IT outsourcing contracts and in managing major, long-term relationships with suppliers. In practice, especially on the latter point, we uncovered considerable immaturity not only among customers, but also among suppliers. It may well be that long term total outsourcing deals are more likely to occur with a maturing of the capability to handle them; however, even supporters of such deals regularly point to the considerable difficulties experienced in getting them right.

More importantly, juxtaposed with the growing evidence, including our own, of the problems with an all-or-nothing approach to IT outsourcing are the benefits of selective sourcing. When companies properly select and contract for specific IT activities by treating IT as a dynamic portfolio, companies maintain management and control of core IT activities – such as strategic planning, scanning the environment for new technologies applicable to business needs, development of business-specific applications, and support of critical systems – while still accessing vendor expertise and economies of scale for well-defined, isolated, or mature IT activities. For example, in 1993 Sun Microsystems signed a three-year, $27 million deal with CSC to handle all of Sun's mainframe operations while the in-house IT staff rewrites its mainframe-based manufacturing and financial applications to run on a new client–server platform. In another example, a major US bank outsourced its data centre operations to IBM to reduce costs while retaining an in-house staff to develop strategic banking systems, many of which are subsequently sold on the market (see Lacity, Willcocks and Feeny, 1995 for a detailed discussion). We believe deals such as these, where vendors take over lower value-added IT tasks while companies manage higher value-added IT applications internally, are bell-wethers to the future of IT outsourcing.

REFERENCES

Ambrosio, J. (1991) 'Outsourcing at Southland: Best of Times, Worst of Times', *Computerworld*, **25**, (12), March 25.

Anthes, G. (1991) 'Perot wins 10-year Outsourcing Deal', *Computerworld*, **25**, (14), April 8, p. 96.

Applegate, L. (1994) 'Managing in an Information Age: Transforming the Organization for the 1990s', In *Proceedings of the IFIP Conference on Information Technology and New Emergent Forms of Organizations*, North Holland, Amsterdam, pp. 15–93.

Applegate, L. and Montealegre, R. (1991) *Eastman Kodak Co: Managing Information Systems through Strategic Alliances*, Harvard Business School Case 9–192–030, Boston, Mass.

Barron, T. (1992) 'Some New Results in Testing for Economies of Scale in Computing', *Decision Support Systems*, **8**, pp. 405–429.

Benjamin, R. and Blunt, J. (1992) 'Critical IT Issues: The Next Ten Years', *Sloan Management Review*, **33**, (4), Summer, pp. 7–19.

Clemons, E. and Row, M. (1988) 'McKesson Drug Company', *Journal of Management Information Systems*, **5**, (1), Summer, pp. 36–50.

Copeland, D. and McKenney, J. (1988) 'Airline Reservation Systems: Lessons from History', *MIS Quarterly*, **12**, (3), September, pp. 353–370.

Hamilton, R. (1989) 'Kendall Outsources IS Chief', *Computerworld*, **23**, (46), November 13, pp. 1–4.

Henderson, J. (1990) 'Plugging into Strategic Partnerships: The Critical IS Connection', *Sloan Management Review*, Spring, pp. 7–18.

Holway, R. (1996) 'The 1996 Holway Report', reported in Jones, R. 'Software and Services Flourishing in UK', *Computer Weekly*, June 6, p. 22.

Hopper, M. (1990) 'Rattling SABRE – New Ways to Compete on Information', *Harvard Business Review*, **68**, (3), May–June, pp. 118–125.

IDC (1992) *Outsourcing Options in Europe*, The Yankee Group Europe, Watford, UK.

Krass, P. (1990) 'The Dollars and Sense of Outsourcing', *Information Week*, (259), February 26, pp. 26–31.

Kettinger, W., Grover, V., Guha, S. and Segars, A. (1994) 'Strategic Information Systems Revisited: A Study in Sustainability and Performance', *MIS Quarterly*, **18**, (1), March, pp. 31–58.

Lacity, M. and Hirschheim, R. (1993) *Information Systems Outsourcing: Myths, Metaphors, and Realities*, Wiley, Chichester.

Lacity, M. and Hirschheim, R. (1995) *Beyond the Information Systems Outsourcing Bandwagon*, Wiley, Chichester.

Lacity, M., Hirschheim, R. and Willcocks, L. (1994) 'Realizing Outsourcing Expectations: Incredible Expectations, Credible Outcomes', *Journal of Information Systems Management*, **11**, (4), pp. 7–18.

Lacity, M. and Willcocks, L. (1996) *Best Practices in Information Technology Sourcing*, Oxford Executive Research Briefings, 2, Templeton College, Oxford.

Lacity, M., Willcocks, L. and Feeny, D. (1995) 'IT Outsourcing – Maximize Flexibility and Control', *Harvard Business Review*, **73**, (3), May–June, pp. 84–93.

Loh, L. and Venkatraman, N. (1992) 'Diffusion of Information Technology Outsourcing: Influence Sources and the Kodak Effect', *Information Systems Research*, **3**, (4), December, pp. 334–358.

Mehler, M. (1992) 'The Age of the Megacontract', *Information Week*, July 13, pp. 42–45.

McFarlan, F. W. and Nolan, R. (1995) 'How to Manage an IT Outsourcing Alliance', *Sloan Management Review*, Winter, pp. 9–23.

Pettigrew, A., (ed.) (1987) *The Management of Strategic Change*, Blackwell, Oxford.

Prahalad, C. and Hamel, G. (1991) 'The Core Competence of the Corporation', *Harvard Business Review*, **63**, (3), pp. 79–91.

Rochester, J. and Douglas, D. (eds) (1990) 'Taking An Objective Look at Outsourcing', *I/S Analyzer*, **28**, (8), September.

Willcocks, L. and Fitzgerald, G. (1994) *A Business Guide to IT Outsourcing: A Study Of European Best Practice In The Selection, Management And Use Of External IT Services.* Business Intelligence, London.

Venkatraman, N. and Short, J. (1990) *Strategies for Electronic Integration: From Order-entry to Value-added Partnerships at Baxter*, MIT Working Paper, Sloan School of Management, Mass.

Yin, R. (1984) *Case Study Research, Design, and Methods*, Sage Publications, Beverly Hills, California.

CHAPTER TWELVE

IT Outsourcing in Europe and the USA: Assessment Issues

LESLIE P. WILLCOCKS, MARY C. LACITY AND GUY FITZGERALD

INTRODUCTION

As outlined in Chapter 11, information technology (IT) outsourcing is a growing phenomenon in the developed economies. In 1992 the Yankee Group estimated global revenues for all types of IT outsourcing as rising to $US49.5 billion by 1994 (Willcocks and Fitzgerald, 1994a). Later estimates by IDC suggest a figure of over US$70 billion by 1998, with the European market at US$8 billion in 1996 (see Chapter 11). In the United Kingdom IT outsourcing spend was £800 million in 1993, and projected to rise to £1.72 billion by 1998 (Fitzgerald and Willcocks, 1993). In practice this figure was exceeded in 1996 with revenues of £1.7 billion and an estimated growth rate of 24 per cent (Holway, 1996). What explains this growth? To add to the discussion in the last chapter, our own research studies suggest that four general drivers seem to be operating. IT outsourcing is often a response to the hype and publicity surrounding the subject; a bandwagon effects leads to senior executives asking: why don't we outsource IT? Secondly, outsourcing may be a response to tough economic and competitive climates and the need to cut, or at least control costs. Thirdly, IT outsourcing may be part of larger and longer term changes in how organizations are structured and managed. Finally, outsourcing may well reflect the desire of senior managers to get rid of a troublesome IT function that finds it difficult to demonstrate its own business value (Lacity and Hirschheim, 1993, 1995; Willcocks and Fitzgerald, 1994a; Lacity, Hirschheim and Willcocks, 1994).

In the cases we have investigated, a mix of reasons for IT outsourcing were advanced. These ranged through financial, technical, and political objectives to a concern to focus effort on core competences. In the last case the thinking reflected that espoused by commentators such as Pralahad and Hamel (1990) and Quinn (1992). Either IT was identified as a non-core competence, and so could be outsourced. Or alternatively, aspects of the IT function were identified as 'core', for example systems that enabled the organization to differentiate itself from the competition, while others were identified as 'commodities' that could be more usefully and economically outsourced. In the vast majority of cases, cost savings of between 10 and 40 per cent were anticipated, and invariably a strong economic logic for outsourcing IT was advanced. However the economic payoff was not always as anticipated. The European survey found that where lower costs were measured, they were running 19 per cent lower on average, ranging between 5 and 20 per cent in most cases. However 18 per cent of organizations surveyed reported higher costs averaging 22 per cent as a result of outsourcing IT. More worrying, 30 per cent of organizations could not, or had not tried to quantify the costs and benefits of IT outsourcing. A related finding was that when organizatons were asked about risks that became reality during outsourcing, the biggest risk was the hidden costs of the contract, closely followed by the credibility of vendor claims (Fitzgerald and Willcocks, 1993).

In all our studies, assessment issues emerged strongly as critically affecting levels of success and failure in IT outsourcing. In particular, many respondents themselves noted four areas of weakness in their practice:

1. failure to to establish adequate measurement of the pre-existing in-house performance;
2. limitations in the economic assessment of vendor bids;
3. failures in contracting in sufficient detail; and
4. inadequate attention to setting up measurement systems to monitor vendor performance.

This chapter, therefore, investigates the assessment issues in these areas, with a view to pointing the way toward how assessment practice could be developed.

RESEARCH: DEFINITIONS AND APPROACHES

This section adds further detail on the research base outlined in Chapter 11. There are slight differences between the two research bases, not least that the one described in Chapter 11 includes data up to 1996. However, the organizations researched remain largely the same. The working definition of IT outsourcing here is the handing over to third-party management, for required result, some or all of an organization's IT, information systems (IS), and related services. As made clear in the previous chapter, outsourcing does not exhaust the ways in which the IT services market can be used. Thus we will continue to make a key distinction between contracts that specify a service and result which the market is to provide ('outsourcing'); and contracts which call for the market to provide resources to be deployed under the buyer's management and control ('insourcing'). Furthermore, contracting under each of these regimes maybe on a spot transaction or a longer-term 'partnering' basis (Lacity, Willcocks and Feeny, 1995). This chapter is specifically concerned with IT outsourcing arrangements. However, the research covered a spectrum of organizations variously involved in short- and long-term deals, insourcing and outsourcing, and also organizations that had contemplated outsourcing only to reject it in favour of the in-house option. Therefore this research enables assessment of the economic attractiveness of IT outsourcing against the alternatives.

This chapter reports the combined findings on major assessment issues from two studies conducted in the 1990–94 period (Lacity and Hirschheim, 1993, 1995; Willcocks and Fitzgerald, 1994a,b). We studied 19 organizations in the USA and 21 organizations in the UK. As can be seen in Table 12.1, the cases represent a wide range of sourcing decisions including data centre operations, systems development, systems support, telecommunications, and/or PC maintenance. In total participants in the 40 organizations made 61 sourcing decisions. Fourteen decisions resulted in *total outsourcing* when participants transferred to third-party vendors IT assets, leases, activities and staff representing at least 80 per cent of participants' IT budgets. Fifteen decisions resulted in *total insourcing* when participants decided to retain internally management and provision representing more than 80 per cent of the IT budget. Thirty-two decisions resulted in *selective sourcing* when participants decided to source selected IT functions from external providers while still spending between 20 and 80 per cent of the IT budget on internal provision.

We interviewed 145 participants. At each case site, we conducted one to three hour-long, face-to-face interviews with individuals directly involved in the outsourcing process on behalf of the client organization. Interviews included 34 senior business executives, and 29 chief information officers (CIOs or equivalent title) who initiated the outsourcing evaluations, six consultants hired to assist contract negotiations, and 30 contract managers responsible for monitoring/administering the resulting contract. We also interviewed 46 IT personnel responsible for gathering technical and financial

Table 12.1   Case study profiles (Continues)

Organiz-ation no.	Industry and size in terms of sales* and MIPs	Sourcing decisions[1]	Year of decisions	Type of contract	Expected cost savings	Cost savings achieved?	Initiator of the decisions
1	US commercial bank* 180 MIPS	Total outsourcing – 10 years	1990	Neo-classical	15–18%	Yes, as of 1994	Senior manager
2	US diversified services* 135 MIPS	(a) Total insourcing	(a) 1988	(a) N/A	(a) 0%	(a) None	(a) IT manager
		(b) Total outsourcing – 10 years	(b) 1988	(b) Relational	(b) 20%	(b) No	(b) Senior manager
3	US Metals* <150 MIPS	Total outsourcing – 10 years	1990	Neo-classical, with major loopholes	16%	Unable to determine	IT manager
4	US transportation* >300 MIPS	Total outsourcing – 10 years	1991	Neo-classical	20%	Unable to determine	Senior manager
5	US mining* 150 MIPS	Total outsourcing – 10 years	1991	Neo-classical, with loopholes	Savings anticipated	Some savings achieved	Senior manager
6	US Aerospace* >300 MIPS	Total outsourcing – 10 years	1993	Neo-classical	No savings estimated	Unable to determine	Senior manager
7	US Chemicals*	(a) Total outsourcing – 7 years	(a) 1984	(a) Relational	(a) and (b) Savings anticipated	(a) No, terminated contract early	(a) Senior manager
	<150 MIPS	(b) Total insourcing – return in-house	(b) 1988	(b) N/A			(b) IT manager

[1] Some companies evaluated outsourcing on multiple occasions
[2] PSB = Public sector body
* = US *Fortune* 500 or *Financial Times* European 1000

309

Table 12.1 Case study profiles (Continues)

Organization no.	Industry and size in terms of sales* and MIPs	Sourcing decisions[1]	Year of decisions	Type of contract	Expected cost savings	Cost savings achieved?	Initiator of the decisions
8	US rubber and plastics* > 150 MIPS	(a) Total outsourcing – 7 years (b) Total insourcing – return in-house	(a) 1987 (b) 1991	(a) Relational (b) N/A	(a) and (b) Savings anticipated but not quantified	(a) No, IT costs rose to 4% of sales	(a) Senior manager (b) IT manager
9	UK Clothing and housewares retailer* > 150 MIPS	Total outsourcing – 10.5 years	1993	Neo-classical and relational	25%	Too early to determine	IT managers
10	UK oil* > 150 MIPS	(a) Selective: diverse services, 3 years (b) Selective: accounting services, 4 years (c) Total outsourcing (3 contracts) Client-servers, WANs, data centres – 5 years	(a) 1988 –1990 (b) 1991 (c) 1993	(a) Neo-classical (b) Neo-classical (c) Neo-classical with relational aspects	(a) 15–20% (b) 20% (c) 20–25%	(a) Yes (b) Most (c) Some savings, less than 20%	(a) IT managers (b) Senior managers (c) Senior managers
11	European electronics* > 150 MIPS	(a) Selective: software development and support – 5 years (b) Total outsourcing: telecommunications and data centres – annually renewable	(a) 1989 (b) 1991	(a) and (b) Neo-classical with rational aspects	(a) and (b) No cost savings estimated, required variable IT costs	(a) and (b) Some cost savings	(a) and (b) Senior and IT managers
12	UK insurance < 50 MIPS	(a) Total outsourcing – 1 year (b) Selective outsourcing – systems maintenance – 1 year (c) Total insourcing – 1 year	(a) 1990 (b) 1991 (c) 1993	(a) (b) and (c) Neo-classical	(a) No (b) 25–30% (c) 30%	(a) No (b) Yes (c) Yes	(a) and (b) and (c) Senior manager and IT managers

[1] Some companies evaluated outsourcing on multiple occasions
[2] PSB = Public sector body
* = US Fortune 500 or Financial Times European 1000

310

Table 12.1 Case study profiles (Continues)

Organiz-ation no.	Industry and size in terms of sales* and MIPs	Sourcing decisions[1]	Year of decisions	Type of contract	Expected cost savings	Cost savings achieved?	Initiator of the decisions
13	UK Inland Revenue Service (PSB)[2] > 150 MIPS	Total outsourcing – 10 years	1994	Neo-classical plus relational aspects	Some savings envisaged	Too early	Government ministers and IT manager
14	US chemicals* 28 MIPS	Total insourcing	1991	N/A	No cost savings estimated	No cost savings achieved	IT Manager and senior manager
15	US diversified services* < 150 MIPS	Total insourcing	1991	N/A	No cost savings estimated	No cost savings achieved	IT manager
16	US petroleum refining* > 300 MIPS	Total insourcing	1988	N/A	No cost savings estimated	No cost savings achieved	Senior manager
17	US petroleum refining* 200 MIPS	Total insourcing	1991	N/A	43%	Yes, within 5 years	Senior manager
18	US petroleum refining* < 150 MIPS	Total insourcing	1990	N/A	0%, remain as is	Yes, costs remained the same	IT manager
19	US shoe apparel* 56 MIPS	Total insourcing	1988	N/A	54%	Yes, within 4 years	IT manager

[1] Some companies evaluated outsourcing on multiple occasions
[2] PSB = Public sector body
* = US Fortune 500 or Financial Times European 1000

311

Table 12.1 Case study profiles (Continues)

Organiz- ation no.	Industry and size in terms of sales* and MIPs	Sourcing decisions[1]	Year of decisions	Type of contract	Expected cost savings	Cost savings achieved?	Initiator of the decisions
20	US public university 106 MIPS	Total insourcing	1992	N/A	20%	Yes, within 1 year	IT manager
21	US food manufacturer* 180 MIPS	Total insourcing	1988	N/A	45%	Yes, within 3 years	Senior manager
22	US tele- communications 32 MIPS	Total insourcing	1991	N/A	46%	Yes, within 2 years	Senior manager
23	UK Water company 20 MIPS	Selective – Customer billing system – 5 years	1991	Neo-classical	20%	Yes	IT manager
24	US petroleum refining > 150 MIPS	Selective – Data centre – 5 years	1991	Neo-classical	16%	Unable to determine	IT manager
25	UK retail and distribution* > 300 MIPS	(a) Selective – corporate telecommunications – 3 years (b) Selective – telecommunications – 2.5 years	(a) 1990 (b) 1992	(a) Classical (b) Neo-classical	(a) 20% (b) 30%	(a) Yes (b) Yes	(a) and (b) IT managers

[1] Some companies evaluated outsourcing on multiple occasions
[2] PSB = Public sector body
* = US Fortune 500 or Financial Times European 1000

312

Table 12.1 Case study profiles (Continues)

Organiz- ation no.	Industry and size in terms of sales* and MIPs	Sourcing decisions¹	Year of decisions	Type of contract	Expected cost savings	Cost savings achieved?	Initiator of the decisions
26	UK chemicals manufacturer* > 150 MIPS	(a) Selective: system support – 2 years (b) Selective: development and support – 2 years (c) Selective: development and support – 3 years	(a) 1985 (b) 1991 (c) 1992	(a) and (b) and (c) Neo-classical	(a) 40% (b) 30% (c) 20%	(a) 50% over 8 years (b) Some (c) Most	Senior and IT managers
27	UK food manufacturer* 76 MIPS	(a) Total insourcing (b) Selective – Factory software development – 2.5 years	(a) 1990 (b) 1991	(a) N/A (b) Neo-classical	(a) 20–30% (b) 25%	(a) Yes (b) No	(a) IT manager (b) Business & IT managers
28	UK consumer product manufacturer* > 150 MIPS	(a) Total outsourcing – 5 years (b) Selective – Data centre– 3 years	(a) 1985 (b) 1988	(a) Neo-classical (b) Neo-classical	(a) 15% (b) 20%	(a) No (b) Yes	(a) Senior and IT managers (b) Business and IT managers
29	US commercial bank* > 150 MIPS	Selective – Data centres – 5 years	1992	Neo-classical	25%	Yes	Senior business manager
30	UK commercial bank* > 150 MIPS	(a) Selective – systems support – 3 years (b) Selective – systems support – 2 years	(a) 1991 (b) 1992	(a) Neo-classical (b) Neo-classical	(a) 15–20% (b) 20%	(a) Yes (b) Yes	Business and IT managers

¹ Some companies evaluated outsourcing on multiple occasions
² PSB = Public sector body
* = US *Fortune* 500 or *Financial Times* European 1000

Table 12.1 Case study profiles (Continues)

Organiz-ation no.	Industry and size in terms of sales* and MIPs	Sourcing decisions[1]	Year of decisions	Type of contract	Expected cost savings	Cost savings achieved?	Initiator of the decisions
31	UK glass and plastics manufacturer* 40 MIPS	Selective – Data centre and systems development – 2 years and renewed for 3 years	1992	Neo-classical with relational aspects	24%	Yes	Senior and IT managers
32	UK brewing and distribution* > 300 MIPS	Selective – central systems development and support – 5 years	1993	Neo-classical with relational elements	Cost increase over 2 years, break-even over 5 years	First year cost increase	IT managers
33	UK clothing and food retailer* 150 MIPS	(a) Selective – data centre – 3 years (b) Selective – PC maintenance – 3 years (c) Selective – mainframe maintenance – 3 years	(a) 1988 (b) 1988 (c) 1990	(a) Neo-classical (b) Neo-classical (c) Neo-classical	(a) None (b) 15% (c) 20%	(a) N/A (b) Yes (c) Yes	IT managers
34	UK food manufacturer* < 50 MIPS	(a) Selective – Factory software development – 2 years (b) Selective – data centre – 3 years	(a) 1988 (b) 1992	(a) Neo-classical with relational aspects (b) Neo-classical	(a) None (b) 30–33%	(a) No, costs doubled (b) Yes, so far	(a) Senior manager (b) IT manager
35	UK electricity supply* < 100 MIPS	Selective – distributed PC networks – 2 years	1992	Neo-classical	30%	Yes, as of 1994	Divisional manager

[1] Some companies evaluated outsourcing on multiple occasions
[2] PSB = Public sector body
* = US Fortune 500 or Financial Times European 1000

Table 12.1 Case study profiles (Concluded)

Organiz-ation no.	Industry and size in terms of sales* and MIPs	Sourcing decisions[1]	Year of decisions	Type of contract	Expected cost savings	Cost savings achieved?	Initiator of the decisions
36	UK public health authority (PSB) < 100 MIPS	Selective – data centre and software packages – 5 years	1991	Neo-classical	20–25%	Yes	IT manager
37	UK county council (PSB) < 50 MIPS	(a) Selective – data centre and telecommunications – 15 years; (b) Selective – office systems support – 4 years	(a) 1991; (b) 1992	(a) Neo-classical; (b) Neo-classical	(a) 20%; (b) 17%	(a) Yes, 20–22%; (b) Yes	(a) and (b) IT, finance and business service managers
38	UK broadcasting corporation* (PSB) < 100 MIPS	(a) Insourcing; (b) Selective – data centre – 7 years	(a) 1988; (b) 1992	(a) N/A; (b) Neo-classical	(a) 25%; (b) 35%	(a) Yes; (b) Yes	(a) Senior and IT managers; (b) IT manager
39	UK aviation authority* < 100 MIPS	(a) Selective – payroll and financial systems – 5 years; (b) Selective – PCs and networks – 4 years; (c) Selective – financial packages – 5 years	(a) 1988; (b) 1989; (c) 1990	(a) Classical; (b) Neo-classical; (c) Neo-classical	(a) 15%; (b) Some; (c) Some	(a) None; (b) Minimal; (c) Minimal	(a) Senior manager; (b) IT manager; (c) IT manager
40	UK water company < 100 MIPS	Selective – data centre – 3 years	1994	Neo-classical	15–20%	Too early	Senior managers

[1] Some companies evaluated outsourcing on multiple occasions
[2] PSB = Public sector body
* = US Fortune 500 or Financial Times European 1000

315

information. During the interviews, we sought to understand the participants' perceptions and motivations, evaluation processes, and consequences of their sourcing decisions. In this sense, we assumed an interpretivist perspective with the goal of understanding the information systems outsourcing phenomenon from the participants' viewpoint (Orlikowski and Baroudi, 1991). All interviews were tape-recorded and transcribed into 1120 single-spaced pages. We then applied the precepts of intentional analysis to the transcripts (Sanders, 1982). In addition to the interviews, we gathered relevant documentation such as the outsourcing request for proposal, outsourcing bids, internal bids, bid analysis criteria, contracts, benchmarks, annual reports and organization charts. We used the documentation to corroborate participants' statements and to analyse contract specifics.

In addition we also utilize in this chapter the findings from a European survey of outsourcing practice conducted in 1993. After piloting, the survey was dispatched to some 1200 senior managers/ directors, mainly in the IT field in both medium and large-sized organizations in Europe. The sample was selected randomly from the large contact base held by Business Intelligence, an independent research organization. The survey elicited a 30 per cent response and a usable response rate of 16.2 per cent. Assessment issues formed an integral part of the postal questionnaire. The survey findings therefore enabled us to provide some quantification and wider context to the issues, evidence and interpretation arising from the case studies.

The chapter is organized to discuss findings on the economics of the vendor bid, setting up a measurement system for outsourced activities, and the major problems experienced on the assessment front after outsourcing. For further detailed findings on assessment issues before outsourcing, the reader is also referred to Willcocks, Fitzgerald and Lacity (1996).

ECONOMICS OF THE VENDOR BID

In this section, we look at bids from IT outsourcing vendors mainly from an economic viewpoint. Clearly, other factors also influence the degree to which any outsourcing arrangements can be sustained. As some examples, the client organization will need to assess the technical capability of the vendor to deliver what it promises, the cultural fit between client and vendor, and the quality of the relationship between the relevant staff in both organizations. A full discussion of such factors appears in Willcocks and Fitzgerald (1994a). While such factors are important and invariably have economic consequences, this section focuses on the more directly economic factors in any vendor bid. A

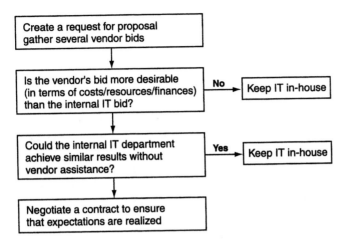

Figure 12.1   Proposed outsourcing evaluation process (Source: Lacity and Hirschheim, 1993)

proposed outsourcing evaluation process is shown in Figure 12.1. This section will use the framework for discussing the more directly economic factors emerging from our research, namely the importance of the pre-existing evaluation process, the sources of hidden costs, some myths in the economics of IT outsourcing, and the central role of the contract in any outsourcing arrangement.

The influence of pre-existing evaluation practice

There is already much advice and indeed some prior academic research on the economics of IT outsourcing, (see for examples Aucoin *et al.*, 1991, Almy, Heise, Landry *et al.*, 1991; Buck-Lew, 1992; Due, 1992; Gupta and Gupta, 1992; I/S Analyzer, 1990). However, there is little work on how to make detailed comparisons with in-house options. A particularly noticeable gap is the lack of attention given to the relationship between prior IT evaluation practice and ability to assess bids from outsourcing vendors. In fact, a major finding from our research is that organizations find it very difficult to assess properly vendor bids against each other, and against any in-house bid, due to poor pre-existing evaluation practice.

As detailed in Willcocks (1994), typical weaknesses in prior IT evaluation practice include:

- not fully investigating risk and its potential cost;
- understating knock-on operating, maintenance and human and organizational costs and budgeting practices that conceal full costs;
- lack of metrics to assess the business contribution of IT;

- use of inappropriate metrics, given the objectives set for specific IT projects; inadequate approaches to dealing with 'intangible' benefits and for tracking benefits over long timescales.

For an organization contemplating outsourcing such weaknesses mean that a great deal of effort will need to be invested in understanding the costs and benefits of the existing IT operation so that these can be compared against vendor bids. Respondents found this best done in the lead up to the request for proposal (see Figure 12.1). Many respondents left it until later; their experiences suggest that it is rarely a good idea to postpone this analysis to the period after contracts have been signed. This can promote both subsequent hidden costs, and also opportunistic behaviour on the part of the vendor. This detailed analysis needs to be carried out even where organizations have already moved to full in-house charging systems, have detailed in-house service level agreements and/or operate in-house IT as a cost or profit centre (Willcocks, Fitzgerald and Lacity, 1996). Our own findings indicate that failure to devote managerial effort to this evaluation task means not only poor assessment of vendor bids; there is also a knock-on effect into setting up inadequate measurement systems for subsequent vendor performance. These issues are pursued further below.

Sources of hidden costs

As noted above, a consistent finding across our case studies was that outsourcing frequently carried hidden costs. As one extreme example, Lacity and Hirschheim (1993) found one petroleum company being charged almost $500 000 in 'excess fees' in the first month into a new contract. More often the hidden costs are less dramatic but accumulate to a significant figure over time. As well as inadequate measurement systems, there seem to be five additional root causes of such hidden costs. They all relate to weaknesses in contracting. These are:

- failure to fully define present IT requirements;
- failure to define fully future requirements, or failure to create mechanisms for protecting price in the face of contingencies;
- loopholes or ambiguities in the contract;
- not allowing the vendor a reasonable profit; and
- unforeseen, rising, in-house contract management costs as a result of weak contracting practice.

The first three weaknesses left client organizations open not only to additional costs for services not previously contracted for, but also to higher prices for those services. Loopholes/ambiguities in the contract may also trigger conflicts with, and also opportunistic behaviour by vendors. For example, a major US bank in 1992 signed a contract stating that the cost of transferring all software licensing agreements would be borne by the client. The first 30 agreements cost very little to transfer, but the last few involved many thousands of dollars. The contract manager felt that the vendor knew the cost implications of the contract, but had not spelt these out to the client. That said, however, vendor opportunism can also be triggered by not allowing the vendor a reasonable profit. Vendor account managers then come under internal pressure to make their margins from the outsourcing deal.

Finally, in-house management costs in terms of new roles, time and effort are frequently higher than anticipated. IT outsourcing was viewed by some respondents as 'spending rather than managing'. However, as Chapters 11 and 17 also point out, in all outsourcing arrangements, key management capabilities need to be retained in-house. At a minimum these cover:

- strategic thinking on IT in relation to the business;
- systems integration;
- eliciting business demand for IT;
- spotting business opportunities for the use of IT;
- an 'informed buyer' role;
- contract monitoring, and
- the ability to lever vendor relations to advantage, (see Willcocks and Fitzgerald, 1994b).

Such costs may not be built into the preliminary assessment of a vendor bid, but they were typical rather than unusual outcomes in most outsourcing arrangements we researched.

Some economic myths in outsourcing

Detailed analysis of in-house IT performance together with assessing *all* the likely costs of outsourcing IT – these help to establish whether the vendor's bid is more favourable than any likely bid by the internal IT department. To help further in this assessment, some possible sources of additional outsourcing costs are indicated in Figures 12.2 and 12.3 below. To add to this picture, it is useful to ask whether an internal IT department can achieve similar results without vendor assistance (see Figure 12.1). There are two central economic myths propagated by many vendors and trade press sources. One myth is that IT outsourcing vendors are inherently more efficient than internal IT departments. The second myth is that savings of 10–50 per cent can be achieved only through outsourcing (Lacity and Hirschheim, 1995; Willcocks and Fitzgerald and Lacity, 1996). Let us look at these propositions in more detail.

For		Questions
Cost savings	**BUT**	• Over what time period? • Can you achieve savings on your own?
Provides scarce IT skills		• At what price • In the contract?
Better quality service		• A point of no return? • Continuity of staff? • How measured?
Assist cashflow problems		• Pay for it later?
Enables focus on core needs and skills of the business		• Reliability of service • Do you need to keep parts of the IS function in-house?

Figure 12.2   Assessing the vendor bid: benefits and issues (1)

For	Questions
Flexibility to go into advanced/new technologies	• In the contract? Price? • Available from suppliers? Control?
Saves money by mopping up excess mainframe capacity	• Shared technology? • Switching costs if contract is unsatisfactory? • Security and contingency issues?
Clear accountability	• How detailed/sketchy is the contractual relationship?
Increased management control	• In-house contract management skills
Manage demand fluctuations better	• Over what range? At what price?

Figure 12.3   Assessing the vendor bid: benefits and issues (2)

Are IT outsourcing vendors inherently more efficient?

In practice, internal IT departments can be cost competitive with external vendors. The argument that vendors are inherently more efficient is usually based on notions of economies of scale. It is often considered that vendors achieve two types of scale economies over in-house departments: through higher mass production efficiency and through labour specialization efficiencies. In practice, it is difficult to measure such efficiencies in IT settings. However, as pointed out in Chapter 11, our evidence is that the advantages vendors bring to bear are generally overstated:

1. Mass production efficiencies will be expressed as lower data processing costs (cost per MIP), and/or lower hardware and software purchasing costs. In practice a number of our respondents reported operating at high efficiency in-house at the 150–170 MIPs range. Some commentators suggest that after 300 MIPs the benefits of transferring to a larger IT shop are negligible (Bergstrom, 1991; Krass, 1990). Three companies in our studies were running 28, 14 and 17 MIP shops respectively, and all were more efficient in terms of cost-per-MIP than large vendor-run data centres. Real Decisions Corporation have found companies reducing data centre costs by 17–25 per cent a year without outsourcing (Bergstrom, 1991).

   On hardware and software costs, the theory is that buying in bulk allows a vendor to buy at cheaper prices. In practice we found many in-house IT functions receiving discounts similar to outsourcing vendors. Smaller companies can also negotiate cheap hardware leases by using older technology, or by using cheaper networked technology. Software companies are becoming harder on charging for the transfer of software licensing agreements. Furthermore, in several of our cases contracts stipulated that the costs of transfer of licensing agreements fell on the client company, not the vendor.

2. Labour specialization efficiencies come from the wider access vendors can have to technical and business talent. In practice many companies outsource to access the vendor's pool of technical talent only to find that (a) they are supported by the same staff, though sometimes at a lower cost, and (b) additional vendor expertise is expensive. As one respondent noted:

   > None of it is cheap. I guess there is a perception that once you have (a vendor) locked in that you have a conduit to all this expertise, but you pay.

We also found examples where, after the first year of a contract a vendor moved their experienced, skilled staff on to newer contracts, or where the better transferred staff with critical business knowledge of a company were nevertheless moved to other contracts run by the vendor. On business talent, many participants who outsourced felt a real loss of business expertise, as talented ex-employees were siphoned off by the vendor to assist in attracting other customers from the same industry. However, even where a vendor may be inherently more efficient on labour costs, the natural cost advantage still needs to be significant to cover the vendor's profit margin.

Can savings of 10–50 per cent only be achieved through outsourcing?
We found organizations achieving savings internally through a variety of measures. The organizations that were more hard-headed about IT outsourcing tended to drive down costs as much as possible internally before then considering outsourcing proposals. The alternative approach tended to allow the vendor to 'pick the low-lying fruit', that is, take, as an additional part of profit on the deal, those cost reductions that could have been achieved internally. As one high-profile example, it is probable that this happened in the 1988–89 Eastman Kodak/IBM deal.

Organizations can also drive down internal costs by consolidating data centres. As one example, Citibank in Europe did this before seeking an outsourcing agreement with a vendor to run those data centres. In several examples where organizations decided against outsourcing, costs were driven down by optimizing resource use, implementing strict cost controls, and by upskilling existing staff rather than seeking access to more expensive technical staff available on the market. Again, even where a vendor may have inherent economies of scale in these areas, these usually still need to be significant in order to offset required profit margins. That said, we found examples where there were political reasons why the IT department could not bring cost savings to bear, or where there were demands to reduce the IT headcount, or where the business required cash from the sale of information assets or needed to move IT from a fixed to a more variable expense. In such cases, the economic logic against outsourcing became intermingled and diverted through a variety of often conflicting stakeholder interests and perspectives.

The centrality of the contract

A major finding was that, if an organization outsources IT, the outsourcing contract is the only certain way to ensure that expectations are realized (see Figure 12.1). In practice weak contracting, based on inadequate assessment of a vendor bid and backed up by poor monitoring systems, not only results in unanticipated, higher costs; it can create major problems for client organizations. In practice it is all too easy for all parties to a contract to agree broadly on what is required from a vendor. We also found parties all too frequently relying on 'partnering' notions to offset any difficulties arising from loose contracting. These rarely proved a sufficient base in themselves from which to run effective outsourcing arrangements (Lacity and Hirschheim, 1993; Fitzgerald and Willcocks, 1994). The issue is succinctly summarized by one of our respondents:

> Outsourcing contracts are agreed in concept and delivered in detail, and that's why they break down.
>
> Vendor manager

When it came to drawing up effective outsourcing contracts we found that indeed the devil is in the detail. Figures 12.2 and 12.3 provide summaries of the typical benefits organizations looked for, and which vendors promised, in the IT outsourcing deals we studied. The anticipated benefits are listed on the left-hand side of the figures. On the right-hand side we list the issues that regularly arose among our respondents in the 40 case studies and in the survey. It became clear from our research that unless, at a minimum, the questions listed here were addressed before IT outsourcing contracts were signed, then unanticipated costs and some significant problems tended to fall upon client organizations. These issues receive further detailed treatment in Lacity and Willcocks (1996, 1997). Some more issues on the economic aspects of contracting are pursued in the next section.

OUTSOURCED–SETTING UP A MEASUREMENT SYSTEM

Once an organization had decided to outsource any aspect of its IT function, it will need to monitor vendor performance. In this section we extend the discussion on the importance of the contract as the fundamental building block for a measurement system, and look at respondents' experiences with different types of outsourcing contracts. We then focus on issues relating to measurement systems and service level agreements, and provide guidelines on these topics.

Tight and loose contracting
Where organizations are setting up and running measurement systems for vendor performance, the most common potential 'bad practice' areas observed were:

- over-reliance on the pre-existing standards and measurement systems; and
- failure to define comprehensively in the initial contract the detailed expectations of both sides on standards and how measurement will proceed.

These usually occurred either through time pressures or a belief in the 'good offices' espoused by the vendor. Much depends on the quality of the relationship between vendor and client. Several respondent organizations were still actually refining measures during the first six months of the contract. This worked reasonably well where, in the early stages of a contract, the vendor was anxious to demonstrate flexibility and good partnering. This was the case, for example, in a 1992–94 Pilkington–EDS deal we investigated. In revisiting the deal in late 1994 we noted the following factors helping to explain the relative success of the contract. The previous service levels on the data centre had been largely detailed before outsourcing. Previous service levels delivered were largely what was required of the vendor anyway. The previous Pilkington IT manager had transferred to the vendor and was managing the contract for them – there was a good vendor–client relationship in place from the beginning. The client knew that it needed a flexible arrangement on vendor performance on the IS development side, and carefully selected the vendor for its ability to deliver this flexibility. Both were clear on the mutual expectations on this point before the contract began. There was also a short-term (three year) contract to minimize the risk. The means for handling changes in service requirements were specified at the start.

However, in several other contracts vendors were more concerned to keep very close to the original contract. This created contract management issues that became exacerbated where the contract was vague or did not cover issues arising later. The problem arose from different perceptions by the vendor and client of the meaning and role of the contract. In many cases, the client believed in the rhetoric of partnership much more than the vendor. The emerging lesson was that participants need to be clear as to what the relationship amounts to and how both sides understand it. Another issue arises here. While clients had a tendency to believe that the quality of the vendor–client relationship would see them over limitations of performance measurement arrangements in the contract, in fact the latter could also come to affect the former adversely. In one contract it took some 18 months of vigorous contract management to finally get the performance measures right and end disputes on service. The contract manager described the situation as follows:

> There was a contract, a legal one with our signatures on it, with various sections in it, but really it did not define what the service was going to be. And worse still, when we invoked penalty clauses, the section in the contract that talked about the penalty clauses was so ambiguously written that we had a bun fight for nearly six months over it. It wasn't the question of how much (it turned out to be something like £30 000, which over a multi-million pound contract was pretty small) but it was the bun fight that was the problem, the fact that they (the vendor) didn't just walk in on the following Monday and say 'we screwed up last week, we were down for three

days, and according to the contract this is what you are owed'. I think that all of that proved to me at that stage anyway, that we needed to get out of this partnership issue and back into a proper business contractual relationship and that is what really set us off, I think, down the right road'.

(Contract manager: UK retail company)

In another case the client was disappointed that the vendor kept rigorously to the contract. The client felt that something more had been promised. The learning points, according to our respondent, were that the safe option in the period just before signing the contract is to get what is said actually written into the contract; and be prepared to spend time chronicling the agreement in monotonous detail. One reason is illustrated in a third case: the vendor kept rigidly to the contract deal because of very slim profit margins. In all three cases described here the vendor–client relationships became adversely affected because of problems with operationalizing the contract.

Measurement: systems and service levels

We have seen that it is possible to operate on a more flexible partnership basis, and also that some areas to be outsourced may be difficult to specify precisely in terms of service and performance required. However, in outsourcing discretion may be the better part of valour. In reviewing 13 organizations contemplating or undertaking outsourcing, Lacity and Hirschheim (1993) suggested the following safety first guidelines on creating a measurement system:

1. Measure EVERYTHING during the baseline period.
2. Develop service level measures.
3. Develop service level reports.
4. Specify escalation procedures.
5. Include cash penalties for non-performance.
6. Determine growth rates.
7. Adjust charges to changes in business.

The experiences recorded in the UK study fit fairly closely with these guidelines. We will review these in the light of all the cases researched in the two studies. Respondents found it highly useful not to start a contract until current information systems services had been measured in a *baseline period*. There are a number of points here. Some respondents left the contract incomplete with a view to carrying out measurement in a baseline period *after* the contract had started, or trusting to a good relationship with the vendor to deal with problems as they arise. Both approaches are hardly low risk and can leave an organization as a hostage to fortune. An early 1990s contract between a major UK retail and distribution company and a vendor of telecommunications services was, as at 1994, producing major cost savings but the measurement system still needed tidying up during the course of the contract because of lack of specific targets when it was drawn up:

> (The vendor) largely wrote it and we signed it. All we were looking for was escalation procedures, what the nap connection charges were, and there was some discussion as to how they would respond and that they wouldn't do this that and the other. Even those comments were ambiguous in the way that they had been written. In undertaking the service level agreement procedure and the definition of our SLAs I think two things were sorted out. First of all, we then developed a service level agreement that was ours. . . . Once we'd done that we then realized that we had no telecommunications targets and strategy relative to the vendor, so we developed them. It was from that point onwards that we wrested control from . . . (the vendor) . . . of our telecommunications strategy, back to where it should have been, which was here all along'.
>
> (Contract manager: retail and distribution company)

Secondly, there may be time pressure to get a contract started. This may cut down on the time in which the baseline period for measurement is allowed to run. Lacity and Hirschheim (1993) recommend a six-month period to allow for fluctuations in service levels due to factors like tax season, seasonal business oscillations, and end-of-year data processing, for example. If service levels are measured monthly and compared, this then allows the setting up of a target variance for each service performance to fluctuate within before 'excess' charges to the vendor will become payable, or underperformance by the vendor can be penalized.

Refining the measurement system after the contract has started can work, provided this was part of the contractual agreement in the first place. Thus a major US-based bank signed an early 1990s outsourcing contract for running its mainframe service. A notable point here is that the pre-existing measurement system was fairly rigorous already.

> Broad inferences were given based upon the service agreements that . . . (the bank's) . . . data centre already had on its businesses. They were not really formal service level agreements. They were merely statements of what the on-line day would be, from when to when, by service, of all the many different services we have across all the different hardware platforms . . . . All that was made available to (the vendor), and established as the initial SLA guidelines. The bank then tasked itself with the vendor's agreement to getting much crisper

SLAs and we spent a lot of time with piloting and doing various other things to try and come up with standard, across-the-region support agreements and service level agreements which everyone could sign up to. We are on to reiteration three about now (1993) and close to signing off what will be the final SLAs'.

(Contract manager, US bank)

A further stipulation about the baseline period is to *measure everything, not just what is easiest to measure*. The problem is less prevalent where what is being outsourced is an area that was being heavily measured before and is on the more traditional 'factory' or production side of IT operations. However there can be a learning curve even here. Thus, WH Smith outsourced telecommunications to DEC, and from the experience was able to formulate much tighter measurement for a 1992 contract between Our Price Records, a company in the group, and the vendor Racal.

A more difficult area to measure, whether outsourced or not, is sytems development. Our own view, argued elsewhere, is that these areas are probably best managed on an 'insourcing' rather than on a strict 'outsourcing' basis (see Willcocks, Fitzgerald and Feeny, 1995). The problem is that the end goal for systems development, and how to get there, can rarely be well-defined. Some organizations, as in the case of Pilkington, handle this by stipulating that the vendor will make defined resources available for a defined period. There also need to be in place measures of the productivity of vendor staff. However these should not be based merely on the speed with which development proceeds through a defined methodology and timetable. The outputs of development also need to be measured in terms of business impact – for example, improvements in cost, quality and service, systems reliability, ease of use, ease of user learning. The elapsed time to business use is also a useful measure, with financial penalties built in for under-performance. Also how far what is developed conforms to corporate architecture and how far software is and will be re-used. These are difficult types of measures to formulate unless there are in-house systems people on the team, who already have key targets and measures in place before outsourcing. Thus in 1988 a UK manufacturing company outsourced micro-vax and software development of warehouse and carousel control systems in the factory. There was a lack of in-house expertise in this area. It emerged that there were complex interfaces with the company's mainframe systems and the mainframe development work was outsourced to further vendors. The company had no complaints about the work of these vendors:

It was lack of appreciation of the complexity of the interface early on because of not high enough calibre staff internally to recognize that.

Also nearly every department was affected in some way by these systems. Yet despite at the outset it was recognized as a business objective to enhance the capability of the site to deal with orders, we found ourselves in a situation where as software was developed and then went to user acceptance testing, it was only then that users realized what the system was doing and then raised very real problems. It has enabled us to rationalize production in Europe but it was longer than it should have been and cost more and it took us longer to become self-sufficient. We were too dependent on a third party for a core, essential business application

(IT manager: UK manufacturing company)

In later development projects this company successfully operated an 'insourcing' approach, bringing external expertise onto in-house teams to ensure transfer of learning takes place. They have also operated with clearer objectives and measures on development performance, not merely on hours worked and effort expended. In addition to the above areas there may be a series of services commonly given by the IT department but not documented. Before outsourcing it is important that these are analysed and included in the service agreement with the vendor along with measures of their delivery. What is not included in baseline period measurement will not be covered by the fixed price offered by the vendor and subsequently may be open to 'excess charges'. Examples of such services may be consultancy, PC support, installation, training services. An overview of service performance measurement by a manufacturing company we have researched helps to indicate the comprehensiveness needed for a measurement system for in-house and vendor performance. Figure 12.4 shows only the higher-level measures that needed to be in place.

Clearly, *specifying service level measures* is critical. Lacity and Hirschheim (1993) point out that, while this is regularly done a common mistake is then to not stipulate 100 per cent service accountability from the vendor. At one helpdesk support contract we researched in a major UK-based oil company, 80 per cent of service requests had to be responded to within 20 seconds and 90 per cent within 30 seconds. Financial penalties were attached to failure to meet these criteria over a specified time period. However the vendor was also made responsible for reporting in detail on this performance and provide explanations where 100 per cent was not achieved. In a more critical area measures would also be needed to ensure that the service requests not handled within the stipulated criteria were subsequently dealt with in an agreed reasonable time. Note also in this example the importance of *detailed service level reports*. Also the importance of agreeing in advance what happens where problems escalate, for

Information processing service performance – % availability; annual rolling availability; unscheduled business interruptions by number of events and time.

Information processing service to distribution – network and database availability; terminal response times; problems processed within stipulated time.

Information processing service to salesforce – successful transmissions at first attempt for salesforce terminals and VANs; successful EDI connections.

Information processing mainframe capacity – % CPU for personal and operational busy hourse for six modes of processing.

Systems development – % efficiency actual versus budget; headcount actual versus budget, monthly project analysis of current and closed projects on time and cost criteria; quality ratios. Detailed monthly project reports.

Systems support – queries resolved versus backlog; query analysis by business function type and volume.

Figure 12.4   Service performance measurement in a manufacturing company

example, providing explanations. This must lead on to *financial penalties for non-performance* as shown in this example from a UK-based bank:

> It was agreed at contract time there would be financial penalties . . . for failure to perform of two kinds. One, if a direct operational loss is caused because of negligence on (the vendor's) part in any one instance and the bank has to pay its clients money in terms of interest charges or penalties, then (the vendor) will idemnify (the company) up to certain limits, and that's on a one-time basis. . . . Secondly, if on an overall average service evaluation, taking its ability to provide a service over the course of a month, it fell below a specified level. So we have two specific financial implications of failure to deliver the service, one over time and one for a particular occasion, and that's well in place.
>
> (IT manager: major UK bank)

It also emerged as important to look to the future when negotiating service levels and their price. A particular issue was underestimation of the rate at which service needs will grow. Based on their own experiences, respondents stressed the need to include realistic growth rates in the contract agreement's fixed price. Specific clauses may also be needed to cover large service volume fluctuations due to merger, acquisitions or sale of parts of the business. Overall it emerged as important for client organizations to make measurement work for rather than against their interests. Thus in one US manufacturing company the contract specified a two-second response time for key applications such as order entry and customer service. It also specified vendor support for up to 20 users at a given time using a 4GL. However, during the first week the 11 4GL users were taking up more than 30 per cent of the machine cycles and making response times for critical applications unachievable. The vendor could have been forced to upgrade the technology provided, but the client, in this case, felt the demand would have been unreasonable. A tight contract reasonably handled by both sides was felt to improve the vendor–client relationship and levels of satisfaction all round.

DISCUSSION: ANTICIPATING SOME PROBLEM AREAS

In this section we signpost some further problem areas encountered. Some of the following issues are quite widely known about, but nevertheless were still undergone by respondent organizations. Other problem areas identified below would seem to be more difficult to predict. All are very real possibilities of which any organization contemplating outsourcing should be aware.

Much effort may be needed to develop an adequate measuring system

This was stressed earlier in the chapter in the context of assessing vendor bids. Here we look at the issue for organizations that have already outsourced. As an example a UK county council signed a £10 million, five-year contract with a major vendor. The contract operated from December 1 1991 and involved mainframe operations and applications service. This was the first major contract of three for the council in the early 1990s. Even though the IT department had been operating largely as an internal trading agency, there was still an immense amount of work needed to get the measurement system in place:

> There was a lot of information available to the out-sourcing companies about the current equipment, current costs of running equipment, staffing costs. A lot of information from us to them. But although we had been operating as a trading organization, there weren't any service level agreements in place to build up a business

relationship between the departments buying the service and the operations area itself. That was why it took five months to get from preferred supplier to contract stage. We actually wanted to have the whole of the contract underpinned by agreed and signed service level agreements before we entered into the contract. Some others choose not to do that, but that's the way we played this one.

(IT director: UK county council)

It is interesting to note here the desire to get the detailed service level agreements in place before the contract is entered into. The process by which the detailed service measures were arrived at is also worth noting:

It was a problem to redefine measurement from scratch. We worked with a preferred supplier to achieve this. The client evaluation team designed the basic service level agreement and then said to the FM (Facilities Management) company does this meet your criteria or is there anything you want to add to this. We had our own staff on the operational side to complete the main part of this document, went to the user departments as receivers of that service to complete their part and then put the documents together to form a single document in initial draft. Then the central client asked the FM company plus the operations staff to meet and thrash out the final versions. We ended up with a mainframe service level agreement, a voice network or telephone service level agreement, and then 97 service department application type service level agreements. A quantity of paperwork.

(IT director: UK county council)

From reviewing our research sites it emerged that user involvement in the establishment of SLAs was particularly important if user needs were going to be properly identified, and if there was to be user buy-in to the measurement activity. However, more detailed service measures and costing procedures can have unanticipated effects on user behaviour as will be discussed below. The sheer detail of the SLAs may also create a monitoring problem. Reflecting on their experiences respondents stressed the importance of focusing on the key measures in any service level agreement.

Outsourcing can require a culture change on measurement

It is all too easy to underestimate how far outsourcing might require a fundamentally different approach to measurement and control. Many organizations had not, at least in their early contracts, moved that far away from their existing measures and standards for IT performance. This can leave latent problems and conflicts that will emerge across the life of the outsourcing contract:

> The performance measures were not strong enough. This was
> because of the culture we operated in. I think they took us and I don't
> blame them, we weren't very professional. I think there have been
> some very good attempts at tightening up performance measurement.
> But once you've got a contract you've got a contract and if you are
> dealing with sharp guys like them, then it's very difficult. But it's no
> surprise to me that the closer we get toward contract renewal, it's
> amazing what we can get.
>
> (IT director: UK public sector organization)

The fact that the respondent here is getting a better deal on service
towards the end of the contract suggests one reason why many
organizations might choose to go for contracts of five years or less in
length. The prospect of contract renewal reinvigorates vendor
motivation to deliver service.

The possibility of vendor opportunism

This issue is hinted at in the previous point. In the UK study we found a
number of organizations operating a multi-vendor strategy explicitly to
limit vendor opportunism. The Pilkington case, detailed earlier, also
shows how a company can get a vendor working in both organizations'
interests. Other organizations often learned over time about vendor
opportunism and how to deal with it. As one example, a manufacturing
company outsourced IT to a major bureau in order to cut costs. A year
into the contract they still had no real in-house expertise to manage the
contract, and no real IT strategy despite the fact that IT was beginning
to impact adversely on the conduct of business. The vendor was
providing trainee contractors for systems development but charging top
rates. Moreover the company was having to train vendor staff about the
company and the industry it was operating in. Subsequently the
company got contract expertise, built up an in-house technical staff
base and renegotiated the vendor role to a much smaller one.

One case researched by Lacity and Hirschheim (1993) is also very
revealing about vendor opportunism. One ten-year contract beginning
in early 1989 was the product of senior management looking at ways to
contain or reduce rising IT costs. A six-month baseline period was
measured, with the vendor contractually bound to deliver the average
service level of this period. However the contract was signed before the
baseline measurement was completed. Therefore the services covered
in the contract were not completely defined. In data centre operations
the contract specified a fixed number of resources, e.g. tape mounts,
CPU minutes, print lines for a fixed price. On applications development
and maintenance the company received a fixed number of manhours of

service. Other utility services were ill-defined in the contract. While the promised 20 per cent reduction off projected in-house IT budgets may be delivered by the vendor on the fixed price, in fact the 'excess' charges as a result of an incomplete contract may well cancel out any benefits. In fact, responses from the operating companies suggest that the vendor reduced its own costs by degradation of service, lack of responsiveness, 'excess' charges, and moving skilled staff transferred from the client on to other contracts. Additionally, despite promises, the vendor failed to develop service levels and performance measures after the contract went into effect. The vendor also took a strict view of the contract's 'change of character' clause, continually interpreting it in its own favour. In a second case there was again failure to negotiate a sound detailed contract:

> The threat of opportunism was readily apparent in the excess charges, degradation of services, loss of IS expertise, antiquated technology and overworked (vendor) staff.
>
> (Lacity and Hirschheim, 1993)

Internal charging systems may create problems

Even in a well-managed outsourcing contract, such as that between a major brewing company and a UK-based vendor, there can be latent problems between users in business units, the IT people managing the contract, and the vendor. In many examples the problems built up around the charging system as it affected users. In this respect the company's experience in the first year of the contract, signed in the early 1990s, is quite a common one:

> The problems are around communications with our business which is the bit we are here to manage really. It's all around: are we buying a service level, is this time and materials, can I use X still on this, can I not use X on this, do things change or not? So it's all around communication with the business divisions and their understanding of the agreement. At the end of the day they will be paying, not directly, but I recharge to them. I am taking it into a central pot and reallocating it. Complexity of recharging is what's causing those communications challenges . . . . They (the business users) are very wary of it because they now realize that it's an outsider who's charging them and maybe there is a risk they will get charged more and people are going to get more commercial.
>
> (Senior manager, UK brewing company)

However the recharging issue can actually become such a bone of contention as to undermine the whole basis of the contract. One example was an £8 million five-year contract begun in the mid-1980s.

The strategic thrust in this multinational was to get rid of national data centres and devolve IT to business units. The company also wished to rationalize head office computing and save on IT costs. The vendor took over all existing IT work for head office and European companies in the multinational. However the inadequate initial analysis of IT costs, together with incomplete specification of performance measures and insufficient detail on what services were required fed into creating large-scale problems in recharging users for services:

> They came to us and said, 'What do you spend on computing at the moment?' and I'll tell you it was difficult to actually arrive at that figure. There were bits of computing going on all over the place, so that was a stab in the dark. The best educated guess we could make was, 'We think all of that costs us that', and they said right we will give you 15 per cent more.
>
> (IT director: multinational manufacturing company)

The initial difficulties were unbundling exactly what the client was paying for, and then determining when excess charges became payable. Also there were problems over 'change of character' where the hardware base was changing along with the services required:

> Immediately problems began to occur. How much computing power were we entitled to before we paid any excess charges? .... Of course, there was a billing cost mis-match because they said 'We will do it for in total about £8M.' So we were going to give them £8M and they were going to provide services. That then gave us the problem of actually charging out the £8M so we had to create an arbitrary invoicing system to recover the £8M .... We wondered, well, the £8M has got to come down hasn't it? They were saying, 'but we are having to take a beating on this, it's all swings and roundabouts'. Well, that's all right, but when you're the guy in the department with a PC, you are thinking, 'it's madness'. They want to cross-charge me £10 000 for a PC, I can go out and buy it for less.

In one example a personnel system had been put in by the in-house team and the user department was charged a certain price for IT staff time to run and maintain it. Under the new charging system the user was charged three times as much for the same service. Clearly these problems could have been less contentious if the vendor was making more than a slim margin on the original deal. Here the lack of clarity in measurement at the contract stage led to opportunities for a pressurized vendor to argue legitimately that many of the services were in addition to those covered by the fixed price agreement. This also brought additional cost pressure on the hastily erected recharging system. At the end of three years the vendor cancelled the contract and each user negotiated separately directly with the vendor. Most of those companies stayed with the vendor, initially, but some drifted away.

Users may become more wary of the IT service

In the cases of the charging systems described above, users clearly became much more anxious about the service they were getting for the money they were being charged. In some respects this is often a healthy development, and may lead to users focusing on necessary rather than 'nice-to-have' services. It may also induce a much greater commercial awareness about computer use in their department. On the other hand there can be some less attractive outcomes in outsourcing situations:

> I think when you talk about service level agreements and the sorts of terminology you start surrounding a lot of the services with, then they tend to get in the way of true fast response, and the question 'How much does it cost?' tends to be an issue. We are already finding that by charging internally for services then the idea that you have to locate a customer who has a budget that can pay gets in the way of getting a fast response. It shouldn't do but it still does. It's magnified beyond reasonable proportions with an external agency.
>
> (Systems development manager, manufacturing company)

IT costs may become too transparent

This would seem to be a contradiction, in the sense that the transparency of costs as a result of outsourcing is usually proclaimed as a desirable outcome. However, where there is still a large in-house IT capability there may arise inflexibilities in the ways in which funds can be utilized, and additional IT work achieved:

> One of the things that some of us were concerned about as part of the deal, but which was overlooked by senior management who signed up to the deal, was the fact that we know the way we operated here in DP. We could always fudge costs. . . . There's always a little bit of fat in any budget that allows us to take on something unexpected. I am talking about the ability to bring on a new software package which might enhance processing in an area, a systems software package, a new tool, which might cost you a licence fee plus £5000 a year in maintenance costs. We could always do these simple things in-house.
>
> (IT manager, financial services company)

The irony here is that the in-house IT staff felt that the vendor had done too good a job of analysing costs and establishing what the price for different services would be. The problems are very much for operational IT staff rather than more senior management who in fact continue to see the non-degradation of contracted service plus large cost savings as very much a good deal:

> When we transferred across it was on the basis of our (existing IT) budget .... They (the vendor staff) had up-front clearly what we were using at the time of the out-sourcing deal. They were very thorough and did their homework. But it's a loss of advantage to us really. We no longer have the ability to demand flexibility of the data centre in the way it manages its cost. We can't force the vendor to find ways to do things on the cheap which is something we would have sat down and found a way of doing, and they feel under no obligation to do this.
>
> (IT manager, financial services company)

CONCLUSIONS

The economics of IT outsourcing uncovered by our research suggests that organizations need to pursue in-house improvements first, identify full IT costs and establish performance benchmarks, pursue further in-house improvements, and only then make in-house versus outsourcing comparisons. If the outsourcing option is initially rejected, it needs to be revisited at regular intervals, not least because the reassessment can act as an external benchmark on in-house IT performance. However, in practice we found a number of other objectives and interests often cutting across this economic logic.

Organizations found it difficult to assess vendor against in-house bids on a comparable basis, especially where prior evaluation practice exhibited the kinds of weaknesses discussed in, for example, Willcocks (1994). However, respondent experiences suggested that the time and effort spent on fully assessing in-house performance, and revamping measurement systems proved vital in feeding into more effective contracting. All too often outsourcing deals can be based on varying degrees of 'voodoo economics'. Another finding was that this evaluation work, to enable comparison with and assessment of vendor bids, is best done before any contracts are signed, even where a specific vendor has been chosen. Organizations cannot safely assume that vendor opportunism will not occur. (A fuller discussion of how vendor opportunism can be managed appears in Lacity, Willcocks and Feeny, 1995). From this perspective, we found the contract to have the central role in determining whether outsourcing expectations would be realized. Hidden costs in outsourcing arrangements were identified, and these were found to be most frequently the outcome of weak contracting. Based on our case study and survey research, the chapter provided guidelines on how to set up and run measurement systems and service level agreements.

It also became clear that even good contracting, based on detailed IT evaluation, and supported by comprehensive service measures and reporting systems, still did not avoid many problems arising during the course of any contract. This stresses again what emerged strongly from all our cases and the European survey: the importance of active monitoring and management of the vendor (see Willcocks and Fitzgerald, 1994b and Chapter 17 for details of management capabilities needed for outsourcing). As one respondent remarked ruefully about a particularly difficult outsourcing experience: 'The one definite thing I have learned is that it's not like ringing for room service'. On the economics and performance measurement issues in IT outsourcing, truly the buck cannot be contracted out.

REFERENCES

Aucoin, P., Almy, F., Heise, R., Landry, R. *et al.* (1991) *Internalizing the Vendor's Resources: Outsourcing in the 1990s*, Report No. C-6-1, Chantico Publishing, Boston, Mass.

Bergstrom, L. (1991) *The Ins and Outs of Outsourcing*, Real Decisions Corporation, Darien.

Buck-Lew, M. (1992) 'To Outsource Or Not?', *International Journal of Information Management*, **12**, pp. 3–20.

Due, R. (1992) 'The Real Costs of Outsourcing', *Information Systems Management*, Winter, pp. 78–81.

Fitzgerald, G. and Willcocks, L. (1993) *Information Technology Outsourcing Practice: A UK Survey*, Business Intelligence, London.

Fitzgerald, G. and Willcocks, L. (1994) 'Contracts and Partnerships in the Outsourcing of IT', *Proceedings of the Fifteenth Annual International Conference in Information Systems*, Vancouver, December.

Gupta, U. and Gupta, A. (1992) 'Outsourcing the IS Function: Is it Necessary for Your Organization?', *Information Systems Management*, Summer, pp. 44–50.

Holway, R. (1996) 'The 1996 Holway Report', Reported in Jones, R., 'Software and Services Flourish in UK', *Computer Weekly*, 6 June, p. 22.

I/S Analyzer, (1990) 'Taking An Objective Look At Outsourcing', *United Communications*, September, Maryland.

Krass, P. (1990) 'The Dollars and Sense of Outsourcing', *Information Week*, February 26, pp. 26–31.

Lacity, M. and Hirschheim, R. (1993) *Information Systems Outsourcing: Metaphors, Myths and Realities*, Wiley, Chichester.

Lacity, M. and Hirschheim, R. (1995) *Beyond the Information Systems Outsourcing Bandwagon: The Insourcing Response*, Wiley, Chichester.

Lacity, M., Hirschheim, R. and Willcocks, L. P. (1994) 'Realizing Outsourcing Expectations: Incredible Expectations, Credible Outcomes, *Information Systems Management*, Fall, **14**, pp. 7–18.

Lacity, M. and Willcocks, L. P. (1996) 'Best Practices in Information Technology Sourcing', *The Oxford Executive Research Briefing*, **2**, Templeton College, Oxford.

Lacity, M. and Willcocks, L. P. (eds.) (1997) *Strategic Sourcing of Information Systems*, Wiley, Chichester.

Lacity, M., Willcocks, L. P. and Feeny, D. (1995) 'IT Outsourcing: Maximize Flexibility and Control', *Harvard Business Review*, May–June, pp. 84–93.

Orlikowski, W. and Baroudi, J. (1991) 'Studying Information Technology in Organizations: Research Approaches and Assumptions', *Information Systems Research*, **2**, (1), pp. 1–28.

Pralahad, C. and Hamel, G. (1990) 'The Core Competence of the Corporation', *Harvard Business Review*, **63**, (3), pp. 79–91.

Quinn, J. (1992) 'The Intelligent Enterprise: A New Paradigm', *Academy of Management Executive*, **6**, (4), pp. 44–63.

Sanders, P. (1982) 'Phenomenology: A New Way of Viewing Organizational Research', *Academy of Management Review*, **7**, (3), pp. 353–360.

Willcocks, L. P. (ed.) (1994) *Information Management: Evaluation of Information Systems Investments*, Chapman and Hall, London.

Willcocks, L. P. and Fitzgerald, G. (1994a) *A Business Guide to Outsourcing IT. A Study of European Best Practice in the Selection, Management and Use of External IT Services*, Business Intelligence, London.

Willcocks, L. P. and Fitzgerald, G. (1994b) 'Towards the Residual IS Organization? Research on IT Outsourcing Experiences in the United Kingdom', In Baskerville, R., Smithson, S. *et al.* (eds.), *Transforming Organizations with Information Technology*, IFIP/North Holland, Amsterdam.

Willcocks, L. P., Fitzgerald, G. and Feeny, D. (1995) 'Outsourcing IT: The Strategic Implications', *Long Range Planning*, **28**, (5), pp. 59–70.

Willcocks, L. P., Fitzgerald, G. and Lacity, M. (1996) 'To Outsource IT or Not? Recent Research on Economics and Evaluation Practice', *European Journal of Information Systems*, **5**, pp. 143–160.

Part Five

Emerging Technology Issues

CHAPTER THIRTEEN

Information Architecture Practice: Research-based Recommendations for the Practitioner

K. PELLY PERIASAMY AND DAVID F. FEENY

INTRODUCTION

Information architecture (IA) has been well-known since IBM introduced 'Business systems planning' (BSP) as an IS planning methodology in the 1970s (IBM, 1981). However, IA's usefulness as an IS planning tool is still the subject of debate. IA is shrouded in many claims and criticisms (see Finkelstein, 1993; Martin, 1990a,b; Teng, *et al.*, 1992; Davenport, 1994; Goodhue *et al.*, 1992). Nonetheless, IA has continued to maintain its position as a top issue in IS management surveys (Boar, 1994, p. 314; Savoia, 1996, p. 112). In these circumstances, there is a need to ascertain IA's usefulness, and identify if and how it can be exploited in information management tasks. The research and recommendations presented in this chapter is an effort in this direction.

This chapter argues that IA is a useful IS planning and implementation tool, particularly for organizations which position IT as a strategic tool. IA's effectiveness and value is dependent on how its conventional components – application architecture and data architecture – and a new component – business system architecture – are targeted, designed, developed and used. The value of data architecture is in project scoping and application development and maintenance. IS planning tasks are better served by the application architecture and business system architecture. The application architecture, in the form of

341

a highly abstracted graphical model, is a suitable tool for communicating the essence of an IS plan – the application portfolio and the relationships between applications – to senior management. A more detailed version of the application architecture is used in IS plan implementation tasks. The business system architecture is a pictorial representation of the fusion of the strategic resources, including IT, for a complete business process which delivers value to its customers. This architecture is an effective tool for integrating IS planning with strategy development and business planning. It is also a tool for performing business process reengineering. Here we argue that the business system architecture, application architecture and data architecture are complementary information management tools, the careful targeting and development of which can contribute to the effectiveness and efficiency of IS planning and implementation. (See Periasamy, 1993, 1994, and Periasamy and Feeny, 1993 for more details of the underlying research).

DEFINITIONS

Information architecture
Information architecture is generally understood to be a high-level blueprint developed during IS planning for the purpose of implementing the resulting plan. This understanding reflects broad direction rather than clear definition. There is confusion and ambiguity as to what exactly constitutes an information architecture. Developments over the years have led to different interpretations of IA. For example, a number of writers use IA synonymously with data architecture/corporate data model (Everest and Kim, 1989; Martin, 1989, 1990a; Teng, et al., 1992). It is, therefore, necessary to develop a definition which reflects current practice and harmonizes with the thesis of this article:

> Information architecture is a set of high-level models which complements the business plan in IT-related matters and serves as a tool for IS planning and a blueprint for IS plan implementation.

Based on conventional understanding and arguments of writers such as Earl (1989) and Sowa and Zachman (1992), an IA in line with the above definition has to have an application component and a data component. That would be the minimum required to serve the three functions stated. The core components of IA are hence defined to include data architecture and application architecture.

Corporate data model
The data architecture which normally features as a component of the IA is the corporate data model (CDM), a high-level graphical model which shows the business entities relevant to an organization and the

relationships between these entities (Figure 13.1 provides an example). The CDM is generally considered as essential for long-term and cost-effective data management and database development (Martin, 1990a).

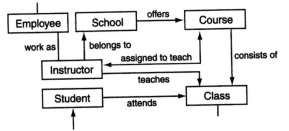

Figure 13.1   Part of a corporate data model of a university

Application architecture

An application architecture (AA) is a graphical model showing the major applications which make up or will make up an organization's integrated information system, and how these applications relate to each other in terms of the data flows between them, (see Figure 13.2 for an example). The AA serves management communication needs during IS planning and later enables development of applications in an integrated manner.

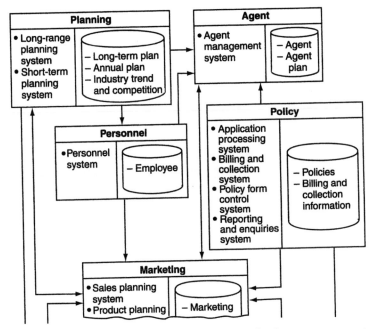

Figure 13.2   Part of an application architecture of an insurance company

RESEARCH METHODOLOGY

The research into information architecture practice required a methodology that progressed from general to specific issues. Hence the research methodology was designed to investigate first the general state and status of IA. The extant literature on IA and IS planning (see References) provided the necessary foundation for conducting a large-scale postal survey into the general usage and perception of IA. The survey was targeted at a stratified random sample of 900 organizations in the UK. It was conducted in 1992 using a structured questionnaire with 34 questions requiring mainly Likert-type scale responses. The 294 completed questionnaires (32 per cent response) from a cross-section of industries, including the public sector, provided an adequate sample size for conducting quantitative analysis and hypothesis testing. The findings of the survey, while helping to clarify the general state and status of IA, also served as a base for proceeding to the next phase of the research, in-depth case studies.

Case studies of six large organizations were conducted in the second phase of the research. The organizations continue to be major players in their respective industries in the UK – petroleum, water utility, motorcar manufacturing, insurance, retailing and rail transport. Five of them were selected because they were generally considered as exemplars of IA practice and/or IS planning, while the sixth, though not satisfying this criteria, was chosen in order to benefit from the organization's recent experience in a major IA project which ended less-than-satisfactorily. These case studies involved in-depth semi-structured interviews with about eight executives in each organization. Those interviewed included the head of IT, senior IT executives, functional heads and senior managers. At least one board member in each organization was interviewed to gain the necessary top management perspective on IA. The interviews followed a consistent format and concluded with the administration of a structured questionnaire on the organization's IA experience. Documentation in the form of business plan, IS plan, systems documentation, IT manuals, minutes, internal surveys, company reports, appraisal forms, and literature in the public domain were examined to extract data relevant to the research. All the data gathered was analysed qualitatively.

LARGE-SCALE POSTAL SURVEY

At the core of the survey was the basic hypothesis that information architecture is a valuable IS planning and implementation tool. The survey, reflecting the perceptions of mainly IT heads and managers, found usage of IA to be significant in medium and large organizations. The architecture was associated with IS planning, and was perceived as being of value to organizations which positioned IT as a strategic resource. Both application architecture and corporate data model, initially identified as core components of IA, were rated as valuable tools but for different purposes.

Survey evidence on corporate data model
The survey found corporate data model (CDM) to be of value more as a tool for implementing the IS plan rather than facilitating the planning process. CDM's strength was perceived to be in the project/technical domain application/database development, data management and communication within the IT department. The survey did not conclusively find CDM to be useless in IS planning. For example, usage of CDM was perceived to add some rigour to the IS planning process. However such IS planning benefits were overshadowed by CDM's perceived weakness in relation to its usage in communications with management; CDM was not only perceived to be complex for communication with senior management but was also regarded as being irrelevant to them. This evidence brings into question the validity of data-driven IS planning approaches.

Information engineering and other forms of data-oriented IS planning methodologies and approaches are strongly advocated by some writers (Finkelstein, 1993; Martin, 1989, 1990(a) and (b). Many of these writers justify their advocacy of data-oriented IS planning by contending that data is stable. Marche (1993), via his empirical work, questions the validity of their contention on data stability, and thereby implicitly challenges the notion of data-oriented IS planning. Other researchers explicitly argue that data orientation is not an appropriate paradigm for IS planning. Goodhue, *et al.*, (1988) note that:

> It is not always clear to the planners or top management whether a strategic data model is being developed to produce a systems plan, create an architecture, or to design new databases.

Goodhue, *et al.*, (1992) report the existence of significant problems in IS planning exercises based on data modelling techniques. They found corporate data models to be complex in format and content, and demanding on planning resources. While claims on CDM's usefulness in IS planning are being increasingly challenged, the position of data modelling *per se* in application/database development and data management remains strong, as found by this survey. Other research evidence, such as March and Kim (1992), support the usage of data models in information systems development and data management.

Survey evidence on application architecture

The survey found the AA to be of value for IS planning and implementation. The AA incorporates rigour into the planning process. It facilitates integrated application development and realization of the organization's integrated IS goal. It serves communication needs within the IT department on IS planning matters. It helps in the planning of IT-related responses to changes in business.

Though the AA was perceived to be relevant to senior management, the general perception was that it is somewhat complex in so far as communications with senior management are concerned. The need is therefore for a less complex AA attuned to senior management characteristics. In this regard, the model needs to be simple and reflect the essence of the IS plan's recommendations on IT applications. However, a macro-level architecture may subsequently manifest itself as a less useful implementation tool. The survey concluded that these conflicting demands could be resolved by developing two levels of application architecture – an overall model for senior management presentation and a detailed model for project implementation. The theories and experiences in the systems development methodology world (Yourdon Inc., 1993) provide a basis for such an approach. The overall AA is targeted at senior management and is used during IS planning in management communication tasks. The detailed AA, based on the overall model, serves technical requirements, project planning and implementation.

IN-DEPTH CASE STUDIES

The five case study organizations which were selected on the assumption that they were exemplars of IA practice were found to develop and use information architecture and to be satisfied with their particular IS planning practice and form of IA. The evidence from the sixth organization, the one which had unsatisfactory IA project experience, was found to lend support to the IA practices of the other five organizations.

Business system architecture

The in-depth investigation into exemplar IA practices revealed the development and usage of another form of information architecture – a business system architecture (BSA). The BSA is a simple pictorial model of how a business system is (to be) implemented (see Figure 13.3 for an example). The architecture is a macro level depiction of a business system and the integral arrangement of strategic resources, including IT, comprising it. A company's basic business strategy, such as differentiated product or low cost operation, can be implemented in a number of ways. The business system architecture depicts a specific

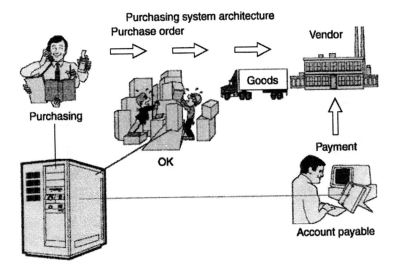

Figure 13.3   An example of a business system architecture

implementation of the basic competitive strategy. The architecture is oriented towards the future. It is unique to the company and is liable to undergo change over time. It can be developed at two levels, an organization-level business system architecture with a number of focused system architectures. One of the case study organizations, a retailer, explains the value of their business system architecture thus:

Whilst the concept of process driven businesses is now well understood, it was with some courage back in 1985/86 that we decided to base its long term IT strategy on an architecture made up of fully integrated processes which crossed all functional barriers. It represented not a set of requirements at that time, but a vision of what food retailing would ultimately become.

The case study investigation found that the exemplars of IA practice perceived the business system architecture to be a useful tool for conducting integrated IS-business planning. These companies see the BSA as a tool for planning holistic responses to the competitive demands of the business. The model's characteristics (simple, pictorial, etc.) are seen as being conducive to this task, particularly in relation to senior and functional management involvement. The following comment from a senior executive reflects the commitment of these organizations to business system architecture usage:

We need to have a very good understanding of the business and where it is going. The (business system) architecture is a way for us to model and articulate this requirement. Everybody understands it, including the chairman.

Case study evidence on application architecture

Two types of application architecture models were found in the case studies: overall application architecture and detailed application architecture. Though they are structurally similar, they differ in their development, content, purpose and usage. The overall AA relates to the business system architecture and focuses on the whole organization, showing at a macro level the major IT applications and their inter-relationships. The detailed application architecture focuses on a particular application and depicts its major sub-applications and their inter-relationships.

The overall AA shows active and planned applications. It is unique to the company and evolves with implementation/modification/replacement/retirement of major applications. Being targeted for presentation by the IT department to senior management, the overall AA employs little syntax, is graphic and seeks to be simple. It is positioned as an IS planning tool. It is of some value at the project level for planning and scoping of applications but is of little use in actual application development tasks. The architecture is developed and maintained by the IT department, as part of functional level IT planning, using information on existing and new applications and the inter-relationships between all the applications. No special tool/technique is used to do this. The following comment from a case study interviewee reflects the general perception on the overall AA by the case study organizations:

> It [overall application architecture] helps to establish our understanding of systems so that we can influence and inform users and managers on application issues.

The case study evidence and findings of the survey together suggest that a properly conceived overall AA, with senior management as the target recipient, can serve as a tool for the IT function to inform senior management on IT's role and overall contribution to the business. Senior management's involvement in IS planning is thus further facilitated. As regards the detailed application architecture, some differences were found in its development and usage among the case study organizations. Only two of the five exemplars of IA practice developed and used detailed application architectures. Nevertheless, comments were consistently made by all six case study organizations that the detailed AA could make a positive contribution to IS planning practice, particularly in linking IS planning to project implementation. One of the senior IT executives interviewed expressed the need for a detailed AA thus:

> We need a planning layer with more detail. We need a model for proceeding from planning to project implementation.

If it was that useful, why was it not being developed as part of standard IS planning practice? The answers from those organizations without detailed AAs was that their IS planning practices focused on management involvement for which the detailed AA was regarded as being irrelevant. They satisfied their detailed AA requirements by developing high-level data flow diagrams or similar models at the outset of application development. Nevertheless, the organizations felt that a detailed AA conceived during planning would be of significant value as it would more accurately reflect application issues which arose during planning. If these issues were not incorporated then into a model, some of them were likely to be forgotten at the implementation stage.

Case study evidence on data architecture

The case studies reinforced the findings of the survey: there was lack of support for the corporate data model while there was unanimous agreement on the value of business area/project data architectures. While all five exemplars of IA practice had business area/project data architectures, only one had a corporate data model (CDM). This organization, however, viewed the CDM as being of little value to IS planning and only of some value to data management tasks. The general experience of the case study organizations was that the effort required to develop a CDM outweighs the benefits it offers. The CDM was seen as complex, detailed, subject to changes, IT-oriented in terms of syntax and form, conveys information on internal hard data, does not inform on applications and is irrelevant to senior management. The absence of a conventional CDM was reported not to have affected the planning or delivery of satisfactory applications and integrated databases in these organizations. Reproduced below are a couple of comments from case study interviewees which convey their general perceptions of CDM:

> It [CDM] is of no real use to me. It is more of a distraction.
>
> Head of business function

> A corporate data model has to cross system boundaries, and frequent renewal makes it of little value .... It should not be part of ISP. It tends to shift focus from business to technique if done as part of ISP.
>
> Principal data management consultant of a very large global corporation

The sixth case study organization's corporate data modelling experience provides additional evidence in this regard. The organization embarked on a major information architecture project with the help of reputed consultants. The project, however, ended in failure. The failure was attributed to the focus on corporate data model and CRUD matrices (see below for more on this issue) as core components of the information architecture that was developed. The corporate data model delivered by the project was poorly received, seen as being overly complex and inaccurate, and ignored by functional executives and even IT professionals. One of the consultants engaged in the project recalled his observation when the CDM was presented to functional executives and management:

> ... many people withdrew in horror when it [CDM] was presented to them.

As the emerging case study evidence on corporate data modelling was one-sided, some effort was made during the research to locate a corporate data modelling success story, but with little success. Relevant literature was examined to locate a success story. Davenport and Short's (1990) discussion of Rank Xerox UK suggested that the company might be an exemplar of successful corporate data modelling practice. A more recent paper by Davenport (1994) which discusses Rank Xerox UK, however, conveys what is becoming a familiar story about corporate data modelling:

> Xerox did data modelling and administration for 20 years, but in the words of the director of information management, 'We got nowhere.' These initiatives were driven by IT rather than by senior business managers; they were always abandoned in favour of specific development projects.

The message emerging from the case studies is that a CDM is not essential or even advantageous, and that data management and integrated database development requirements could be adequately satisfied by an organization's set of business area data models.

The case study organizations were unanimous in their support for business area/project data architecture. A business area data architecture is often developed at the outset of a project and serves as the project data model, hence the concatenated name 'business area/project data architecture'. The data architecture is developed by the project team using an appropriate systems development methodology. The development is done in consultation with the organization's data management group. The data model is meant for business area/project database development, integration of databases and data management. The business area/project data architecture's value to application development is reflected in the following comment from one of the project managers interviewed:

> Even if it [CDM] had existed, it wouldn't have helped that much. What my team needed was a project-level data model.

Case study's message on CRUD matrices

A CRUD matrix is a process/data matrix where the relationships between process and data classes are expressed in terms of create (C), read (R), update (U), and delete (D). CRUD matrix development is core to IS planning methodologies such as BSP (IBM, 1981) and information engineering (Martin, 1989, 1990(a) and (b)) for developing information architecture. The case study research hence investigated the usage of this matrix. The investigation found that the sixth case study organization's IA project had delivered a set of CRUD matrices. These matrices were used in management discussions and workshops during the IA project but were poorly received by their recipients. A senior IT executive interviewed clarified his experience thus:

> It [CRUD matrix] is great as an analysis technique but is difficult as a means for getting people involved. They were not with it. People couldn't understand 'entity'. They encounter difficulty when relating 'entity' to real life things. They wonder what creating an entity means.

Of the five exemplars of IA practice, only one was found to have CRUD matrices. Their experience with CRUD matrices was similar to that of the sixth case study organization. Their CRUD matrices were poorly received by functional management and executives. The models were not seen as being relevant to senior management. The main users of these models were IS planners in the IT department. The case study evidence suggests that, while the CRUD matrix may be a tool for IS planners, it is not an appropriate means for getting management and functional executives involved in IS planning.

RECOMMENDATIONS FOR PRACTICE

The research evidence suggests that information architecture is a useful tool for IS planning. The value is particularly significant to an organization which positions IT as one of its strategic resources and conducts integrated business–IS planning. The information architecture which can offer such value should consist of business system architecture, overall and detailed application architectures, and business area/project data architecture. These models are different in appearance and content but are inter-related. They are used in an ongoing manner from business–IS planning to project scoping/planning by different teams of people with complementary purposes. Each IA model has targeted users and serves specific purposes.

For effective exploitation of information architecture, it should consist of a set of hierarchically related models supporting all the main activities from business–IS planning to project implementation (see Figure 13.4). A model spans at least two activities and is developed in one activity for use in another activity. The set of models, when appropriately targeted and developed, help to vertically integrate activities from strategy development and business–IS planning to application development. Usage of the business system architecture, application architecture and business area/project data model also contribute to horizontal integration, integrated functional effort, integrated IT applications and integrated databases respectively. Vertical and horizontal integration is central to holistic planning and strategy development, the paradigm on which integrated business–IS planning is founded.

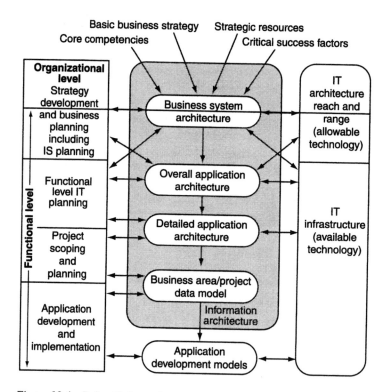

Figure 13.4   Role of information architecture in integrated business – IS planning

Developing and using business system architecture

The business system architecture is jointly developed by executives from the functional units involved in a strategy implementation, often under the initiative and coordination of senior IT executives. No special tool or technique is used. The company's basic business strategy together with the inventory of strategic resources, core competencies, critical success factors and technology opportunities serve as key business inputs for developing a business system architecture. These inputs are considered in the light of technology as defined by the company's IT architecture and infrastructure. The objective is to produce an integrated model of the proposed strategy implementation for consideration by senior management. Development of a few business system architectures, one per business line, is possible. As a business system architecture is relevant to all participating functions, it is not only part of an information architecture but is also part of the participating functions' plans and blueprints.

The business system architecture provides a means for the company's functional units to collectively depict to senior management the strategies which they will deliver as a team. Attention is paid to simplicity, business-oriented content and aesthetics, taking into consideration the architecture's target recipient. The business system architecture is walked through during strategy development workshops/ presentations. Senior management as a group are able to discuss and deliberate on strategy implementation options by referring to the architecture, and holistically considering all strategic resources including IT. In this way, senior management contributes to the architecture and helps to update and finalize it as a blueprint for implementation.

Development and usage of application and data architectures

The application architectures and business area/project data models serve as technical blueprints for planning, developing and delivering IT applications consistent with the business system architecture. They are tools employed by the IT function in carrying out its tasks and responsibilities. The business area/project data model is developed during the planning and scoping of application development for a business area. An application architecture, on the other hand, is developed during IS planning by abstracting from a business system architecture the sub-applications and their relationships, and depicting them graphically. If necessary, additional details are incorporated to make the model more detailed, or sub-application architectures are developed to supplement the abstracted application model. The overall application architecture is set at the organizational level and targeted at senior management. It is developed by considering only the key applications depicted in the business system architectures, and graphically modelling them and their relationships.

The application architecture and data architecture are complementary, serving specific purposes which range from management tasks at the business–IS planning level to technical tasks at the project level. The overall application architecture is for providing senior management with a macro-level perspective of the organization's IT applications and their contributions to the business. The detailed application architecture is for use at the project level and serves to integrate IS planning with application development. The business area/project data architecture is used in application/database development tasks. At the application development level, the IA models are replaced by application development models (data flow diagrams, logical data models, etc.) which are not part of an IA but which can potentially inherit relevant planning information from the IA models.

Exclusion of corporate data model from information architecture

Though there is wide support in the literature for corporate data modelling (for example, Finkelstein, 1993; Martin, 1990a,b; Teng, et al., 1992), it is recommended that it should be excluded from information architecture practice. While it is possible that some organizations may be successfully developing and using corporate data models, the evidence from this research and that provided by some writers such as Davenport (1993, 1994) and Goodhue et al., (1988, 1992) are in unison on suggesting that a corporate data model is not worth the required development effort. Even James Martin, the guru of information engineering, concedes in an interview that the concept of a consolidated corporate data model is impractical (Ross, 1988). Collectively, the set of business area/project data architectures developed by an organization can serve to meet its data management and integrated database development needs, the forte of corporate data modelling as claimed by some.

Role of IT architecture

The IT architecture, defined in terms of reach and range (Keen, 1991), provides information on technologies allowed by the company's technology plan. This information is necessary for identifying new technologies or technical resources in respect of an IT application. The IT architecture is consulted in the course of developing the business system architecture and overall AA. New technologies identified in this manner later cause the IA to impact the IT architecture and infrastructure. Information on available technologies and resources, as defined by the IT infrastructure, is considered in the development of the business system architecture and overall AA. There is a two-way relationship in how IA and IT architecture/infrastructure influence each other, though in the first instance it would have likely been the IA which would have determined the core, characteristics and standards of the IT architecture and led to its emergence. This relationship and the specific manner in which it operates further helps to increase the effectiveness of IA as a complement to integrated business–IS planning.

Targeting of models

The effective exploitation of information architecture calls for multiple types of IA models, each of which is specifically positioned and targeted. The models are inter-related but focus on distinct purposes and recipients. Senior management's requirements in relation to business–IS planning are best served by the pictorial business system architecture rather than detailed technical models. In contrast, models for project implementation such as the business area/project data architecture need to be detailed and adhere to some syntax/standard for them to be of practical value to the application developers. A useful guide for deciding on the form and content of an IA model is to gauge its relevance and usefulness in relation to its targeted recipients and their behavioural/communication characteristics and expectations.

An enhanced information characteristics continuum based on the work of Gorry and Scott Morton (1971) is offered as a reference framework for deciding the form and content of not only IA models but IS models in general. Essentially, the continuum (see Figure 13.5) is clustered around 'syntactics, complexity, specification, detail, text and written presentation' at one end, and 'semantics, simplicity, clarification, macro issues, pictorial/graphic and verbal presentation' at the other end. Models closer to the 'semantics' end are meant for senior management while those nearer the 'syntactics' end are for operational and project-level personnel. In developing a model, its purpose and recipient need to be identified first. Reference to the information characteristics continuum framework using these two parameters provides guidance on the appropriate form of the model and the characteristics of its contents.

Business process reengineering and information architecture

The information architecture model which is directly relevant to business process reengineering (BPR) is the business system architecture. This model is similar to the business process maps advocated by Davenport (1993, 1994) and Hammer and Champy (1993) for performing business process reengineering. By adopting business system architecture as a standard component of information architecture, an organization is effectively equipping itself to progressively reengineer its business by modelling the fusion of strategic resources and competencies into effective business processes.

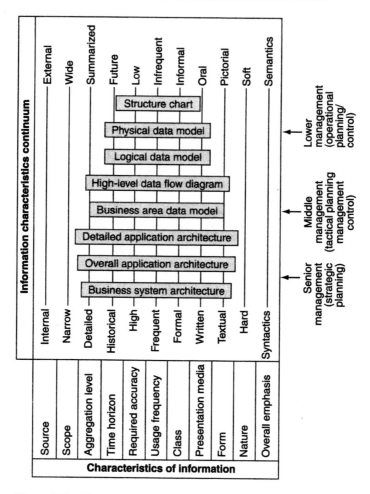

Figure 13.5   Management information characteristics framework

IMPLICATIONS FOR PRACTICE

In the current dynamic business environment, the planning and implementation of an IT application requires it to be considered in the context of its larger business system. In this regard, a holistic IS planning framework with a redefined information architecture as a key component is recommended. The adoption of the framework depicted in Figure 13.4 involves rethinking and repositioning of planning processes and tasks rather than investing in new tools, techniques and such like. The premise of the framework is on focusing and targeting of IA models and not that the current planning techniques/models are wrong. Current skills and investments in data modelling, application architecture development, data flow diagramming, development of matrices, etc., thus maintain their values in the practice of the redefined information architecture.

In using the holistic IS planning framework and the redefined information architecture, due consideration has been given to current developments in IS methodologies, tools and techniques, in particular object-oriented techniques and CASE tools. Object-oriented techniques and CASE tools are primarily aimed at application development and not at the business at large. They are seen as means for specifying, developing and maintaining software of high quality in an efficient and effective manner. Thus their domain is predominantly IT. It is maintained that unless object-orientation, CASE tools or other such concepts/techniques/tools are applicable across the organization, they are unlikely to be relevant or find ready acceptance in business planning and other organizational level activities. As it stands, they are of little relevance to business planning and its integrated IS planning. Their domain of usage is application development and maintenance. Just because they have been found to be useful in application development, it does not necessarily follow that they will be equally useful in other tasks or areas.

CONCLUSION

Information architecture, while contributing to the practice of holistic business–IS planning, also satisfies the necessary reductionist requirements via its set of hierarchically-related component models. The business system architecture is the tool offered by information architecture for modelling the fusion of strategic resources and competencies into requisite strategies and business processes. Though originating from an IT consideration, the business system architecture has more to do with the business as a whole and less to do with IT specifically. For planning tasks which are specific to IT, the information architecture provides application architecture and business area/project data architecture. These IA models collectively facilitate the progression from business issues to IT specifics in an ongoing integrated manner. The underlying paradigm in the redefinition and repositioning of information architecture is 'designing and developing models with the target in perspective'.

Acknowledgement   The authors would like to express their thanks to the consultancy business of IBM United Kingdom for their financial support for this research.

REFERENCES

Boar, B. H. (1994) *Practical Steps for Aligning Information Technology with Business Strategies*, John Wiley & Sons, New York.

Davenport, T. H. (1993) *Process Innovation*, Harvard Business School Press, Boston, Mass.

Davenport, T. H. (1994) 'Saving IT's Soul: Human-Centred Information Management', *Harvard Business Review*, March–April, pp. 119–131.

Davenport, T. H. and Short, J. E. (1990) 'The New Industrial Engineering: Information Technology and Business Process Redesign', *Sloan Management Review*, Summer, pp. 11–27.

Earl, M. J. (1989) *Management Strategies for Information Technology*, Prentice-Hall International, Hemel Hempstead.

Everest, G. C. and Kim, Y. (1989) *Perspectives on Data Planning and Information Architecture*, Working Paper MISRC-WP-89-04, MISRC, Carlson School of Management, University of Minnesota, Minnesota, November.

Finkelstein, C. (1993) *Information Engineering: Strategic Systems Development*, Addison-Wesley Publishing, New York.

Goodhue, D. L., Quillard, J. A. and Rockart, J. F. (1988) 'Managing the Data Resource: A Contingency Perspective', *MIS Quarterly*, **12**, (3), Sept., pp. 373–392.

Goodhue, D. L., Kirsch, L. J., Quillard, J. A. and Wyobo, M. D. (1992) 'Strategic Data Planning: Lessons from the Field', *MIS Quarterly*, **16**, (1), March, pp. 11–34.

Gorry, G. A. and Scott Morton, M. S. (1971) 'A Framework for Management Information Systems', *Sloan Management Review*, Fall, pp. 55–70.

Hammer, M. and Champy, H. (1993) *Reengineering the Corporation*, Nicholas Brealey Publishing, London.

IBM (1981) *Business Systems Planning: Information Systems Planning Guide*, IBM, GE20-0527-3, IBM, London.

Keen, P. G. W. (1991) *Shaping the Future: Business Design through Information Technology*. Harvard Business School Press, Boston, Mass.

March, S. T. and Kim, Y. G. (1992) 'Information Resource Management: Integrating the Pieces', *Data Base*, **23**, (3), pp. 27–38.

Marche, S. (1993) 'Measuring the Stability of Data Models', *European Journal of Information Systems*, **2**, (1), pp. 37–47.

Martin, J. (1989) *Information Engineering, Book I: Introduction*, Prentice-Hall, Inc., Englewood Cliffs, NJ.

Martin, J. (1990a) *Information Engineering, Book II: Planning and Analysis*, Prentice-Hall, Inc., Englewood Cliffs, NJ.

Martin, J. (1990b) *Information Engineering, Book III: Design and Construction*, Prentice-Hall, Inc., Englewood Cliffs, NJ.

Periasamy, K. P. (1993) 'The State and Status of Information Architecture: An Empirical Investigation', in DeGross, J. I., Bostrom, R. P. and Robey, D. (eds.), *Proceedings of the Fourteenth International Conference on Information Systems*, The Society For Information Management, Orlando, Florida, December, pp. 255–270.

Periasamy, K. P. (1994) *Development and Usage of Information Architecture: A Management Perspective*, Unpublished D.Phil. Thesis, Wolfson College, University of Oxford, Oxford.

Periasamy, K. P. and Feeny, D. (1993) *Gaining Value from Information Architecture*, Research and Discussion Paper RDP 93/4, Oxford Institute of Information Management, Templeton College, Oxford.

Ross, R. G. (1988) 'An Interview with James Martin', *Database Newsletter*, 2 part interview in **16**, (3), (May–June), and (4) (Jul.–Aug.).

Savoia, R. (1996) 'Custom Tailoring', *CIO Magazine*, June 15, p. 112.

Sowa, J. F. and Zachman, J. A. (1992) 'Extending and Formalizing the Framework for Information Systems Architecture', *IBM Systems Journal*, **31**, (3), pp. 590–615.

Teng, T. C., Kettinger, W. J. and Guha, S. (1992) 'Business Process Redesign and Information Architecture: Establishing the Missing Links', *Proceedings of 13th International Conference on Information Systems*, Dallas, Texas, pp. 81–89.

Yourdon Inc. (1993) *Yourdon Systems Method*, Prentice-Hall, Englewood Cliffs, NJ.

CHAPTER FOURTEEN

A Worldwide Client–Server Implementation: *Plus Ça Change …?*

MARY C. LACITY, LESLIE P. WILLCOCKS AND
ASHOK SUBRAMANIAN

INTRODUCTION

The Client–server 'paradigm'

Client–server computing may be described as a paradigm of computing characterized by distribution of processing power among a network of processors. More important, the distribution is made to ensure 'division of labour' among the processors with each processor specializing in providing certain functions. End user applications (clients) utilize the services provided by these processors (servers) in order to accomplish their purpose. This co-operative sharing of work among clients and servers is the essence of the client–server computing paradigm (Bachteal and Read, 1995).

In order to distribute functions across the network, tasks must be partitioned into discrete functions. There are numerous ways in which the partitioning of tasks may be accomplished. Thus client/server systems can be designed and implemented in various forms depending on the manner in which the tasks are partitioned. The Gartner Group (Attachmate Corporation, 1995) developed a model that has been frequently used to describe a range of client–server systems (see Figure 14.1). The model essentially views computing tasks as belonging to one of three logical categories – data management, application logic (or business rules) and presentation management. The *data management* component comprises database related activities such as storage and retrieval of data. The *application logic* or business rules component

360

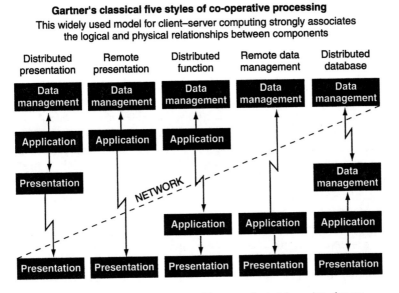

Figure 14.1   Client–server computing (Source: adapted from Attachmate Corporation, 1995)

represents the processing performed on the data to yield the required results. The *presentation management* component is the user interface to the system.

The model describes five different implementations of this three-tier architecture. Each implementation distributes different components across the network. Thus, for instance, one implementation could have the presentation manager in a client computer and the application and data on a network server. Another implementation could distribute the application and presentation to the client computer, and the database to a network server. Thus, client–server systems form a continuum, ranging from systems where the client application merely functions as a presentation manager, typically implemented with a user-friendly graphical user interface (GUI) as a front end to traditional mainframe-based systems, to those systems which optimally distribute processing responsibilities between client applications and servers. The Gartner group estimates that 90 per cent of client–server systems developed today are of the first type where the presentation component is in the client machine and the data and application are in the server (Attachmate Corporation, 1995). This is very similar to the architecture of mainframe-based systems.

Client–server growth
There is much evidence that organizational adoption of client–server

computing has become one of the more significant phenomena in the information technology field. According to recent surveys 71 per cent of all new applications are being developed for desktop or mid-range computers as compared to 29 per cent for mainframe computers. Moreover, 68 per cent of organizations use specialized servers in their computing architecture in contrast to 9 per cent which use mainframes only (Allen, 1995; Computerworld Client/Server Report and Directory, 1996). In the UK a 1995 survey of 750 IT professionals found 43 per cent of respondent organizations had already implemented client–server and 34.5 per cent were considering implementing the approach. Only 5.8 per cent had considered client–server and rejected it (Green-Armytage, 1995). In the US Gerber (1995) has estimated that 40 per cent of information technology dollars are being spent on client–server development, deployment, and support. If infrastructure costs such as hardware, systems software, and networking gear are included, client–server expenditures rise to 60 per cent. In a survey of 207 US companies Kole, Roukas and Tate (1995) found that 66 per cent were planning to implement client–server on an enterprise level. The study concluded that the scope of client–server systems between 1996–98 would increase from intra-departmental to global systems. Seemingly, these statistics are strong evidence of the significance of client–server information systems and the rapid adoption and diffusion of client–server systems in the 1990s.

But, as for many 'advances' in IT, the public sources, including trade journals and newspapers, regularly underplay the organizational issues associated with adopting new technologies. As argued in the Introduction to this book, and shown in Part 3, there is an inherent assumption that adoption will lead to business success. Invariably the business case is logically argued and grounded: through enhanced data sharing, integrated services, cost reduction due to downsizing, interoperability and data interchangeability, location independence of data and processing, and centralized management, client–server promises to transform data into knowledge, to empower users, to increase the quality and speed of decisions (see for example King, 1994; Simpson, 1995). Moreover, given advances in technology, such as increases in input/output over networks, storage capacity and cost, graphical user interfaces, relational databases, and the proliferation of local area networks, these business benefits can be affordably achieved (Muller, 1994; Renaud, 1993; Wagner, 1995).

By 1995–96, however, studies had uncovered a range of organizational and technical barriers and implementation issues associated with client–server technology. Thus the Gartner Group conducted a survey in 1995 of 100 companies that had implemented client–server. Over half of the implementations were late and over-budget, although the final implementations did produce business benefits (Lyons, 1995). A Study by Sentry Market Research shows only a 3 per cent increase in client–server adoption in 1995 over the previous year across 712 large enterprises in North America and Europe. The reasons cited include unexpected complexity of infrastructure demands (Pontin, 1995). 1996 survey research found a range of difficulties registered by respondents, including skills shortages, lack of executive management support, lack of money and complete development tools, and mistaken reliance on a centralized management model to keep distributed management costs in line (Forrester Research, 1996). Sometimes the difficulties have resulted in abandonment of moves to client–server. As one high profile example in the UK, after a £235 million client–server investment programme, in 1996 North West Water abandoned plans to implement its main Oracle database on a distributed Unix platform, and reverted to a mainframe-based strategy (Collins, 1996).

However, despite a number of large-scale client–server surveys, and much prescriptive, together with some relatively rudimentary, case study work (see for example Bochenski, 1994; Levis and von Schilling, 1994; Mill, 1994; Renaud, 1993) there has been all too little systematic, let alone academically rigorous, study of client–server implementations within the context of specific organizations. In this chapter, therefore, we present findings from a detailed case study of a worldwide client–server implementation at a silicon manufacturing company, here called Silicon Inc. to retain the confidentiality requested by our respondents. We selected the case of Silicon Inc.'s worldwide implementation of customer ordering, manufacturing planning, plant scheduling and product specification system because it had been widely recognized, and portrayed externally (by Computerworld), as a successful project. Our aim in studying this case in considerable detail was to investigate academically the dimensions and degrees of 'success'; the factors that were cited by managerial respondents as responsible for effective implementation; and whether there were difficulties and issues that arose distinctive to large-scale client–server implementation in a work organization, or whether such difficulties were typical of any major new information-based technology project.

RESEARCH METHODOLOGY

Case study approach
The strengths and limitations of case research in the study of information systems, and the reasons for pursuing a case research strategy, are by now well established in the literature (see Benbasat *et al.*, 1987; Eisenhardt, 1989; Lee, 1989; Yin, 1989). There is also now a

considerable supportive literature on the adoption of qualitative and interpretive methods in information systems studies (see for example Lacity and Janson, 1994; Van Maanen, 1979; Walsham, 1995). Additionally a number of researchers have successfully justified and applied a single case study research strategy for examining phenomena in the information systems field (see for example Markus, 1983; Smith, 1990; Walsham and Waema, 1994). Informed by this literature the present research adopted an interpretive and qualitative longitudinal single case research strategy in order to explore the under-researched area of client–server implementation. While client–server surveys of varying degrees of rigour have regularly appeared, together with short case histories largely in trade magazines, client–server has rarely been the subject of a detailed, academically conducted case study.

The detailed interview protocols appear in the appendix to this chapter and these indicate the declared purposes of the research. The research sought to elicit descriptive contextual information together with respondent opinion on a range of issues in a project widely considered 'successful'. We sought to explore the dimensions of this 'success' and also the difficulties experienced in the project. Within this prior structuring of concerns and questioning the research we then proceeded inductively to build the case study from interview material, documentation, organizational records, and a review of physical evidence in the form of systems and their operation in various organizational contexts. This allowed us to develop our own analysis as an overlay on the several accounts produced by the organizational respondents at Silicon, Inc. We then sought to compare and evaluate the lessons and difficulties that emerged from our analysis with those to be found in the wider literature on client–server implementation. The comparison allowed us to suggest ways in which client–server may be distinctive, and more difficult to implement, or encounters similar problems and requires implementation approaches not dissimilar for all new information-based technology projects of any size.

Interviewing

We interviewed different stakeholders within Silicon, Inc., including business unit managers, IT managers, and IT staff. The specific titles and pseudonyms of the participants are:

- Robert, the director of MIS, who inherited the project in 1991 when he became head of IS.
- Steven, the manufacturing services support systems supervisor, is a current business manager over the users of the system.
- Michael, the strategic manager of marketing, was the lead user and project manager of the entire project.

- David, the manager of business information systems, headed the business applications development, implementation, and support.
- John, a senior analyst, worked on David's team.

These individuals held different views on the client–server project and provided longitudinal accounts of the decision-making process, and explained the context in which the client–server implementation was embedded. All interviews were conduced in person at the company site and were tape-recorded and transcribed, but participants were assured of anonymity so as to promote open discussions. We also gathered a number of documents including the acquisition request, user and technical documentation of the client–server project, annual reports, and the organizational chart.

Interviews followed the same protocol, proceeding from an unstructured to a structured format. During the unstructured portion, participants were asked to tell their client–server story. The unstructured format allowed the participants free rein to convey their interpretations. After participants completed their stories, they were asked semi-structured questions designed to solicit information on specific sourcing issues that may have been absent from their previous recollections. The interview protocols appear in the Appendix to this chapter. Participants were also asked specific questions about their company and IT department. Pertaining to their company, participants described the organizational structure, the major products and services produced, competition in their industry, their financial situation, corporate goals, and business successes and failures. Pertaining to IT, participants described their IT activity in terms of headcount, budget, chargeback system, user satisfaction, challenges, goals, and reputation.

CASE STUDY: SILICON, INC. 1989–95

Context and history

Silicon, Inc. was started in 1989 as a result of a merger between a North American and a European company. Since then, Silicon has become one of the largest manufacturers of silicon in the world, with 11 plants spread throughout the United States, Asia, and Europe. As at the end of 1995 Silicon, Inc. employed 5000 people worldwide. Annual sales were almost $1 billion and expected to continue to grow as the world demand for silicon increases. Silicon, Inc. exclusively makes custom products, taking special orders from the world's largest electronic companies. These customers are extremely sophisticated in engineering, computing technology, and manufacturing. Their demands for custom wafers require as many as 200 parameters for a product specification. Given their rate of innovation, customers' requirements change on average every six months. Thus, Silicon, Inc. rarely makes the exact same product twice.

To compete in this industry, silicon manufacturers must be able to meet the custom needs of their highly technical customers in a timely manner. Back in 1989, Silicon was at a competitive disadvantage because customers were frustrated by its inability to commit to orders, fill orders on schedule, or change orders in a timely fashion. The problem stemmed from a lack of shared information about each of the manufacturing plant's capabilities, capacities, and schedules. When a customer called the centralized sales office to ask whether X product could be manufactured by Y date, Silicon, Inc. took up to three weeks to call the customer back and confirm the order. The old business process first required a headquarters person taking the order to determine which plant had the capability to manufacture silicon with the requested properties. Once the targeted plant was notified, that plant then determined what supply they needed to make that product. This often generated another internal order to another Silicon, Inc. plant. That second plant would then determine its ability to deliver the supply, and call back to Plant A, which would then be in a position to determine its ability to deliver the product. Plant A passed this information back to headquarters, which would then call back the customer to see if they still wanted the order. Many times, the customers found silicon manufacturers who responded quicker, thus representing a lost sale to Silicon, Inc. Michael describes the situation as follows:

> It was a mess because you couldn't get accurate information. The cycle time to place an order after a customer calls in and says I want 2000 more of Part Number Six for delivery in June, it would take us six or seven days[1] to process that because we would have to first receive the order in, then they'd have to figure out where to source the slices, and then the slice people say, 'Oh we need crystal.' Now we have to submit an order for the crystal people. They would have to find out where they were going to make it. In the meanwhile, no one was talking to the people in specifications and the customer says, 'I'll take material from site A but not from site B.' And we were in a constant swirl there.
>
> Michael, strategic manager of marketing

Although an IT solution seemed obvious, traditionally IT was perceived as a necessary cost burden, rather than a business enabler,

---

[1]The cycle time was stated as closer to three weeks to respond to customers by the other four participants

with senior management reticent to invest large sums in IT. Robert explains:

> There is an agonizing that goes on about the cost of this. Each year, going through the budgeting process, every year the budget goes up for two reasons. One, we are doing more and more, and two, we are getting bigger. We have more sites to support. And we need more people to do all of that. But it's not without some anxiety about where is the end of this?
>
> Robert, director of MIS

In addition to senior management perceiving IT as costly, they also perceived that service was poor. The IT managers blamed an outsourcing arrangement for the high costs and low service levels. At the time of the merger in 1989, Silicon, Inc. was forced to migrate off the mainframe of its previous parent company. Rather than build an internal data centre, Silicon, Inc. opted to sign with a service bureau for a $100 000 per month fee. David, manager of business information systems, explains why service from the vendor was poor:

> We were just one little fish in a big pond. So what we wanted was inconsequential to their other clients, which were significantly larger than we were in terms of revenue. So we tended to get – we got support – but it was slow. A lot of times the people we were dealing with had no idea the questions we were asking. We knew a lot more about what we wanted than they did. It became difficult to explain to them ... it was easier for us to code up the macro and hand it to them than to explain, 'I want an LU2.6 terminal that will do SNA/RJE to an AS 400.' They would scratch their head and say, 'We've never done that before.'
>
> David, manager of business information systems

Thus, from a service and cost perspective, people at Silicon, Inc.'s US operations were dissatisfied with their mainframe supplier. At the same time, the European operations were looking to replace their mainframe systems. At that time, they had over-customized a manufacturing software package to the point where the vendor would no longer support it. The software was also lacking and needed functionality as a result of the merger, such as dealing with multiple currencies and price breaks. The chief financial officer (CFO) in Europe had a vision that software running on smaller platforms was the future of IS, whereas these antiquated mainframe systems were becoming increasingly obsolescent. More specifically, he wanted to replace mainframe manufacturing systems with an integrated package which runs on a smaller platform (AS/400). The need for such an integrated, worldwide information system prompted the World-Wide Systems

Project in 1989. From this time on senior management's views on IT began to shift from seeing IT as a cost burden to viewing IT as a significant business investment, albeit one whose costs could not be limitless.

Client–server project

The original acquisition request (AR) for the worldwide systems project stated reduced cycle time to respond to customers as the primary justification. There was an attempt to quantify the costs and benefits, but the benefits, in particular, represented very rough estimates. On the cost side, the original AR requested $6 million for a two-year project. The expected cost benefits were loosely stated as $15 million a year for projected increased sales due to better customer service and a saving of approximately $500 000 a year to migrate off the mainframe. Michael gives his impressions of the projected benefits:

> It was a bit loose, there is no doubt about that. It's almost one of those things where faith is an issue. Especially, when you deal with, 'How is this going to affect the customer relationship?' Those are very difficult to put dollar values on, but just about everybody grasped that going from six days to less than a day has to be cost beneficial. But how much? We don't know.
>
> Michael, strategic manager of marketing

Michael, as strategic manager of marketing, was put in charge of the project. He recruited 'volunteers' from the major user groups – order processing, product specifications, and production scheduling. These users were seen as vital for ensuring that the project not only met its business objectives, but to also foster faith in the system:

> The working group took a lead role in co-ordinating among their peers to make sure that what we were building was what they wanted and needed. We had some oversight groups that made sure that was the direction we wanted to go in.
>
> Michael, strategic manager of marketing

Business applications

In the beginning (1989), the project team's first major task was to evaluate the specific software production solution proposed by the European CFO. The more the team studied the package, the more they realized it didn't fit their business model. In particular, Silicon, Inc.'s custom-made products required scheduling that conflicted with the assumptions of the package. Michael explains:

> The deeper that we got into it, the more we started realizing that it

didn't do scheduling. They used the classical MRP [material requirements planning] type of system where there is an infinite schedule situation, which works real well in an environment where you are going to be making product to a forecast, putting it on a shelf and then drawing from the inventories to satisfy the customers. Well, that is not our business. Our business is a custom order fabrication type business. So we had a problem with scheduling.

Michael, strategic manager of marketing

The parts of the package that *did* match Silicon Inc.'s business needs were not significantly different from their current mainframe applications. If they bought this package, they would have to retain every user worldwide to perform essentially the same functions, with no added business benefit. The project team decided to augment the home-grown systems with packaged software to add functionality for order processing, planning, scheduling, and multiple currencies. These packages would be integrated with 'non-mainframe' versions of the current systems. The search for these additional software packages created a spin-off project team, headed by David, and they evaluated several packages in the US and Europe. From a business standpoint, the best software was MIMI, which stands for 'manager for interactive modelling interfaces.' Michael describes the MIMI system from a user perspective:

It looked like it had most of the things that we were interested in. It was based on finite capacity as opposed to infinite capacity. It was based on a premise that you would have master models and submodels and they all talked together. Initially, we were looking at it more using the automated tools as opposed to the Star Wars tools as I call them, the drag and drop things. And we started going to some of their seminars and learning more and more about the product. The people in scheduling were getting excited about this. Especially when we got into a mode where it was very graphic-oriented. And I don't know if you have seen it, it's pretty interesting. When you start thinking about what's going on, you are essentially grabbing a block which is a schedule for a particular product with all the underlying data hiding underneath the block. If you decide, 'I don't want to put that on that piece of equipment, I want to put it on this piece of equipment,' you just point, click, drag, drop, and it spreads out the other schedules and recalculates all the underlying data like the start date, the start time, the quantities of the raw materials. It's pretty fantastic.

Michael, strategic manager of marketing

From a technical perspective, however, the package was lacking because it was a single-user system. Each user had his/her own model stored in RAM, much like a stand-alone spreadsheet package. When David was charged with enhancing this package to share models across user groups, the client–server solution emerged:

> So, we looked at the tool and determined a major problem with it. That is, it was single user. It was essentially like a LOTUS spreadsheet. Everything was in memory. Your couldn't share tables across users. So the only way to use this tool, which was an excellent finite capacity scheduling system – it had artificial intelligence, a backwards chaining inference engine, linear programming, a macro language, SQL links – the only way to use this in a multi-user mode was to take the tables that needed to be shared and put them into a relational database that sat in the middle of all of these various models as they are called ... or programs or macros, whatever you want to call them. And then have all that data updated on a server that was sitting in the middle of all of the MIMI clients. We were suddenly client–server, although we didn't know it at the time. So it just evolved as the reason we did this. The reason we did this: there was no other way to get around the deficiency of the system at that time.
>
> David, manager of business information systems

In 1991 the MIMI system was implemented. Robert's team downloaded the mainframe data containing all the parametric product specifications to the MIMI server. The MIMI system processed the specifications to create a standard set of parameters with a consistent set of measures (such as converting all quantities to the metric system). This functionality was known as *central specification*. After central specification, the data would be used as input for *central planning*. The central planning model looked at the product specifications and plant characteristics to determine which Silicon, Inc. plant should manufacture it. Robert explains:

> The central planning model looked at bottle-necked resources, and the relative capacities and capabilities of the plant sites on a worldwide basis and then determined what the allocation for manufacturing the product would be to each of the plant sites, of which we have several throughout the world, each with different capabilities and capacities. The central planning model determined the best way to divvy out the manufacture of the product.
>
> Robert, director of MIS

The next step was *local recipe generation*. Once a plant was assigned to manufacture a product, the central specification data would be used to generate a local recipe to determine exactly how the plant will manufacture the product. This business requirement led to the purchase of another software package running on a client–server platform. David explains:

> That took information that took information from the central specifications database and at a specific site ... we would generate a recipe, which is in essence taking information from this homogenized central spec data, looking at it and generating a 'here's how you would make it' route within the plant for that part that would be done in that plant. And then generate a document which was used at the shop floor through either a terminal inquiry or on hardcopy paper or both.
>
> David, manager of business information systems

At this point in 1991, order-processing on the mainframe still served as the front end to all the downstream client–server systems. In addition, outputs from the client–server systems were uploaded to the mainframe so the sales offices could answer customer queries about scheduling. The fourth generation languages which queried this data generated over 700 mainframe reports per month. Both the order-processing and reporting were the last to be migrated off the mainframe in 1992, and migrating the reports reduced the charges by $20 000 per month, which pleased senior management. Once the 700 reports were migrated, however, several technical problems surfaced, such as rollback, transaction backout, locking records, and slow response time. For example, Silicon Inc. had to shut the US mainframe down over night to run the batch extracts, which was making the mainframe useless for most of the day in Asia. Once again, David engaged the vendor as a 'strategic partner' to improve the product. The product was enhanced to concurrently run batch and online and the mainframe was only brought down one hour a night to do backups.

In November 1992, David and his group began the migration of the customer order entry and management system off the mainframe. They wanted to purchase a new product which essentially ran mainframe programs in a UNIX environment. David and John, a senior analyst, took the vendor's course in this new technology. During breaks, David compiled some of his programs and felt that the product showed promise to meet their needs, but the current version had many technical bugs. Silicon Inc. and the vendor became 'strategic partners', which mutually benefited both parties. Silicon Inc. received an immense discount on the vendor's resources, including use of the vendor's data centre to convert the 700 programs and access to their top technical specialists, in exchange for the vendor using Silicon, Inc. as a software test sight. David explains:

> They would give us facilities, machine, consulting resources and the

early release code and direct access to the developers. As it turned out, it was an excellent opportunity for both of us because we would shake out a lot of bugs in their code while we were converting our system. So we did that – that took four months.

David, manager of business information systems

The order entry and management system, which was the last piece of the worldwide system, was fully implemented at the end of 1994.

Technological infrastructure

Initially, when the mandate to eliminate the mainframe came from its European headquarters, Silicon Inc. chose the AS/400 mid-range computer as its computing platform. This was, primarily because it was viewed favourably by the CFO. In addition, the software package considered initially in 1989 was designed to run on an AS/400 computer. Subsequently, when David and his group determined that the software package was not suitable, the AS/400 was no more the computing platform of choice. The MIMI package was evaluated and found to be an effective tool for the fixed capacity scheduling and planning required to support Silicon Inc.'s operations. Because MIMI was designed to operate in the UNIX operating system environment the choice of the computing platform to be selected was restricted to UNIX-based computers. Specifically, the RS/600 RISC computers were selected. The RS/600 uses the AIX operating system which is IBM's version of the UNIX operating system. Its RISC architecture makes the RS/6000 an effective computer for intensive mathematical applications such as fixed capacity scheduling. It also serves as an effective communication bridge between AS/400-based applications and the older VAX computers still existing in some departments within the organization.

As at end of 1995 the worldwide system comprised several RS/600 application and database servers linked by a dual ring fibre distributed data interface (FDDI) metropolitan area network (MAN). This configuration supported an aggregate data rate of 200 Mbps between the servers. A few servers, which are primarily used for testing applications, are connected to the FDDI ring using Ethernet local area networks (LANs). Client stations are also connected to the servers on the FDDI ring using Ethernet LANs which support a data rate of 10 Mbps. One of the RS/600 computers on the FDDI ring functions as a router to route traffic to and from the client stations and the appropriate servers. It also functions as a terminal server to support traffic from VT100, VT220 and IBM 3270 ASCII terminals.

As described earlier, Silicon Inc.'s worldwide system is a collection of client applications that obtain services from a collection of servers interconnected by a high-speed network. The entire system may be viewed as comprising two sub-systems – the planning and scheduling system and the order entry management system. In the planning and scheduling system the primary application software is MIMI. The MIMI software is a client–server package. The server modules contain relevant data and provide mathematical modelling functions. The client modules are essentially the GUI front ends that function as the user interface to the system. The planning and scheduling system is supported by six RS/6000 servers:

1. one server contains the central specifications data in a relational database;
2. one server that contains the MIMI mathematical models used for central planning;
3–4. two servers provide local shop-floor scheduling services for each of the manufacturing sites;
5. one server provides the chemical recipes used by each manufacturing site for growing silicon; crystals of various specifications are stored on yet another server;
6. one server is used for testing new MIMI models.

The services of each of these servers is utilized by client MIMI applications. These clients utilize local recipe data and local scheduling services to develop work plans for each shop floor. Some of the client applications are specification queries from local sites which are supported by the database servers. MIMI client applications that perform central planning and scheduling utilize the services of the central specifications database server and the central planning applications server.

The main application software in order entry management system consists of the CICS/600 transaction control system and ENCINA – a product that provides enhanced transaction processing functions. These layers of software operate over the distributed computing environment software (DCE). DCE is a product that provides essential services in a distributed computing environment such as file services, directory services and security. These layers of software work co-operatively to enter, control and manage all aspects of transaction processing such as user authentication, order entry, data validation, transaction backout and recovery, etc. The order entry management system consists of five RS/6000 servers:

1. one server functions as a terminal server to handle data entry and queries from terminals used by sales personnel and also serves as a router to route traffic to and from other DCE clients and servers;
2. one server functions as the CICS server that provides the core transaction processing service;

3. one server functions as the database server that contains the transaction data;
4. one server provides the report writing function. These reports are generated in a batch mode;
5. one server provides data backup and archiving services.

This current architecture was developed gradually over a period of five years. Along the way numerous technical problems were encountered and addressed. The technical problems were primarily due to the newness and lack of maturity of the technology both for the vendor as well as for Silicon, Inc. For example, in the planning and scheduling system, the MIMI software was not originally designed to support multiple users. However, because there was no other comparable tool available David and his group had to modify MIMI to suit their needs. In the order entry system the CICS and ENCINA products had never been tested with realistic transaction loads. Thus, when it was initially tested at Silicon, Inc. the system proved to be inadequate. For example, when a transaction was aborted and backed out, the system would get bogged down for hours. As David described it ... 'we would put in a transaction that would do 20 000 I/O per logical unit of work and hit the rollback button and two days later it would come back ... which we decided wasn't an acceptable response time (sarcastically).' Problems such as these were gradually ironed out with the close support and co-operation of the vendor. Finally, on respondent accounts and on what we have seen of the technology in operation, what has emerged is a very open system with connectivity across the organization. Moreover it would appear to be a system designed to grow and evolve with the changing needs of Silicon, Inc.:

> So if I want to characterize what this project was, more than anything else, it was an infrastructure building project. We built a worldwide infrastructure for data communications, client–server computing – and quite honestly, if someone came in tomorrow and said, hey guys, we are done with IBM, no more RS/6000, switch everything to ALPHAs – Great! give me a week; give me OSFI; buy the packages for that version – I'm done. We built an open architecture that allows us to plug the pieces in any way we want ... we built this to be open, modularized so pieces could be swapped in and out.
>
> David, manager of business systems

CASE ANALYSIS AND DISCUSSION: CLIENT–SERVER 'SUCCESS' AND EMERGING ISSUES

The participants all agreed that the project was a financial and business success, although admitting they could not quantify accurately the outcomes. In this section we analyse the 'success' of the project from two perspectives: cost savings and better business decisions. We then carry out two further analyses. First, six critical success factors are distilled from the case material (see Table 14.1). The fact that these have been consistently cited in the extant IT project implementation literature for over a decade suggests that, from a management perspective, in many ways there is little that is new in how client–server implementation needs to be handled. However, secondly, we identified from the literature ten technical and managerial features of client–server environments considered distinctive, and rendering implementations more difficult than for previous technologies. Here each is investigated against the Silicon, Inc. experience, and an assessment made of the difficulties encountered and how they were handled.

Table 14.1   Silicon, Inc.: outcomes and critical enabling factors

Outcomes	Silicon, Inc.: critical enabling factors
Financial • Cost up to $12 million – twice original estimate • Operating costs reduced by $600 000 per year • Most of the investment cost would have gone in maintaining/upgrading existing IS anyway • 'Significant' improvements in business process operations **Business** • Reduced response time to customer queries (weeks to hours) • Reduced manufacturing cycle time from 27 to 19 days • Reduced inventory from 60 000 to 20 000 wafers a day • Late changes to order by customer possible • High customer acceptance • Contributed to signifcant increased sales	1. Business process re-engineering drives technology choice 2. Insourcing preferred 3. Vendor partnering – timing and type of relationship 4. Incremental implementation 5. Senior level support and participation 6. Close user – IS professional relationships 7. IS perceived as a business investment in a R&D-type project rather than a cost centre

Financial outcomes

The original acquisition request called for an investment of $6 million for a two-year project. The project took twice as long and – according to some participants – cost twice as much as originally estimated. (Others note that broadening the project scope accounts for the increased cost.) Despite this overrun, all participants agreed that it was a project that had to be done in order for the business to survive, and thus was worth the cost. The most concrete financial justification for the project was moving off the mainframe. In terms of operating costs, the mainframe environment was costing $1 200 000 a year. By end of 1995 Silicon, Inc. operated 15 RISC machines for only $50 000 a month. These numbers, however, do not include the investment costs of development, training, or implementation. When Michael was asked about these other costs, he responded:

> Yeah, but the biggest problem we had, we had gone into a mode that we knew we were going to discontinue support of the old software and old methodologies. So, yes it's true we had to add bodies in to support the new applications, but had we decided to continue on with the old applications, we would have had to have as many bodies, if not more, to continue to support it on the old platforms using the old methodologies. We made a conscious decision early on, that if it wasn't true, that's what we were going to state to everybody. Anyway by and large, everybody bought it. It took us a long time to convince management that probably 85 per cent of the project's cost is the maintenance after the fact. It's not the first bring-it-up-on-line, the computers, it's the fact that everybody wants to continue to tweak them. You had to be careful not to get too carried away with that. But, by and large, the tweaks are beneficial. So, yeah, it's true you have to support it, you have to have facilities, people dedicated to it, but it's not going to run itself. You can't walk away from it, no matter what. So you are going to pay that burden.
>
> Michael, strategic manager of marketing

Other participants readily admitted that they could not concretely quantify cost savings (other than reduced operating costs.) However, the improvements to the business processes have been so significant, participants were all confident the project was a financial success in the sense that the business would have severely suffered without it.

Business outcomes

All five of our respondents perceived that the project was a success because it:

- Reduced the response time to customer queries from several weeks to less than a few hours. (No participant estimated the worth of this benefit).
- Reduced manufacturing cycle times from 27 days to 19 days due to better planning. (No participant estimated the worth of this benefit).
- Reduced inventory from 60 000 wafers a day to 20 000 wafers a day.

(Steven estimates this saving at $200 000 a year in reduced inventory carrying costs).

In addition to processing new orders faster, Robert explained that the reduced cycle time also includes customers' requests to make changes to existing orders:

> That [reduced cycle time to respond to customer queries] has been a big improvement in our relationships with our customers. They obviously want to know, 'Can you deliver on time?' because the industry is tight on supply right now. And we also are better able to meet that date, which is obviously part II. And a lot of changes are always coming in. That's the other side of it. Nobody realizes that you take an order and sure you commit it to a date, now they call up two weeks later and say, 'Hey we really need twice that much. We really need it two weeks earlier. Can you do it?' And that's where the new COMPASS system has enabled us to answer those questions quickly and accurately, which before was a total guess. On paper, there was no way to determine if indeed it could be done. We would guess and miss and we had a lot of unsatisfied customers. Right now we don't have everything 100 per cent on time, but given the market conditions and the tremendous demand, and the record production levels we are running right now, our on-time delivery is very respectable. The customers are understanding. And when we are going to miss, we will be able to communicate that to them ahead of time which is helping the situation. So that's probably our biggest business impacter.
>
> Robert, director of MIS

Michael and Robert capture the participants' reluctance to put a dollar value on these business benefits:

> Many of our customers come back and say, 'It's almost phenomenal, the change.' There was a lot of frustration before because we took so long to commit. Things of that nature. How do you put a price tag on that? It's almost impossible to set a price that you know that in a world where people are getting more and more used to things being instantaneous, the closer you are to instantaneous, the happier they are, the more likely they are happy to make orders with you.
>
> Michael, strategic manager of marketing

> It's just one component of many that continues to increase sales. A resounding success. If success is measured by customer acceptance, they will all speak highly of it. Day and night they use it to do their job more accurately, more quickly, the cycle time issues. And also the benefit, the business benefit, it's hard to tell because a lot of

things keep changing in this industry so you can't just say, 'Okay we put that in and our sales went up 10 per cent.' You can't ever do that because at the same time you've brought on a new plant site. There are so many things happening. But I am very confident that system enabled us to stay on top of our growing situation. Being able to utilize our facilities more effectively than we would have otherwise.

Robert, director of MIS

Although all of the respondents (all of whom played a vital role in the project) considered the project a resounding success, all admitted that senior management did not pay that much attention to the project's achievement. For example, Steven noted that they really didn't understand the effort needed to implement the system. For him, senior management was glad that the software operated and that the recipes were correct, but they still did not perceive it as a considerable IS success. Other participants comment on senior management's perceptions:

Senior management is glad the project is over. They were glad we didn't kill the business. By and large, they are pleased.

Michael, strategic manager of marketing

But when you try to explain exactly what technology went into this and what we really accomplished as compared to anybody else, or compared to another way of doing it, it's hard to get that across. And I sense that only in the way that they talk about the project. In some ways – as an omission – there isn't a lot of talk about the project. They say, 'Oh you did a good job,' but not really a good feeling of why it is it was accomplished. They wouldn't necessarily come back I don't think and say, 'You need to do more of that client–server' because there isn't an understanding of what it is and why we want to do it.

Robert, director of MIS

When the participants were asked how senior management could give a luke-warm reception to the project given the business success, three answers were offered. John noted that the culture of Silicon, Inc. is to expect fantastic results, thus there are few 'pats on the back' for project successes of any kind. Robert noted that senior management was focused on other business initiatives, such as opening new manufacturing plants. David felt that senior management failed to understand the amount of work required to create a seamless transition:

They [senior management] see it as a success that it is over with. They are not as excited about it as we are, we being MIS. The main reason I would say that is because from a user standpoint, it was a non-event. Which is in my mind, part of the reason it's a success.

There was a minimal perceived interruption to the business and the business flow as a result of this project. Yet it put in place an infrastructure that will allow us to move into the future. So, from my standpoint, it's a fantastic success. It will make my life much easier in the future. From management's perspective, it looks like a duck, it quacks like a duck.

David, manager of business information systems

Critical success factors

All participants agreed that the client–server project was successful, although the level of enthusiasm differed among stakeholders. Participants were asked to relate the critical success factors (CSFs) to the design, development, and implementation of the system. We have categorized their responses into seven CSFs which will now be discussed.

Business process re-engineering drives technology choice

It's a business problem that we solved using this technology as opposed to the other way around. He thinks, from what he has seen, if you are installing C–S just to install C–S, you are crazy, because there is a high learning curve to get over. With all the advances recently, the learning curve is not as high as it used to be, but we got into it early.

Michael, strategic manager of marketing

All the participants stressed that the worldwide systems project was a result of a business crisis because Silicon Inc. could not service their customers. The project teams sought to redesign the business processes to reduce the time needed to place, change, and fill customer orders. The resulting system centralized order processing, central specification (the homogenizing of customer orders to standard units of measurement), and central planning (assigning orders to specific plants) while decentralizing the local recipes and schedules. As at 1996 we would probably call this project business process re-engineering, although that term was not common in 1989. But Robert notes that Silicon, Inc. has always looked at business processes before applying any automation.

We understand that there are processes to doing everything. And we always look to fix the process before we automate it. That is key. That is true of a lot of our IS projects. We've got to look at the process first then try to write a program around it because the process is usually what the problem is. As opposed to the software. Some companies go out and buy new software like SAP and they use it –

they say they are putting new software in – but they are really putting it in to re-engineer the company to be more like what this software says you should be. That's where the benefit comes. Quite frankly, I don't think it's the software as much as they get the organizational processes re-done in a more streamlined way.

Robert, director of MIS

All participants stressed that the worldwide systems project actually *evolved* into a client–server solution. Thus, it was a tool to enable a change in business processes:

It being a client–server project is an afterthought. It was not a direction. It just so happened that that was the vehicle that we saw as the most economical, most expandable, and didn't lock us into a particular methodology.

Michael, strategic manager of marketing

That project was probably a little different in the way it came about. I came in the middle so I am trying to think back how exactly it got started. There was just a very obvious need for a new system for scheduling and planning. It started out ... they were looking at the process and asked what it was they wanted to do. No preconceived notion about what system to use. I'm sure [David] has said this before because he and I feel really good about the way we ended up with client–server. That project never envisioned client–server in the beginning. It was strictly a project to find a better automated way to do this process. This came from an obvious pain in the company. The customer was beating us up because we couldn't respond fast enough. So they started in with trying to find an artificial intelligence package. That was the first step. It happened to run on the RS/6000 quite well so we got into RS/6000. This was four years ago. And it was just by evaluating the need and trying to apply software solutions that it became more and more obvious that we were generating a C–S solution. That sounds abstract, but the key point is that no where in that did we say, 'We are doing client–server.' We kind of woke up and discovered that we were implementing a client–server solution after we were into it. It was more like after we were into it, this tool seemed to fit our need, then we woke up to the fact that this was client–server. And I say that over and over because I think that is the right way to enter in C–S.

Robert, director of MIS

Insourcing

Participants perceived that outsourcing vendors do not have the same motivation to make service users or to keep IS costs as internal IS employees. By insourcing, Silicon, Inc.'s IS staff were more responsive to users because they understood the business consequences of their requests. Robert explains:

It's [manufacturing] a very difficult job. Anyone who hasn't been there, can't appreciate that. That 24 hour-a-day, 7 day-a-week demand to have the place produce. No matter what happens. I don't care if the power fails or it snows or we are running out of supplies. It's all the responsibility of manufacturing to get that done. If they have an IS group that is not supporting that, that is not responsive or doesn't sense the urgency that manufacturing always feels, and there is a big difference there. That's where a lot of the animosity I think comes from between IS and the rest of the company comes from. Many times the people in the IS group haven't sensed the urgency that the others are feeling. If the IS function doesn't perform in an urgent way, you obviously have bad feelings.

Robert, director of MIS

In a summary report to management, David cited insourcing as one of the major benefits of the client–server project because it reduced costs and increased service:

At [Silicon, Inc.] we determined that by bringing the application in-house and integrating it to the scheduling systems, we would reduce lead times and improve customer service.

David's summary report to management

Moving off the mainframe was an economic advantage and a simplifier of our lives. We have one less vendor out there to worry about. And we've improved the realiability of that system.

Robert, director of MIS

Although Silicon, Inc., did not outsource the development, implementation, or support of the client–server system, that did not preclude Silicon Inc. from accessing needed talent from external vendors. However, the subsequent success of these arrangements may be partly explained by these vendors being engaged in a form of partnering that resulted in complementary rather than conflicting goals (see Henderson, 1990; Willcocks, 1995; also Chapter 11).

Form of vendor partnering
All participants perceived the vendor partnership as a critical success factor:

There is little doubt in our case (of) extremely close support on the part of the vendors. They were practically living here with us in many cases for quite a while. We had some of the top people with

IBM working on the CRM side. And physically sitting in cubicles out here and working with the programmers.

Michael, strategic manager of marketing

We were in a client partnership program. The deal was that if they got it going for us we would run around singing their praises.

John, senior analyst

I think that [the vendor] contributed heavily in the consulting role, not only giving us advice, but they sent in six people out here, three for a long period of time. A number of them showed up for weeks at a time to get us kicked off. We were having trouble with memory management. A number of things came up that they were good at responding to. Some of our other software vendors weren't quite as responsible after the fact that you own their software, they weren't willing to contribute.'

Steven, manufacturing services support systems supervisor

We actually helped them debug it and make it a viable product. That was a partnership unlike any I had really seen in the past years I've been in IS. They gave us support to make it happen. But of course, we were checking their product out which needed a lot of checking. So it goes two ways.

Robert, director of MIS

The timing of the partnership was also key. Silicon, Inc. needed resources to migrate off the mainframe and the vendor needed a customer to help debug their new software. As at 1996 Silicon would not be able to duplicate that deal, although they would search for other opportunities to exploit complementary goals.

Incremental implementation

The project represented the single largest acquisition request for IS at Silicon. Given senior management's trepidation over IS expenditures, the project team had been anxious to implement pieces of the system as soon as a significant business function was complete. The major subsystems implemented were: scheduling (1991), central specifications (1991), central planning (1991), migrated 700 reports (1992), and order entry (1993–94). Participants explained how this incremental approach led to project success:

Being able to have successes along the route and not necessarily everything is installed at once. This piece is installed and running and doing what's its supposed to. In this particular case, it allowed us to drop the charges by $15 000 a month for the mainframe. In this particular case, we now give manufacturing better visibility as far as what the work load is going to be for the next six weeks which helps them figuring out overtime, figuring a way to avoid overtime. It can't be a sit back, wait a year and a half and all of a sudden, boom, here it is. It has to be something that comes in pieces of discernible enough sizes that people can see it's there and working and doing what we want it to do.'

Michael, strategic manager of marketing

At least this wasn't a thing that waited until the third year before it was turned on. Along the way, benefits were starting to come out. And that helped the situation. It wasn't like they waited three years with a totally manual system. Several steps, every six months, new features were being added. That's one of the advantages of client–server approach. You keep adding new features, we added new servers. We kept this very fluid mix of boxes out there. We kept changing the arrangement because we kept seeing a benefit each time as we learned, we found better ways to do things. So I think the project allows you that kind of advantage. You turn things on gradually. You see benefits gradually. The customer likes that. They feel good right away.

Robert, director of MIS

By 1995 the worldwide systems project had been going on for five years. Although the major components had been installed in 1991, new functionality has been constantly added to accommodate changes, such as new manufacturing plants and new technologies. Thus, all participants stated that the project *still* isn't completed.

Senior-level support and participation
From the beginning, the worldwide systems project had had at least one senior level manager in full support of the project. This support led to project funding, despite the 'abstractness' of the costs and benefits outlined on the acquisition request:

I think the answer is that it wasn't as defined as we would like it to be today when it started out. I tried to be complete in our direction, the tools, the hardware before we write an AR. We don't write some abstract thing and hope for the best. That one was a little like that, abstract and hope for the best. It was a very big project with a lot of dollars in that. It had the backing of people who were influential enough to get it through in spite of its abstractness. It's not typical of how we run projects today. But, because of its abstractness, it allowed us to experiment a bit on how we were going to get there.

Robert, director of MIS

The European CFO drove the project at the beginning. His white paper outlining the future of IS called for a migration off the mainframe to smaller platforms (although he did not specify client–server), integrated manufacturing and financial systems, and a worldwide telecommunications infrastructure served as the initial vision of the project. To ensure that this vision would be realized, Michael, a high-level business manager was put in charge of the project. The other participants credited his political ability as a critical success factor. David, for example, explained how Michael competently traversed through Silicon, Inc.'s matrix organization:

> The credit really goes to [Michael] in my mind and the CFO. They drove it. They made it work. [Manufacturing] group were on the sidelines, dragged in kicking and screaming. What made a difference – our organization is like this, a mess, and it still is ... it's democratic. Getting consensus can be difficult. We didn't always get consensus throughout the project. But what allowed us to be successful was the fact that [Michael] knew how to navigate the matrix organization. He pulled in the right people at the right time to get decisions made. There was a lot of this matrix organization that made it possible to get access to the right people to get things done. Because so many people work for so many other people, you have to build the right strategic alliances to the right parts of the matrix. You have to pull the matrix however you want to pull it. But that's something that helped. Manufacturing had dotted lines into marketing, marketing had dotted lines into planning, etc. But high-level user involvement was a key to success. But it was also who was involved.
>
> David, manager of business information systems

Close user–IS relationships

In addition to high-level support and involvement, close user–IS partnering was also cited as a critical success factor. Project teams required full-time commitments from both groups. Users and IS team members 'worked in the same bull pens', as one respondent described it, so their close physical proximity promoted constant communication. Participants explained:

> I think the people that were involved had worked together for a good period of time. They had an appreciation for each others' skills. They weren't ashamed to say, 'I don't know this answer but we can talk to this guy ...'. We really understood each other well enough that we could rely on each others' strengths. [David] is a very good resource. You can't top his IS knowledge and the things he can come up with. He is very creative. I consider myself a very good resource from the manufacturing side. I had some management skills. I ran the

modification building here for some period of time. Things of that nature. With all of here together as a team, it caused it to be a success.

Steven, manufacturing services support systems supervisor

I come back to teamwork a lot. This company is not built on isolated units. We are very much working together as teams. There is no IS project that doesn't have users right on the project team. So it was two ways. We certainly had an outstanding IS group on this group, including the contract people.

Robert, director of MIS

In my opinion, we could not have pulled this project off by having MIS sit in one area and have the users sit in another area. Physically we were only 20 or 30 feet apart. Literally, the programmers were sitting by the schedulers, next to the people who write the plan orders, the people who deal with the commercial issues. If there hadn't been that close coupling, that would have led to frustration. It would have led to more false starts. We have a pretty active users group. Basically, the way we try to structure it, as we start tackling different segments, there was involvement from people who did the work, who were going to do the work in the future. One of the people who now maintains part of the system was a plant operator. She's been taught how to use SQL rules, how to use expert systems, things of that nature. There has been real imparting of knowledge to the users and soaking up that knowledge. I think if it had been done in a vacuum, it would have never happened. There had been too many frustration/fights/battles and the users would not have been able to see that progress was being made. Having them be able to report back to their supervisors and saying, 'Yeah, it's moving forward, it's getting there.' I think that was a critical factor.

Michael, strategic manager of marketing

IS seen as a business investment, not just a cost centre

These seven critical success factors suggest that Silicon's client–server project possessed many of the characteristics of other large-scale IT implementations (Willcocks and Griffiths, 1994; see also Chapters 9 and 10). However, Silicon, Inc., also shares another common characteristic in that it was considerably over-budget and over-due (Saarinen and Vepsalainen, 1993; Willcocks and Griffiths, 1994). Although this can hardly be cited as a critical success factor, the enabling feature in the Silicon, Inc. case was the willingness of business and technical management at senior and operational levels to continue to invest resources, time and effort beyond original estimates into what turned out to be, *de facto*, a research and development project with considerable significance for the organization's short- and long-term business performance. While IT expenditures were always subject to budgeting reviews at Silicon Inc., some sense of senior management's changing perception of IT as an investment, rather than merely a cost to be minimized is revealed by the following comments:

> IS is seen as an enabler of transformation. We are a valued competency that enables this business to succeed .... I think we have a real benefit (in Silicon, Inc.) in that we do have a lot of people who do recognize that. That comes about in the sense of us getting approvals. And being given the OK to try new things and technologies, which do cost money and do have some risk.
>
> Robert, Director of MIS

> It was paid for by the chief financial officer but ... the chairman of the board of our parent company ... he really was the sponsor. He was the one pushing it ... they wanted us to get into a mid-range system. It was really more an edict from the top than a push from the bottom.
>
> David, manager of business information systems

CLIENT–SERVER: DISTINCTIVE IMPLEMENTATION ISSUES?

These critical enablers are, of course, very familiar (for more detailed accounts see in particular Chapters 2, 7, 8, 9, 10, 11 and 17). This suggests that there will be little difference between the implementation experiences of client–server and those on any relatively large new information technology-based project, at least in a relatively large complex organization like Silicon, Inc. However, one final comparison will be made. Table 14.2 shows the major technical and managerial difficulties that feature regularly in the literature as distinctive to client–server implementations as opposed to other organizationally-used IT-based technologies. Here we compare these against Silicon Inc.'s own client–server experiences.

Technical issues

We reviewed published case studies, survey research and the prescriptive literature on client–server implementation. These sources suggest a number of distinctive technical issues:

- Client–server represents a distinctively different and organizationally new set of technologies (Friend, 1995; King, 1994; Muller, 1994; Orfali et al., 1994).

Table 14.2 Distinctive client–server issues: A comparison with Silicon, Inc.

Client–server issues	Silicon, Inc. experience							Remarks
	Factor present			**Level of difficulty incurred**				
	Minor	*Major*	*n/a*	*Negligible*	*Some*	*Considerable*	*Project threatening*	
Technical								
Involves distinctively different and organizationally new set of technologies		✓					✓	Skills shortages managed as R&D project
Not one technology: complex integration/testing problems		✓			✓			Vendor partnering and close user–IS relationships in systems development
Hardware/software compatibility issues	✓				✓			Strong supplier relations and restricted choices made
Sizing, configuration and capacity issues		✓				✓		Present but not experienced as technically difficult
Centralization/decentralization debate creates short/long-term technical issues	✓				✓			Managed incrementally
Main payoffs from enterprise-wide technical planning	✓				✓			Grow into this type of planning
Managerial								
Creates lack of clarity about responsibilities of business users, roles, skills		✓			✓			Incremental implementation enable adjustments
Not one technology: everyone has to know something new		✓				✓		Run as a learning project
Usually introduced as part of wider organization change		✓			✓			Management as re-engineering project
Requires matrix management and new approaches to managing problems		✓			✓			Existing matrix management redeployed

387

- Client–server is not one technology but several. The resulting complexity raises distinctive and more problematical, integration and testing issues. These are made worse by lack of appropriate client–server development methodologies and generally accepted standards in networking (Bochenski, 1994; Friend, 1995; Levis and von Schilling, 1994; Renaud, 1993).

- Relatedly, client–server presents a range of distinctive hardware/software compatibility issues (Forrester Research, 1996; Mill, 1994).

- Sizing, configuraton and capacity planning become more difficult with client–server (Collins, 1996).

- Lack of mature products and tools to support a diverse and complex client–server computing environment (Forrester Research, 1996; Levis and von Schilling, 1994).

- Client–server invariably intervenes in a dynamic IT centralization-decentralization debate and can confuse rather than clarify the technical directions and options (Mill, 1994; Ross, 1995; Tayntor, 1994).

- More than other technolgoies client–server requires an enterprise-wide technical planning and management (Forrester Research, 1995; Kole, Roukas and Tate, 1995).

In reviewing the case documentation and interview transcriptions, it was clear that all these technical issues were present in the client–server implementation at Silicon, Inc.. However, even if distinctive of client–server environments, on our analysis none of these factors emerged as particularly critical barriers to the Silicon, Inc. implementation (see Table 14.2 – the ratings represent our own view derived from respondent opinion). One key to success was accepting early on that the organization had low 'technology maturity' (see Feeny, Earl and Edwards (1996) and in Chapter 7). For Silicon Inc. client–server was relatively new and unstable in specification and application, and in the first two years there was relatively little relevant in-house technical experience. This implied the need for insourcing and the taking of a 'user' focus, that is using multi-functional teams rather than leaving development to technical specialists. It also meant that external vendors needed to be used on a buy-in or close partnering rather than on a strict contractual basis (Feeny, Earl and Edwards, 1996; Lacity, Willcocks and Feeny, 1995). All these approaches were in fact adopted effectively at Silicon, Inc., but represent prescriptions applicable to any new systems development, rather than exclusive to client–server environments. Some flavour of the approach is suggested by the following, but note that the technical rather than the organizational issues of implementation are downplayed by the respondent:

We had no choice but to use in-house people because they understood the business logic. The technical skills required (were) minor to the understanding of the business logic. Training the staff on a new paradigm was at times difficult especially when they were getting stuck in their old roles. We had to isolate them from their old roles and immerse them in the new technology. Eventually, everyone made the transition.

David, manager of business information systems

What was interesting in the Silicon, Inc. case was that as far as IT was concerned the technology was both centralizing and decentralizing, and yet the enterprise-wide technical planning and management approach stressed as necessary and distinctive for client–server implementations by many sources developed gradually rather than being present at the beginning:

There was just an obvious need for a new system for scheduling and planning .... The customer was beating us up because we could not respond fast enough. So we started in with trying to find an artificial intelligence package ... it happened to run on the RS/6000 quite well so we got into RS/6000. This was four years ago. And it was just by evaluating the need and trying to apply software solutions that it became more and more obvious that we were generating a C–S solution. ... The key point is that nowhere in that did we say 'We are doing client–server'. It was more like after we were into it, this tool seemed to fit our need, then we woke up to the fact that this was client–server. And I say this over and over because I think this is the right way to enter into client–server. Now today, we obviously know more about it, you will think C–S more quickly than you did four years ago.

Robert, director of MIS

This was not a technology looking for a problem, this was a solution that used a technology. It's a business problem we solved ... if you are installing C–S just to install C–S you are crazy, because there is a high learning curve to get over.

Michael, strategic manager of marketing

Clearly during the 1989–95 period there had been so much learning due to the partnering arrangements, the in-house approach and close user–IS relationships that any distinctive technical difficulties had been largely surmounted: the outstanding issue remained the perennial one for all IT functions, namely cost containment:

The concept of fully integrating the company worldwide so that we are managing all our resources, all our inventories and that we can produce on the spot demand – all that requires very integrated systems. To do all that and accomplish that within the budget constraints is my biggest challenge. I don't feel a great challenge to keep up with technology. I have an organization, I believe, that is very capable of being on that leading edge of technology. But applying that cost effectively to our company is the challenge.

Robert, director of MIS

Managerial difficulties

Published sources also suggest a range of managerial issues distinctive to client–server implementation:

- creates lack of clarity about the responsibility of business users, their roles and the new skills needed (Forrester Research, 1996; Levis and von Schilling, 1994);
- not one technology, therefore everyone has to learn something new. For example, problem and change management must be conducted differently with more interest groups involved than before (Renaud, 1993; Ross, 1995);
- usually introduced when the organization is itself centralizing or decentralizing. The background of organizational change exacerbates the technology management issues. Alternatively the organization traditional structure and culture creates barriers to moves to a distributed technical environment (King, 1994; Levis and von Schilling, 1994; Renaud, 1993; Tayntor, 1994; Tebbutt, 1996);
- requires matrix management involving many parties and new approaches to managing problems (Levis and von Schilling, 1994).

Again, while all these barriers can be easily read into the case, what is interesting is how none really emerged as critical obstacles. The reasons for this, at least for the first three points, would seem to lie with the critical success factors delineated from our review of documents and the interview transcripts (see above). In particular, these seemed to lead to an overarching emergent approach that mitigated risk while promoting widespread organization-wide learning:

We went from low risk to high risk and learned along the way. Learned a lot along the way.

David, manager, business information services

However, on the fourth point, Silicon Inc. management clearly recognized the distinctive implications of client–server for how implementations should be pursued:

Getting consensus can be difficult … what allowed us to be successful was the fact that (Michael) knew how to navigate the matrix organization. He pulled in the right people at the right time to get the decisions made. There was a lot of this matrix organization (that) made it possible to get access to the right people to get things done. Because so many people work for so many other people you have to build the right strategic alliances to the right parts of the matrix. You have to pull the matrix however you want to pull it. But that's something that helped.

David, manager of business information systems

In this case the pre-existing matrix organization was an important enabler, but could have been a major obstacle if there had not been managers actively utilizing it to pursue client–server project objectives.

DISCUSSION AND CONCLUSION

The critical success factors associated with Silicon's client–server application were mostly little different from the managerial lessons derived from studies of other new IT-based projects. Once applied these enabled most of the technical and managerial barriers usually cited as distinctive to client–server to be handled without any becoming major obstacles. Additionally there was at Silicon, Inc. a wide acceptance of three factors that made for effective implementation: that there was relatively low technology maturity as far as client–server was concerned; that the project was closer to research and development; and that the degree of organization-wide learning over the course of the project would be fundamental to the level of success achieved.

Certainly, the plethora of IT research has demonstrated the need for top management support, the need for IT to be perceived as an investment rather than as merely a cost centre, re-designing business processes before implementing IT, building in-house capability, accessing vendor resources, user participation on development teams, and phased implementation strategies to reduce risk. We also see many of the same problems surfacing, such as IT projects late and over-budget, primarily caused by similar problems: failing to freeze user specifications and underestimating the costs of training, support, and maintenance. In this sense, we can see that Silicon's case is representative of many large-scale IT projects.

Business process re-engineering drives technology choice   Ever since Hammer and Champy's seminal book, *Re-engineering the Corporation* (1993), practitioners have been told, 'don't automate, obliterate.' Their message is simple: improve the business process before implementing IT solutions. However, their methods call for radical change: *'It is about beginning again with a clean sheet of paper ... marginal improvement is no improvement at all but a detriment.'* Although these authors argue for radical change, research has suggested that practitioners opt for a more moderate approach to BPR, one of gradual process improvements, rather than obliterating the past (Willcocks, 1996a; Willcocks and Currie, 1995; also Chapter 10). However, Silicon's BPR project can better be characterized as a process improvement rather than radical re-design. Silicon, Inc. still went through the same process of order-entry – central specification – central planning – local specification – local planning. The process improvements comprised integrating information for faster customer response. Thus, although participants used the rhetoric of 'BPR driving technology', a better description may be 'process improvement before automation.'

Insourcing the development of new technology   The sourcing strategy for client–server implementations was seen as a critical success factor by participants – how could they acquire the skills necessary to build and support this new technology? Many companies are opting to outsource the development of client–server applications rather than build in-house capabilities. For example, First National Bank of Chicago has signed a seven-year, multi-million dollar contract with CSC to install SAP on client–server platform. Holiday Inn announced a partnership with IBM to build and install client–server-based reservation systems in 1900 hotels by mid-1997 (Wagner, 1995). Silicon, Inc. rejected outsourcing the project because they felt that internal IT staff had the necessary business expertise, although they wished to access vendors' technical expertise (see Chapter 7 for a confirmation of this approach).

Unique vendor partnership   In recent years, there has been much research on strategic partnering with IT vendors. In many cases, the rhetoric of 'strategic partners' is used to describe many client/vendor relationships, although closer scrutiny fails to reveal how many such contracts are 'strategic' (Willcocks, 1995). Silicon, Inc. however, is an exemplar for a strategic partnership because the contract truly defined *complementary* goals (see also Chapter 11). Silicon received resources and talent in exchange for de-bugging the vendor's new product. Although Silicon participants stressed that such an opportunity is unique, the lesson to search for complementary goals holds (Lacity, Willcocks, and Feeny, 1995).

Incremental implementation   Incremental implementation is the phased delivery of a system. The benefits of incremental implementation include verifying user requirements, verifying system design, capitalize on learning, demonstrating value to secure management approval for full-scale implementation, or gaining user acceptance of the system, (Janson and Smith, 1985; Naumann and Jenkins, 1982). We saw evidence that Silicon Inc.'s incremental implementation served to keep senior managers and users interested in the project as well as to make adjustments as learning occurred (see also Part 3 of this book).

Senior level support   As the Introduction and Chapters 1 and 2 make clear, IT research points to top management 'support' as one of the most vital critical success factors in the successful implementation of IT. In particular, IT researchers have distinguished four theoretical constructs comprising senior management's attitudes and behaviours towards IT:

1. *Project champion*: 'Champions are managers who actively and vigorously promote their personal vision for using IT, pushing the project over or around approval and implementation hurdles. They often risk their reputations in order to ensure the innovation's success' (Beath, 1991, p. 355).
2. *Project sponsor*: 'Sponsors have the funds and authority to accomplish their goals' (Beath, 1991, p. 355), (a less active and less enthusiastic role compared to a champion).
3. *Senior management participation*: 'Activities or substantive personal interventions in the management of IT' (Jarvenpaa and Ives, 1991, p. 206), (active behaviours).
4. *Senior management involvement*: 'The psychological state ... reflecting the degree of importance placed on IT' (Jarvenpaa and Ives, 1991, p. 206), (moral support).

At Silicon, the CFO served as project champion, Michael served as a project sponsor. Through their efforts, other senior managers came to support and participate on the project as needed during the development.

Close user–IS partnering   IT research in Chapters 7 and 8 demonstrated that close user–IT partnering is a critical success factor. Additionally, Mumford (1981) describes three types of user roles on project development teams:

1. *Consultative*: users are consulted about what they want, but decision-making is done by another group, typically IT.
2. *Representative*: a group of users is elected to represent the needs of their co-workers in the design process.
3. *Consensus*: users not only make decisions, but assume full responsibility for the success of the project.

Others have pointed to the significance of close user–IS partnering to project success, and the different ways in which it can be achieved (see Chapter 8; Skyrme, 1996). At Silicon, lower-level users served as representatives on the project team and higher-level users accepted responsibility for the success of the project.

IS perceived as a business investment   As at 1989 IT was largely perceived as a cost centre. However the client–server project itself came to have two drivers: not just to reduce mainframe costs, but also, more primarily, to achieve a significant business objective. Clearly, some senior managers were influential in supporting the client–server development through considerable cost rises. As the project progressed it became increasingly recognized organizationally that it was a strategic project linked intimately with business direction and operational performance. This wider recognition of the business value of IT as an investment is frequently cited in the literature as a fundamental reason why strategic projects come to be proposed endorsed and supported, despite very often fairly unclear financial cost and benefits, as in the Silicon, Inc. case (see for example Introduction and Chapter 1; Grindley, 1995; Keen, 1991; Parker, Benson and Trainor, 1989).

Anticipated versus actual costs   At the same time Silicon's project was not immune from many of the problems encountered on traditional IT projects. This was particularly the case on cost. One aspect of this was the project itself costing as much as twice the original estimates. A further aspect is how far client–server actually saves money directly. When client–server technology was first sold by vendors, it was largely paraded as a cost-saver. Thus it was widely suggested that companies could invest in the technology for about $100 000 compared to a multi-million dollar mainframe, and that the price performance curves were about 30 per cent improvements per year compared with 20 per cent for mainframe improvement. These arguments were used to rationalize the investment in client–server at Silicon – the most concrete financial justification for the project was moving off the mainframe. In terms of operating costs, the mainframe environment was costing up to $1 200 000 a year. By late 1995 Silicon, Inc. operated 15 RISC machines for only $50 000 a month. These numbers, however, included only the hardware and software investment and neglected the costs of learning the technology, maintenance, and support. These, of course, could be considerable. Thus International Data Corporation estimated that companies spent more than $800 million on client–server training out of a total training market of $6.6 billion. Another study by Forrester Research estimated that 'for a little over $500 000 over a period of one to two years, an organization can get 20 developers 100 per cent trained in client–server technologies' (Lipp, 1995, p. 58).

Aside from these points, there is still a question mark over whether client–server itself can save on organizational costs. In the Silicon, Inc. case the direct financial impact could not be clearly ascertained; as in other organizations there are probably a series of IT-related costs that are hidden, and not easily identified as relating to the costs of client–server operations (Willcocks, 1996). What is perhaps more impressive is the widespread recognition among respondents of considerable business gains that would impact on Silicon's profitability and revenues even if the contribution of client–server to this could not be isolated let alone quantified. This adds a further dimension to the rather mixed picture emerging from other studies on cost savings and business gains emerging from client–server implementations (see for example Kole, Roukas and Tate, 1995; Simpson, 1995).

Finally, it is useful to indicate some limitations of this research and some possible future directions. Clearly, research into one case study acknowledged as a success could be counterbalanced by further work looking at those considered failures. A wider, multiple case study approach taking into account a variety of sizes of project and outcomes could also produce some rich comparison, and, indeed this is the direction of our own future research in this area. Furthermore one would welcome more detailed work on the degree to which client–server has distinctive characteristics that make its implementation more, or less difficult, to achieve. Our research here is detailed in many places, suggestive in some others, but as yet there are all too few in-depth studies that investigate this potentially very rich, and useful, direction.

REFERENCES

Allen, L. (1995) 'Client/Server Q&A', *Mortgage Banking*, **56**, (2), November 1995, pp. 95–96.

Attachmate Corporation (1995) 'How to Revitalize Host Systems for Client/Server Computing', *Datamation*, June 1, S1–24.

Bachteal, P. and Read, J. (1995) 'Client/Server Solutions', *CA Magazine*, **128**, (9), pp. 41–43.

Beath, C. (1991) 'Supporting the Information Technology Champion', *MIS Quarterly*, **15**, (3), pp. 355–373.

Benbasat, I., Goldstein, D. and Mead, M. (1987) 'The Case Research Strategy in Studies of Information Systems', *MIS Quarterly*, September, pp. 368–386.

Bochenski, B. (1994) *Implementing Production-Quality Client/Server Systems*, Wiley, Chichester.

Cole, B. (1995) 'SAS Redefines Approach to Data Warehousing', *NetworkWorld*, **12**, (49), December 4, pp. 29, 32.

Collins, T. (1996) 'NWW Backtracks on £235 m. Project', *Computer Weekly*, March 7, pp. 1,4.

Computer Weekly (1996) *Client/Server Report and Directory*, Interactive Information Services, London.

Cox, J. (1995) 'Client/Server is Pricy but Effective', *NetworkWorld*, **12**, (49), December 4, pp. 29, 32.

Edwards, B. (1996) 'The Project Sponsor', In Earl, M. (ed.) *Information Management: The Organizational Dimension*, Oxford University Press, Oxford.

Eisenhardt, K. (1989) 'Building Theories from Case Study Research', *Academy of Management Review*, **14**, (4), pp. 532–550.

Feeny, D., Earl, M. and Edwards, B. (1996) 'Organizational Arrangements for IS: The Role of Users and Specialists', In Earl, M. (ed.), *Information Management: The Organizational Dimension*, Oxford University Press, Oxford.

Forrester Research (1996) *Managing Client/Server*, Forrester Research, Boston, Mass.

Friend, D. (1995) 'Client/Server Versus Cooperative Processing', In Umbaugh, R. (ed.), *Handbook of IS Management*, Auerbach Publications, New York.

Gerber, C. (1995) 'Client/Server Price Tag: 40% of IS Dollars', *Computerworld*, **29**, (45), November 6, p. 7.

Green-Armytage, J. (1995) 'Client/Server Wins over Majority of Management', Tate Bramhalad Survey reported in *Computer Weekly*, October 12, p. 22.

Grindley, K. (1995) *Managing IT at Board Level*, Pitman Publishing, London.

Hammer, M. and Champy, J. (1993) *Re-engineering the Corporation: A Manifesto for Business Revolution*, Nicholas Brearley Publishing, London.

Henderson, J. (1990) 'Plugging Into Strategic Partnerships: The Critical IS Connection', *Sloan Management Review*, Spring, pp. 7–18.

Janson, M. and Smith, D. (1985) 'Prototyping for Systems Development: A Critical Appraisal', *MIS Quarterly*, **9**, (4), pp. 305–316.

Jarvenpaa, S. and Ives, B. (1991) 'Executive Involvement and Participation in the Management of Information Technology', *MIS Quarterly*, **15**, (2), 1991, pp. 205–227.

Keen, P. (1991) *Shaping the Future*, Harvard Business Press, Boston, Mass.

King, W. (1994) 'Creating a Client/Server Strategy', *Information Systems Management*, Summer, pp. 71–74.

Kole, A., Roukas, G. and Tate, P. (1995) 'The Real Costs of Client/ Server Computing', *Technology Managers Forum International*, New York, October.

Lacity, M. and Janson, M. (1994) 'Understanding Qualitative Data: A Framework of Text Analysis Methods', *Journal of Management Information Systems*, Spring, pp. 95–112.

Lacity, M., Willcocks, L. and Feeny, D. (1995) 'Information Technology Outsourcing: Maximizing Flexibility and Control', *Harvard Business Review*, May–June, pp. 84–93.

Lee, A. (1989) 'A Scientific Methodology For MIS Case Studies', *MIS Quarterly*, March, pp. 32–50.

Levis, J. and von Schilling, P. (1994) 'Lessons from Three Implementations: Knocking Down Barriers to Client/Server', *Information Systems Management*, Summer, pp. 15–22.

Lipp, J. (1995) 'Building Skills for Client/Server', *Business Communications Review*, **25**, (11), November, pp. 57–59.

Lyons, D. (1995) 'Controlling Client/Server Process', *InfoWorld*, **17**, (49), December 4, p. 73.

Markus, L. (1983) 'Power, Politics and MIS Implementation', *Communications of the ACM*, **26**, (6), pp. 430–445.

Mill, J. (1994) 'The Trouble with Client/Server', *Computer Weekly*, October 13, pp. 32–33.

Muller, N. (1994) 'Applications Development Tools: Client/Server, OOP and CASE', *Information Systems Management*, Summer, pp. 23–27.

Mumford, E. (1981) 'Participative Systems Design: Structure and Method', *Systems, Objectives, Solutions*, **1**, (1), pp. 5–19.

Myers, M. (1995) 'Studying the Real Cost of Client/Server Projects', *NetworkWorld*, **12**, (49), December 4, p. 34.

Naumann, J. and Jenkins, A. (1982) 'Prototyping: The New Paradigm for Systems Development', *MIS Quarterly*, **6**, (3), pp. 29–44.

Orfali, R., Harkey, D. and Edwards, J. (1994) *Essential Client/Server Survival Guide*, John Wiley, New York.

Orlikowski, W. and Baroudi, J. (1991) 'Studying Information Technology in Organizations: Research Approaches and Assumptions', *Information Systems Research*, **2**, (1), March, pp. 1–28.

Parker, M., Trainor, E. and Benson, R. (1989) *Information Strategy and Economics*, Prentice Hall, Englewood Cliffs, NJ.

Pontin, J. (1995) 'Client/Server Adoption Stalls, Study Finds', *InfoWorld*, **17**, (46), November 13, p. 34

Pontin, J. and Scannel, E. (1995) 'IBM Maps Out Future for OS/2 Warp Client and Server', *InfoWorld*, November 20, p. 16.

Renaud, P. (1993) *Introduction to Client/Server Systems – A Practical Guide for Systems Professionals*, Wiley, Chichester.

Ross, R. (1995) 'Shifting to Distributed Computing', In Umbaugh, R. (ed.), *Handbook of IS Management*, Auerbach Publications, New York.

Saarinen, T. and Vepsalainen, A. (1993) 'Managing the Risks of Information Systems Implementation', *European Journal of Information Systems*, **2**, (4), pp. 283–295.

Simpson, D. (1995) 'Cut Costs with Client/Server Computing? Here's How', *Datamation*, October 1, pp. 38–41.

Skyrme, D. (1996) 'The Hybrid Manager', In Earl, M. (ed.) *Information Management: The Organizational Dimension*, Oxford University Press, Oxford.

Smith, C. (1990) 'The Case Study: A Useful Research Method for Information Management', *Journal of Information Technology*, **5**, (2), pp. 123–133.

Tayntor, C. (1994) 'New Challenges or the End of EUC?', *Information Systems Management*, Summer, pp. 86–88.

Tebbutt, D. (1996) 'IT to the Rescue: The Thin Blue Line', *Computer Weekly*, February 29, p. 33.

Van Maanen, J. (1979) 'The Fact of Fiction in Organizational Ethnography', *Administrative Science Quarterly*, **24**, (4), pp. 539–550.

Wagner, M. (1995) 'Firm Thrives on Client/Server Consulting', *Computerworld*, **29**, (46), November 13, p. 87.

Wagner, M. (1995) 'Holiday Inn Books Client/Server', *Computerworld*, **29**, (47), November 20, p. 6.

Walsham, G. (1995) 'Interpretive Case Studies in IS Research: Nature and Method', *European Journal of Information Systems*, **4**, (2), pp. 74–81.

Walsham, G. and Waema, T. (1994) 'Information Systems Strategy and Implementation: A Case Study of a Building Society', *ACM Transactions on Information Systems*, **12**, (2), pp. 150–173.

Willcocks, L. (1995) *Collaborating to Compete: Towards Strategic Partnerships in IT Outsourcing?* Oxford Institute of Information Management Research And Discussion paper 95/4, Templeton College, Oxford.

Willcocks, L. (1996a) 'Does IT-enabled Business Process Re-Engineering Pay Off? Recent Findings On Economics and Impacts', In Willcocks, L. (ed.), *Investing in Information Systems: Evaluation and Management*, Chapman and Hall, London, pp. 171–192.

Willcocks, L. (1996b) *Investing in Information Systems: Evaluation and Management*, Chapman and Hall, London.

Willcocks, L. and Currie, W. (1995) *Does Radical Re-engineering Really Work? A Cross-Sectoral Study of Strategic Projects*, Oxford Institute of Information Management Research Report RDP 95/8, Templeton College, Oxford.

Willcocks, L. and Griffiths, C. (1994) 'Predicting Risk of Failure in Large-scale Information Technology Projects', *Technological Forecasting and Social Change*, **47**, (1), pp. 1–23.

Yin, R. (1989) *Case Study Research: Design and Methods*, Sage, London.

APPENDIX TO CHAPTER 14: INTERVIEW PROTOCOL

Table A14.1   People to interview

Subscript	Senior level IT manager	IT manager/staff member involved in client–server implementation	Senior business manager for whom the client–server was built	Supervisor of users of client–server application
	(Robert)	(David and John)	(Michael)	(Steven)
Generic interview script	X	X	X	X
Motivation for client–server project	X	X	X	X
Outcome of client–server project	X	X	X	X
Objective information	X			
Perceptions of IT within organization	X	X	X	X
Technical issues		X		
Project management issues	X	X		

Generic interview script

Specify goal of the research to the participant:
The goal of this research is to identify critical success factors for implementation of client–server technology. Even companies who consider their client–server projects as generally successful, often identify things they would do differently next time. We hope to extract the lessons your company learned while developing and implementing C–S technology.

Note: if talking to someone knowledgeable on C–S: During the course of the interview, we will be asking you to explain your *own* perceptions and interpretations of client–server projects in your organization.

Note: if talking to a senior business person: We want to talk to you about the role of IT within your industry and company, because we suspect that client–server projects add more value in some industries than others. During the course of the interview, we will be asking you to explain your *own* perceptions and interpretations of IT's role within your organization in general, and if you have first-hand knowledge, your view of client–server projects.

Explain the confidentiality policy:
We tape record the interviews for our own research purposes but only we will review the transcripts. We do not publish these transcripts or identify you or your company. To put your mind at ease, we will give you a copy of our confidentiality agreement. You may have the tapes back after six months if you wish. The output of our research will be general lessons learned from the companies we study.

Administer the confidential agreement to the participant
Do you have any questions before we begin?
We first need to ask you some questions about yourself:
Participant information:

- Job title
- Years in current position
- Years in company
- Previous positions held

What role, if any, did you play in the sponsoring, development, or implementation of client–server technology?

Note: if the participant doesn't know anything about the client–server project per se, administer the questions from: Perceptions of IT within organization

Else ask: We are primarily interested in your version of the story of your company's experiences with client–server technology. Most participants feel comfortable providing an historical account, beginning with who conceived and sponsored the project, how the project was justified, sold within the organization, how it was developed, implemented, and subsequently accepted (or rejected) in the organization. The more descriptive you can be the better.
(Note: Participants usually respond well to this question and will likely talk at length. It is usually best to only interrupt to ask for specific examples. Whenever the respondent gives a platitude, ask for a specific example to illustrate the point. At the end of his/her dicussion, ask the participant to cover any of the following points which may have been absent from the story).

Motivation for the client–server project

Sponsorship

Who sponsored this project? What do you think was the sponsor's reasoning for investing in this project?

- Discovered a legitimate business use of C–S
- Bandwagon: mimicry; coercion; norms
- Experiment
- Consultant or trade-press sell job
- Vendor push, perhaps software driven
- User pull
- Part of a business process re-engineering (BPR) effort (This may lead to many questions).

If part of BPR, explore this issue with the goal of being able to categorize:

- Level 1: Localized exploitation of technology to existing business processes
- Level 2: Internal integration of IT capabilities across an entire existing business process
- Level 3: Use of IT as a lever for designing an organization's core processes
- Level 4: Exploitation of IT to redesign processes extending beyond one organization to a network of organizations
- Level 5: Use of IT to redefine the organization's business scope

How was the project justified? With traditional measures?

How was the project budgeted? With traditional budgets or slack resources?

Was this project treated differently than other IT projects?

Would you say that the sponsor perceived this project as possessing high or low risk?

Outcome of the project

Would you characterize this project as a resounding success, a qualified success, or a failure? Why? Are there any objective measures of success? If so, what are they?

Do you think senior management holds this same perception? What is their perception based upon?

Would you characterize senior management's expectations of client–server as realistic or unrealistic? Why?

Do you think users perceive the project as successful? What is their perception based upon?

Would you characterize user's expectations of client–server as realistic or unrealistic? Why?

Do you have any feel for the tangible and intangible costs of this project? (projected and actual cost)

- Training IT and users
- Organizational learning
- Investment in hardware and software
- Unstable technology
- Loss of business critical data
- Support costs

What do you perceive as the tangible and intangible benefits of the system?

- Organizational efficiency and effectiveness
  - Facilitate (easy to do) cross-functional work groups (or are users all localized?)
  - Quickly enables the creation of cross-functional work groups?
- Potential cost savings
  - Downsizing from mainframe
- Software issues
  - Flexibility for users to develop own applications
  - Access to better software

What do you perceive as the critical factors associated with client–server applications?

Perceptions of IT within the organization
What critical events have affected your industry in the past five years?
How has your company reacted to these events?
What is your company's current competitive positioning within the industry?
Does IT currently contribute to this positioning?
In general, how would you characterize your company's use of IT?
- Industry leader/close follower/middle of the pack/somewhat behind/laggard
What are your perceptions of IT?

- A support function, cost minimization as the primary agenda
- A support function, service excellence as primary agenda
- A valued core competency?
- An enabler of business transformation?

Do you feel your organization is getting value for the money spent on IT?
Do you know if you spend more or less on IT than your competitors?
How did you formulate that perception?

What do you think senior management's perceptions of IT are?

- A cost to be minimized?
- A valued support function?
- A valued core competency?
- An enabler of business transformation?

What do you think senior management's perceptions of IT performance is based on?

- Personal experience with IT?
- Benchmarks?
- User surveys?
- Talking to people outside the organization like peers in the industry or consultants?
- Talking to people within the organization?
- Trade press?

Would you characterize senior management's expectations of IT performance in general as realistic or unrealistic?

How would you characterize the relationship between the senior IT manager and senior management along a scale of 1 to 5, 1 being a trusting, fertile, synergistic and comfortable relationship, 5 being a very poor relationship.

What do you see as the biggest challenge facing the senior level IT manager?

In what ways are he or she meeting this challenge?

In what ways does he or she still have a way to go before meeting this challenge?

If talking to senior manager: Do you have a vision or specific plan for IT over the next five years?, ten years? How long have you had this vision?

How would you characterize users' satisfaction with the IT department:

- Highly satisfied with service levels and costs.
- Highly dissatisfied with service level and costs
- Somewhere in between?

What is your company's future competitive positioning in this industry?

What role, if any, will IT play in your company's future positioning?

Technical issues

Functional description of the C–S system/application:

Name of the system/application

How many servers?

How many clients? (users)
What applications run on the C–S?

- Transaction processing
- EUC (WP, spreadsheets, graphics)
- Communication (EMAIL)
- Decision support systems/expert systems
- Group decision support systems (LOTUS NOTES; PLEXIS; WINDOWS for Workgroups)
- Executive information systems
- CAD/CAM/process control

Relationship to legacy systems:

- Provides terminal capabilities with a GUI interface to mainframe systems
- For queries only? for updates?
- Migration from legacy system off the mainframe
- What was the rationale for distributing various components?
- Totally new business application

Characterize the level of distribution of the C–S:

C–S Components:	Local: desktop machine	Distributed: any server
Interface	#	#
Business rules (programs)	#	#
Data	#	#

Note: ascertain whether the three components, if distributed, reside on the same server.

How does this system support business objectives?
Users of the C–S system versus legacy systems
Number of current users
Number of planned users
Who formulates access privileges? What is the rationale?
Who is responsible for maintaining the integrity of the data?
Who is responsible for training users?
Characterize user training: hours, formal/informal, customized/generic, frequency offered
Percentage of current users trained

Technical description of the system

\# of MIPS
\# of transactions per day
Client operating system (DOS; MAC OS; UNIX)
Server operating system (WINDOWS NT; Novell Netware; UNIX; IBM VM, MVS)
Client–server application development tool (POWERBUILDER; UNIFACE; SAP; ORACLE FORMS; EDA SQL)

How was the decision made to select this software? Are these corporate wide standards?
Do you have corporate standards for hardware and software
Formal/informal
Driver: connectivity, costs, flexibility, interoperability
Developed by whom?
Enforcement in general
Enforcement on the project

Project management issues
Development of the system:
Year
In-house/grass roots
Number of IS team members

Project teams:
What criteria was used to select team members? (High flyers/losers)
How were teams organized?
Who/how were teams evaluated and rewarded?

System development methdology:
Traditional SDLC,
Prototyping
Trial and error

System design issues: Do you match user interface with task characteristics? (GUI versus Pre-specified screen layouts)

Did users participate in development, if so how?
Did you hire consultants, if so, what for?
Projected and actual development time
Implementation issues:
Did anyone resist implementation?
Data ownership and sharing issues (turf protection)
Why? How did you address this?

Support of the system:
Number of people allocated to support system
Is the nature of this support different in terms of roles, responsibilities,

or procedures from the support of legacy systems?

Are there any planned enhancements?

What are the major problems so far? How are they being addressed?

Even successful C–S projects have problems – what were the major challenges that arose during this project?

How were these challenges handled? If your organization had to do it over again, what would it do differently?

(Objective information needed only once)

Company description:

Market share

What are you company's primary products or services?

Can you generally describe or draw your organizational structure or provide a copy of an organization chart?

Number of employees

Annual reports

IT organization

Can you generally describe or draw an IT organizational structure or provide an organizational chart?

How do you think this structure enhances or hinders communication between users and IS? Between senior management and IS?

Can you estimate the IT budget in absolute dollars or percentage of revenue?

How many people comprise the IT staff?

How is IT accounted for? Overhead? Profit Centre?

How do you charge users for IT? (describe the chargeback system)

In general, can you characterize your information systems planning process? Do you think this process can be improved to better align IS strategy with overall business strategy? (Was the C–S project included in this process?)

Size in terms of MIPs and location of data centres

Estimate the number of PCs/terminals

Do you outsource any IT activities, if so, what?

In general, what are the core proficiencies of your IS staff? As related to the C–S project, what are the core proficiencies of your IS staff?

In general, what are the major skills of your IS staff that you would like to be improved? In relation to C–S, what are the major skills of your IS staff that you would like to see improved?

CHAPTER FIFTEEN

The Internet as a Strategic Resource: Evidence from the European Retail Sector

JONATHAN REYNOLDS

INTRODUCTION

The strategic importance and viability of electronic channels to market has been a continuing subject of debate amongst retailers and marketers for over 20 years (Quelch and Takeuchi, 1981; Reynolds and Davies, 1988; Hoffman and Novak, 1995; Quelch and Klein, 1996). The recent emergence in the 1990s of the Internet into the popular consciousness has encouraged the proponents of electronic commerce to argue that the appropriate technical vehicle has, at last, arrived. Certainly, the exponential growth of the phenomenon has led to an unprecedented level of rhetoric over likely changes in industry structure and over future market size and share. But, of course, as discussed in the Introduction of this book, there can be considerable discontinuities between such rhetoric, the capability of the technology, how it is used, and whether the outcome is an underpinning of an organization's strategic direction.

In this chapter we seek to anchor this debate in evidence on the promise, capabilities and use of the Internet in a leading economic sector. We critically review the extent to which European retailers have sought to involve themselves in the use of the Internet for a variety of purposes. The chapter is based upon a series of interviews and site visits conducted during the early part of 1996. The research suggests that European retailers need to be aware of:

- the very different characteristics and requirements of electronic channels to market;

- the very varied picture of experience, barriers and opportunities across Europe; and
- the potentially wide range of positioning opportunities available.

In considering opportunities for electronic commerce, we argue that the primary decision for a retailer is to determine whether its marketing assets are directly transferable to an electronic channel. If this is shown to be achievable, then the next key decision is whether any Internet presence is to be purely informational or transactional in nature. This distinction is a critical one. To assist retailers in evaluating opportunities and positioning themselves appropriately in the electronic channel, we provide a series of frameworks against which a retailer's level of sophistication in relation to its Internet presence and content can be assessed.

We believe that practice is, as ever, more complex and ambiguous than technologists would have us believe (Kelly, 1994). It is easy to advocate caution, but we nevertheless argue that retailers must be wary of embracing an electronic channel simply because others are. As one senior retail manager commented:

> There is an element of keeping up with the Joneses here. None of us wants to be left behind just in case the whole thing unexpectedly goes up like a rocket.

Retailers seeking to invest in Internet ventures need to devote as much (if not more) care and attention to researching and understanding the market, to the design and crafting of their offers and to their skills and capabilities in delivering the offer as they would in the development of more conventional physical storefronts. We would suggest that a similar argument can be applied beyond the retail sector to any organization seeking to utilize the Internet as a strategic resource.

NEW CHANNELS TO MARKET

The proponents of electronic commerce are correct insofar as market conditions are more favourably disposed towards electronic channels than ever before. European-wide trends towards *market fragmentation* suggest that channels to markets which permit the more careful targeting of identifiable market segments (as electronic channels do) will represent considerably more efficient business development strategies for retailers (Mueller-Heumann, 1992). Retailers are already responding to increasingly fragmented markets through technology with attempts to generate more information about their customers' behaviour, through database marketing and loyalty scheme initiatives.

Fragmentation of markets is paralleled by *media fragmentation* with a proliferation of promotional choices available (see Figure 15.1). Electronic promotional channels in principle provide unrivalled opportunities for switching from a model of one-to-many to one-to-one marketing communications: for immediate feedback on marketing plans and for closer monitoring of consumer behaviour. The combination of combined media and market fragmentation is an increasing complexity of potential purchase decisions for the consumer, the resolution of which is itself a retail marketing opportunity. Finally, the generational effects working to ensure that significant groups of young people are sensitized to and comfortable with technologies, which are increasingly converging in their specifications and functions, and which provide a degree of *technical change* which is wholly favourable to the success of electronic channels to market (see Figure 15.2).

Over 9.4 million computers were linked to the Internet 'network of networks' worldwide in January 1996, representing a 95 per cent increase on the previous year (Network Wizards 1996, http://www.nw.com/ – see also Figure 15.3). With a single host computer supporting anything from a single to a thousand users, estimates of total numbers of users connected vary up to 30 million worldwide.

At the time of writing while the US dominates, Europe now has some 23 per cent of connectivity. The Internet's functional

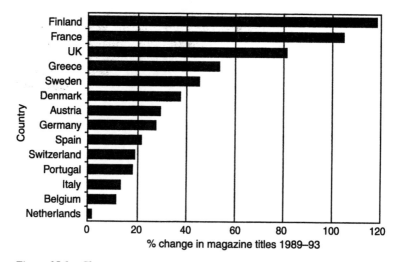

Figure 15.1   Change in major magazine titles, Europe 1989–93 (Source: Oxford Institute of Retail management, 1996, adapted from NTC; Young and Rubicam Media in Europe)

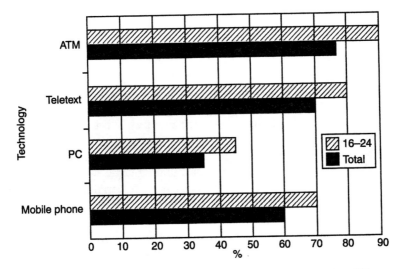

Figure 15.2   Percentage of respondents feeling confident about using different technologies (Source: Henley Centre Planning for Social Change Survey, 1996)

characteristics consist of:

- electronic mail;
- file transfer and remote computer login facilities;
- discussion groups;
- multi-player games and communications systems; and
- global information access and retrieval systems, largely by means of the worldwide web (WWW).

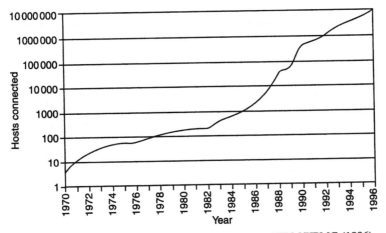

Figure 15.3   Internet domain survey, 1996 (Source: OXIRM/KPMG (1996), adapted from Networks Wizards, 1996)

It is this final function which has been largely responsible for the extensive growth of hosts and of commercial interest. Commercial hosts now outweigh educational connections worldwide.

However, despite the phenomenal growth of the Internet as 'A set of common protocols, a physical collection of routers and circuits, distributed resources and even a culture of connectivity and communications' (Hoffman *et al.*, 1996), much of the debate still centres around the medium's strategic *potential* rather than its actual performance, accessibility and content. There is little in the way of robust forecasting or modelling of such a very recent phenomenon.

The key to understanding the potential strategic attraction of an Internet channel to market for retailers is the emerging user profile: hitherto hard-to-reach but very desirable market segments. While much of the research evidence is US-oriented, what European evidence exists confirms that while 'use of the Internet has been largely confined to a technically-minded business audience who have ready access to PCs' (OXIRM/KPMG, 1996), as PC ownership spreads more widely through European domestic markets, it is the level of educational attainment which appears the fundamental demographic driver of WWW access and activity. In terms of lifestyle groups active on the Internet, SRI's *actualizers* ('individuals characterized by higher incomes and educational levels') and *experiencers* ('innovative, stimulation-seeking and fashionable young people') are most prominent (http://future.sri.com). However, these segments are among the most demanding and sophisticated in their use of conventional retail channels and therefore potentially provide a significant marketing challenge to retailers on the Internet.

REVIEWING CURRENT PRACTICE

Current practice refers here to the late 1996 period. The US is often cited as a reliable predictor of a future European retail environment. Despite the US origins of the Internet and the global nature of the phenomenon and the best efforts of the European Commission, our research shows that the European experience of the Internet and retailers' exploitation of it is very much a patchwork quilt affair. Europe is developing in a relatively piecemeal way and in many ways differently from the US. As Figure 15.4 shows, Internet penetration and usage varies widely between countries, as does retailers' degree and sophistication of use.

This is not simply a question of different stages of development, although southern European countries, by and large, do lag behind northern and western Europe in their experimentation with electronic

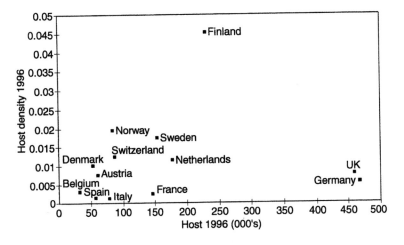

Figure 15.4   European Internet host density (Source: RIPE/NCC, 1996)

channels, in much the same way as these countries exhibit rather different conventional retailing structures. In a number of countries, the Internet is not perceived as the only, or indeed the most attractive, choice by many retailers. (In France, of course, Minitel has been the dominant electronic channel for several years. However, current IT investments by retailers such as Quelle and Ahold in Germany and the Netherlands and La Redoute in France are devoted as much to CD-ROM and CD-I as to Internet routes to market). There is considerable debate over the technical obstacles to widespread domestic Internet usage in these countries, particularly over bandwidth (or speed of connection), as well as over the likely profitability of the channel for retailers. This is much less the case in the UK, for example, where there has been considerable experimentation with retail web sites, and much less work with CD-ROM. In addition to this is the extensive interest in European-oriented home shopping channels, particularly in Germany, Italy and France, which has come rather later than in the US. There, HSN and QVC established a relatively small but stable share of the retail market before exponential Internet growth was triggered. The consequence is that retailers in European countries have a variety of choices to make over channels at similar stages in development and by no means all are convinced that the Internet channel is the correct, or only, channel to market worth backing.

In seeking to exploit opportunities on the Internet, European retailers are faced with a proliferation of interested parties, working at various levels in an attempt to provide the infrastructure and network support facilities required to enable value-added information providers to function effectively. Strategic alliances characterize the classic business development model in this industry and retailers must take care to evaluate the comparative strengths and weaknesses of the competing alliances which are now seeking to dominate domestic network connectivity across Europe. The growth of network service providers (which include US online service providers like AOL and CompuServe as well as national telecom companies such as BT and France Telecom), in particular, provides a confusing choice of prospective partners.

Summarizing current practice by retailers across Europe at present is a complex, dynamic and somewhat serendipitous activity. This is largely because the Internet is an inherently passive marketing medium: the user often discovers services by chance and, in many ways, this is part of the attraction. The market is also characterized by experimentation, rapid development and equally rapid degradation and abandonment.

The best developed markets tend to possess more sophisticated directory and indexing services. The most active of the larger countries by far is the UK with an estimated 300 retail sites (excluding 150 computer hardware and software suppliers/retailers), followed by the Netherlands (three malls and nearly 50 stand alone sites) and Austria (source http://www.ukdirectory.co.uk/shop). Nearly every country in Europe had at least one major retail chain pioneering a web site: in Italy, La Rinascente; in Spain, El Corte Inglés; in Austria, Quelle; in France, FNAC, Decathlon and Virgin Retail; in the UK, Tesco and J Sainsbury. Only in Ireland, Belgium and Norway appear to have little if any retail presence. However, other organizations are also providing or hosting retail services: Barclays Bank in the UK, media group Bertelsmann, through its link-up with AOL in Germany; software house Conteste in Portugal; manufacturer Benetton in Italy. Established direct response players, notably the mail order houses, have also generally provided larger and more sophisticated sites (Quelle, Wehkamp). Greater innovation has been exhibited by those retailers already seeking to meet conventionally the needs of Internet target market segments (Virgin, Levi Strauss, Body Shop, Benetton). However, the nature of the medium means that Internet presence, style and content can be easily emulated and first-mover advantages based purely upon presence can be easily and quickly eroded. We deal with three example countries (Germany, France and the UK) in more detail below.

COUNTRY STUDIES

Germany

German retailers appeared to have been thrown onto the defensive by recent suggestions that the growth of electronic commerce posed a threat to conventional retail channels. The original remarks were attributed to Michael Fuchs, president of the country's Wholesale and Foreign Trade Association. Speaking at the end of March 1996, he claimed that Germany's customers were using the Internet to find lower prices for their goods worldwide.

Where once a German company would offer to supply goods abroad at a given price and be fairly sure of winning the order, it was now likely to find the potential customer quoting more competitive prices from perhaps five other suppliers and putting it under pressure to improve its terms.

Retailers were also vulnerable, he suggested, because a shopper with a credit card can sit at their terminal and order goods from anywhere in the world. The German Retail Association was already on record (October 1995) as taking a dim view of home shopping, believing that it would not even reach one per cent of the German retail market by the end of the century. The group's secretary has been quoted as saying that:

. . . home shopping lacks the soul that is present when you go shopping

(Hubertus Tessar)

This is not the view of analysts and commentators. It has even been suggested that it is no accident that countries with more restrictive conventional shopping hours have a high proportion of retail sales going through conventional non-store channels. Germany had twice the estimated per capita direct mail sales of the UK in 1995 and still in late 1996 had among the most restrictive trading legislation for conventional retailing across Europe, although there has been considerable debate underway over reform and liberalization. In the meantime, by 1996 German mail order groups were comprehensively exploring the potential of electronic channels. Quelle now (1996) has major investments in the three major electronic routes to market: home shopping channels (through the joint venture with Pro-7); CD-ROM (through the launch in 1995 of its disk-based catalogue) and on the Internet in Austria as well as in Germany.

Prospects for the German home shopping market seemed buoyant, according to reports produced simultaneously by research groups Datamonitor and Simba Information in April 1996. Datamonitor forecasted that Germany would be the dominant market in Europe by 2000, accounting for 50 per cent of all on-line services. Both reports pointed to the high existing level of PC penetration in Germany (estimated at 25 per cent), with 1.35 million subscribers on-line, and to the higher bandwidths potentially available through the existing cable TV network. The 1995–96 period saw substantial growth of interest in

German Internet connectivity. Much of this growth in domestic Internet usage would come from the activity of the European on-line service provider companies: AOL, CompuServe and Microsoft Network. AOL was launched in Germany, UK and France between December 1995 and March 1996. Germany has been a prime target because of its high penetration of PCs. By mid-1996 there were around 1.3 million domestic Internet subscribers in Germany. CompuServe believed that it had 100 000 subscribers in Germany.

By the end of 1996 the biggest investments were being made by AOL/Bertelsmann, the German arm of the US service provider America Online. At time of writing (late 1996) its service was a fully German operation, although its home shopping services (*Markplatz*) were poorly developed. New German retail web sites included Neckermann (www.neckermann.de) offering selected articles only; and Quelle (www.quelle.de – orders could be placed via its web site for delivery in Germany only).

France

In the case of France, *l'aventure du Minitel* had provided a useful testing ground for retailers and other service providers seeking to gauge consumer reactions and determine profitable fulfilment strategies. Yet, as at late 1996, there were remarkably few traditional retailers, other than existing mail order operations, using Minitel for anything other than informational services. (Mail order company La Redoute reported some 15 per cent of its revenues from Minitel transactions ($310 million), running at some 25 000 transactions per day).

It seems that the French Internet market has been held back significantly to date by the high penetration and levels of usage of older generation Minitel terminals. As at 1996 France had only two-thirds the number of servers of Finland, or ten times fewer per capita. While a number of French retailers had extensive services on offer through their Minitel gateways, relatively few had web sites. Among these, operators such as FNAC and Decathlon offered largely sample catalogue ranges and company history. Only recently has France Telecom announced a development route towards a hybrid Minitel/web terminal, likely to be combined with Netscape browsing capabilities, setting itself up as an Internet service provider. This has been called:

> ...the most aggressive Internet plan of any telco.
>
> (Jim Clark, Netscape)

The initiative was also undoubtedly a consequence of inexorable trends in the global market. While the 14 million French Minitel users were undoubtedly sensitized to the benefits of on-line services, and French retailers have equally been able to experiment with the economics and practicalities of electronic commerce, as at late 1996 there was a substantial transition to be effected to the emerging technical platform standard.

There has been, therefore, considerable disagreement over the likely growth of Internet commerce in France. Consultants Inteco have forecasted that well over 3.5 million French homes would have high-speed access to the Internet by 1998, with twice this number having CD-ROM drives. It suggested that those companies which have gained experience over the seven or eight years of Minitel usage would be well-placed to take advantage of this new market. But Carrefour is on record as suggesting that Internet would not necessarily be a success among the general public in France. The company commented that despite the fact that as at 1996 the Internet had over 100 000 users in France (largely acquired over the previous 12 months) only 10 per cent of accesses were made from home. (During a 1996 transport workers' strike, Internet usage by telecommuters rose by 28 per cent in ten days). Jean-Pierre Masclet, La Redoute's associate director of IT, was critical of bandwidth restrictions for domestic users and had made clear his company's preference for image and catalogue delivery via cable (by mid-1995 La Redoute's first applications were already on trial with Multicable Lyonnaise des Eaux). As at 1996, French households were already known for their concern over the cost of Minitel services. Masclet also felt that cost barriers would also impede the growth of domestic Internet connections:

I can't see people paying by the minute to look in our catalogue.

As a consequence, and unlike Les Trois Suisses, which had already made a firm commitment to its web site, La Redoute, as at 1996, had invested in catalogue distribution via CD-ROM and CDi, although it will use HTML – hypertext mark-up language – the formatting language from which worldwide web pages are constructed and a familiar interface for Internet browser users. In 1996 it even advertised its CD-ROM product on the Internet site. The choice of HTML permitted a relatively painless migration to the Internet should this prove commercially viable.

United Kingdom

Outsider the US, as at 1996, the country which had experienced the largest amount of rhetoric about the Internet and its commercial potential was the UK. In this case we have an opportunity to assess in some detail the level of activity two years into the kind of growth which the US experienced in the early 1990s. Media coverage was substantial over the 1995–96 period; a cursory search on Reuters Textline in mid-1996 revealed 11 500 stories containing the word 'Internet'.

At the end of 1995, there were over 300 retail sites on the web based within the UK (excluding computer hardware and software vendors), according the UK 'Yellow Pages' service UKDirectory (Figure 15.5). These varied from independent operators, such as Lossie Seafoods, the The Body Shop, Austin Reed and Toys R Us. Sixteen virtual shopping centres opened, including Barclays' BarclaySquare, Highland Trial (offering net access to Scottish products) and the London Mall. CompuServe opened its only customized non-US merchant service in the form of the UK Shopping Centre. Tenants included WH Smith, Dixons, Tesco and Virgin. Estimates suggest that the BarclaySquare site received more than 200 000 visitors between its opening in May 1995 and March 1996. By late 1996 most UK food retailers had an Internet presence.

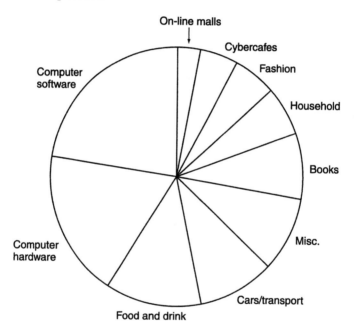

Figure 15.5   UK retail web sites, 1996 (Source: UKDirectory, 1996)

However, after the rhetoric we must address the reality. Not unexpectedly, hard data is difficult to come by so soon after the commencement of many of the schemes, but even by late 1996 early figures were not enormously encouraging. For example, after a year of trading, J Sainsbury reported that, while it was satisfied with the experience, sales of wine, flowers and – most recently – chocolate, were 'not like hot cakes'. The finance director of Argos revealed in

March 1996 that, after nine months on-line, the Argos web site had sold just 22 items, with the biggest selling product being wine racks: 'biggest-selling product in terms of, hello, we have sold more than one ... we have sold about three....'. Tesco suggested that although it was happy with the response so far, it did not expect a major shift over to home shopping on the Internet, 'as everyone anticipates'.

This is not to suggest that such figures imply any kind of failure. Rather, in the Netherlands and France, and despite the large number of retail sites, it does nevertheless suggest some disagreement over medium and long-term prospects for the channel. As at late 1996 the most thoughtful retailers regarded their web sites as experiments from which to learn. Looking forward, some UK retailers were entirely pragmatic as this comment from electrical retailer Dixons shows:

> By the end of the century I would be surprised if the home sector [including all electronic channels to market] was delivering for us the equivalent in sales of one average store.... That could mean sales of up to £3 million so it could still be worth our while doing it, depending on the cost. But it will not have much impact on our high street operations.

Interflora the florists expected sales through electronic media to account for up to 1 per cent of all sales within the first year of operation. They compared it to their initial experience with telemarketing, which by late 1996 represented a substantial share of revenues. J Sainsbury were on record in *the Times* (March 27 1996) as believing that home delivery would gain between 5–10 per cent of the UK food market in the long term. (Although, as at late 1996 the company had interests in other non-store routes to market, including its role as supplier to Supermarket Direct, a London-based telephone order home shopping firm).

STRATEGIC OPPORTUNITIES FOR ELECTRONIC COMMERCE

Looking at the situation at the time of writing, namely late 1996, there are a wide variety of experiences and opportunities offered to retailers through Internet presence. This is indeed an exciting, if chaotic, environment and is likely to stretch the most creative retail talents. In determining opportunities for action and investment by European retailers, we propose that there are two basic positioning strategies: purely *informational* against more *transactional*. Our view is that there are some key opportunities for European retailers related to these strategies within the market into the next century:

Informational

- The opportunity to better inform the consumer's buying decision (by clarifying choice in the emerging transactional environment).
- The opportunity to better understand the needs of an increasingly sought-after market segment.
- The opportunity ultimately to build brand presence at an early stage in a new and potentially powerful distribution channel.

Transactional

- The opportunity to use existing skills to develop value-added retail products and services specifically designed for the electronic environment.
- The opportunity to make shopping for essential goods easier (by substituting home-based ordering and delivery of distress items and countering the disliked aspects of essential shopping activity).
- The opportunity to improve the quality of the non-essential shopping trip (by providing additional choice within the home).

We have touched upon certain challenges and caveats surrounding different categories of web presence, but we have yet to review formally the obstacles to retail presence on the Internet. To what extent are the retailer's competencies aligned with the needs of electronic channels to market (one-to-one relationships and customized individual delivers, for example)? European retailers have already made it clear that they have a set of anxieties about establishing an Internet presence. The top four concerns in 1995, according to a report by Hoskyns CGS (OXIRM/KPMG,1996), were:

- too few users;
- an inappropriate market segment;
- inadequate financial security; and
- lack of delivery infrastructure.

Perhaps some of these concerns will prove to be misplaced. The concern over payment systems, for example, is likely go be a short-term one – it is a largely technical debate driven by psychological overtones in terms of perceived consumer behaviour. We suggest that there are four categories of strategic concern for European retailers seeking to establish themselves within an Internet, web, or on-line service provider channel. These have to do with the potential lack of fit, in both economic and cultural terms, of conventional retailing within the Internet environment; concerns to do not so much with creativity, but with implementing, operating and maintaining an electronic channel to market.

The retail brand

The strength of nearly all retail brands lies in their physical manifestation through conventional store portfolios across Europe. Consumers test the values of those brands in a tangible way whenever they enter a store to purchase an item, even though the retail brand itself is a mixture of intangibles: image, reputation, word of mouth. These intangibles are in effect 'tangibilized' through the shopping experience and the service encounter.

One question which we must pose is the extent to which an established brand can be safely and durably transferred to an electronic channel. What cues do customers then use to make a judgement about the retail brand's quality? Do they rely upon their memory of the last store visit? How long can that be sustained and what can be used to replace it? How, in other words, do retailers recreate added value in an electronic environment. For example, such attributes as *quality*, *value*, and *convenience* may not only mean quite different things in an electronic channel, but may be entirely inappropriate at the global level at which they subsequently attract scrutiny. Few retailers would internationalize their conventional activities in quite such a cavalier manner.

Part of the answer has to do with image and content, just as we have demonstrated in the previous section. This is why many of the flat, low investment, information-poor sites are such risky investments for conventional retailers. Those companies with established direct mail brands are, by and large, long-established organizations which have spent decades in investing and maintaining their brands through catalogues, customer service, agents and direct marketing.

Distribution networks

The capability of a retailer to profitably fulfil transactions in the very different economics and logistics of the electronic trading environment is also open to question. Experiments with small-scale picking and packing have yet to find cost-effective technological routes to the customer. The 'distribution network' argument has been most commonly conventionally applied to grocery retailing. There is little scope in the much smaller margins of this sector to provide for the additional costs of a labour intensive, distribution-intensive process. That there are so few grocery shopping schemes extant on the high-density Minitel network, for example, is largely a consequence of the uneconomic characteristics of the logistics operation. Yet even for non-food operations, conventional retailers must put in place a cost and fulfilment structure which is diametrically opposed to conventional ones: linked to low service levels, cheap out-of-town sites and the economies of scale which accrue to contemporary distribution of retail floorspace.

Market share

While the focus of this study has been at the European level, the phenomenon of the Internet itself is essentially a global one. Substantial market shares within one set of territorial or market boundaries start to become meaningless in a global context. Fortune begins to favour truly global players. Evidence demonstrates to date that there are relatively few truly global retailers. We ask to what extent have retailers who have sought an Internet presence genuinely thought through the impact and global exposure which Internet presence brings with it? Service providers are already anticipating the need to curtail presence on request, often to a more local level of accessibility. BarclaySquare, for example, is beginning to set up different regional versions of itself to allow access by smaller players. Nevertheless, several hundred leading European retailers' home pages are now on view in markets which they would not normally consider conventionally.

Supplier relationships

Many of the truly global players are, of course, supplier companies. In the eyes of many European retailers, suppliers – rather than their conventional competitors – will become the real enemy in a game where the rules have been changed. The threat of disintermediation hangs over those who do not seek an electronic presence and, even for those who do, the question arises over whether an electronic retailer can continue to provide the same kind of buffer between their customers and their suppliers as is presently the case. In involving its suppliers directly in its Microsoft Network initiative, we must ask whether Wal-Mart is not simply providing them with the eventual means to reach customers directly, without the retailer's assistance. For those who do, without the barrier of inconvenience and physical distance to overcome, their value-added service may need to be consistently demonstrated to a sophisticated consumer to justify their intermediary role.

Finally, to assist retailers with the evaluation of their prospective Internet presence, and to help in determining what precisely constitutes *added value* in an electronic context, we propose a series of frameworks against which a retailer's positioning strategy can be judged. In summary, these can be resolved as four spectra:

1. In terms of **focus**, is the strategy targeted to the needs of a specific market segment or individual (narrowcasting) or is it undifferentiated (broadcasting)?

FOCUS

Broadcasting ——— ◆ ——— Narrowcasting

2. In terms of **dynamism**, is the strategy innovative or emulative of others?

DYNAMISM

Emulative ——— ◆ ——— **Innovative**

3. In terms of **content** is the site striking, rich, lavishly and thoughtfully-designed, or unimaginative and infrequently updated?

CONTENT

Poor ——— ◆ ——— **Rich**

4. In terms of **interactivity** is the retailer seeking to establish a set of relationships through interaction with individuals, or seeking to perform an essentially non-interactive, public relations role?

INTERACTIVITY

Non-interactive ——— ◆ ——— **Interactive**

It is possible to position general characteristics, or a service or site against each of these four dimensions, either singly or in combination. In Figures 15.6 and 15.7 we examine the relationship between *focus* and *interactivity* and between *dynamism* and *content*. A selection of retail web sites are positioned subjectively. (Hotwired is the only non-retail site identified on these charts. http://www.hotwired.com is the on-line presence of the magazine *Wired*). These matrices provide a useful mechanism for differentiating on qualitative grounds between different Internet investments.

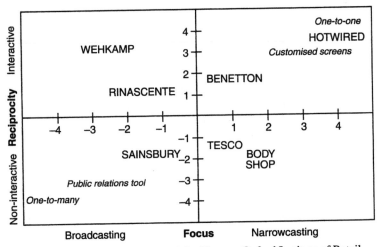

Figure 15.6   Focus versus interactivity (Source: Oxford Institute of Retail Management (1996))

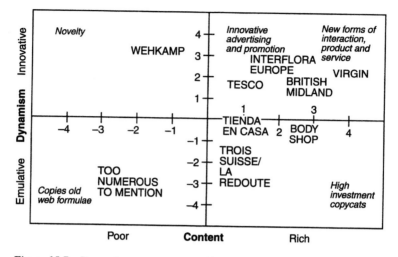

Figure 15.7   Dynamism versus content (Source: Oxford Institute of Retail Management (1996))

CONCLUSION

This chapter has sought to show that behind the rhetoric of the Internet and its associated features, serious questions are raised for conventional retailers. The Internet and its derivatives will prove an appropriate and attractive distribution channel for certain groups of consumers. Paradoxically, these groups are likely to prove among the most demanding and critical of future European consumers. While retailers have an opportunity to play a role in a digital future, this role is circumscribed most importantly by the realities of supply chain economics within the electronic channel and by other difficulties experienced in re-orienting their asset base.

A truly profitable, transactional presence on the Internet appears somewhat more problematic than many of its proponents would have retailers believe (*The Economist,* 1995; Reynolds, 1994). European retailers may not find this conclusion of itself surprising, but they should not find in it grounds for complacency. The sources of sustainable competitive advantage through new technologies remain the same as described in Chapter 3 of this book. The choice of consumers in the marketplace will be extended with or without the assistance of traditional retail organizations. The success of electronic channels to market is not likely to be determined solely by retail presence or absence and the challenge of profitable operation while a complex one, may not be avoidable in a future business environment.

REFERENCES

Henley Centre for Forecasting (1996) *Planning for Social Change Survey*, HCF, London.

Hoffman, D. L. and Novak, T. P. (1995) *Marketing in Hypermedia Computer-mediated Environments: Conceptual Foundations*. Working Paper 1, Project 2000 Research Programme. http://www2000.ogsm.vanderbilt.edu.

Hoffman, D. L. and Novak, T. P. (1995) *The CommerceNet/Nielsen Internet Demographics Survey: Is it Representative?* http://www2000.ogsm.vanderbilt.edu.

Hoffman, D. L., Novak T., Chatterjee, T. P. and Chatterjee, P. (1996). 'Commercial Scenarios for the Web: Opportunities and Challenges', *Journal of Computer-mediated Communication*; **1**, (3), (http://jcmc.huji.ac.il)

Hoskyns C. G. S. (1995). Reported in OXIRM/KPMG (1996). See below for details.

Kelly, K., (1994) *Out of Control: The New Biology of Machines*, Fourth Estate, London.

Mueller-Heumann, G., (1992) 'Market and Technology Shifts in the 1990s', *Journal of Marketing Management*, **8**, (4), pp. 303–314.

Network Wizards (1996). Website is at (http://www.nw.com).

Oxford Institute of Retail Management (OXIRM/KPMG (1996) *The Internet: Its Potential and Use by European Retailers*, Templeton College, Oxford.

Quelch, J. A. and Klein, L. R. (1996) 'The Internet and International Marketing', *Sloan Management Review*, Spring, pp. 60–75.

Quelch, J. A. and Takeuchi, H. (1981) 'Non-store Marketing: Fast Track or Slow?', *Harvard Business Review*, **58**, pp. 103–112.

Reynolds, J. and Davies, R. L. (1988) *The Development of Teleshopping and Teleservices*, Longman, London.

Reynolds, J. (1994) 'Is there a Market for Teleshopping? The Home Network Case', In McGoldrick, P. (ed) *Cases in Retail Management*, Pitman, London.

The Economist Magazine, (1995) 'The Internet – The Accidental Superhighway', *The Economist*, July 1.

RIPE/NCC (1996). Website is at (http://www.ripe.net).

UKDirectory (1996). Website is at (http://www.UKDIRECTORY.com).

CHAPTER SIXTEEN

Information Systems in Global Businesses

MICHAEL J. EARL AND DAVID F. FEENY

INTRODUCTION

In the literature of international business, a recurring theme is the need for co-ordination of operations and their management in global organizations. Such co-ordination is indeed central to the whole concept of globalization. Co-ordination of activity in order to achieve supra-national efficiencies is argued by many writers to distinguish the global business from the 'multinational' (Bartlett and Ghoshal, 1989a) or 'multidomestic' (Porter, 1986). And co-ordination in the strategic planning domain is at the heart of the 'strategic intent' which defines global businesses for Hamel and Prahalad (1989).

These authors have expanded on the nature and complexity of global co-ordination required in the successful organizations of the future. Such organizations must exhibit the simultaneous achievement of global scale, responsiveness to markets and governments, worldwide transfer of learning and innovation (Prahalad and Doz, 1987; Bartlett and Ghoshal, 1989). In place of organizational uniformity, each geographical unit will have a distinctive role within the overall business (Hamel and Prahalad, 1985; Bartlett and Ghoshal, 1989(a) and (b)). In the 'transnational' corporation of Bartlett and Ghoshal, the organization is neither centralized nor decentralized; it represents an integrated network in which there are intensive and complex interactions between physically remote but interdependent units. Clearly this takes even further the complexity and issues discussed earlier in Chapter 6.

As Porter (1986) recognizes, the ability to co-ordinate globally is seen to be dramatically increased through advances in information technology (IT). The widescale use of IT is also implicit in Bartlett and

Ghoshal's (1987) vision of the transnational as an organization in which there is 'collaborative information sharing and problem solving, co-operative support and resource sharing, collective action and implementation'. So information systems would seem to be an important component of global competitive strategy. Egelhoff (1988) has touched on this in his work on the complexity of global organizations. He has applied information processing models of organization, such as the work of Galbraith (1973), Huber (1989) and Thompson (1967) to multinational companies (MNCs) and concludes that high information processing requirements are likely and could easily be ignored in formulating international business strategies (Egelhoff, 1991). Hagstrom (1991) shows through case study research in the SKF company that information and communication flow requirements tend to grow as the multinational organization evolves.

However, there has been little empirical research done through the information systems perspective (i.e. looking at IT applications and studying the IS function[1]). Ives and Jarvenpaa (1991) executed a survey to test emergent alignment of IS management with global business strategies, but otherwise few authors so far have examined in any detail the practice of exploiting IT to enable co-ordination in a globally managed business. In this chapter we examine some of the forms in which IT may contribute, the enabling conditions, and the obstacles to success, based on case study research in four European-based corporations.

THE POTENTIAL ROLE OF IT IN GLOBAL BUSINESS MANAGEMENT

Before exploring these case studies, we sought to establish more specifically what might be the theoretical contribution of IT. The start point was consideration of the three imperatives of global operation identified above – global efficiency, local responsiveness and transfer of learning.

The search for *global efficiency* implies that the organization must be able, within each relevant function, to co-ordinate and consolidate its activity to achieve available economies of scale. A key requirement would seem to be the collection of comparative performance information from locations around the world to support decisions on how to effectively allocate resources and source requirements. This need may be facilitated by building a global data network, collecting

---

[1] We use IT to describe information technology and IS as shorthand for information systems. IS is also used to describe the information systems function. As acknowledged by the editors throughout the book, we are conscious how varied and loose terminology is in the domain.

and providing access to information which conforms to some globally applied data standards. Organizations often wish to go further, to implement standard application systems worldwide, in order to ensure the integrity of information, facilitate the transfer of activities and people, and perhaps achieve scale economies in systems development and processing. Conceptually, however, the base requirement is for the definition and communication of standard data.

Achieving *local responsiveness*, on the other hand, implies limits to standardization. The expectation is that organizations will want to identify some level of standard/core product, but also provide a variety of optional features which may be present or absent in the delivered product depending on local legal or market conditions. Thus the 'world car' or 'global TV' becomes tailored to suit the requirement of each market segment – 'glocalization'. in the vernacular. Global IT investment to support this environment may include production scheduling and control systems to support the management of high variety; IT and communications networks to facilitate the efforts of dispersed marketing/engineering/manufacturing groups who are tasked with developing the next generation of global core products or creating the required local derivatives. These capabilities will need to be planned and developed at global level, to interface with and supplement local systems which meet local needs.

The co-ordination required for *transfer of learning* would seem to be along functional dimensions, across multiple locations involved in research and development, marketing, service etc. Communication networks supporting informal dialogue among professionals are the obvious IT contribution, providing electronic mail, and computer and video conferencing facilities. Construction of globally accessible knowledge bases or knowledge systems may follow, as examples of best practice or scarce expertise are recognized and codified for distribution to others who can use or build upon them.

Finally, the potential IT contribution may be extended if the organization is alert to new opportunities, beyond the alignment of IT investment with established business needs in the manner described above. For example, Ghoshal (1987) has described how an organization may extend its economies of scope through *external alliances* between companies with different skills and cultures. Inter-organizational IT systems can provide new opportunities to operationalize this concept: in the vertical dimension, Benetton, the Italian clothing retailer use IT to support what Johnston and Lawrence (1988) call 'value adding partnerships' with manufacturers and retailers; in the horizontal dimension, Konsynski and McFarlan (1990) have described the global 'information partnerships' between airlines, hotel chains, and car rental companies.

Figure 16.1 summarizes these propositions on the potential contribution of IT to the pursuit of global business strategies. It served as a framework for analysing the history, current use and development of global information systems in our case study companies. The ideas it contains seem straightforward enough, but we were already aware from prior work with global businesses of a significant gap between the propositions and common practice. While this gap might be merely a function of deficiencies in the framework, an alternative explanation was that global information systems represent difficult organizational and implementation problems. Consequently, IT organization and management issues became a particular focus of our fieldwork.

Business imperative	IT contribution
Global efficiency	Data networks Data standards Common systems
Local responsiveness	Production systems to manage variety Networks to support collaborative development
Transfer of learning	Functional communications networks Knowledge bases/systems
Global alliance	Interorganizational systems

Figure 16.1   Global information systems

THE RESEARCH DESIGN

Given the complexity and emerging nature of the global business field, it was our view that a large-scale empirical study was inappropriate at this stage. Instead we sought to build insights into the reality, potential, and problems of IT contribution through in-depth investigation of a small number of businesses which were known to have pursued global management capabilities over a number of prior years.

Four such businesses were selected, to represent a variety of global business contexts and potential co-ordination needs. For the first, in re-insurance, transfer of learning was the primary global driver. For the second, in electronics, supra-national economies of scale in R&D and manufacturing were paramount. In the white goods industry our case study business was among those promoting global competition, seeking out economies of scale and scope while maintaining responsiveness to residual heterogeneity between national markets. By contrast, in the chemicals industry, the product was already a global commodity – but our case study business had set out to improve responsiveness in an industry traditionally organized to achieve efficiency. Figure 16.2 illustrates the approximate positioning of the case study businesses on the familiar efficiency/responsiveness grid. It demonstrates that we were examining a mix of stable and evolving industry positions, but in all four cases there was some level of attempt to simultaneously achieve global efficiency and market responsiveness – and indeed the transfer of learning. In this sense each business aspired towards the transnational positioning of Bartlett and Ghoshal.

Our case study businesses also exhibited a mix of organizational structures, driven by a combination of business need and organizational heritage. In Figure 16.3, Porter's (1986) co-ordination/configuration

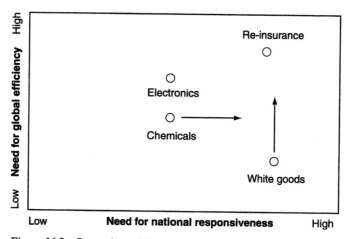

Figure 16.2   Strategic positioning of case study companies

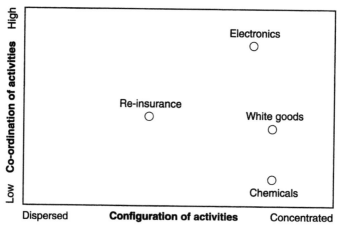

Figure 16.3   Organizational positioning of case study companies

framework is used to suggest their overall positioning in this respect. While Bartlett and Ghoshal focus on organizational capabilities required and achieved, Porter is concerned with organizational arrangements. His framework is primarily designed to explore the operation of value chain activities (an aspect we shall return to in our analysis) but it serves here to demonstrate the contrasting co-ordination/configuration patterns of our case studies.

In combination, Figures 16.2 and 16.3 confirm that our case study businesses were concerned with global management capability, beyond multinational/multidomestic operation. The need for co-ordination was implicit in at least some dimensions of their functional activities, and hence a potential IT contribution existed. Our basic questions for these businesses became:

1. What information systems (applications of IT) are in place or under development to support the global strategy of the business?
2. What IT infrastructures (networks, databases) are in place or under development to enable the desired levels of cross-border functioning?
3. How is the IT function being managed in the global context, and with what results?

To address these questions we conducted in each business a series of interviews at senior management levels, examined archival evidence of information systems evolution and plans, and sampled experience of operational activity. General management executives were interviewed to establish an understanding of industry context, business strategy, perceived and potential contribution of IT. IT management was questioned about IT history, strategy, organization and key issues. Operational management described usage of information systems in place, and experience of co-ordination needs, policies and problems. Summaries of the case studies are now provided.

SKANDIA RE-INSURANCE BUSINESS

In 1991, Skandia International – a major insurance company within the Skandia Group – operated in 18 countries with 3800 employees. Only 350 of these employees were located in Sweden, the Group's headquarters. Roughly 70 per cent of Skandia International's revenues came from the re-insurance business which was the focus of the case study. Gross premium income from reinsurance was MSEK 9341 (US$1.5 billion) in 1990, placing Skandia fourth in the world behind the giant Munich Re, Swiss Re and General Re.

The re-insurance market was seen as naturally global; large (more than $40 billion) but mature and cyclical. The market was in slow decline as direct insurers reduced their purchases of re-insurance through backward integration. Entry barriers were low ('a tough mind and a pen') so that during cyclical upturns new entrants increased rivalry and created overcapacity. In 1991 there were an estimated 1250 competitors worldwide. In this difficult market. Skandia's strategy was summarized as follows by (former) CEO Hans Dalborg:

> We strive for profitability before volume and are realigning ourselves towards areas in which we can offer clients superior services. We are focusing our efforts on advanced actuarial techniques and products as well as on administrative and consulting services. At the same time we are introducing powerful computer and communication systems while making improvements on the personnel side. Together these measures will help us keep costs in check and will give us a base for new product development. The objective is to keep volume where it is, or expand in a controlled way in areas where profit potential is very good – concentrating on technically advanced niches.

Skandia operated a relatively flat organization structure with most employees operating from a network of local offices as underwriters or support staff. Each local office was a profit centre, operating within the strategy and policies laid down by Stockholm headquarters. As can be detected from Dalborg's statement, these global policies extended beyond business goals and strategy to the field of information systems. In the words of Corporate Controller Sten Lundqvist:

> The essence of our offensive competitive strategy is to build information in a structured way over many years, and then take risk and return decisions.

A corporately developed and owned system called SARA (System for Advanced Reinsurance Assistance) tracked reinsurance treaties and conditions; accounted for and managed money flows; stored treaties, risks and claims; handled credit. SARA was available on-line at all local offices, supported by a standard set of analysis and enquiry tools. Underwriters accessed SARA for decision support, entered deals and updated the central database on-line to Stockholm. In 1991 Skandia was encouraging and co-ordinating experimental investments in expert systems, triggered by an initiative in the US, to help distribute underwriting expertise to new and dispersed staff. The database therefore was the repository of experience-based knowledge on risks, claims and prices. It was updated and disseminated to offices over the global data network. The decision support tools, some with resident expertise in them, enabled underwriters to be both responsive and shrewd in taking on risks. SARA and its related systems were thus fundamental to the global business strategy and operations of Skandia.

While IT resources and investment had reached a peak during the development of SARA, the company continued to regard IT as a strategic resource. Skandia was one of the three initiators of RINET – the value-added network being developed for information exchange in international insurance and re-insurance. Skandia set out to be a leader in improving information flows in the industry because it had an incentive to do so.

These examples demonstrate how IT was itself a globally co-ordinated function within Skandia's re-insurance business. Corporate policy vested ownership of all local equipment and support staff with corporate IS; there were globally defined technical architectures for the IT networks and applications; two preferred IT vendors were recognized worldwide, with central co-ordination of purchasing; a central register was maintained for all data and programmes. This strong co-ordination of IT in the re-insurance business was very much a conscious choice, not a chance legacy of history. A recent proposal from the US business unit to devolve IT responsibility had been firmly rejected because of the perceived business benefits flowing from existing arrangements. By contrast, IT organization for Skandia's life and general insurance business had long been decentralized, in line with the nature of those businesses which were responding to a variety of local national markets (A more detailed analysis of Skandia's strategic position can be found in Earl, 1994).

PHILIPS DISPLAY COMPONENTS

In 1991, Display Components was a major business unit within the components division of the Philips Corporation, with annual revenues of around Fl 4 billion (US$2.3 billion). With global responsibility for development and manufacture of picture tubes for TV sets and computer monitors, Philips DC employed around 19 000 in factories and offices around the world.

Like Skandia, Philips DC competed in a market that was large (100 million tubes/annum worth US$15 billion) global in nature, and relatively mature. Western Europe was the largest market area, followed by North America and Japan. Because of economies of scale in development and production competition was concentrated, with four global companies accounting for more than 50 per cent of industry output. Philips DC was the leading producer, closely followed by Toshiba and Matsushita. These same corporations were of course prominent in TV set-making, but in practice set-making and tube-producing subsidiaries operated on a trading basis with set-making plants sourcing their TV tubes from producer plants in the same region.

The market for Computer Monitors was smaller, around US$9.5 billion in 1991, but growing strongly at around 25 per cent per annum. The market was heavily concentrated in the Far East, reflecting that region's strength in microcomputer systems. Competition was less concentrated in this segment, with Philips DC perceived to be 'one of the pack'. The strategic question for Philips DC in 1991 was summarized by executive management as 'choosing where we want to be and what we want to have'. The concern was that Philips DC was too influenced by a Europe in which its dominant market share could only decline over time. Future business success was dependent on capturing market share elsewhere – particularly in the Far East which included the large Japanese TV market and the critical market for computer monitor tubes. To this end, Philips DC had a number of strengths to deploy. Its current product offering was rated (at least in Europe) as better than industry average on every customer criterion except price, and Philips were perceived technology leaders over time. Philips already had a manufacturing presence in all of the four key continental markets of the world. But three aspects of market responsiveness were identified for special attention:

1. Since success increasingly came from being the chosen partner of successful set-makers, the Philips culture needed to develop further from a technology to a customer orientation.
2. 'Closeness to the customer' must extend in a physical sense to the R&D function; poor performance in the Far East was linked to the lack of a development group based there.
3. Product time-to-market must be significantly reduced, with rapid handover from development to manufacturing despite the geographic separation involved.

Industry scale economies and globally-oriented Japanese competition had resulted in Philips DC becoming the first business to move away from the corporation's historic emphasis on autonomous national subsidiaries: during the 1980s decision-making was increasingly centralized into the Philips DC head office. However, by the end of 1991 a new organizational pattern had emerged to balance global coherence with customer responsiveness. Under this new regime, (which also reflected wider corporate changes towards profit centre autonomy, cost and quality emphases) three levels of responsibility were emphasized.

1. Business unit HQ was responsible for R&D and strategic marketing, therefore controlling the global core product stream.
2. Four geographic regions were each responsible for the manufacture, sale and distribution of the core products within their territories.

3. Each plant had a mission to manufacture and distribute one or more core products to customers in its region, tailoring core products where necessary to meet customer needs.

At the beginning of 1992 it was not clear that IT was yet anchored securely in the new organization. A number of IT studies and developments were in progress but they were not explicitly focused on global issues or the emerging global business strategy. IT resources were thinly scattered across HQ, regional, and plant levels; IT managers were rarely embedded into the key management teams at each level; DC was largely dependent for IT development and service on resources elsewhere, a legacy of the historic IT structure which was aligned to corporate, national and more recently divisional levels within Philips.

A further legacy of this structure was a set of common transaction processing systems across the corporation, notably in order processing, production planning and control, and logistics management. While the imposition of these systems in the 1970s and 1980s had caused resentment in some businesses, it did create an unusually coherent infrastructure which in principle global business units could exploit to considerable benefit. For example, Philips DC had no difficulty in taking an order from a customer anywhere in Europe and allocating it to whichever plant was appropriate. However, by 1991 a number of operational systems were due for replacement and questions were being raised over future levels of standardization: could a regional requirement for the co-ordination of logistics, for example, be met through regional data standards and local systems, or did it necessitate a common worldwide logistics system? A higher-order information management agenda was put forward by one member of the Philips DC executive management team, who believed IT had a further and critical contribution to make in four areas:

1. Enabling the co-ordination of increasingly geographically dispersed product development, based on distributed access to a consolidated design database.
2. Providing information to support the optimization of supply versus demand, across the various production sites.
3. Supporting goods flow management within the vertical manufacturing and supply chain.
4. Providing better information on global activity of competitors to management.

THE ELECTROLUX WHITE GOODS BUSINESS

With 43 factories in 15 countries and a turnover of more than US$5 billion, white goods was the dominant business of the Electrolux

Corporation in 1991. It was also a pioneer of globalization in an industry where received wisdom had held that national differences prevented products such as refrigerators and washing machines from selling across borders. Electrolux had built its global business through more than 200 acquisitions, including large units like Zanussi (1984), White (1986), and Thorn EMI Appliances (1987). These acquisitions had been energetically and rapidly integrated into a complex new organizational structure. Despite setbacks (Baden-Fuller and Stopford 1991), Electrolux had been sufficiently successful to convince others of the global potential of white goods, notably Whirlpool with its acquisition of the domestic appliance business of Philips. The industry now comprised a combination of global giants such as Electrolux, Whirlpool and Matsushita; and aggressive national/product specialists such as GEC's Hotpoint and Merloni's Ariston – though these latter companies were increasingly seeking global alliances.

Electrolux has been a case study target for others interested in international business, including Ghoshal and Haspeslagh (1989), and Lorenz (1989) who wrote a series of articles which positioned Electrolux as the epitome of Bartlett and Ghoshal's transnational organization. Features of the organizational structure for white goods in 1991 included:

1. Product divisions, responsible for development and manufacturing; each had a specific international mission, delivered through a number of dispersed sites.
2. International marketing units which each controlled a number of national and international brand names; working through nationally-based sales companies which operated an arms-length/trading relationship with product divisions.
3. Country organizations, 'headed by strong country managers' with 'primary responsibility' for all the development, manufacturing, and sales units in their territory.
4. Centralized service functions, including IT, which provided specialized expertise across the corporation.

In most respects the culture stressed decentralization, with production sites, sales units and service functions all operating as profit centres. It is clear that a number of tensions are built into such a structure, which can be pictured as a multi-dimensional matrix. But, according to Bartlett and Ghoshal, Electrolux operated not as a formal matrix but through overlay of a series of microstructured mechanisms on top of a distributed asset structure! Certainly there was little evident co-ordinating bureaucracy: rather an emphasis on a culture which expected agreement seeking, galvanized by a series of corporate strategic directives, and monitored by a small number of high-level executives such as the three responsible for international marketing. The strategy this 'impossible' organization was designed to deliver had the classic transnational components (Ghoshal and Haspeslagh, 1989):

- achieving global scale volume to ensure long-term survival;
- building/maintaining 'adequate' share in all markets through local presence and responsiveness;
- developing 'insurmountable' competitive advantage through faster development of better products by multidisciplinary design teams; and through transferring leveraging product concepts, components, manufacturing techniques across markets and borders.

The most transnational of our case studies also showed the most extensive exploitation of IT, at least in terms of the global information systems framework of Figure 16.1. The Electrolux Forecasting and Supply system (EFS) supported business-wide co-ordination of demand, production and distribution – across functions, profit-centres and national borders. A common financial reporting system provided comparative information for performance assessment. Standardization on the ODETTE protocol for electronic data interchange (EDI) allowed co-ordination of internal and external suppliers across different plants. The IT contribution to faster development was based on a common/shared CAD system; and IT was integral to the extensive investments in manufacturing automation made at the plants at Susequana and Porcia to achieve flexibility of production. Only in respect of the transfer of learning was an IT contribution less in evidence, with little apparent enthusiasm for using the electronic mail system; but the presence of a group subsidiary to supply and install all factory level automation ensured transfer of learning within that field. This alignment of IT investment with business need had been achieved even though the IT function was not formally integrated into the organization and management structure of the white goods business – as already noted IT at Electrolux took the form of a corporate subsidiary and profit centre, with minimal IT resources located in production and sales units. But a number of factors were seen to underpin its achievement:

1. White goods was (by far) the dominant customer of the IT unit, and therefore critical to its success.
2. IT initiatives consistently paralleled and evolved with major business initiatives (for example EFS was first created in support of an inventory reduction drive); this ensured the line management support required to implement tough changes such as the imposition of standard product coding.
3. The centralized nature of the IT group simultaneously ensured that a standard and coherent technical architecture was put in place as applications developed.

4. The central IT group remained lean (150 employees in a corporation of 153 000) and committed to pragmatic evolution rather than revolution; standards and new developments went no further than necessary, for example EFS interfaced with existing local order processing systems.

Overall, the IT effort at Electrolux demonstrated the focus and drive which may be considered the hallmarks of effective IS strategy-making.

EUROCHEM

In 1991 Eurochem[2] comprised four business units producing commodity chemicals with a combined turnover of around £2.3 billion. Each business unit had global responsibility for its product range. But a combination of scale and scope economies, history, health and safety and environmental factors meant the business units shared production sites. Indeed, in a common industry pattern, production sites and technologies and facilities were often shared with rival chemical companies.

The 1991 organization resulted from a series of evolutionary steps which had rationalized the acquisitions made in the 1970s and 1980s. The progressive emphasis in these steps had been to devolve from central functions into business units to increase accountability and cost control in a commodity-based industry. Most service functions had now been migrated to business unit control to establish value for money; one of the most recent changes was the devolution of the IS function. Alongside this process of decentralization, group business strategy continued to stress leadership in process technology as the route to cost advantage and market leadership. Since price was determined by market conditions, low-cost production was essential to long-term survival. However, a common ordering pattern was for customers to select a chemicals supplier to meet their forward needs during a contract period, with actual deliveries being made against call-offs, and at prevailing market prices. Therefore, in the shorter term and at business unit level customer service was an important parameter of competitive strategy.

It was a particular attempt to create a service edge that had attracted our interest in Eurochem. In 1984 the company decided to develop a new computer-based order processing system which would provide 'comprehensive facilities to manage order processing, distribution,

---

[2] The company, in the chemical sector, requested anonymity on the basis that our findings were a fair representation but captured a business in transition.

stock control, and invoicing' across the business, replacing a plethora of systems inherited through acquisition. In the classic pattern of IT innovation (Feeny and Willcocks, 1997; Runge and Earl 1988; see also Introduction and Chapter 3 of this book), the system was championed by a senior line manager in the commercial function who saw it as the solution to a business problem ('we like your products, but we can't get hold of them'); and won the support of an executive sponsor who steered the proposal through the Board. Another parallel with IT innovations elsewhere was set when the project development was put under the original champion, who contracted with external hardware and software suppliers to the exclusion of the in-house IT department. For a number of reasons, the order processing system went through an often traumatic development history, with major overruns in timescale and budget; but by 1991 the system was installed and in use across the commodity business.

Opinions of the benefits and value of the system varied widely. In the opinion of the original champion, it had not only succeeded in putting Eurochem on a par with, or ahead of, the best chemical company and distributor competition; it had also been a stimulus to the internationalizing of the company. Others were much less convinced, complaining that it was a high-cost system which would be of limited value until it became a more authoritative source of inventory and market data. More mundanely, a sales office manager opined that the system was too slow to provide the planned immediate response to customer telephone calls. Some of the specialty chemicals businesses doubted that they required this sort of system.

With the latest changes to the IS organization, the ownership of the system had been devolved from group level to the business unit processing bulk chemicals. With its thousands of customers and hundreds of products, this was the business where the system's capabilities were most relevant. The business unit agreed to provide the system service to its sister businesses, some of whom were expressing dissatisfaction with it and expressing the belief that they could find a cheaper/better alternative to meet their own particular needs. Of course, if any one business discontinued its use of the order processing system, there would be adverse cost consequences for the others. The question would also arise of whether a common system had in fact been necessary for interfacing the four businesses to the plants that served them. In short, the original rationale, the anticipated benefits and the current need for a common order processing system were not agreed across the chemical businesses.

While order processing attracted most of the attention, it was not the only common system in Eurochem. It had in fact been preceded by the creation of a management accounting database. More recently a standard maintenance and materials system had come up for consideration; but a proposed common approach to payroll had been rejected as poor value for money. There was a seemingly ever stronger profit centre focus, and an accompanying devolution of most IT resources and responsibilities to business units (a small IT policy unit remained at the centre, reporting to the controller, but subsequently this unit was closed down and an investigation initiated into how to downsize the entire IS function across the businesses). It therefore seemed unlikely that new initiatives which involved cross-business co-ordination and co-operation would either emerge or be supported.

DISCUSSION

Global alignment

Our four case study businesses demonstrate more differences than similarities, as the research design intended. But collectively we believe they illustrate that information systems are necessary to support or enable certain global business strategies. In Figure 16.4 we compare the descriptive evidence against our normative matrix presented in Figure 16.1. Different levels of investment in IS for co-ordination are evident, but each company has recognized at least some need. (The question marks represent systems not yet agreed and developed or systems which in principle could have supported a global business imperative).

| Business imperative | Investment in information systems at | | | |
	Skandia	Philips	Electrolux	Eurochem
Global efficiency	General ledger SARA re-insurance assistance system	Order processing Logistics system production Planning and control ?Supply/demand balance	EFS FCS CAD EDI	MAS ?Order processing
Local responsiveness		Order processing Logistics system ?Competitor information	EFS FMS EDI	?Order processing
Transfer of learning	SARA re-insurance assistance system Re-insurance decision support and expert systems	?Design database	?CAD	
Global alliances				

Figure 16.4   Investments in global information systems

Each type of global thrust, or business imperative, is represented except the development of global alliances. As we anticipated, companies differed in terms of their particular global strategies.

At Skandia, operating in a global marketplace, the intent was to differentiate by building and exploiting a worldwide platform of knowledge within parameters of low-cost operation. SARA and the ledger systems, therefore, support global efficiency, but more particularly SARA and its surrounding decision support systems provide transfer of learning. Our model in Figure 16.1 predicts these IS investments plus the emphasis on worldwide standards which the central IS group enforced.

Electrolux also demonstrates the model fairly well. By design and some good fortune, they have developed or acquired information systems and technologies to support the three dimensions of the 'transnational'. EFS, the financial control system, and EDI standards all facilitate the pursuit of global efficiency. EFS and EDI also provide the co-ordination to serve local responsiveness from one or two production sites. The flexible manufacturing technologies also aid responsiveness. The CAD systems provides functional co-ordination across sites to transfer design and development knowledge.

In Philips DC we find information systems present which are capable of supporting the same three transnational thrusts. However, their management team, with new and increased responsibility through the parent's decentralization programme, were only just beginning to agree the critical success factors required to operate globally and perhaps thereby agree on IS requirements. The systems inheritance in production and logistics looked promising.

Eurochem neither fits nor deviates from our model because their (global) business strategy was not clear. Organizational devolution in response to corporate business was prompting hard questions, not only about its strategy, but the appropriate structure and the requisite information systems. This is not a context in which alignment is likely to be found, nor be capable of evaluation.

Our study could have ended with the above descriptions and evaluation. We could have concluded that global business strategies are likely to benefit from or need investment in IT and IS and claimed support for our normative model of global information systems requirements. However, not all the companies were investing equally in IT and two clearly demonstrated better adjustment between IS and their global business strategy than others. Indeed, collectively, the four cases do not provide overwhelming evidence that a global IT platform is necessary to do business globally as the industry hype often claims. We offer two explanations for this situation one relatively commonplace, the other more novel.

First there needs to be a *global business vision* in place, shared among the top team. Such a vision was readily apparent at Skandia, where in a global marketplace the intent was to differentiate by building and exploiting a worldwide platform of knowledge, within parameters of low-cost operation. A vision was also in place at Electrolux, where global economies and local responsiveness were being pursued in parallel, but with a clear and consistent sense of how these goals would be achieved. The requirement was not clearly fulfilled in the other two cases. In Philips, increased responsibility and authority at business unit level had led to clarification of the nature of global competition in display tubes, and there was an emerging consensus on the consequent critical success factors. Corporate performance problems and a severe downturn in its chemicals markets had more recently impacted Eurochem: once again, organization devolution was seen to be prompting hard questions about strategy – and indeed the nature of the Eurochem group; but answers to these questions were not yet clear.

It is the gospel of consultants and many academics that before a firm can formulate its IS strategy it needs a business strategy. So the need for a global vision may be only a special case of the wider problem. Indeed it may not be just that information systems should not be forgotten in global strategy-making, as Egelhoff (1991) suggests, but more fundamentally that you cannot consider appropriate IS requirements until the vision of competitive strategy at a global level is developed and agreed. However, it is well documented that information strategists often find business strategies absent, disputed or unclear (see Introduction; also Earl, 1993). The IS function often has to work with the organization to explicate both levels of strategy, or to await for them to emerge (Earl, 1993). Consequently it is clear that whether an IS strategy is derived form a business strategy, is formulated integrally with it, or emerges by an incremental and evolutionary process, it only happens through organization.

The second condition, therefore, is that the *IS organization structure* promotes integration of business and IS strategy (see also Chapter 6). This integration was particularly clear at Skandia where the IS function's centralized structure and wide-ranging powers both enabled and reflected its role in business strategy. At Electrolux the positioning of IS as a service business and profit centre was consistent with corporate culture; and the dominance of the white goods business ensured that IS gave the highest priority to understanding and meeting its needs. We are not clear that a smaller business unit would have been equally well served by these arrangements. In contrast, our other two case study businesses were clearly handicapped by a lack of organizational integration. At Philips, years of change had left the IS function fragmented and struggling to catch up with the business unit structure; lack of IS representation on key management teams was a particular problem during a period of formative strategic thinking; and even the agreed IT initiatives were making slow progress, lacking resources and active support from business management. Finally, at Eurochem the IS function faced a major repositioning challenge. From being a group level function with executive support for development of the order processing system, it had to migrate to business unit level, where doubts about its contribution and performance had always existed. But unless it repositioned quickly and successfully, it would be unlikely to make much contribution to the group's new thinking and development.

The importance of a shared business vision and alignment/integration of the IS function may, then, seem simple or obvious propositions. However, it is not unusual for quite different issues to be emphasized by writers on global IS management. For example, McFarlan (1992) has referred to disparity of standards in equipment provision and service around the world. We would suggest that this is no more than a technical, operational issue, the IT equivalent of the controller's need to handle multi-currency accounting. As in other functional areas perhaps, the challenging issues are managerial and organizational. In the case of IT and IS, however, there is undue complexity because information and information systems not only cross national borders, but operate between functions, business units, profit centres, and sites. This is the inevitable corollary of the role of information systems in global businesses being that of co-ordination. Information management, as we discuss below, has to cross many levels and borders of the organization.

Information management in the global business

The need for alignment between business and IT organizations has already been noted in the global context by Ives and Jarvenpaa (1991), but this was a top-level mapping, associating different configurations of IT and IS with the different globalization categories of Bartlett and Ghoshal, namely international, multinational, global and transnational. Beneath these labels, and in contrast to the neat and tidy configuration implied by the familiar strategic business unit (SBU) of the 1980s, the organizational arrangements for global business management are both varied and complex. Whereas the global business unit (GBU perhaps) in principle has the characteristics of the SBU – product homogeneity, market delineation, identity of competitive forces, strategic control of resources – the four case studies demonstrate how organizational forms may vary as these ideas are played out across national borders. In Skandia Re-insurance, there is a relatively simple and single line of business, a centre-driven strategy, profit centre discipline, and a hub and spoke configured organization. By contrast Electrolux dub themselves 'an impossible organization but the only one that works'. The organization is multi-dimensional, with different market, product, functional and geographic axes, overlaid by a strong profit centre control architecture. It can be sensibly described at the level of the white goods business, but in reality it comprises many interacting entities and its operation relies on myriad boundary-crossing activities and mechanisms. Meanwhile, in Philips and Eurochem, organizational history has left complicating legacies which hinder the working out of a neat and tidy configuration. The GBU, then, is apparently a complex phenomenon with which to achieve alignment.

The four case study businesses were all moving towards the transnational model of Bartlett and Ghoshal (1989), which involves simultaneous pursuit of several global capabilities. One consequence suggested by these authors (and by Porter, 1986, and others in the history of international management) is that the organizational design of functions becomes critical: each function may have to be designed differently, dependent on which global driver is most relevant to its domain. Since IT is a means to different ends – supporting functional activities or enabling them to be done differently – the IT function has first to align with a mix of functional strategies. But crucially IT can then be instrumental in welding these organizational axes together; the co-ordination role is essentially this, enabling cross-boundary as well as cross-border integration and interaction. For example, at Philips and Electrolux information systems were necessary in interfacing geographically-based sales units into product-based manufacturing plants; at Eurochem the interface was between product-based businesses and geographically-oriented plants! So how to organize the IT function to both align with and integrate across different functional strategies is both a critical and non-trivial question – and may be the single most important issue in understanding the implications of globalization for IT.

Curiously, achieving the required organization fit may become easier if the question is first made more complex, if the different aspects of IT management are identified for potentially separate organization design decisions. We suggest that each of our case studies, even the more successful, might have benefited from adoption of Earl's (1989) distinction between three strands of information strategy:

1. Information systems (IS) strategy – the choice of applications, of *what* is to be delivered to the business.
2. Information technology (IT) strategy – the choice of technical platform of *how* applications are delivered.

3. Information management (IM) strategy – the adoption of policies which determine *who* holds what mission, authority and responsibility.

Our case studies suggest that IM strategy must be determined at or above the top organizational level of the global business. Skandia had identified that, because the re-insurance (as distinct from the insurance) business had global character, a very strong mandate must be given to the IT director, together with appropriate administrative arrangements. In Electrolux, the IS function was corporate and so had little difficulty in taking an aggregate view of the white goods business. In consequence at Skandia and Electrolux global IS strategy was being delivered (for example the SARA and EFS systems respectively); and global IT strategy was in place and robustly protected – not just by the IS function but by top management. By contrast at Philips DC and Eurochem, the IM issues were not yet resolved and this helps to explain why the business/IS strategy connections were not consistently made, and why questions of whether certain applications should be common across the business were so difficult to address.

The rationale for this proposition about IM strategy ownership should be clear. From the case study evidence, we propose that global information systems are needed to cross both borders and boundaries within the transnational organization. To develop the appropriate IS strategy, a business vision must be set and shared at the level of the global business. To deliver the IS strategy, an IT strategy/architecture is required – data standards, application interfaces, computer compatibilities, communications topologies – which is independent of any one function, country, profit centre or operating unit. Top-level ownership of IM strategy provides the platform, the decision framework, from which all this can be achieved.

Having a global IM strategy does not of course mean that all applications must be global and common, or that every piece of equipment must be prescribed by a monolithic global architecture. On the contrary, a successful global IM strategy enables application and technology to be made at various organizational levels without prejudicing global business strategy. The third framework developed during our research (depicted in Figure 16.5) concentrates on these

System Objective	System scope		
	Global	Regional	Local
Efficiency Responsiveness Learning transfer			

Figure 16.5   Information systems ownership

questions of IS and IT strategy ownership level. Conceptually it is employed after the application set has been developed through the first two frameworks; in practice, it seems to stimulate further application thinking in its own right.

Two examples can briefly illustrate the framework's use. At Electrolux, EFS is essential to delivering the global aspirations of the white goods business; both IS and IT specifications must be set at global level. On the other hand, order entry is seen as a local application: its functionality (IS aspects) can be determined by local management, but interface into EFS requires that each local system must be designed within a global technical (IT) specification. Secondly, at Philips DC, re-organization of the logistics function raises the question of what combination of IS and IT responsibilities for the relevant applications will best align with daily operational control which is local and policy co-ordination, a regional responsibility.

We believe that our four case studies demonstrate something of the need for, and nature of, alignment between global business and information strategy. The resolution is not as straightforward as speculative practitioner and academic articles suggest (for example Reck, 1989; Karimi and Konsynski, 1991; Alavi and Young, 1992). The frameworks we have introduced address the need to surface, analyse and action a set of information management issues as a function of the business strategy and organization. When Egelhoff (1989; 1991) calls for greater attention to information requirements in global businesses, we have to agree. However, firms may need the sorts of frameworks of analysis we have proposed to identify and justify requisite information systems. They certainly need to address information management strategy – the IS organization and ownership questions – at the organizational design stage. The contrasting and changing contexts we have encountered emphasize the importance of this type of analysis. They also leave unanswered the question of whether the 'transnational' is yet a robust prescription for the challenging economic environment of the 1990s. However, information systems appear to be one important means for achieving the potential advantages implied by the transnational model.

IMPLICATIONS AND CONCLUSION

The aim of the study reported here was to explore how IT was being deployed in pursuit of global business strategies in four firms. Each case study business had some characteristics of the 'Transnational' and each was at a different stage of evolution. We now venture some implications of our findings for research and practice.

Implications for research

The global information systems challenge appears to be more complex than commonly suggested, and the solutions far from neat and tidy. The critical questions seem to be ones of information management strategy, in particular about organizing the IS function appropriately. These are not new questions; nor are they technological *per se*; in some ways they are general management questions. It is perhaps interesting to note that Bartlett and Ghoshal (1991) later argued that management and organization studies have contributed significantly to understanding international business. They may be of similar value in studying international aspects of information systems.

One way of doing such managerial research is through case studies. They allow multi-disciplinary, integrative enquiry. We suggest they also can provide a necessary dynamic lens on global IS. It seems likely from our four case studies that the archetypal IT applications – as, say, predicted by our framework in Figure 16.1 – are not yet widely in place. Firms are still discovering their global IS requirements and thus IT applications are evolving. Longitudinal case studies – not least further monitoring of events in the four firms reported here – therefore could be valuable if theory development is in part making sense of firms' actions.

Another direction for research is to extend investigations into the transnational organization. The multidimensional thrusts of the transnational form seem to involve high co-ordination and thus require intensive information processing. IT would seem to offer considerable potential in meeting these challenges. Our studies show some, but not widespread, investments in IT as transnational strategies unfold. Thus related questions arise. What is the contribution of IT in practice *and* what other means of information processing – social and organizational in particular – are commonly deployed? Then it becomes important to know which mechanisms are more effective and yield more sustainable advantages. Two other research opportunities may be mentioned. The use of inter-organizational systems to enable or support global alliances was not the concern of this study. It could be a rich area of enquiry. Finally, in examining how IT can enable new ways of doing and managing global business, individual IT applications may be a more fruitful level of analysis than the business unit.

Implications for practice

We have argued from case study evidence that there are no easy and straightforward prescriptions for practitioners involved with global information systems. However, we have concluded that a useful starting point is to formulate a global business strategy first, before any sensible IT decisions can be made. (We also have opined that few, rather than many IT applications will be required). 'Strategy before systems' is a beloved adage of consultants and is hardly noteworthy advice. However, perhaps only one of our case firms, Skandia, had managed to adopt this rational approach where a CEO had formed and pursued a business vision that was significantly dependent on IT.

Such top-down, business-led strategy-making in IT is rare and difficult to achieve. Commonly a much more organizational approach is required (Earl, 1993) where management teams work continuously – or are specially brought together – to analyse business problems, agree business imperatives and identify a strategic theme, including the IS requirements, which is implemented over several years. There were elements of this in Electrolux, it was perhaps beginning in Philips, and maybe it was needed in Eurochem.

This perspective on IS strategy-making leads to a third implication for practice. If a global business strategy is in place and the IS strategy has been aligned with it, the information management (IM) strategy must then also match to ensure implementation and prevent global IT policies being eroded by local behaviours. Skandia is an exemplar. However, if the global business strategy is not yet clear and therefore no IS strategy has been formulated – or if determination of the IS strategy is hindered by legacies from the past – our cases suggest that attention is then best directed to IM strategy. By defining the roles, relationships and processes for managing IS, alignment of global IS and business strategies may then evolve. In particular, it seems crucial to ensure that these IT decisions are made at or above the level where the global business strategy is to be formulated and debated.

The final recommendation for practice is that in resolving these questions, our frameworks for analysis can help. They were prompted and refined by the case study evidence and could help managements identify and address the key questions of global information strategy.

Conclusion

Co-ordination of operations and management is commonly seen to be the hallmark of global businesses. Information technology in principle extends the horizons of co-ordination and reduces its cost and thus information systems are likely to be important investments for any global business. Some were present in each of our case study firms.

The co-ordination need is found to be across business entities, functional boundaries and national borders. Thus information often becomes a shared and common asset and information systems have to cross many organization domains. This creates considerable management challenges and organizational complexity for the IT function. It is this complexity – often in a context of slowly evolving global business strategy – that stands out. There may be some special difficulties in applying IT globally – regulatory constraints, national infrastructure development, multiple vendors, conflicting standards – but they seem likely to be trivial compared with the management and organizational issues which arise. This complexity provides an opportunity for those firms whose competitive strategy is partly based on global IT applications. Sustainable advantage may be gained by those who effectively resolve these questions. The complexities of information management may also provide an arena for those researchers who wish to study the realities of how transnational organizations function.

REFERENCES

Alavi, M. and Young, G. (1992) 'Information Technology in an International Enterprise: An Organizing Framework', In Palvia, S., Palvia, P. and Zigli, R. (Eds.), *The Global Issues of Information Technology Management*, Idea Group Publishing, Harrisburg, PA.

Baden-Fuller, C. W. F. and Stopford J. M. (1991) 'Globalization Frustrated: The Case of White Goods'. *Strategic Management Journal*, **12**, pp. 493–507.

Bartlett, C. and Ghoshal, S. (1987) 'Managing Across Borders: New Organizational Responses', *Sloan Management Review*, **29**, (1), pp. 43–53.

Bartlett, C. and Ghoshal, S. (1989a) *Managing Across Borders: The Transnational Solution*. Harvard Business School Press, Cambridge, Mass.

Bartlett, C. and Ghoshal, S. (1989b). 'A New Kind of Organization', *PA issues*, (10), PA Consulting, London.

Bartlett, C. and Ghoshal, S. (1991) 'Global Strategic Management: Impact on the New Frontiers of Strategy Research', *Strategic Management Journal*, Special Issue Summer, pp. 5–16.

Earl, M. (1989) *Management Strategies for Information Technology*, Prentice-Hall International, London.

Earl, M. (1993) 'Experiences in Strategic Information Systems Planning', *MIS Quarterly*, **17**, (1), pp. 1–24.

Egelhoff, W. (1988) *Organizing the Multinational Enterprise: An Information Processing Perspective*, Ballinger Publishing, Cambridge, Mass.

Egelhoff, W. (1991) 'Information Processing Theory and the Multinational Enterprise', *Journal of International Business Studies*, Autumn, pp. 341–368.

Feeny, D. and Willcocks, L. (1997) 'Rethinking Capabilities and Skills in the Information Systems Function', In Currie, W. and Galliers, R. (Eds.), *Rethinking MIS*, Oxford University Press, Oxford.

Galbraith, J. (1973) *Designing Complex Organizations*, Addison-Wesley, Reading, Mass.

Ghoshal, S. (1987) 'Global Strategy: An Organising Framework', *Strategic Management Journal*, **8**, pp. 425–40

Ghoshal, S. and Haspeslagh, P. (1989) *Note on the Major Appliance Industry in 1988*. INSEAD – CEDEP Case Library, INSEAD, Fontainebleu.

Hagstrom, P. (1991) *The 'Wired' MNC: The Role of Information Systems for Structural Change in Complex Organizations*, Institute of International Business, Stockholm School of Economics, Stockholm.

Hamel, G. and Prahalad, C. (1985) 'Do You Really Have a Global Strategy?', *Harvard Business Review*, July–August, pp. 139–148.

Hamel, G. and Prahalad, C. (1989) 'Strategic Intent', *Harvard Business Review*, May–June, pp. 63–76.

Huber, G. (1989) 'A Theory of the Effects of Advanced Information Technologies on Organization Design Intelligence and Decision-Making', *Academy of Management Review*, **15**, pp. 47–71.

Ives, B. and Jarvenpaa, S. (1991) 'Applications of Global Information Technology: Key Issues for Management', *MIS Quarterly*, March, pp. 33–49.

Johnston, R. and Lawrence, P. (1988) 'Beyond Vertical Integration – The Rise of the Value-Adding Partnership', *Havard Business Review*, July–August, pp. 94–101.

Karimi, J. and Konsymski, B. (1991) 'Globalisation and Information Management Strategies', *Journal of Management Information Systems*, **7**, (4), Spring, pp. 7–26.

Konsynski, B. and McFarlan, F. (1990) 'Information Partnerships – Shared Data, Shared Scale', *Harvard Business Review*, September–October, pp. 114–120.

Lorenz, C. (1989) 'Electrolux Management', *The Financial Times*, 19/21/23/26/28/30 June.

McFarlan, F. (1992) Multinational CIO Challenges for the 1990s', In Palvia, S., Palvia, P. and Zigli, R. M. (Eds.) *The Global Issues of Information Technology Management*, Idea Group Publishing, Harrisburg, PA.

Porter, M. (1986) 'Competition in Global Industries: A Conceptual Framework', In Porter, M. (Ed.) *Competition in Global Industries*, Harvard Business School Press, Cambridge, Mass.

Prahalad, C. and Doz, Y. (1987) *The Multinational Mission: Balancing Local Demands And Global Vision*, Free Press, New York.

Reck, R. (1989) 'The Shock of Going Global', *Datamation*, August 1.

Runge, D. and Earl, M. (1988) 'Using Telecommunications-based Information Systems for Competitive Advantage', In Earl M. (Ed.)

Information Management: The Strategic Dimension. Oxford University Press, Oxford.

Thompson, J. (1967) *Organizations in Action*, McGraw-Hill, New York.

Part Six

Key Trends: Capabilities and Learning

CHAPTER SEVENTEEN

The IT Function: Changing Capabilities and Skills

DAVID F. FEENY AND LESLIE P. WILLCOCKS

INTRODUCTION: FEWER CAPABILITIES FOR INCREASED CHANGE

In an increasingly complex and fast-changing world, businesses succeed, it is claimed, through sustained commitment to excellence within a narrow domain. It is simply not possible for any organization to remain competitive, let alone world-class, if it dissipates its management attention across many markets and activities when each of them is subject to potential transformation. Thus we see corporations divesting subsidiaries in order to focus their future on a smaller number of business which exploit their 'core competences' (Hamel and Prahalad, 1990). Phrases such as 'virtual' and 'hollow' corporations, and examples such as Benetton, the Italian clothing retailer and Nike, the sportswear company, capture the prescriptions of Quinn (1992) and others – that successful businesses focus on creating advantage through a small number of 'core' activities, while other activities are outsourced to world-class supplier/partners.

These ideas are being translated into the IS/IT domain, which arguably represents an extreme example of growing complexity and rapid change. It seems obvious that no business, however rich in resources, can retain competitiveness in IS/IT activity through all this turbulence when compared to third-party providers whose management are wholly dedicated to the area. Hence top management are seen to be debating whether IS is core or non-core/peripheral to the future of their business; and what arrangements for IS best reflect their analysis. Huge IS outsourcing deals have been concluded by organizations like General Dynamics, Xerox, and the UK's Inland Revenue. Yet often these deals are labelled 'strategic partnerships' (McFarlan and Nolan 1995), recognizing that IT exploitation remains a 'critical' (but 'non-core') element in the future of the business. We suggest that this uneasy juxtaposition of terminology points to the need to apply the analysis in quite a different way. Instead of questioning whether 'IS' is 'core' or 'non-core', the debate should really be about *which IS capabilities are core to the business's future capacity to exploit IT successfully?*

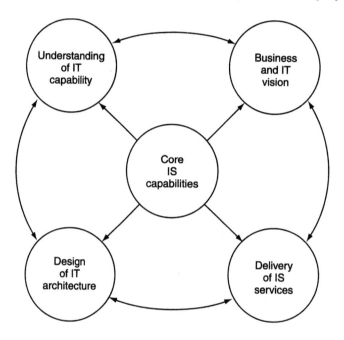

Figure 17.1   Enduring challenges in IT exploitation

Decomposing the question a little further, we can identify four enduring challenges in the organizational exploitation of IT. They are depicted in Figure 17.1. Each represents an area which must be successfully addressed over time, in the face of rapid change and future uncertainty.

- The challenge of *understanding IT capability* is not just about keeping track of a myriad of different technologies, each of which exhibits unprecedented speed of change. As other authors have noted over the years (e.g. Curley & Pyburn, 1982; Walton, 1989), these technologies are non-directive. Their uses are defined by the consumer not the producer. Understanding the functional characteristics of the multi-media workstation is not the same as understanding the range of applications in which such workstations may be sensibly deployed.

- The challenge of *business and IT vision* is similarly twofold. The obvious component is alignment of information systems to support business strategy. However, as IS authors have regularly argued, developments in IT may enable new and superior business strategies. Recently Pine *et al.*, (1993) have suggested that the operations function of many businesses may be transformed using IT to deliver mass-customization, the simultaneous achievement of low unit costs and high customer specificity. Similarly Rayport and Sviokla (1994, 1995) have argued that IT is transforming the focus of the marketing function from the 'marketplace' to the 'marketspace', allowing new distribution, product offering, and brand exploitation opportunities.

- The challenge of *delivery of IS services* of low-cost and high-quality is being transformed by the emergence of a large and vibrant services market. While authors such as McFarlan and Nolan (1995); Lacity *et al.*, (1996) and Earl (1996) have provided contrasting prescriptions for reacting to this opportunity, there seems little doubt that businesses will experience high degrees of change in the sourcing of IS services for many years to come.

- The challenge of *designing IT architecture*, the choices of technical platform on which to mount IS services, is again twofold. It is linked closely to change in technology capability and supplier health. Do groupware products and the Intranet concept represent complementary propositions or alternative directions? How may low-cost/network driven workstations impact on existing client–server architecture and its providers? To the chagrin of organizations seeking stability over time in their technical platforms, product sectors are quite commonly dominated by companies which scarcely existed a few years ago. The business life cycle of IT companies seems to average years rather than decades. The challenge is then compounded by the need for IT architecture to remain open to change in the demands of the host business. With the blurring of organizational boundaries, there may be profound change required in what Keen (1991) has called the 'reach' and 'range' of the platform, with a wide selection of IS services needing to be provided to a large number of users beyond the historic confines of the business.

What each of these challenges have in common is the need to continuously re-assess and re-interpret a basic remit within a turbulent context. Today's assessment of the role of IT within the business or the appropriate IT architecture will inevitably and rapidly be overtaken by events. Yet a business without the ability to securely update and alter its judgements in these areas will soon be severely handicapped – strategically and economically. In defining and researching 'core IS capabilities', we have been searching for the minimum set of capabilities that will enable a business to consistently address the four challenges of Figure 17.1. Beyond this minimum, the organization may decide from time to time to operate in-house or to contract for service or resources to achieve its IS activities. Provided it possesses the core set of IS capabilities, its future ability to successfully exploit IT should not be prejudiced.

THE RESEARCH BASE

Our view of core IS capabilities has been developed from three strands of research carried out in the period 1992–96.

- The first strand concentrated on the role, persona, and experiences of the CIO. Based on face-to-face interviews in 61 organizations, Earl and Feeny (1994) provided a profile of the CIO's potential to add value to the business. These interviews also provided insights into the capabilities which leading CIOs believed to be crucial to the IS function.

- In the second strand, Feeny et al., (1997) investigated four of the capabilities which were consistently highlighted by CIOs. Twelve participating organizations identified 53 individuals who were considered to demonstrate outstanding ability in one of the target areas. Data on these individuals was captured using personal background and perceived ability questionnaires, critical event interviews, and a variety of psychometric testing instruments. The research provided insights into both the way target capabilities were delivered, and the profile of individuals who delivered them.

- An extensive third strand has involved research into IS/IT outsourcing experience. Data from 142 organizations has been collected by questionnaire, and face-to face interviews have been conducted with multiple stakeholders in 30 case study organizations. An overview of the findings on outsourcing practice was reported in Lacity et al., (1996). Most significantly for our purpose here, many of the case study organizations were found to be directly addressing the question of what they typically referred to as the scope of the 'residual' in-house IS function.

Looking across these research strands, we find organizations converging from two different directions on the concept of core IS capabilities. In the first two research areas, most organizations studied were clearly positioning IS/IT as a strategic resource for the business. CIO attention in these organizations was focused on identifying and developing the capabilities most directly associated with creating business value through IT. They were less interested, and less developed in their views, in the capabilities required to successfully engage the market of IS/IT service providers. However, organizations studied in the third research area generally exhibited the opposite tendency. Having made significant commitments to IS/IT outsourcing, their learning was concentrated on how to manage external service providers. While they recognized the need to address future business and IT vision challenges, this represented a longer-term agenda. Furthermore, they were conscious that the investment in IS capabilities required for the longer-term challenge would have to be carefully justified and vigorously argued to business executives who thought they had 'outsourced all that stuff'.

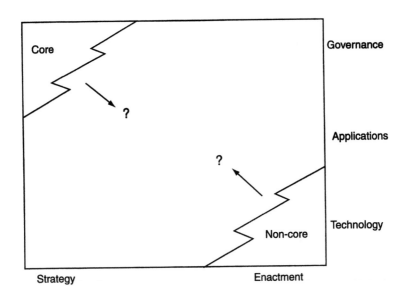

Figure 17.2   Mapping choice in IS/IT activity

We can depict these contrasting perspectives through Figure 17.2. It suggests that organizations address the challenges of IT exploitation through their decisions and actions in three dimensions. In the governance dimension they determine responsibilities and accountabilities for IS/IT, allocate resources, promulgate standards and best practice approaches, monitor adherence. In the applications dimension, they select and develop the systems which will create value for the business. In the technology dimension they design, build, and operate the infrastructure on which those systems are mounted. Each dimension represents a spectrum, from strategy-making through to enactment. And each dimension contributes to meeting the challenges of successful IT exploitation. For example, the development of business and IT vision requires:

- The deployment of appropriate IS resources within the business, and the establishment of effective relationships and processes to integrate business and IT thinking (governance dimension).
- The consequent selection and development of systems investments which enable the chosen business strategy (applications dimension).
- The selection of an IT architecture which can respond to the reach, range, and performance requirements of the vision implied by the business strategy (technology dimension).

Using Figure 17.2 to illustrate our contrasting perspectives, we can see that organizations committed to IS/IT outsourcing tend to start from the assumption that core IS capabilities are focused on the requirement to develop governance strategy. They are learning through experience that a much wider set of core capabilities is required to sustain success in IT exploitation in the longer term. On the other hand, organizations which have positioned IT as a strategic resource have tended to assume that almost all IS/IT activity should be in-house and regarded as core. Over time, as they focus their attention on capabilities related to creating business value, they have started to expand their definition of 'non-core' activities away from the technology/enactment corner, and to make more use of external providers.

Figure 17.2 provides one potential template for any organization to develop further insights into the concept of core IS capabilities. By debating the degree of control required to safeguard future ability to exploit IT, and the extent of the spectrum which must be 'owned' for each dimension, management can trigger a more detailed study of the capabilities required to achieve the target level of ownership. Our own analysis of the learning being achieved across our research base has led us to identify the nine core IS capabilities described in the next section.

NINE CORE IS CAPABILITIES

The nine core IS capabilities can be identified and defined by reference to three of our enduring challenges of IT exploitation – Business and IT vision, design of IT architecture, and delivery of IS services. These three are shown in Figure 17.3 as overlapping circles, highlighting the importance in core IS capabilities of making the connections between challenge areas as well as addressing the specifics of each. In this perspective the fourth challenge – understanding IT capability – can be thought of as an overlay across the entire picture. An appropriate understanding of IT capability needs to permeate every aspect of core

IS capabilities, a theme to which we shall return later. Embedded in the diagram we have positioned the core IS capabilities, each of which is now discussed in turn.

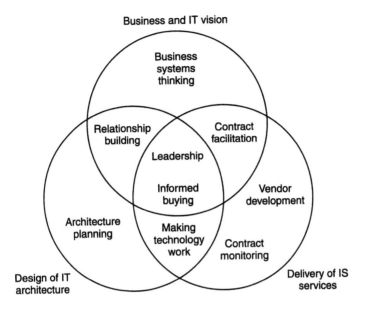

Business and IT vision

Business systems thinking

Relationship building

Contract facilitation

Leadership

Informed buying

Vendor development

Architecture planning

Making technology work

Contract monitoring

Design of IT architecture

Delivery of IS services

Figure 17.3   Nine core IS capabilities

Capability 1 – IS/IT leadership

Integrating IS/IT effort with business purpose and activity

At the centre of Figure 17.3, in the overlapped space of the three challenges, is the need for effective IS/IT leadership. Leadership devises the organizational arrangements – structures, processes, staffing – to address each challenge area and to manage the interdependencies between them. It sets the goals and direction in each area. IS/IT leadership also influences the overall business perception of IT's role and contribution, through the creation of shared vision and the establishment of appropriate values and culture within the IS function. Leadership is of course the traditional role of the CIO or director of IT, and it has become fashionable in some quarters to question the future of that role. But our experience consistently reinforces the view reported in Earl and Feeny (1994), that the CIO is personally instrumental in organizational exploitation of IT. In one research example, the incoming CEO of an energy utility found that his company's entire IS function had been outsourced by his predecessor. The new CEO recruited a high-calibre CIO and charged him with recreating sufficient in-house IS capability to safeguard the company's ability to pursue his future business directions.

Capability 2 – business systems thinking

Envisioning the business process which technology makes possible

The single most common concern we have found in case study companies is the lack of progress in integrating business development with IT capability. Many are still making IS/IT investments to support ageing and inefficient processes, or as additions to new processes which have been designed without current IT capability in mind. Business systems thinking is the core IS capability required to meet the challenge of business and IT vision. In companies which have it, like one of the major retailers in our research, the IS function is automatically included as equal partner in every significant business development initiative. By contrast, in a large aerospace business we found the CIO frustrated at her inability to get IS representation on any of the business process reengineering task forces underway. The business expected to involve IS at a later stage, after the primary thinking and design was complete, and the CIO was unable to convince them that any member of her staff could make valuable contributions at a more formative stage.

Capability 3 – relationship building

Getting the business constructively engaged in IS/IT issues

While the business systems thinker is the individual embodiment of integrated business/IT thinking, a further core IS capability is the relationship building which facilitates the wider dialogue between business and IS communities. Over many years researchers and commentators have pointed to both the importance of this dialogue and the difficulty of achieving it. There has been regular reference to a culture gap between 'techies' and 'users'. While this gap can be experienced in the context of delivery of IS services, we have found relationship building's most important contribution to be in the creation of mutual confidence, harmony of purpose, and successful communication between those focused on the business and technical agendas – hence the positioning shown in Figure 17.3. We have seen many instances where a single individual had transformed the relationship between an area of the business and the IS function. As a departmental head in one retailer commented: 'Things are quite different now; we feel our new contact point with IS is really one of us'. Successful relationship building paves the way for business systems thinking activity, and the development of a higher value-added agenda in the exploitation of IT.

Capability 4 – architecture planning

Creating the coherent blueprint for a technical platform which responds to present and future business needs

The need for architecture planning may be self-evident, as will be the challenge of achieving it. The question is more whether it is correct to position architecture planning as a core IS capability. Case study organizations with recently-made commitments to a largely outsourced IS environment commonly assumed that the task of architecture planning now resided with their suppliers. We challenge that assumption. Without in-house expertise in this area, it is difficult to see how the business can understand the viability of addressing new demands, or the potential for meeting existing demands on a new technology platform with better economics. Nor is it obvious, in the latter respect, that an external supplier will place priority on migration to a lower-cost platform – unless it results for them in higher profits rather than lower revenues. We would rather point to an automotive manufacturer which now has many years experience of outsourcing the majority of its IS/IT activity. Through its own significant investment in architecture planning, this company both protects its ability to exploit IT, and is able to negotiate architecture evolution with its suppliers from a position of strength.

Capability 5 – making technology work

Rapidly achieving technical progress – by one means or another

In the overlap between the challenges of IT architecture design and delivery of IS services – where the rubber hits the road – we identify the core IS capability of making technology work. Making technology work requires much of the insight found in the architecture planning role, allied to a pragmatic and short-term orientation. In today's environment of complex/networked/multi-supplier systems, the technical 'fixer' makes two critical contributions: to rapidly trouble-shoot problems which are being disowned by others across the technical supply chain; and to identify how to address business needs which cannot be properly satisfied by standard technical approaches. The need to retain this sort of capability is recognized even among organizations that have 'totally outsourced' IT. As a senior manager in an oil company commented: 'We have retained in-house some significant technical consulting expertise, we regard it as important. It's not so much a doing organization now, but it's one which is capable of debating technical development routes with our outsourcing partners'.

Capability 6 – informed buying

Managing the IS/IT sourcing strategy which meets the interests of
the business

A second core IS capability at the centre of Figure 17.3, taking
account of all three challenge areas, is identified as informed buying.
It involves analysis of the external market for IS/IT services;
selection of a sourcing strategy to meet business needs and
technology issues; leadership of the tendering, contracting, and
service management processes. In an organization which had decided
to outsource most IS/IT service, the informed buyer is the most
prominent role behind that of the CIO. One interviewee described the
role in this way: 'If you are a senior manager in the company and you
want something done, you come to me and I will select the vendor
and draw up the contract. If anything goes wrong it's my butt that
gets kicked by you'. However, we have found increasing recognition
of the informed buying role even in companies which retain most
IS/IT activity in-house. There are two trends in evidence here. First,
business management now require reassurance that the in-house
option is truly appropriate and competitive versus the external options
of which they are now aware. Secondly, as data centres and other
operational activities are consolidated to achieve efficiencies, in-
house services are being provided on the basis of more explicit, quasi-
contractual, agreements. The informed buyer must command the
confidence of the business, and those responsible for IT architecture,
in securing service agreements for IS delivery.

Capability 7 – contract facilitation

Ensuring the success of existing contracts for IS/IT services

Arrangements for delivery of IS services can nowadays involve
considerable complexity. Typically a large population of users within
the business are receiving a variety of services from multiple supply
points (external and internal) under a set of detailed and lengthy service
agreements. The contract facilitation core IS capability provides a single
point of contact through which the user can ensure that problems and
conflicts are resolved fairly – and above all promptly – within the
framework of agreements and relationships. It is another action-oriented
capability, which we have found to be identified more often through the
experience of practice rather than the theory of planning. If service
agreements and service suppliers were perfect, contract facilitation
would not be a core IS capability. But as one role model interviewee
noted: 'The users have been bitten a few times when they have dealt
directly with suppliers, and it's a service we can provide, so now we do'.

Capability 8 – contract monitoring

Protecting the business's contractual position, current and future

As organizations move to exploit the burgeoning external market for IS services – in either a revolutionary or more evolutionary way – contract monitoring becomes a core IS capability. While the contract facilitator is working to 'make things happen' on a day-to-day basis, the contract monitor is ensuring that the business position is at all times protected. Effective contract monitoring involves holding suppliers to account against both existing service contracts and the developing performance standards of the services market. In other words it enables production of a 'report card' for each supplier which highlights achievement against external benchmarks as well as the standards embedded in the relevant contract. While all of our outsourcing case study companies recognized contract monitoring as a core IS capability, there was evidence that the extent of the task may be underestimated if outsourcing results from snap decision-making at executive level. The more detailed development of a major outsourcing deal in the defence industry led to a senior IT manager commenting: 'We need a significant number of people in-house to monitor vendor service performance. In one business unit alone we have 16 people working on contracts, six exclusively on the monitoring side. Admittedly we are still in the settling-in period, but I can't see the work declining that much'.

Capability 9 – vendor development

Identifying the potential added value of IS/IT service suppliers

The last of our core IS capabilities, and usually the last to be discovered by our case study companies, concerns vendor development. The single most threatening aspect of IS/IT outsourcing is the presence of substantial switching costs. To outsource successfully in the first place requires considerable organizational effort over an extended period of time. In one example, it took more than 50 man-years of effort to arrive at a contract for a ten-year deal worth around $700 million. Implementation requirements of considerable magnitude followed. To subsequently change suppliers may well require an equivalent effort. Hence it is in the business interest to maximize the contribution of existing suppliers. It is this realization that leads organizations to identify the need for vendor development, which looks beyond existing contractual arrangements to explore the long-term potential for suppliers to add value, creating the 'win-win' situations in which the supplier increases its revenues by providing services which increase business benefits. A major retail multinational has a number of ways of achieving this, including an annual formal meeting: 'It's in both our interests to keep these things going and we formally, with our biggest suppliers, have a meeting once a year. These are done at very senior levels in both organizations, and that works very well'.

Non-core IS capabilities

By implication, our analysis suggests that many of the traditional capabilities of IS functions should be regarded as non-core. There is now ample research evidence that much IS delivery and development activity can be successfully achieved through the use of external resources. In 'The Value of Selective IT Sourcing', Lacity *et al.*, (1996) provide a set of frameworks to guide decisions on where and how to engage the external market for IS services. Through the core IS capabilities we have now described, organizations can exercise these frameworks to utilize over time a pragmatic blend of internal and external resources in non-core IS roles.

When we have shared our analysis in detailed workshops with large organizations during the past 12 months, only one further candidate for core IS capability status has consistently been urged upon us. Many IS managers clearly feel that project management is a core IS capability, and they support this belief with reference to the well-documented problems of large IS development projects. We suggest a more radical vision. If the IS function – through development and deployment of leadership, relationship building, and business systems thinking capabilities – successfully meets our challenge of Business and IT Vision, we find there *are* no large IS projects. Projects are now business projects, with IS and other dimensions, and project management responsibility passes to business managers. In Rockart's phrase (1988), 'the line takes the leadership'. Furthermore, with IT investment now concentrated into business projects which are both urgent and critical to the business agenda, IS requirements are compressed and time-boxed. When the emphasis is on the achievement of an 'adequate' system within a short project timescale, rather than on a 'complete' and 'state of the art' system, project management is considerably less demanding. Our analysis does not therefore overlook project management capability. But it does position it as a transitory requirement, pending the achievement of true core IS capabilities.

CORE IS CAPABILITIES AND THE SKILLS TO ACHIEVE THEM

Many of the IS functions with which we have been working are developing new frameworks for defining and developing the abilities of their IS professionals and managers. Often these frameworks are based on 'competency' models which have originated in consultancy companies focused on human resource management, and which may be deployed more widely across the IS function's host organization. In most such frameworks, each competency represents a generic unit of ability or characteristic such as 'analytical thinking', 'self-control', or 'results orientation'. Each of our core IS capabilities would be constructed through a combination of such competency units. However, in this emerging field there is as yet little general agreement on the labelling or definition of the building blocks, or even on the level at which a competency is most appropriately identified.

A second strand of contemporary analysis focuses on skill sets. Authors such as Lee *et al.*, (1995), Todd *et al.*, (1995) and Earl (1995) have all recently explored the implications of change in the IS function by reference to 'technical', 'business', and 'inter-personal' skills. As with competencies, there are contrasting definitions of the terminology, but general agreement that IS professionals and managers need to demonstrate a (changing) mix of skills in these three broad areas. We can review our core IS capabilities against these reference domains, adding two dimensions which we have consistently found to be important – the time and value orientations which underpin delivery of each capability.

Core IS capabilities and technical skills

While the need for technical skills is self-evident in two core capability areas – architecture planning and making technology work – our research evidence indicates that technical skills remain important across the spectrum of core IS capabilities.

- At the CIO level (leadership capability) Earl and Feeny (1994) have referred to the requirement for 'a profound knowledge of IT', and the 'lengthy apprenticeship in the IS function' common to value-adding CIOs.
- Feeny *et al.*, (1997) found that high-performing relationship builders matched outstanding technical specialists in the length of their IS experience and their achievement in technical aptitude tests. Most business systems thinkers in the sample had a similar profile.

Even in supply management capabilities such as contract monitoring we can make a prima facie case for technical skills, and point to case study evidence that these capabilities are being provided in practice by people with substantive IS experience. Closer analysis and interpretation suggests that the common requirement is best captured as 'understanding IT capability'. A lengthy immersion in IS enables the individual to build mental models which capture the fundamentals and provide a lasting base from which to interpret new developments. The critical step is – at some time – to have reached in IT the equivalent of what Bohn (1994) calls stage 7 knowledge – the 'know why' stage. Delivery of one of the core IS capabilities can then be pursued by someone who is confident of meeting the challenge of understanding IT capability over time, at whatever level is required. Even the technical specialists in our research seem to rely more on their meta models of technology than on formal training in the latest products.

Core IS capabilities and business skills

Significant business skills would seem to be a prerequisite for delivering at least five of our core IS capabilities – leadership, business systems thinking, relationship building, informed buying, vendor management. How then do we explain the predominantly IS careers of those in our research sample who are seen to perform so well in these capabilities? To unravel the paradox, we distinguish between the accumulation of business *experience* and the capacity for business *understanding*. We find that building relationships between IS and (say) marketing is dependent not upon the demonstration of marketing expertise which rivals the marketing professionals, but rather upon convincing those professionals that you understand their goals, concerns, language, and processes. And that you are trying to help them towards achievement of their goals, not to belittle their existing practices. Similarly, business systems thinking which stimulates new ideas for managing the supply chain requires an ability to conceptualize and envision business processes – not to develop detailed command of the minutiae of present wisdom and operations. In this analysis, supported by data from the study of Feeny et al., (1997), IS professionals now deliver core IS capabilities by exploiting assets which previously enabled their successful IS careers: the ability to rapidly absorb new information; to build mental models of how things work (in this case the business and the organization rather than the technology); to use those models to explore what might now be.

Core IS capabilities and interpersonal skills

In four of our areas of core IS capability – relationship building, contract facilitation, leadership, and informed buying – we have found interpersonal skills to be at a premium. Reference back to Figure 17.3 is helpful here. It shows each of these capabilities positioned in the overlap between two or three of the challenge circles, and therefore each represents the need to build bridges between the various communities involved in the exploitation of IT. Thus contract facilitators must empathize with both business users and service providers, and show that they understand and respect the concerns and values of each in facilitating problem solving. CIOs/leaders and informed buyers have the ultimate challenge of guiding all three communities towards an appropriate way forward. The one exception to this logic appears to be in 'making technology work'. Although positioned in an overlap, we have not found technical fixers recognized as particularly gifted in interpersonal skills. It seems that awkwardness and lack of tact is tolerated here provided there is a high level of confidence in their ability to make things work. One CIO in our research referred to these people as his Michelangelos. Perhaps difficult behaviour is accepted and even expected where genius is recognized.

Core IS capabilities and time horizons

Further reference to Figure 17.3 enables us to highlight another facet of delivering core IS capabilities, the time horizon which is appropriate to each capability area. For those capabilities embedded in a single circle of the diagram – business systems thinking, architecture planning, contract monitoring, vendor development – the emphasis is on identifying and protecting the longer-term position: the target business process, making the technical architecture robust over time, the lasting arrangements with service providers. By contrast relationship builders, technical fixers, and contract facilitators must be committed to shorter-term progress within the constraints imposed by the longer-term interests of their colleagues. If technical fixers fail to 'make technology work' quickly, they forfeit the confidence and respect of those they serve. Relationship builders and contract facilitators similarly need a bias for action to keep things moving at the speed the business expects. In this respect Figure 17.3 also demonstrates graphically the position of CIOs/leaders and informed buyers who must constantly balance long-term interests against short-term imperatives. There are difficult judgements to be made. But, as Earl (1993) has identified, simultaneous attention to long-term vision and short-term performance is a matter of survival for CIOs.

Core IS capabilities and motivating values

When Feeny et al., (1997) studied a subset of core IS capabilities in depth, they were surprised to find how many of the study group of 53 were apparently multi-talented. Just under half were perceived by their colleagues (managers, peers, subordinates) to excel in at least two of the capability areas. It seemed that today's business systems thinkers or relationship builders were often yesterday's high performers in making technology work. What had changed over time was their motivation or value set, the challenges which captured their imagination.

We can usefully borrow some thinking here from the research team for Massachusetts Institute of Technology (MIT) Management in the

Nineties programme. When they reported on their work (Scott Morton, 1991), they organized their findings around a conceptual framework which depicted management processes addressing four elements – strategy, structure, individuals/roles, technology. Each of these elements provides its own sort of intellectual challenge:

- Strategy   How does the business currently create value, and how might it create more value?
- Structure   How does the organization work, and how therefore should the issue at hand be progressed?
- Individuals/roles What are this person's goals/values/style, and how therefore can their support be achieved?
- Technology   How does this technology work, and what therefore must be done to achieve the target result?

We can describe the values embedded in our nine core IS capabilities as fascination for various combinations of these challenges. For example, successful business systems thinkers are dedicated to the strategy challenge, determined to make a difference to business added value. Relationship builders are absorbed by the individuals/roles and structure challenges. Informed buyers are intrigued by the interactions of strategy and structure, including the extended structure represented by the organization's suppliers. Figure 17.4 provides a mapping of capabilities against values. It is inevitably tentative at this stage of our learning, but captures the indicators of our research to date.

We believe further development of this thinking is a priority. Throughout our research studies we have found high performers in the core capabilities to be very achievement oriented. But they are self-driven/inner-directed rather than motivated through formal job specifications and reward systems. Their satisfaction derives from pursuit of things that fascinate them, and hence an understanding of

	Motivating values			
Core IS capability	Strategy	Structure	Individuals	Technology
IS/IT leadership	✓	✓	✓	
Business systems thinking	✓			
Relationship building		✓	✓	
Architecture planning				✓
Making technology work				✓
Informed buying	✓	✓		
Contract facilitation		✓	✓	
Contract monitoring		✓		
Vendor development	✓		✓	

Figure 17.4   Capabilities and values

motivating values is key to the development and retention of individuals who excel in core IS capability areas.

CORE IS CAPABILITIES – IMPLICATIONS AND CONCLUSIONS

The introduction to this book discusses the particular challenges of IT exploitation, and proposes some fundamental principles of successful information management. Prior chapters have further developed various aspects of information management and presented more detailed research-based insights. In this chapter we have sought to identify some of the wider consequences for IS human resource management. The core IS capabilities are defined as those which are necessary and sufficient to ensure that the organization retains its ability to exploit changing markets of technology and services, its opportunity to achieve business advantage through IT over time. Much of course remains to be done in this respect. There are far-reaching implications of a core IS capability model.

The most obvious and pragmatic challenge is to understand how best to operationalize the model. How does the business translate core IS capabilities into organization structure, job specifications, management processes, etc? How does it decide how many people are required to deliver each necessary capability? Clearly the answers to these and other questions will be very much a function of the size, shape, nature, culture of each business, but we can suggest some initial guidelines. Organizational design will need to be driven by separate consideration of the drivers for each capability area. Wherever there is strategic business leadership within the structure, there needs to be matching IS/IT leadership – a pattern of CIO-type positions which maps onto the business leadership structure of the corporation as a whole. The number of business systems thinkers required will be a function of the number of business development projects (business process re-engineering initiatives and the like) active within the organization. Every operational unit of the organization will need a clearly identified relationship builder who has sufficient time to devote to the development and maintenance of constructive business/IS relationships. Deployment of the various supply management capabilities must be proactively planned ahead of the organization's developing use of external service providers. Architecture planning will be a central or dispersed function depending on the chosen IS governance policies, the judgement of what standards are required to support the target level of corporate coherence across its business units.

To what extent can multiple core IS capabilities be delivered by a single individual? We have already referred to evidence that some people are multi-talented. The same evidence of course demonstrates that others are not. We can expect that some will be able to combine relationship building with business systems thinking. CIOs probably need to. But some combinations probably will not work. Analysis of the previous section suggests that combinations will be particularly problematic if they consist of capabilities which are associated with conflicting time horizons or motivating values. It is very difficult to be simultaneously fascinated by both business added value potential and the interstices of technology. Similarly the proper instinct of a contract facilitator to find a timely solution to a service problem potentially conflicts with the contract monitor's concern to avoid setting undesirable precedents.

Must all core IS capabilities be delivered by the organization's employees? Is this practical in the context of a small business? It may be possible to achieve at least some of the capabilities through an 'insourcing' route, where the delivering individuals belong to external organizations (or other units of the host corporation), but are retained to work under the direction, and towards the goals, of in-house management. For example, architecture planning might be successfully provided by a highly-qualified individual who is neither from the host organization, nor from the providers of its outsourced IT services (see Lacity et al., 1996 and Chapter 11 for further definition of the insourcing concept).

Most critically in the long run, the core IS capability model implies migration to a relatively small IS function, staffed by highly able people. What is the migration route from what may currently be a large IS function, populated mainly by individuals with less exceptional abilities? Having somehow achieved migration, how must the IS function's culture, structure, career paths, reward systems etc, be changed if a small number of highly able people are to thrive and prosper rather than get frustrated and depart? And will these arrangements, despite the small size of the IS unit, provide each individual with the scope to properly retain and develop the capability for which he or she is valued?

Despite so many unanswered questions, we suggest that planning for a rather different future IS function is a high-priority task. All too often in our case study organizations we have witnessed a reactive rather than an anticipatory approach to IS human resource issues. The proviso to our exhortation is that it is the planning that is urgent. Implementation may probably be later rather than sooner. The core IS capability model is envisaged as a blueprint for *sustaining* the organization's ability to exploit IT. If that organization has yet to put in place the fundamentals of successful information management, the blueprint is important but the implementation must – at least to some extent – wait. The final chapter of this book describes an evolutionary model of information management, and the organizational learning which must be achieved before a core IS capability regime can be fully effective.

REFERENCES

Bohn, R. E. (1994) 'Measuring and Managing Technological Knowledge', *Sloan Management Review*, Fall.

Curley, K. F. and Pyburn, P. J. (1982) 'Intellectual' Technologies: The Key to Improving White-Collar Productivity', *Sloan Management Review*, Fall.

Earl, M. J. (1993) 'The Chief Information Officer: A Study of Survival', *London Business School, Centre for Research in Information Management*, WP 93/3. London Business School, London.

Earl, M. J. (1995) 'The Changing Shape and Skills of the IS Function', *London Business School, Centre for Research in Information Management*, WP 95/3.

Earl, M. J. (1996) 'The Risks of Outsourcing IT', *Sloan Management Review*, Spring.

Earl, M. J. and Feeny, D. F. (1994) 'Is Your CIO Adding Value?', *Sloan Management Review*, Spring.

Feeny, D. F., Abl, V., Millie, E., Minter, A., Selby, C. and Williams, J. (1997) 'Defining New Skills and Competencies', *Oxford Institute of Information Management, Research and Discussion Paper*. Templeton College, Oxford.

Hamel, G. and Prahalad, C. K. (1990) 'The Core Competence of the Corporation', *Harvard Business Review*, May–June.

Keen, P. G. W. (1991) *Shaping The Future: Business Design Through Information Technology*, Harvard Business School Press, Boston, Mass.

Lacity, M. C., Willcocks, L. P. and Feeny, D. F. (1996) 'The Value of Selective IT Sourcing', *Sloan Management Review*, Spring.

Lee, D. M. S., Trauth, E. M. and Farwell, D. (1995) 'Critical Skills and Knowledge Requirements of IS Professionals: A Joint Academic/Industry Investigation', *MIS Quarterly*, September.

McFarlan, F. W. and Nolan, R. L. (1995) 'How to Manage an IT Outsourcing Alliance', *Sloan Management Review*, Winter.

Pine, B. J., Victor, B. and Boynton, A. C. (1993) 'Making Mass Customisation Work', *Harvard Business Review*, September – October.

Quinn, J. B. (1992) *Intelligent Enterprise: A Knowledge and Service Based Paradigm for Industry*, Free Press, New York.

Rayport, J. F. and Sviokla, J. J. (1994) 'Managing in the Marketspace', *Harvard Business Review*, November–December.

Rayport, J. F. and Sviokla, J. J. (1995) 'Exploiting the Virtual Value Chain', *Harvard Business Review*, November–December.

Rockart, J. F. (1988) 'The Line Takes the Leadership – IS Management in a Wired Society', *Sloan Management Review*, Summer.

Scott Morton, M. S. (1991) *The Corporation of the 1990s: Information Technology and Organizational Transformation*, Oxford University Press, Oxford.

Todd, P. A., McKeen, J. D. and Gallupe, R. B. (1995) 'The Evolution of IS Job Skills: A Content Analysis of IS Job Advertisements 1970–1990', *MIS Quarterly*, March.

Walton, R. E. (1989) *Up and Running: Integrating Information Technology and the Organization*, Harvard Business School Press, Boston, Mass.

CHAPTER EIGHTEEN

The Five-year Learning of Ten IT Directors

DAVID F. FEENY

INTRODUCTION

In this final chapter we focus on the themes of learning, leadership and continuity and change in the IT function. The learning theme has become particularly prominent in the management literature in the 1990s. Leadership has been a perennial issue, as indicated in Chapters 1 and 2. The theme of continuity, however has been far outstripped by the widespread emphasis on the need for change – in the IT function, as well as the organization at large. Here we revisit these themes and develop a framework for understanding how an IT function may evolve.

In 1986 ten UK IT directors agreed to participate in a research study carried out by the Oxford Institute of Information Management (OXIIM). Each of them not only headed the IT function of one of the largest organizations in the country, but also was considered on a personal level to be a leader in the field. The ten were interviewed about the role and significance of IT within their companies; the issues they perceived to be critical to successful IT exploitation; their current and expected future pattern of activity; their experience and opinions of various approaches to IT education for business executives. A particular outcome of the research (Hirschheim *et al.*, 1988) was the development of a three-stage model that described an apparently common pattern of evolution in the leadership and management of the IT function: from an inwardly focused drive to establish the professional credibility of the IT function; through a re-orientation period which stressed business management understanding of IT potential and the alignment of IT strategy with business need; to a 'mature' phase in which organizational and technical infrastructures were central issues.

Evolution and leadership were the two themes which stimulated the follow-up research study described in this chapter. What had happened to the ten individuals involved in the original study, what had been the fortunes and further experiences of a group identified as leading practitioners? And what further evolution in information management had occurred in the organizations they represented – was it consistent with the model developed in 1986? During a six-month period the author revisited each of the original group and interviewed them about their experiences during the period 1986–91, their analysis of events, and the lessons they drew from them. Only one of the ten remained in the same role and organization; while several others had prospered, three had departed from their 1986 positions under pressure, and two more had resigned in frustration. All ten had been through an eventful five years! The objective of this chapter is to report on the group's individual and collective experiences, positioning their learning in ways that are hopefully helpful to fellow IT practitioners and academics.

The report makes particular reference to two other recent studies: an investigation of the determinants of the CEO/CIO relationship (see Chapter 2); and a study of CIO survival by Earl (1992; 1996) – another co-author of the 1986 paper. All three studies centre on the responsibilities and demands placed on CIOs of large organizations. The personal and longitudinal orientation of the study reported here may be seen to complement and enrich the issue-based approach of the other two.

'THE GROUP OF TEN'

The objective of the 1986 study was to gain insights into 'best thinking and practice' in selected areas of information management, particularly in linking IT to business needs. The ten subjects in that study were therefore selected on the basis that they were perceived to be exponents of best practice, and leading practitioners in leading UK organizations. The selection was carried out (subjectively of course) by faculty of OXIIM, with assistance from IBM United Kingdom (sponsors of the original study), and drew upon an extensive combined range of contacts. The selection was moderated by the objective of representation across industry sectors; and in fact the ten interviewees came from nine different sectors spanning industry and commerce.

The most accurate way to describe the resulting survey group was probably 'ten of the leading IT executives in the UK'. Each headed a large IT function in what is commonly referred to as a 'blue chip' company; on average they had been in post for 4.6 years in 1986. While they held a variety of titles, they each justified the soubriquet 'CIO', and for convenience that is how they will be referred to here. Half of the ten operated as corporate CIOs within an organization composed of multiple semi-autonomous businesses; the others presided over IT in what were essentially single-business corporations.

In 1991 three of the ten were in CIO positions (but only one with his 1986 company); a fourth now combined the CIO role with responsibility for the human resources function; two had become chief executives of IT-related services businesses; four were now operating as independent consultants. All, however, remained active in information management and retained strong views on information management issues. Despite having been selected as perceived leaders among their peer group, five had left their 1986 positions without an immediate destination: three had been required to leave, two had resigned in frustration. It seems even leaders are vulnerable in a role which is consistently reported to be high risk (for example Grover *et al.*, 1993; Rothfeder and Driscoll 1990). However, it is important to distinguish between survival and achievement. For example, one of the CIOs who had been fired pointed to the latest corporate annual report, which described two of the information systems he created as among the corporation's five substantial strengths on which the future would be built! As Feeny *et al.*, (1992) (see also Chapter 2) and Earl (1996) have described, the fortunes of a CIO are impacted by far more than operational performance.

RESEARCH PROCESS

Each of the group of ten was interviewed for between one and two hours between November 1991 and May 1992. Interviews started with a reminder of the responses given by that individual in 1986:

- positioning/role of IT in the business;
- principal issues/concerns identified;
- current pattern of activity for the CIO;
- anticipated future pattern of activity.

Interviewees were then invited to describe their experiences from 1986–91, highlighting perceived achievements and frustrations; to provide their own analysis of the event described; and to volunteer any perceived general lessons/advice to peers. In the final phase of interviews, more structured questions sought out data on organizational factors and personal characteristics which prior authors have suggested to be related to CIO success. In addition all but one of the ten agreed to provide data on their management team role profile, using the instrument devised by Belbin (1981).

Given the objectives of the study, and the small size and special nature of the group, the first phase of analysis comprised scanning of the interview notes to identify major issues and themes. Issues and themes which were *recurring* (in the sense they were picked out for special attention by five or more interviewees) and *consistent* (in that their significance was not specifically denied by other interviewees) are described in the following section, 'Research findings'. The five areas covered are listed in Table 18.1 as 'critical issues in information management'. The fact that at least half of a group of perceived leaders wanted to discuss those issues when summarizing and analysing their experiences suggests that they are of potential importance to others.

Table 18.1   Critical issues in information management

- Executive relationships and visions for IT
- Agenda of applications and infrastructure
- IT delivery performance
- Evolving IS organization
- Changing IS skill needs

Finally an attempt was made to synthesize the findings, to suggest a possible explanation for major differences of emphasis across the interviews, and to make sense of the findings collectively as well as individually. The evolutionary model of 1986, with some amendment, was found to provide an overall framework which suited this purpose.

RESEARCH FINDINGS

Executive relationships and visions for IT

The single most common finding from the ten CIO interviews was the emphasis placed on their relationships with business executives, particularly with the CEO. When describing the highlights of a five-year period, all of the CIOs made frequent references to these relationships, and used them to explain success and failure. Four of the five 'non-survivors' singled out a change of CEO as the root cause of their difficulties and subsequent departure. Four others described how progress in IT exploitation was stalled for a period while they worked to improve relationships with key executives.

In Earl's (1992) study the same phenomenon emerges. 'CEO relationship' and 'Executive relationships' are two of the five primary factors he identifies as determinants of CIO survival. The ten CIOs in this study confirm these findings and add colour through their comments. One recalled how his CEO had asked: 'Once we were in the forefront of IT use in our industry; why have things changed?' 'The change coincided with your appointment as CEO' was the candid response. Another described his five-year experience succinctly: 'With CEO A anything was possible. With CEO B (his successor) nothing was possible'.

In our parallel study which focused on CEO/CIO relationships, Feeny et al., found that successful relationships were associated with a number of attributes of the CEO, the CIO, and the organizational context (see Chapter 2). The current study provided particular support for three of these attributes – the CIO's team role profile, the CEO's vision of the role of IT, and the CEO's attitude to change.

Feeny et al., found that CIOs who enjoyed successful relationships with their CEOs consistently showed a team role profile which included both of the leadership styles identified by Belbin (1981) – the entrepreneurial and the consultative, labelled shaper and chairman/co-ordinator by Belbin. We suggested that the consultative style might be a necessary complement to the entrepreneurial, protecting the CIO from charges of arrogance by more powerful business executives (see Chapter 2). The current study provided support for this proposition. Of the nine CIOs who completed the Belbin self-perception questionnaire, seven had a profile in which the consultative style was prominent. The other two – both 'non-survivors' – had each experienced difficulties in their relationships with executives. 'I now realize', said one, 'that I used to construct win/lose situations with my peers. I had territorial pride and was determined to fight the IS corner, to establish that our position was the right one. Instead of allies, I generated enemies. In my new job I go to great lengths to construct win/win relationships, and it is paying off'.

Table 18.2   Visions of the role of IT

- Vision to automate
- Vision to control
- Vision to empower
- Vision to transform

The ten CIOs also provided strong support for the linkage suggested by Feeny et al., between CEO relationships and Visions of the Role of IT. The CIOs were presented with descriptors of the four alternative visions headlined in Table 18.2, which were adapted by Feeny et al., from the work of Schein (1989). All ten aligned themselves with the 'vision to transform', in which the use of IT is embedded within initiatives to achieve radical change in some aspect of the business.

They also consistently associated the 'vision to transform' with executives with whom they held positive and successful relationships (12 examples were discussed in some detail). On the other hand unsuccessful relationships were associated with executives subscribing to the 'vision to automate' (four detailed examples) in which IT is positioned as a cost-displacement technology, leading to incremental gains in efficiency; or with executives thought to hold the 'vision to control' (four further examples) in which the role of IT is to enable closer supervision of the business, and micro-management by the executive team. Eight of the ten CIOs were immediately comfortable with the vision descriptors, and positioned executive colleagues within the categories with apparent ease and certainty. One CIO described as his single most critical success factor the ability to convert executives from an 'automate' to a 'transformation' vision of the role of IT. He provided rich accounts of his endeavours in this direction, his orchestration of what typically were lengthy campaigns. On one occasion he had brought in a psychologist to advise him on a particularly difficult situation. His efforts contrasted sharply with those of another CIO who had gone for a 'quick win' with a special 'IT day' for the new CEO. This CIO found to his cost that persuading an executive to change his values, attitudes and vision for IT takes sustained effort over a significant time period.

The third link with the earlier research concerns the CEO's attitude to change, which Feeny *et al.*, positioned as one of four determinants of the CEO's vision of the role of IT. Two CIOs who had worked with conservatively minded CEOs provided graphic support to this contention. The first reported that when a new CEO – whom he positioned as having low change orientation and the IT vision to control – was appointed, 'all the movers and shakers, including myself, left the company'. The second also experienced the arrival of a CEO with low change orientation, identified as having the IT Vision to Automate: 'He was uncomfortable with new ideas; I was regarded as 'pushy' and 'a bit of a nutter'. For CIOs who want to achieve excellent relationships, with a shared vision of IT as agent of transformation, it seems that a start point is to identify areas in which there can be mutual agreement on the need for business change.

Agenda of applications and infrastructure

In seven of the ten interviews, CIOs devoted considerable time to the issue of linking IS effort to the needs of the business – encapsulated by one CIO in the phrase 'having the right agenda'. The emphasis was on not just achieving the linkage, but *being seen* to achieve it. Business executives must be clear about the connections between IS development activity and their own critical success factors. Language was important:

If the business was currently focused on improving its cost structure, then IS initiatives must be presented in ways which demonstrated their impact on costs rather than 'irrelevant' improvements to customer service.

'Having the right agenda' required flexibility and prescience in the CIO and the IS function. IS had to expect that business priorities would sometimes change quickly and dramatically. The CIO's credibility depended on his ability to respond to the new situation. Thus an automotive CIO credited his survival to his success in keeping IS 'tied-in' to the business, as the emphasis moved from distribution channels, to time-to-market, to cost reduction in line with industry pressures. The CIO of a brewing group prospered when colleagues were pleasantly surprised by the IS function's ability to accommodate a corporate restructuring without delay. Similarly a banking group CIO won plaudits through timely support for two major new product initiatives. In contrast, the retail CIO began to be marginalized when he persisted with a home-shopping initiative in which the rest of the Board had lost interest.

IS flexibility was achieved not just by a willingness to change priorities; it depended on forward planning of data standards and IT infrastructure, hence the importance of prescience. Infrastructure developments typically represented large investments which were not directly linked to the business cycle, with the result that cost/benefit cases were hard to establish. One ex-CIO was proud of the communications network he had implemented under a visionary CEO; he saw himself as the I. K. Brunel of his corporation. But the business now showed little appreciation of his achievement. None of the CIOs had found a way to make the business fully understand the importance they themselves attached to infrastructure, to express cost/benefits in terms that proved robust over time. The successful CIOs had therefore become opportunist. They created their own vision of infrastructure, and implemented pieces of the vision on the back of applications commissioned by the business. For example, in the automotive company, the CIO felt the new systems for automotive distributors represented a 'platform for the next 20 years' as well as satisfying the immediate needs of the business. It seems that the 'right agenda' may be a canny blend of visible winners and invisible future enablers.

So how is this 'right agenda' identified? 'Proactively, by insiders' would summarize the response of these CIOs. First, they were clear that business imperatives were not proclaimed on corporate billboards, at least not in a form which could be directly translated into action. Key business themes had to be teased out and interpreted through a relentless probing of fellow business executives, in formal and informal encounters. It was a process of listening and testing, with CIOs continually seeking out occasions for the former, and at times proposing their own understandings of business direction for reaction and confirmation from colleagues. There is clearly a link here back to the issue of executive relationships. And most CIOs stressed how important it was to be a member of the top management team, to maximize the opportunities for dialogue.

Several CIOs contrasted their approach in the 1990s with their experience of the 1980s, when consultants/gurus/academics were invited in to proclaim how IT could be used to achieve competitive advantage. These 'outsiders' came in for something of a roasting for encouraging an 'instant success syndrome'. One CIO described how consultants had raised unrealistic expectations which took years to overcome. Others were dismissive about the lack of lasting impact from such incursions. Collectively the CIOs agreed that business themes and concepts like continuous quality improvement were the effective vehicles for advancing the exploitation of IT in their organizations. If 'outsiders' had a role to play, it was in facilitating, not driving progress, making contributions within an overall approach which was orchestrated by the CIO.

At this point it is worth contrasting the experience of CIOs within multi-business corporations with their peers who operated in a single business context. None of the five CIOs in the former category had survived the five-year experience. 'Having the right agenda' had been a particular problem for them. Most business themes, the effective springboard for that agenda, arise at business unit rather than corporate level. Corporate added value strategies, the identification of how the centre contributes operationally beyond the business units, tend to be poorly developed. Hence there is often a minimal business agenda to which these CIOs can connect. The relevant CIOs in this study certainly suffered through involvement in infrastructure projects which the businesses regarded as expensive overheads; or became enmeshed in problems of cross-business priorities which corporate management seemed reluctant to address. In addition these CIOs were mostly remote from the top management team, and lacked strong sponsors to defend them when budgets and activities come to be questioned. It seems that the CIO role is altogether more comfortable if it is within the context of a single business corporation, rather than a multi-business group.

IT delivery performance

Five CIOs brought up the topic of IT delivery performance, the quality of existing operational services and the successful completion of new projects. In three instances the CIOs were reflecting on reasons for the success they had achieved; in the other two the CIOs were diagnosing the causes of their downfall. Delivery performance is another of the five primary factors identified by Earl (1996) as determinants of CIO survival.

All five CIOs agreed that delivery was fundamental to their credibility, that a successful track record must be in place before they could move on to a more ambitious agenda for IT use. But they had adopted contrasting positions in terms of how it would be achieved. Both the 'non-survivors' had left delivery in the hands of others, one because of his belief in empowerment of his subordinates, the other because the culture of the organization was to leave key aspects of delivery in the hands of business units (which failed to resource it properly). In this latter case the deployment by the businesses of new recruits onto help-desks led to an accumulation of day-to-day problems for which the users 'had no tolerance'. And the corporate CEO was unforgiving. Despite the formal lines of responsibility he saw the CIO's job as being 'to deliver, not to have new ideas'.

By contrast, the three achievers all assumed that what could go wrong would (or at least might) go wrong. 'You can never take your eye off delivery', 'I still get daily reports on everything that has gone wrong', 'There is a natural process of inefficiency in IT', 'It is a fallacy to believe that technology is getting any easier' were some of the quotes. These CIOs talked of 'walking the floor' and 'dropping in on people' to get early warning of impending problems. And they gave examples of how they had got involved in sorting out problems on the user side to achieve success. It was not enough for the IS function to perform; problems were interpreted as IS failures no matter what the real cause. Perhaps significantly, these successful pessimists all came from IS backgrounds, whereas both non-survivors were transplants from general management to the CIO position.

The successful CIO's also emphasized the importance of constructing projects to enable rapid delivery. One spoke of instilling in IS a culture of only tackling the 20 per cent of the requirement which brings 80 per cent of the benefit. Another described with pride a major project which had been rolled out 'incredibly/ridiculously fast'. The third talked of the importance of managing the not invented here (NIH) syndrome: 'The best IT people always want to invent. This is immensely frustrating for users who are aware of the existence of packages'. Despite their emphasis on delivery, the successful CIOs actually spent little of their personal time on delivery issues. 'My own managers see little of me; the great majority of my time is spent outside the IS function'. 'I built a superb team below me'. This is consistent with the earlier finding of Feeny *et al.*, (1992), that CIOs can achieve delivery performance through a combination of key management appointments, an appropriate regime, and perpetual (but not necessarily time-consuming) watchfulness.

Evolving IS organization
In eight of the interviews IS organization was a major discussion point (on this topic see also Chapters 6 and 7). Among these CIOs there was a strong consensus on the *direction* in which IS organization should

evolve; but there was also an emphasis on the importance of the *timing* of change, of the need to resist change until certain fundamentals were securely in place. 'I am still convinced we had the right idea' said one (non-survivor) CIO, 'but it was ahead of its time'.

The target IS organization was described in terms of three components: a strong 'front office' which interfaced directly with the business; a 'back office' which managed the delivery of services across the business; and a 'market' of internal and external IT service businesses which increasingly represented the source of supply. These comments can be usefully compared to our findings in Chapters 6 and 17. The front office is aligned with the structure of the business, mapped onto the business units and functions in a way that reflects the organizational philosophy and power structure. Its first task is to establish and maintain excellent business/IS relationships at all key points, to win the confidence of business decision makers and influencers. With that confidence as a base, the role of the front office is to contribute to 'top level dialogue' – to educate, inform and stimulate the thinking of the business about how IT can contribute to business need. One CIO illustrated the position he wanted to achieve with a recent comment from the director of marketing: 'Now that we know each other and you understand what I am trying to do, why don't you start telling me what I should be asking from IS'. The front office is focused on the first two critical issues discussed in this chapter – executive relationships and visions for IT; and the agenda of applications and infrastructure.

The front office also plays a role in tackling the third critical issue, IT delivery performance. Its contribution here is to manage *perceptions* of performance, to ensure that those perceptions are surfaced and shared between business and IS management. Success in IT delivery performance comes form a combination of actual achievement and perceived achievement.

The actual achievement is the responsibility of the back office. While the traditional development and operations functions have both provided and managed the supply of service, the future back office emphasizes the management of supply. It is responsible for identifying and securing sources of supply, monitoring and managing supply in accordance with agreements negotiated. While only one of the organizations represented had yet experienced large-scale outsourcing of the IT function, most were making targeted but significant use of the external market for IT services. The CIO's collectively expected a continuing trend towards a market-based model of IT supply. There were several instances of the organization's own operational IT resources being structured into an IT service business which became one of a number of possible supply sources. The evolving IT organization therefore comprised a sizeable front office, distributed across the corporation; a relatively small back office, distributed or centralized; and an extensive services market in which some providers might be within corporate ownership. Chapter 17 further elaborates our own thinking on some of these issues, but concentrates particularly on capabilities and skills in the IS function (see also below).

While there was consensus on future IS organizational shape, timing of any transition was a major issue. Of particular importance was timing of devolution of IS responsibility and resource into the business, the release of IS resources from central control. Four CIOs described how responsibility for IS strategy and delivery had been devolved to businesses whose executives placed little value on IT. In consequence, as authors like Parsons (1983) have predicted, their IT units were poorly directed and resourced, and performance suffered. But despite the transfer of responsibility, these problems were still perceived to reflect badly on the CIOs concerned. A related issue was the problem of enacting corporate priorities for resources across the businesses once the transition had occurred. 'Devolution became anarchy' for one frustrated CIO. By contrast, the more successful CIOs retained control of resources (and thereby performance quality) while working with business unit executives to develop their understanding of IS strategy to meet their needs. One such CIO related how he had intensively 'educated' business unit executives, then devolved responsibility for IS budgets while retaining control of resources. When the corporate CEO made a somewhat arbitrary assault on total IS expenditure, budgets were vigorously defended by the business unit heads. In the final section of this chapter, these various experiences are related back to the evolutionary model identified by Hirschheim *et al.*, (1988) from the original study.

Changing IS skill needs
In five interviews a significant part of the discussion was devoted to changing IS skills needs, related to the evolving IS organization. The front office/back office concepts place new demands on the IS function and require a significant re-think of human resource management policies. Our own thinking on this, influenced in part by the present study, is elaborated in Chapter 17. However, here we describe our respondents views on these issues.

Recruitment using traditional technical criteria was seen as particularly inappropriate to the needs of the front office. The first requirement here is for *relationship building* by people who are 'reasonably extrovert, with empathy and political judgement'. One CIO cited an example of an executive colleague who put out a call for help with a problem encountered on his executive information system. The 'techie' who answered the call fixed the problem with expertise and dispatch. But no communication or learning occurred. The executive remained unclear as to what had gone wrong, how it had been fixed, how the problem might be avoided in future. The IS function had learned nothing about how the executive was using the system, what he was (or was not) achieving, how further use of the system might be of value. Proper operation of the front office would have turned the call for help into an opportunity for exploring satisfaction and mutual learning. Social skills and 'marketing' instincts were the necessary attributes. An analogy could be drawn with the successful barber, who not only gets the hair cut but also senses quickly how to put each customer at ease. He consequently delivers a good experience which leads to customer satisfaction and repeat purchase.

The second front office requirement is to make an IS contribution to the top level business dialogue, to strategic analysis, business process re-design and the like. The necessary skill was universally described as 'systems thinking' – the ability and inclination to view organizational activity holistically, with a recognition of connections, relationships and interdependencies. Systems thinking is a well established field of academic study (see for example Emery (1969), which is receiving renewed attention through the work of authors such as Senge (1990). The CIOs in this study believed that the IS function was both the natural home and the breeding ground for systems thinking skills. One CIO argued that all his company's new employees should spend their first year or two within IS in order to develop a systems approach. Certainly the IS function is one of those which can provide a cross-functional perspective and a focus on systemic organizational change.

In relation to the back office, the CIOs recognized – but devoted surprisingly little discussion time to – the need for *procurement skills*. It was not clear whether these skills were thought to be readily available (perhaps through transfer of experience acquired in other parts of the business); or whether use of a market model of IT service supply was currently too limited to highlight potential problems and deficiencies.

The other skill area which did draw considerable comment was technical proficiency. Some reference was made to the need for skills in new technologies, such as I-CASE and Client–server (for a detailed case study on this see Chapter 14). But most emphasis was placed on the need for a small core of IS employees who demonstrated *technical excellence* across a whole range of technologies. These were people whose performance was not 'above average', but 'many times the average'. One CIO referred vividly to his precious 'Michelangelos', the supremely talented and versatile few whom he deployed on projects which would differentiate the firm from its business competitors.

As we pointed out in Chapter 17, perhaps the most challenging question that emerges from these CIOs' comments on new IS skill needs is how these skills are to be acquired. For many years now, IS functions have developed skills in new technologies through investment in training programmes. But as Figure 18.1 depicts, training and experience are not the only determinants of capability. What is striking about the new skills/capabilities being targeted is that at least three of the four – relationship building, systems thinking, technical excellence – would seem to be more a function of cognitive style and/or personality than the result of training or experience.

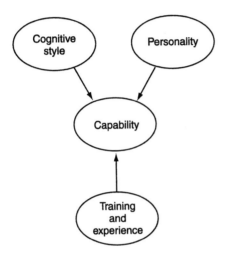

Figure 18.1   Sources of capability

It is also unclear to what extent the target new capabilities are mutually compatible versus mutually exclusive. Can a single individual exhibit both technical excellence and systems thinking capabilities? Should organizations be seeking out multi-talented individuals, or planning for multiple and distinct patterns of recruitment and development? And how many of an organization's existing IS employees are likely, given the chance, to demonstrate high ability in at least one of the target capabilities? While we deal with these issues in more detail in Chapter 17, there is still an urgent need for further research to assist organizations in their future human resource planning of the IS function.

SYNTHESIZING THE LEARNING

One way to make collective sense of the findings of the present study, and the learning of the ten CIOs, is to return to the model derived from the interviews conducted in 1986 (Hirschheim *et al.,* 1988). The model

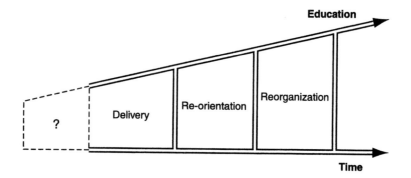

Figure 18.2   Leadership of a 'strategic' IS function

is reproduced as Figure 18.2. It suggests three stages of evolution, with contrasting emphases and success factors in each stage.

The objective of the first phase, labelled delivery, is to establish the credibility of the IS function. During this phase the CIO is required to spend most of his or her time 'inside' the IS function, generating the professional skills and management arrangements which result in consistent achievement of its commitments by the IS function. Education is targeted at developing the capability and service orientation of IS employees, required to deliver excellent operational service and successful completion of development projects. The delivery phase creates the necessary platform for more ambitious exploitation of IT.

In the second phase, labelled re-orientation, the objective is to create the perception of IT as a strategic resource. The CIO now spends most of the time 'beyond' the IS function, working with senior levels of business management. The prime targets for education, formal and informal, are business executives who are exposed to ideas of IT-enabled competitive advantage and exhorted to integrate business and IT planning. The re-orientation phase culminates in an 'IT literate' executive team who are equipped to take leadership of future IT exploitation (as espoused, for example by Rockart, 1988). Responsibility for IS resourcing can now be devolved to business unit heads who understand IT's contribution.

The third phase, labelled reorganization, emphasizes relationships and boundary management. The CIO's task here is to ensure that organizational arrangements for IS enable the function to integrate effectively and efficiently with the business – to participate in strategic thinking, achieve timely development of new systems which support business initiatives, provide operational services now critical to the functioning of the business. As the model implies, reorganization is seen as the mature phase for a business which positions IT as a strategic resource.

In the follow-up study, each CIO was asked to verify the positioning we had identified for each organization in 1986; and to assess the current positioning of that organization, whether or not he still belonged to it. Table 18.3 summarizes their responses.

Table 18.3   Organizational evolution

Organization	1986	1991–92	Evolution
A	Re-orientation	Re-orientation	No
B	Re-orientation	Delivery	No
C	Re-orientation	Reorganization	Yes
D	Delivery	Delivery	No
E	Re-orientation	Reorganization	Yes
F	Reorganization	Re-orientation	No
G	Re-orientation	Re-orientation	No
H	Reorganization	Reorganization	Yes
I	Re-orientation	Reorganization	Yes
J	Re-orientation	Reorganization	Yes

Five organizations (C, E, H, I, J) were seen to have evolved successfully in their use of IT, in line with the suggestions of the model. However, five others (A, B, D, F, G) were described as having stalled or regressed in relation to the model. At first sight this is scarcely a consistent endorsement of a framework which purports to explain evolution! But closer examination of the experiences described, particularly in organizations which failed to evolve, provides a more insightful picture.

For example, organization A is the European business of a US-based multinational. The CIO recounted how every two or three years a new group of top executives arrive from the US to gain European experience before (hopefully) promotion back to corporate headquarters. The CIO is therefore in constant re-orientation mode, working on relationships and attitudes with a changing executive team.

In organization B the CIO's experience was even worse. In 1986 he worked for the CEO with whom 'anything was possible'; by 1991 the CEO with whom 'nothing was possible' had arrived. In the meantime a once successful delivery performance had deteriorated because key aspects of service responsibility had been devolved to business units which failed to resource them properly. The new CEO's view was that IT had a limited role, within which it should perform a lot better and cost a lot less.

Organizations F and G had each progressed at some time from the re-orientation to the reorganization stage. But in both cases a corporate restructuring had occurred which defined new and smaller business units. In consequence, the emphasis had returned to re-orientation, working at the level of the new business unit management teams.

A possible interpretation is that the five 'unsuccessful' organizations had each failed to establish conditions for the *continuing* success of one phase before progressing to the next. Achievements were fragile because they were dependent on particular individuals who had in due course moved on. Conditions for success had not been *institutionalized* through *organizational* rather than *individual* learning.

By contrast the secure progress of organizations such as C, E, H was seen to be based on their ability to embed the necessary learning in organizational arrangements and procedures. They had fixed the process rather than the problem. When new business or IT managers were appointed (provided they were promotions from within) they brought with them the same attitudes and capabilities as their predecessors. The organization did not regress. With this interpretation we can suggest that the model remains a helpful framework provided that 'time' is replaced on the horizontal axis by 'organizational learning'. And it is then possible (Figure 18.3) to refine the model by positioning within it the findings of the follow-up study.

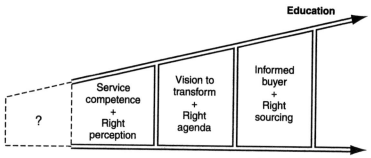

Figure 18.3   Evolution in the management of IS

In this refined model, the requirements of the delivery phase can be seen as establishing both the necessary service competence and the 'right' perception of service. In other words the IT function must not only achieve, it must be seen to achieve – both back office and front office capabilities (relationship building) must be in place. Furthermore there must be established an organizational regime which ensures that the capabilities are securely in place, that attention can safely be transferred to any subsequent phase.

The two components of the re-orientation phase are described as positioning IT through the vision to transform, and establishing how this gets interpreted into the 'right' agenda of applications and infrastructure. The first component requires a lengthy and widescale educational (in the broadest sense) process which succeeds in convincing present and future executive management that IT should be associated with transformational business change. Once this shared vision is in place, business/IS relationships at executive level become much more straightforward (see Chapter 2; also Earl, 1996). Interpreting the vision into the 'right' agenda for the business draws upon the strong relationships and exploits skills in systems thinking.

Finally the re-organization stage can be interpreted as establishing the 'informed buyer' and making the 'right' sourcing decisions. The informed buyer is here an aggregate of both components of the front office, plus the procurement skills identified within the back office (see Chapter 17 for a detailed discussion). Whatever 'outsourcing' takes place it is considered essential that the organization retains these components in-house, so that relationships can be maintained, the 'right' agenda is updated in the light of business change and new technology, and contractual arrangements are tailored to reflect the organization's current needs and future security. Within this study no one emphasized the need for the informed buyer more strongly than the former CIO who was now chief executive of an IT services company. He did not wish to do business with naïve customers, and he gave detailed examples of the efforts he had made to ensure that particular customers put in place strong IS leadership and competent supporting capabilities. As Chapters 11 and 12 make clear, what has changed since 1986 is that the available market for IT services has greatly expanded. It makes sense for the informed buyer to adopt a market model of supply, with little theology about any general superiority of internal or external sources.

CONCLUSIONS

In assessing the findings of this study it is important to recall that they reflect the learning of ten people who were identified in 1986 as leading practitioners and opinion setters. If some have since fallen from grace, this may tell us as much about business executives and the perils of the CIO role as it does about the individuals concerned. All ten were reflective and analytical about their experiences, willing to acknowledge mistakes and weaknesses as well as to defend their beliefs and achievements. Their learning should be of real value to others.

Perhaps the biggest single message from the study was the importance of organizational learning to the successful exploitation of IT. This is a point emphasized also by our other findings on the importance of capabilities, detailed in Chapter 17 (see also Feeny and Willcocks, 1997). This is not of course a new message – authors from Gibson and Nolan (1974) onwards have referred to it. But it is a message that came through more vividly and forcibly than hitherto. Organizational learning would also seem to be a widely neglected consideration in practice, as we pointed out in Chapter 17.

The second strong message concerns the IT vision to transform. In this study, and in Feeny *et al.*, (1992), having an executive team which subscribes to the transformational vision was seen as a key enabler. This would also apply for any operationalization of the sort of IS function described in Chapter 17. But how do you 'convert' an executive who currently believes in the IT vision to automate? This is one issue which must deserve a further investment in research.

Reinforcing our position in Chapter 17, the other area for research, and major finding from this study, is the need for new skills and capabilities in the IS function. Unless we can understand how to recruit and develop these capabilities, the IS function may once again be perceived as failing to deliver to its promised potential.

REFERENCES

Belbin, R. (1981) *Management Teams: Why they Succeed or Fail*, Heinemann, London.

Earl, M. (1992) *The Chief Information Officer: A Study of Survival*, London Business School Working Paper, London.

Earl, M. (1996) 'The Chief Information Officer: Past, Present and Future. In Earl, M. (ed.), *Information Management: The Organizational Dimension*, Oxford University Press, Oxford.

Emery, F. (1969), *Systems Thinking*, Penguin Books, London.

Feeny, D. and Willcocks, L. (1997) 'Rethinking Capabilities and Skills in the Information Systems Function', In Currie, W. and Galliers, R. (eds.), *Rethinking MIS*. Oxford University Press, Oxford (forthcoming).

Feeny, D. Edwards, B. and Simpson, K. (1992) 'Understanding the CEO/CIO Relationship', *MIS Quarterly*, **16**, (4), pp. 435–448.

Gibson, C. and Nolan, R. (1974) 'Managing the Four Stages of EDP Growth', *Harvard Business Review*, January–February.

Grover, A., Jeong, S., Kettinger, W. and Lee, C. (1993) 'The Chief Information Officer: A Study of Managerial Roles', *Journal of Management Information Systems*, **10**, (2), pp. 107–130.

Hirschheim, R., Earl, M., Feeny, D. and Lockett, M. (1988) *An Exploration into the Management of the Information Systems Function: Key Issues and an Evolutionary Model*, Information

Technology Management for Productivity and Competitive Advantage, IFIP TC-8 Open Conference, Singapore, March.

Parsons, G. (1983) *Fitting Information Systems Technology to the Corporate Needs: the Linking Strategy*, Case Study 183176, Harvard Business School, Boston, Mass.

Rockart, J. (1988) 'The Line Takes the Leadership – IS Management in a Wired Society', *Sloan Management Review*, **29**, (4).

Rothfeder, J. and Driscoll, L. (1990) 'CIO is Starting to Stand for Career Is Over', *Business Week*, February 26.

Schein, E. (1989) *The Role of the CEO in the Management of Change: the Case of Information Technology*, Management in the Nineties Working Paper (89–075), Sloan School of Management, MIT.

Senge, P. (1990) *The Fifth Discipline: The Art and Science of the Learning Organization*, Doubleday, New York.

Index